PLANTS

2400 Copyright-Free Illustrations of Flowers, Trees, Fruits and Vegetables

Edited by

Jim Harter

DOVER PUBLICATIONS, INC.
Mineola, New York

Bibliographical Note

This Dover edition, first published in 1998, is an unabridged republication of *The Plant Kingdom Compendium,* published by Bonanza Books, New York, in 1988.

DOVER *Pictorial Archive* SERIES

This book belongs to the Dover Pictorial Archive Series. You may use the designs and illustrations for graphics and crafts applications, free and without special permission, provided that you include no more than ten in the same publication or project. (For permission for additional use, please write to Permissions Department, Dover Publications, Inc., 31 East 2nd Street, Mineola, New York, 11501.)

However, republication or reproduction of any illustration by any other graphic service, whether it be in a book or in any other design resource, is strictly prohibited.

Library of Congress Cataloging-in-Publication Data

Harter Jim.
[Plant kingdom compendium]
Plants : 2400 copyright-free illustrations of flowers, trees, fruits and vegetables / edited by Jim Harter.
p. cm.
Originally published: The plant kingdom compendium. New York : Bonanza Books, 1988.
Includes bibliographical references.
ISBN 0-486-40264-9 (pbk.)
1. Plants in art. 2. Wood-engraving—19th century. I. Title.
NE962.P56H37 1998
769'.434—dc21 98-24685
CIP

Manufactured in the United States of America
Dover Publications, Inc., 31 East 2nd Street, Mineola, N.Y. 11501

CONTENTS

Introduction

vii

SECTION 1:

Botanical Images

1

SECTION 2:

Appendices of Botanical Images

APPENDIX A:

Additional Trees

248

APPENDIX B:

Edible Foods, Nuts, Fruits, Vegetables, Legumes, Grains, Beverages, Herbs and Spices

274

APPENDIX C:

Medicinal Herbs, Narcotic and Psychotropic Plants, Plants with Miscellaneous Uses

304

APPENDIX: D

Vases and Urns, Decorative Flowers and Plants, Window Gardens, Greenhouses, Gardening, and Gardening Tools

319

APPENDIX E:

Decorative Borders and Motifs

333

Glossary of Plate References

340

Bibliography

373

INTRODUCTION

As an artist, illustrator, and graphic designer with long experience in working with nineteenth-century engraved images, my intention in putting together this book has been to make available for others an ultimate resource book having the finest available plant images that the late Victorian period had to offer. This book is not only intended to provide fine images of many different plant species and varieties, but also, whenever possible, to offer a range of two or more alternative choices from which the artist or designer can make his or her selection. This book, of course, is equally intended for those others who have a great appreciation of the beauty and infinite variety within the plant kingdom and who, I hope, will find the old pictures reproduced in this volume both interesting and pleasing to the eye.

Much of this material is now quite rare—and expensive if one has the good fortune to come across it. The earliest material in this book is from *A History of British Forest Trees, Indigenous and Introduced,* published in 1842. The most recent material dates from the early 1900s; however the great bulk of it dates from 1875 to 1895, when wood engraving had reached its zenith. During most of the nineteenth century, wood engraving was the primary method by which pictorial images were reproduced throughout the publishing industry. By 1875 this process had become greatly refined so that very realistic and graphic representations of images could be achieved. However, by 1895, this method had largely been replaced by the halftone photographic method, which was less costly and less time consuming, and which continues in use to this day. Because nineteenth-century engravings have a high graphic quality and, at the same time, are in the public domain and thus copyright free, they continue to have a special appeal.

As one might imagine, the task of trying to organize a project of this size required making certain choices and compromises. After considering various possibilities, I decided to organize the book alphabetically by category according to the plant families and to include a final section with a number of specialized appendices.

For the most part, the plant's Latin name is specified. However, on occasion, due to the varied source material, the French or German name is used instead.

As images need to find a composition all their own on a page, to achieve an ideal visual harmony, a strict sequence of images has not been adhered to. This applies to both the arrangement of images within any given family, and also to the combination of families on a page when there is a scarcity of images for each of those separate families.

In other instances, due primarily to the scarcity of images for certain families, but also for aesthetic reasons, I chose to combine several different families on the basis of certain shared characteristics. This includes the following:

A. All cannibal plants of various families are included with the Venus's-flytrap and sundew in Droseraceae.

B. Most fresh water plants and water grasses are included with the water lilies in Nymphaeaceae.

C. All flags and water algae are included with the seaweeds of Fucaceae.

D. Most examples of very primitive plants such as yeasts, mosses, molds, and lichens are included with mushrooms in Agaricaceae.

E. The Coniferales and other related families are included under the group name Gymnospermae. However, family Cyadaceae is included separately elsewhere in the book.

F. The various families of the ferns are combined under the fern group name Felices.

While the bulk of the material was being organized in this way, it became apparent that a number of appendices would need to be included. This was done so that material that was omitted from the primary section for various reasons might still be included, and also to present certain categories of images, such as fruits and vegetables, in such a way as to be more easily accessible. These appendices are as follows:

Appendix A: Additional trees.

Appendix B: Edible foods; this includes various fruits, nuts, vegetables, grains, legumes, herbs, and spices. Certain other food items including the edible mushrooms are contained in the primary section of the book.

Appendix C: Medicinal herbs, narcotic and psychotropic plants, and plants having other uses.

Appendix D: Plants used in decoration; including floral arrangements, window gardens, wreaths, and also items relating to gardens and greenhouses.

Appendix E: Plant images used in graphic design including borders and motifs.

Despite my best intentions and choice to organize the book to include as much good material as possible, in the interest of space, I had to eliminate a variety of images. I will leave it for other diligent seekers to find such images on their own. I would also like to warn the reader that this book should not be taken as a complete, scientifically-accurate-in-every-detail, encyclopedia of the plant kingdom. Classification within the plant kingdom has changed substantially since the time these engravings were produced.

Although classifications have been updated wherever possible, some of the renderings themselves may be inaccurate, and there is a possibility that a few images might be misclassified. I have done extensive research to verify that each image is assigned to its correct family, but it was not humanly possible to fully investigate every image contained within the book.

The search for the old books, periodicals, and seed catalogs necessary to put this book together led me to many out of the way places and through various flea markets, antiquarian book stores, and other such sources, both in this country and in Europe. During the course of this adventure I was happily amazed to find that such a great wealth of this sort of material actually existed. I hope that in looking through these pages, you—the artist, designer, or plant lover—can enter into this adventure as well and go back in time to this late nineteenth-century world and into its fantasy of the plant kingdom.

JIM HARTER

SAN ANTONIO, TEXAS
1988

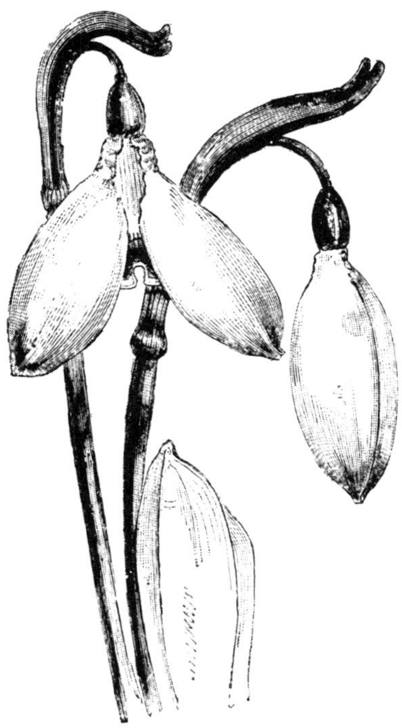

SECTION 1

Botanical Images

1

2

4

3

5

6

ACANTHACEAE

1

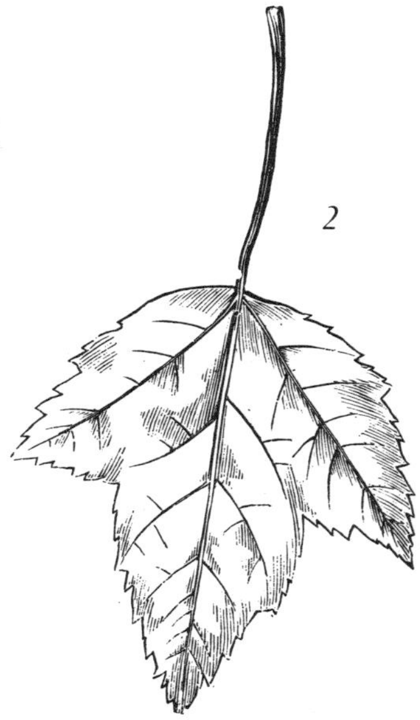

2

3

4

5

6

7

8

9

10

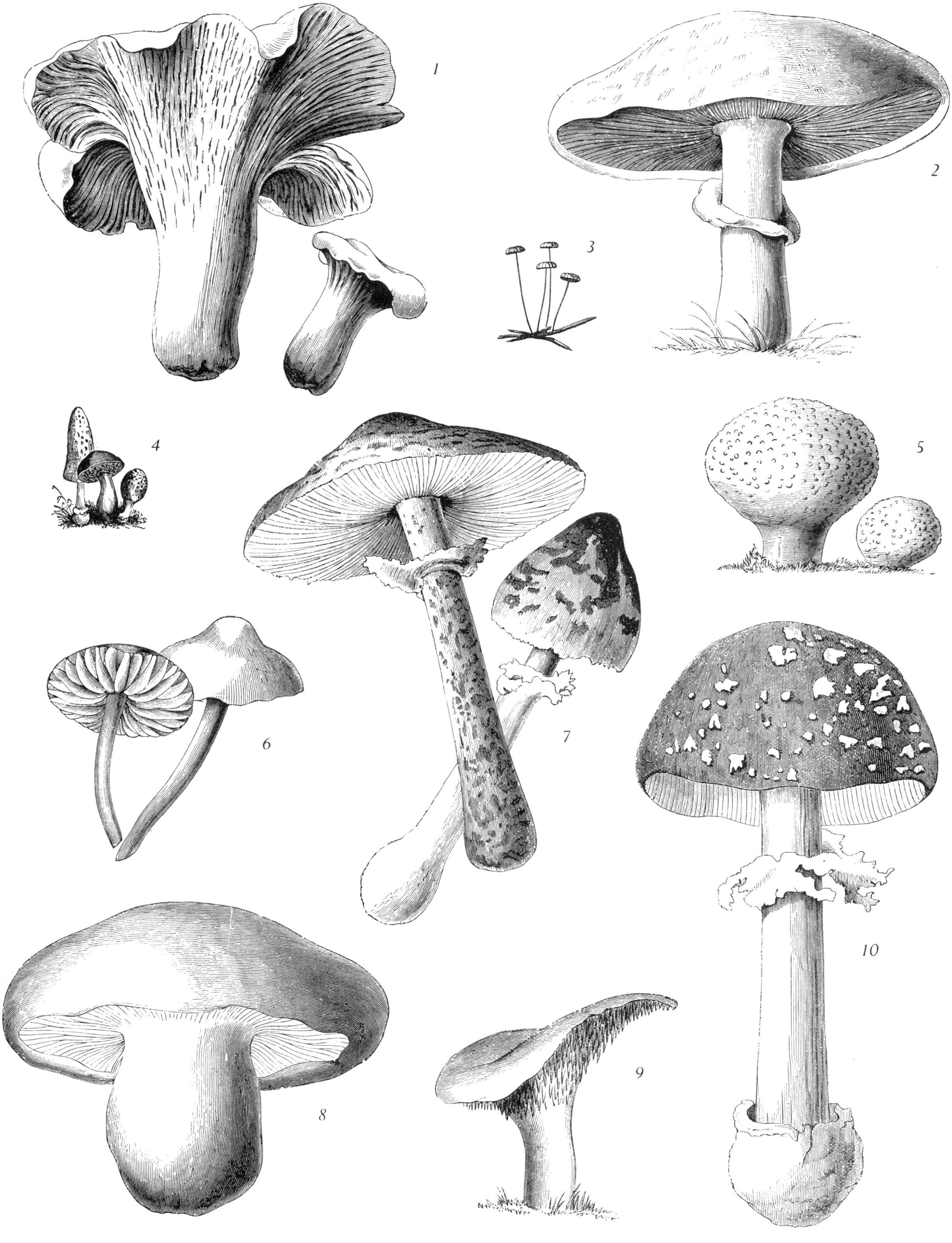

4 ***AGARICACEAE (Mushrooms, Toadstools)***

AGARICACEAE (Mushrooms, Toadstools)

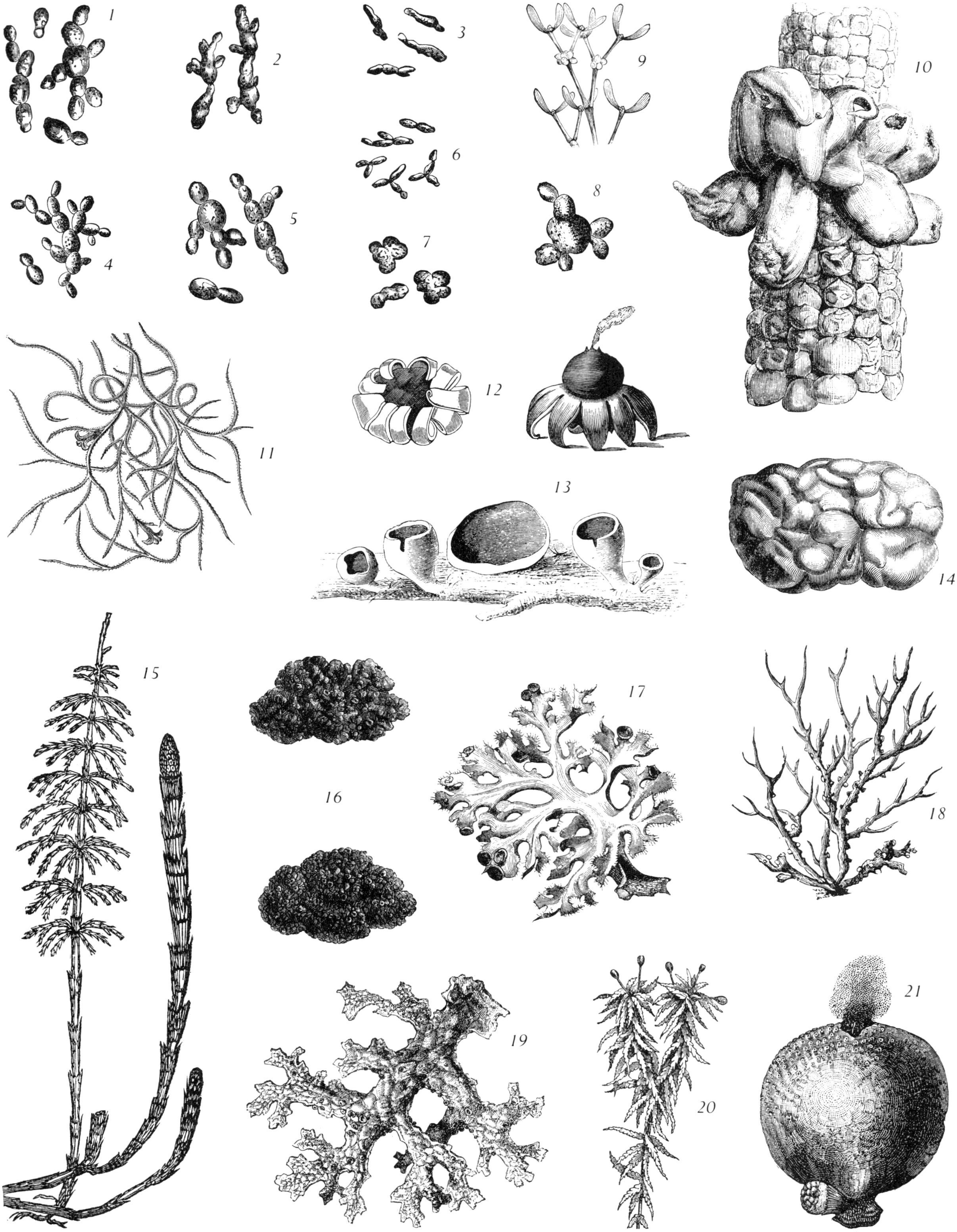

 AGARICACEAE* (*Mushrooms, Toadstools*) *and other primitive plants

1

2

3

4

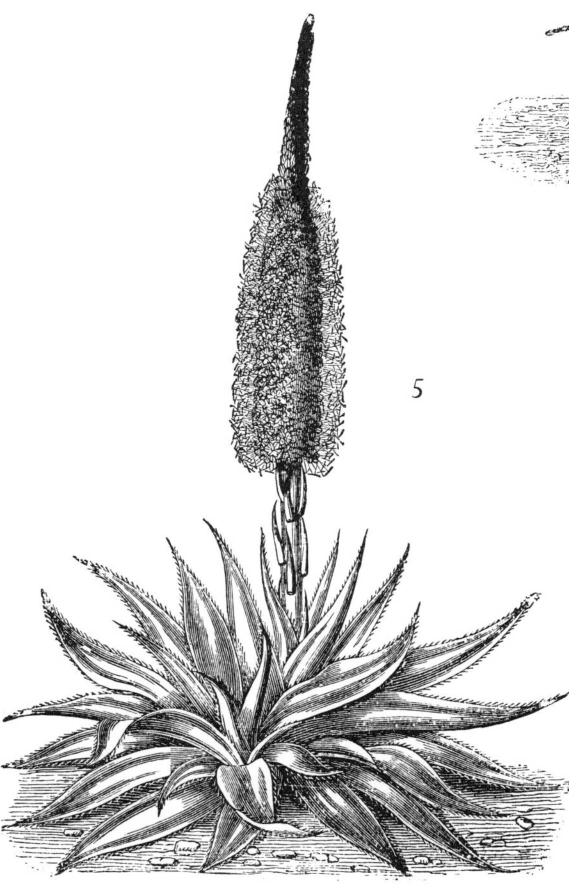

5

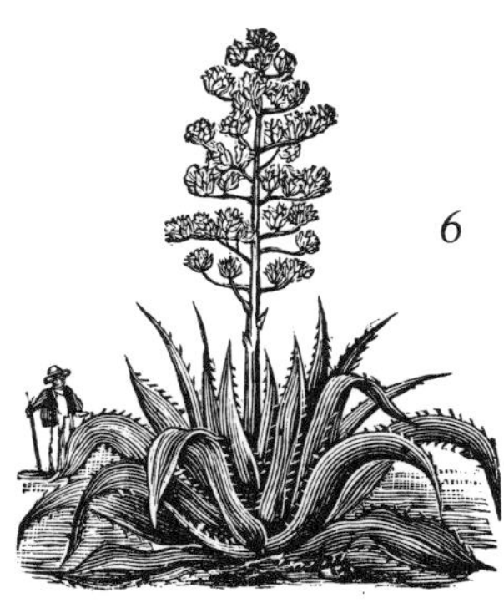

6

7

AGAVACEAE (Agaves)

8 ***AGAVACEAE** (Agaves)*

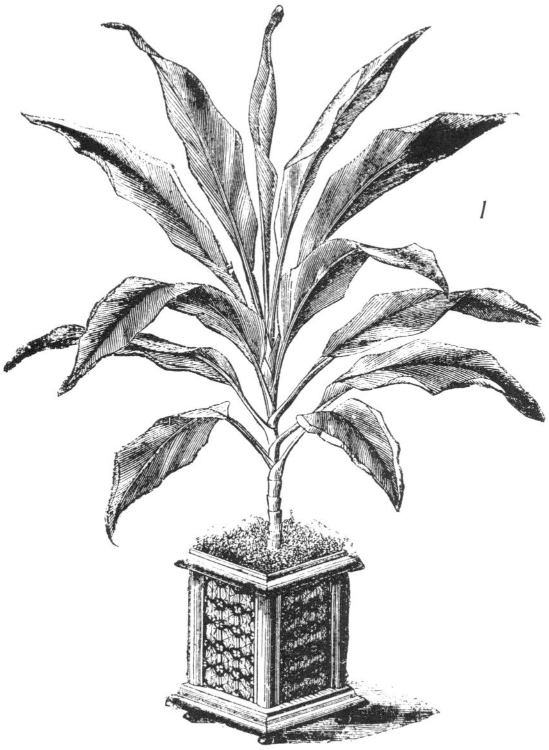

1

2

3

4

1

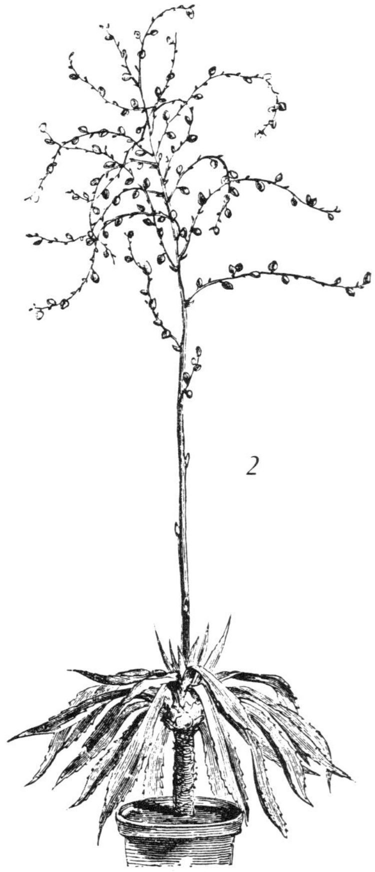

2

3

4

5

6

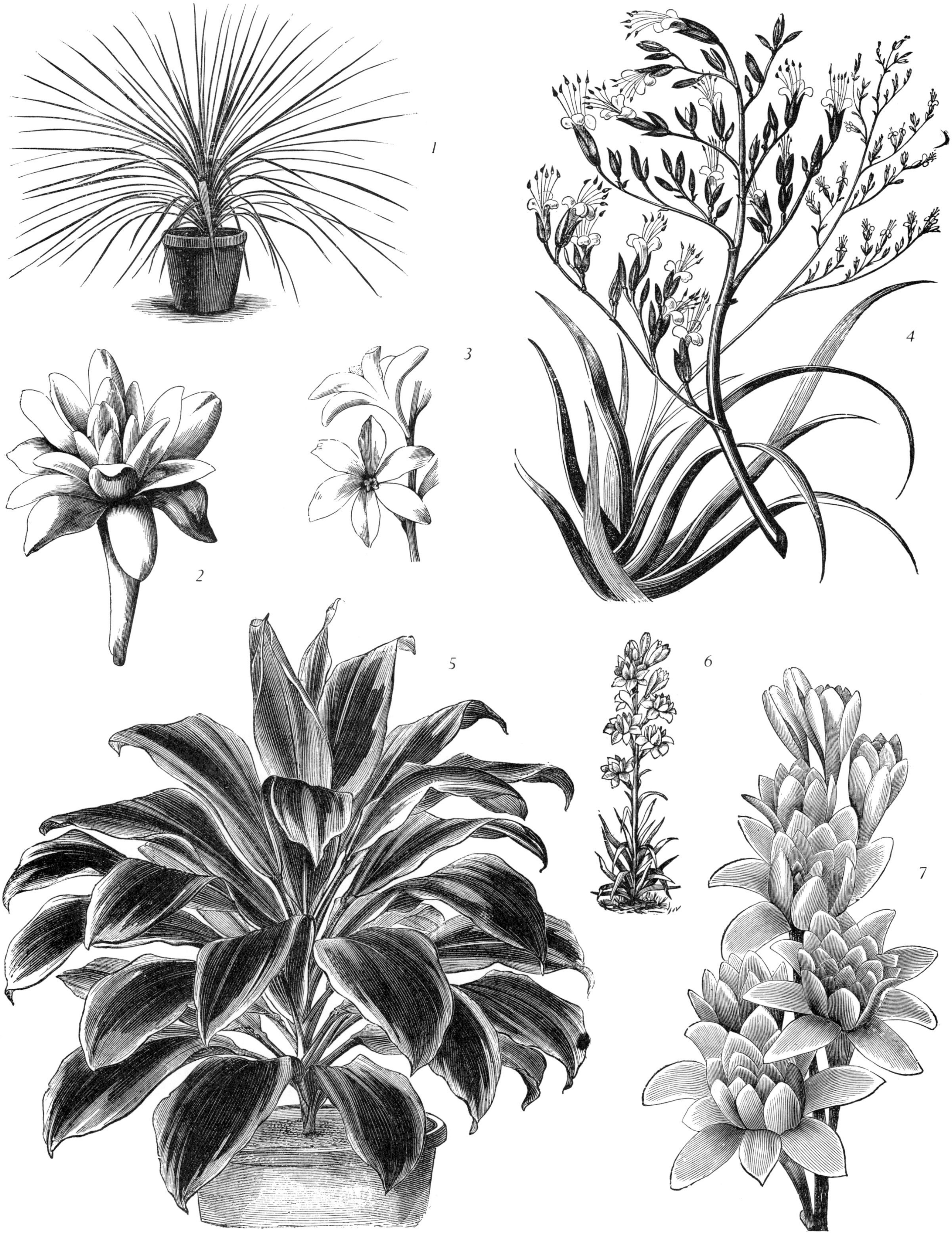
1
2
3
4
5
6
7

 AGAVACEAE (*Dracaenas*)

1

2

3

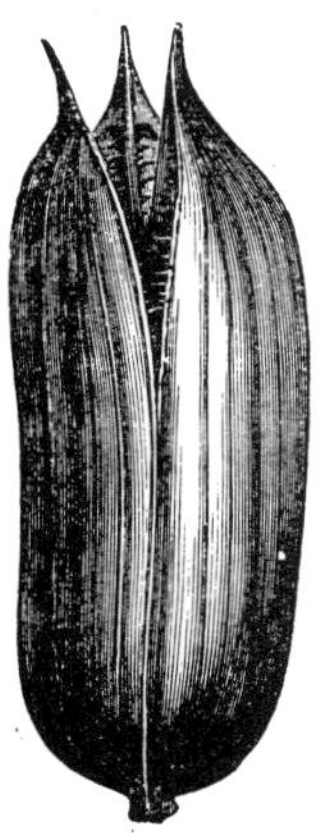

4

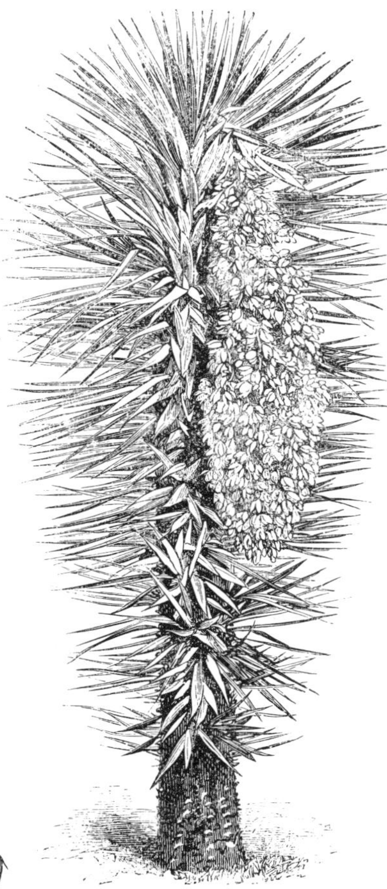

5

6

7

1

2

3

4

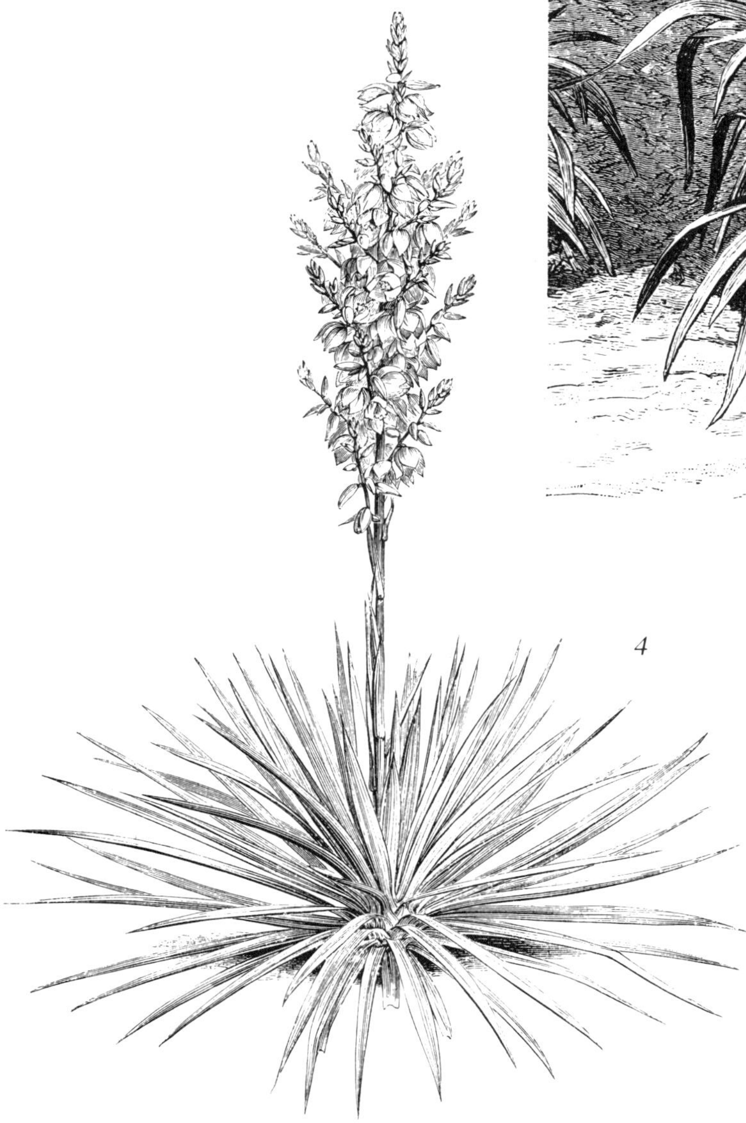

5

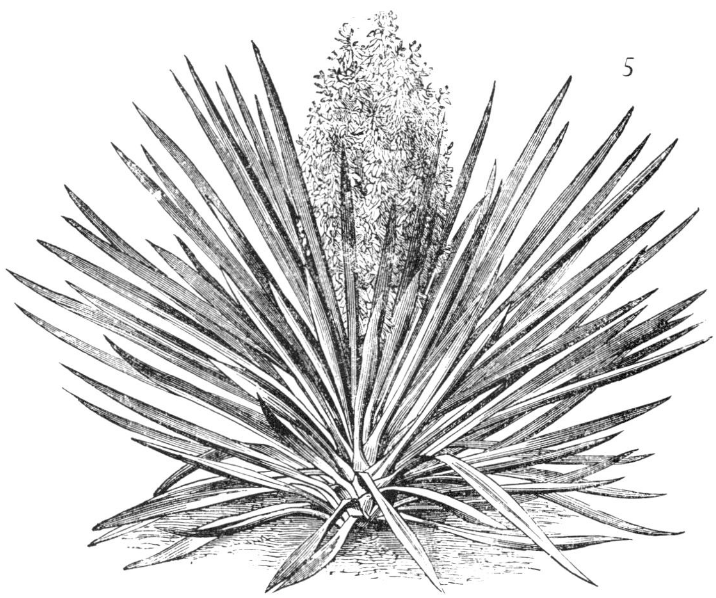

1

2

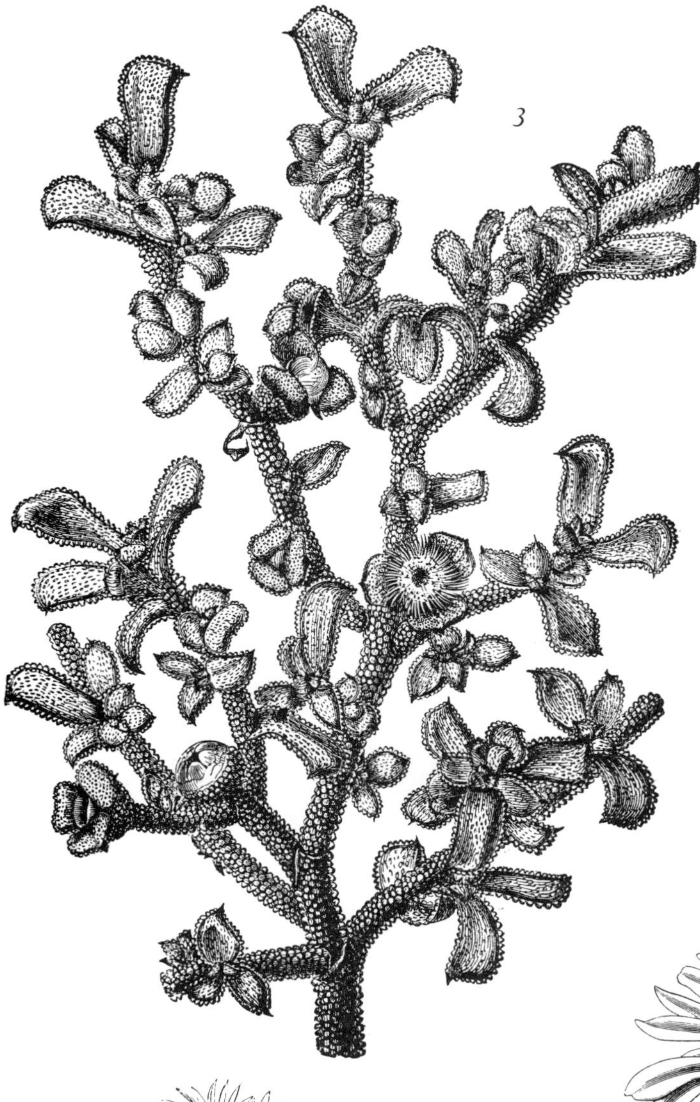

3

4

5

6

7

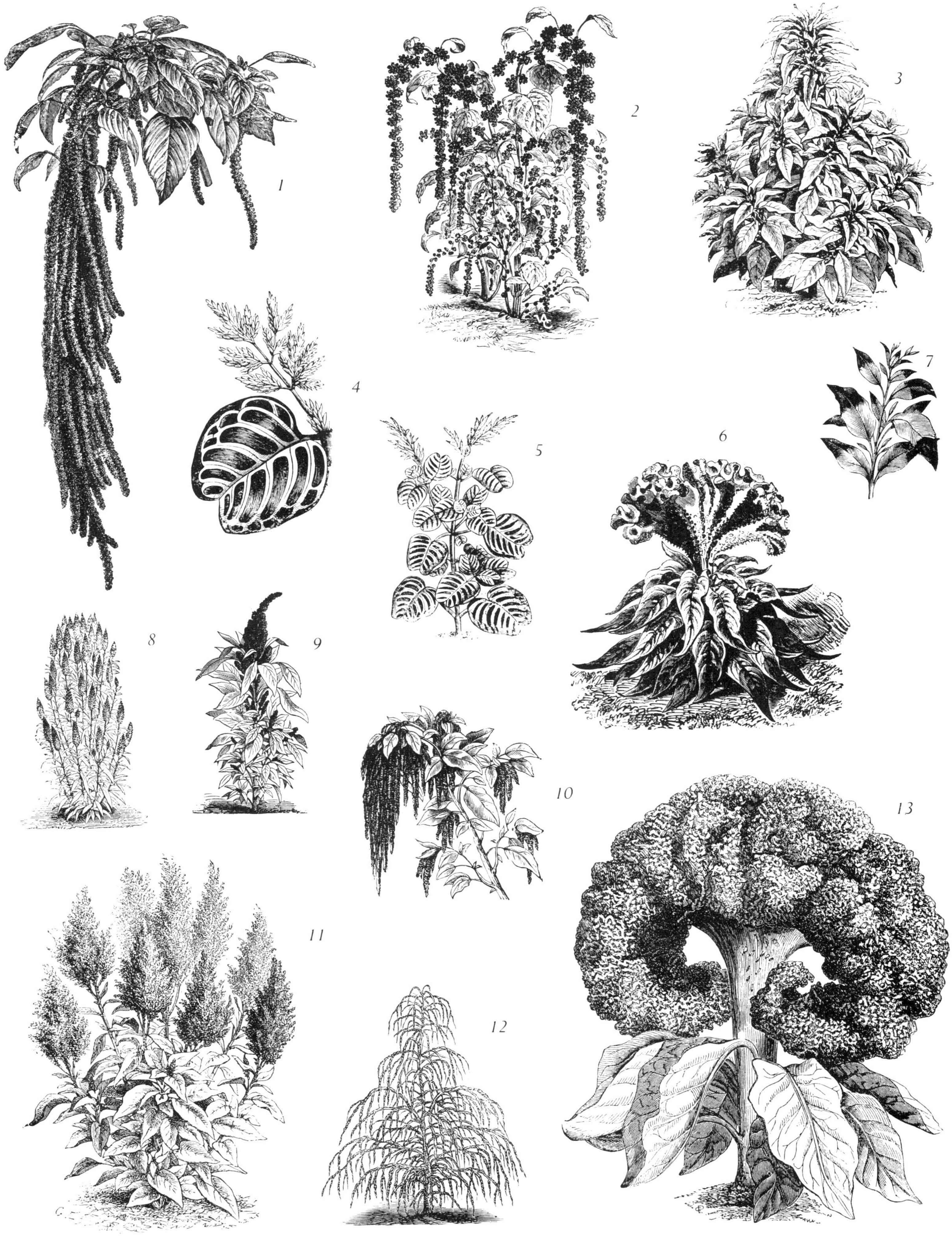

 AMARANTHACEAE (*Amaranths, Cockscombs, Celosias*)

1

2

4

3

7

5

6

1

2

3

4

7

6

5

9

8

AMARYLLIDACEAE (*Amaryllis, Daffodils*)

1

2

3

4

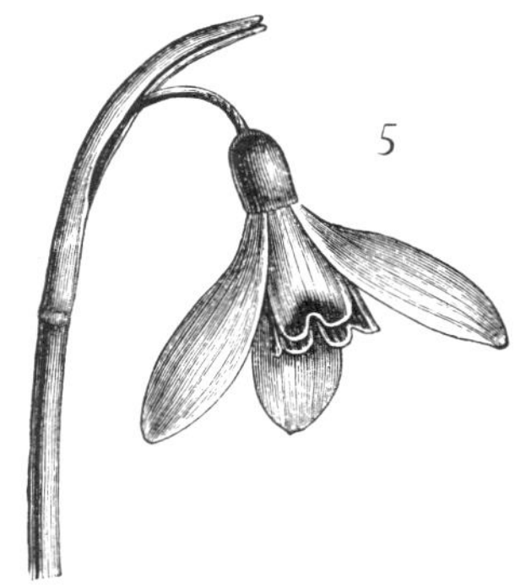

5

6

7

1

2

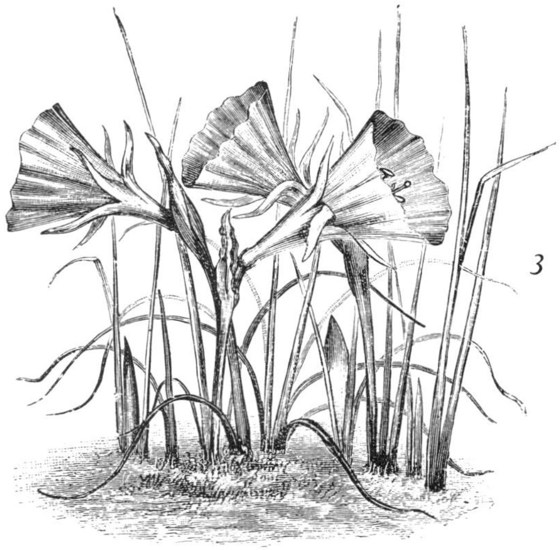

3

4

5

6

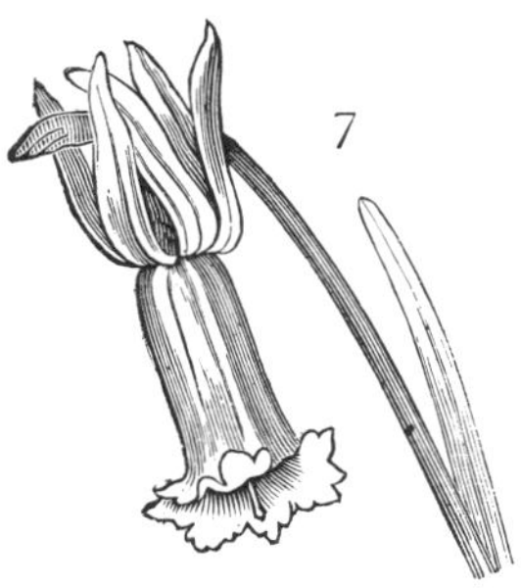

7

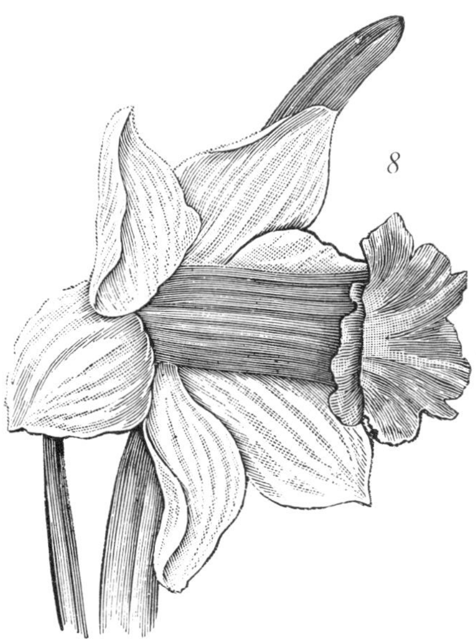

8

9

10

1

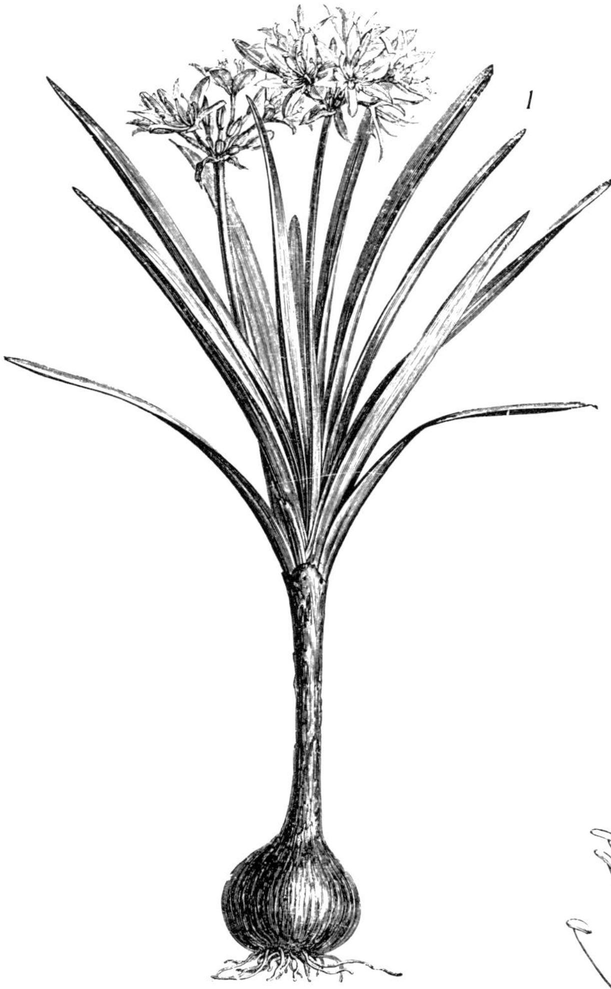

2

3

4

5

1

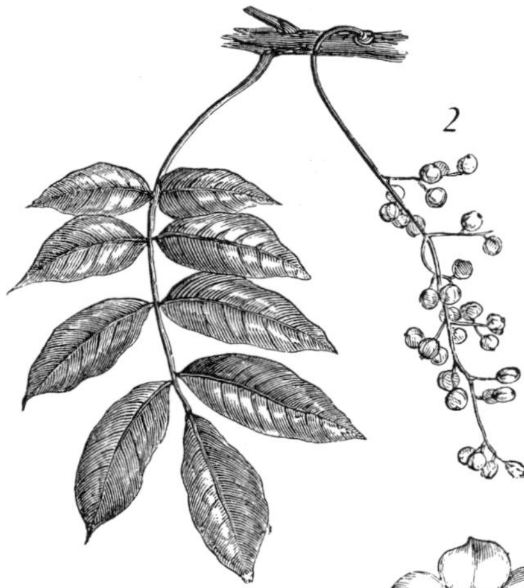

2

3

4

5

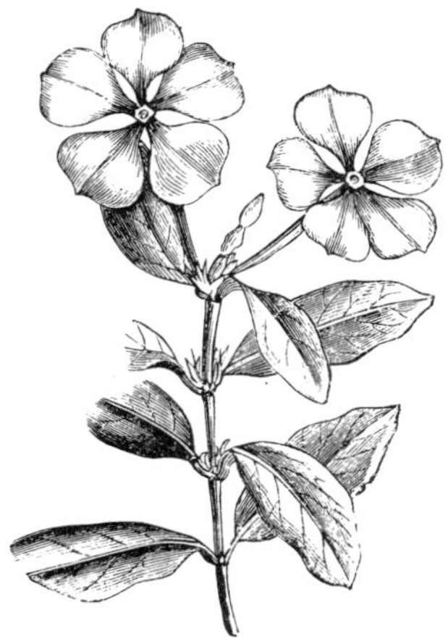

6

7

8

9

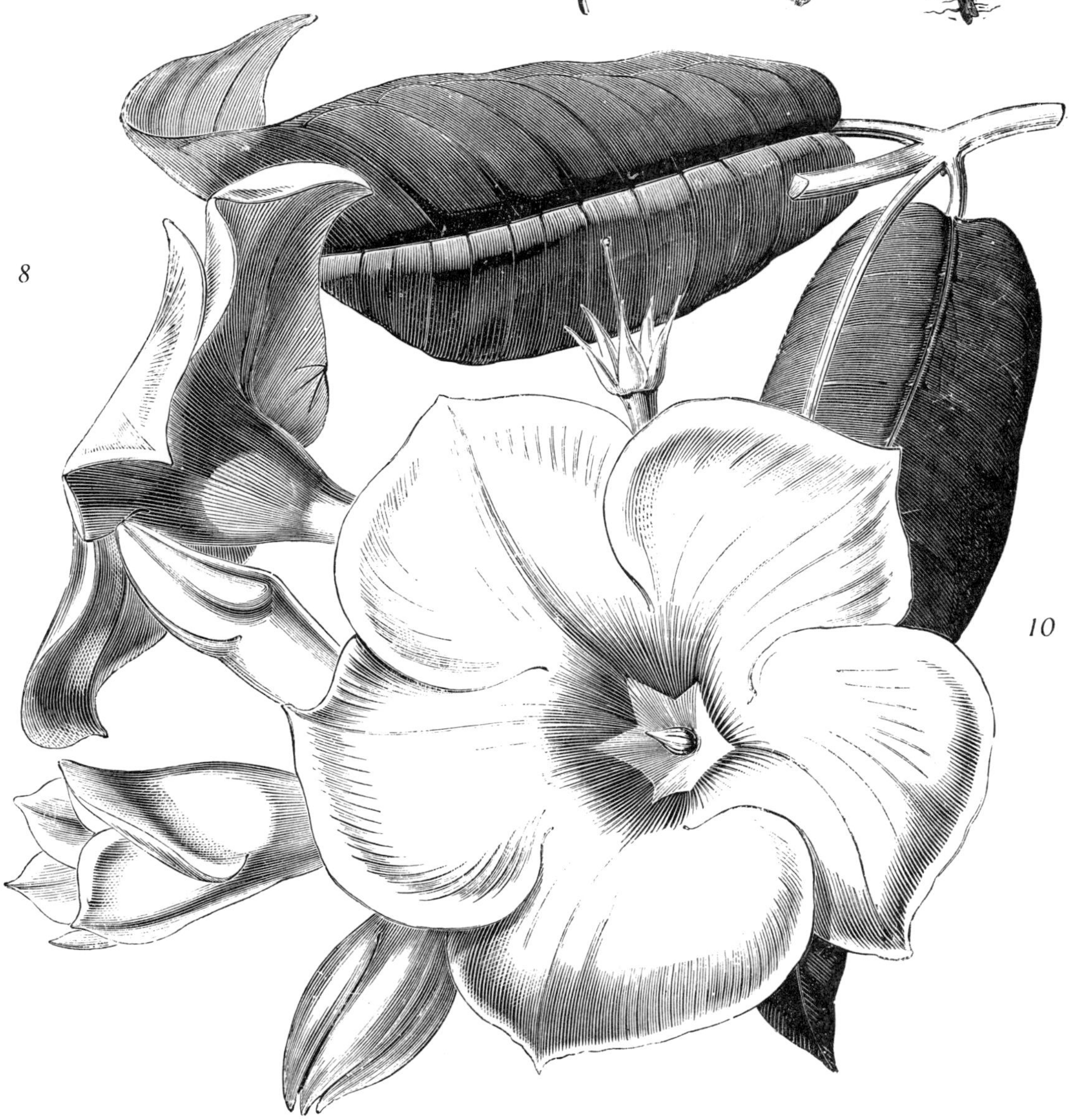

10

***ANACARDIACEAE* (*Cashews, Mangoes, Poison Ivies*) and *APOCYNACEAE* (*Periwinkles, Oleanders*)**

1
2
3
4
5
6
7
8
9
10
11
12
13
14
15
16

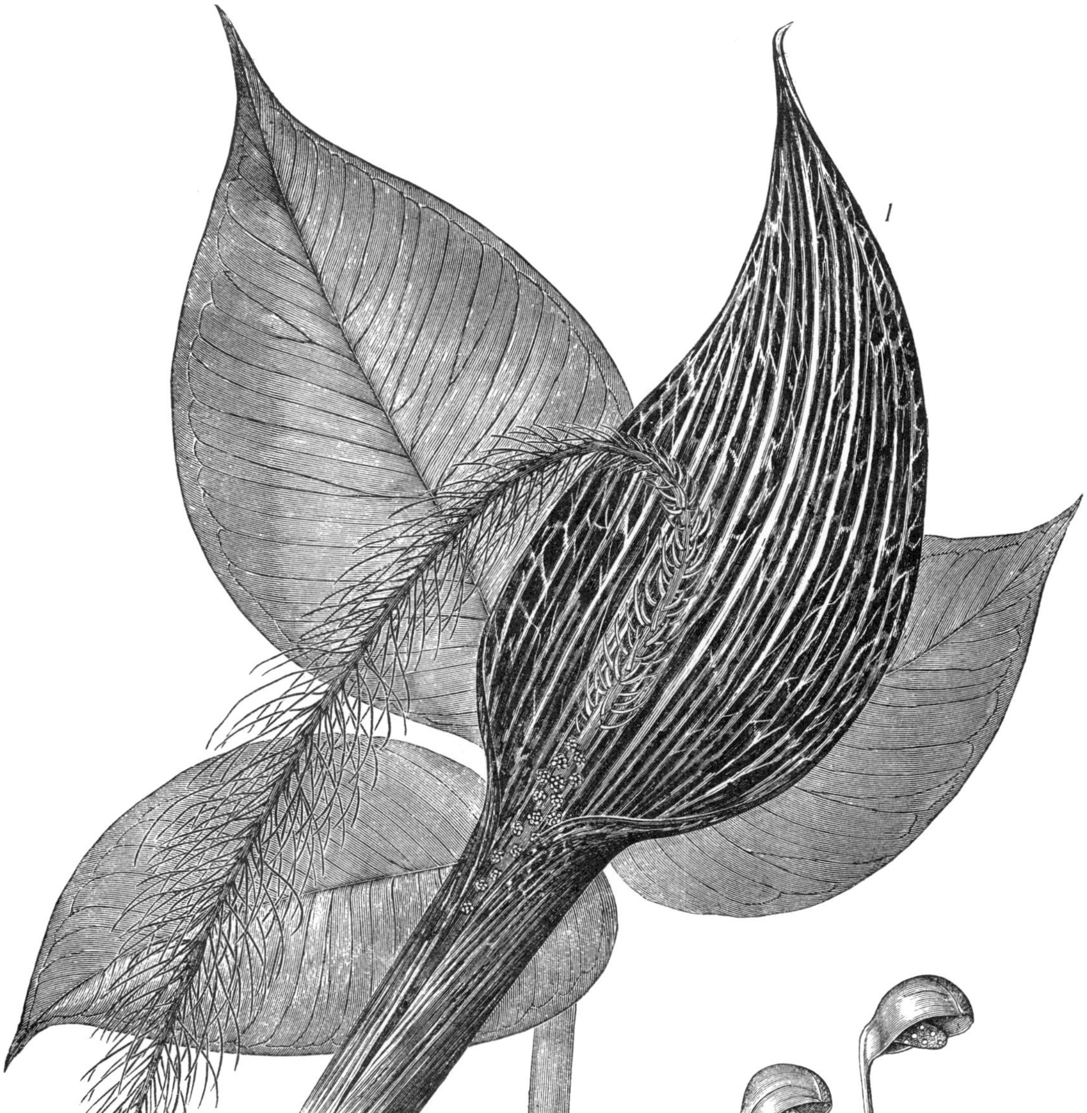

1

2

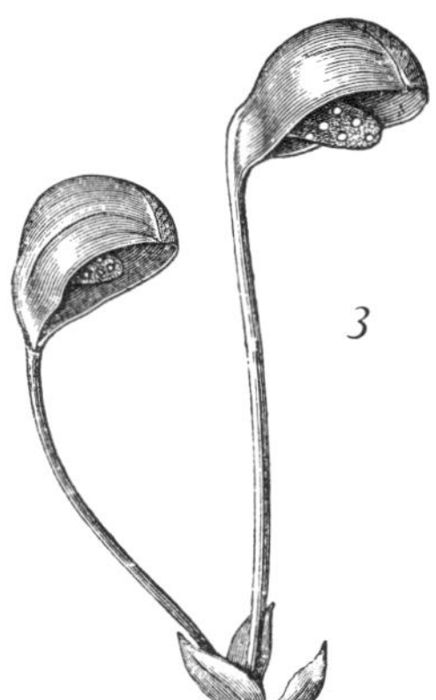

3

4

5

6

1

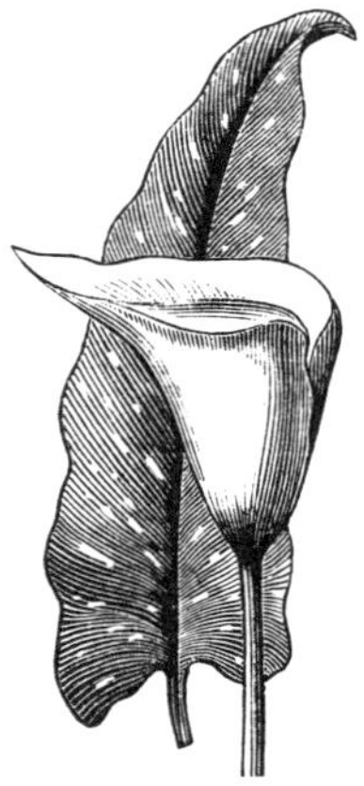

2

3

4

5

6

7

8

9

1

2

3

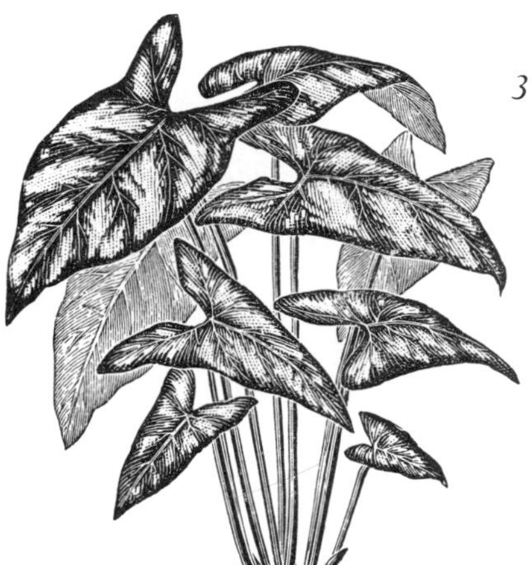

4

1

2

3

5

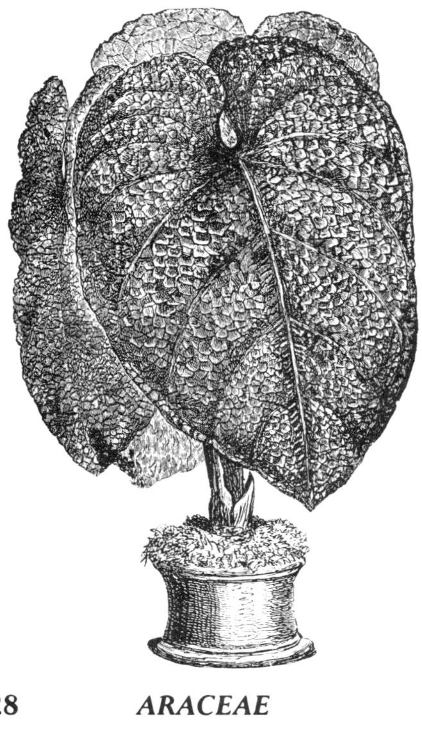

4

1

2

3

4

5

6

1

2

3
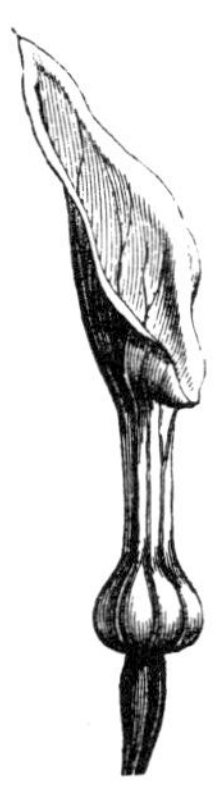
4

5
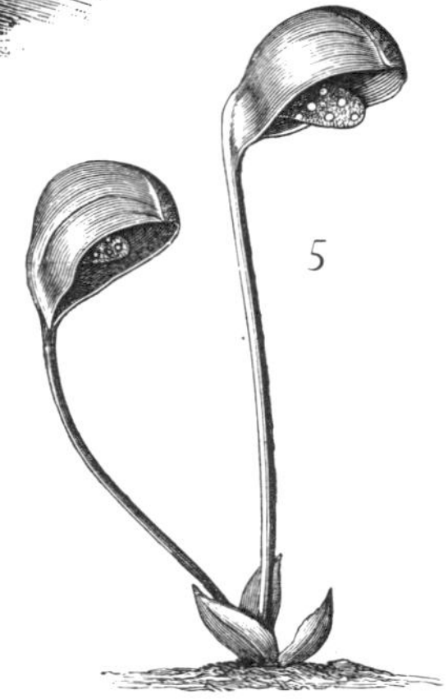
6

7

8

1

2

3

4

5

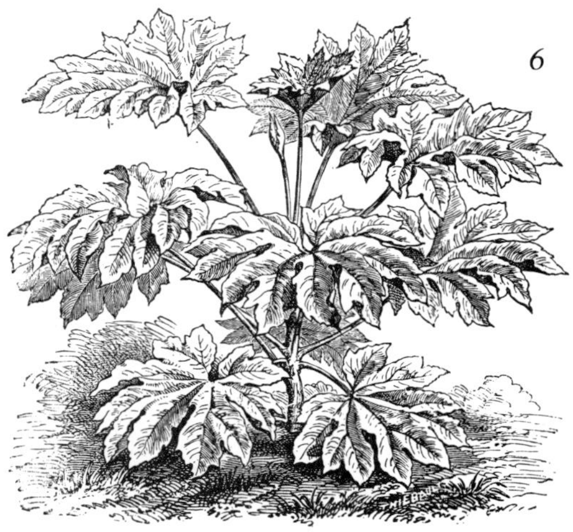

6

7

ARACEAE (Aroids) and ARALIACEAE (Ivies, Ginsengs)

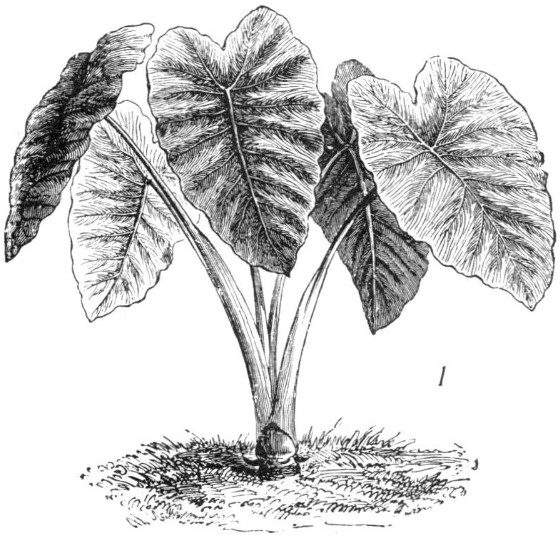
1

2

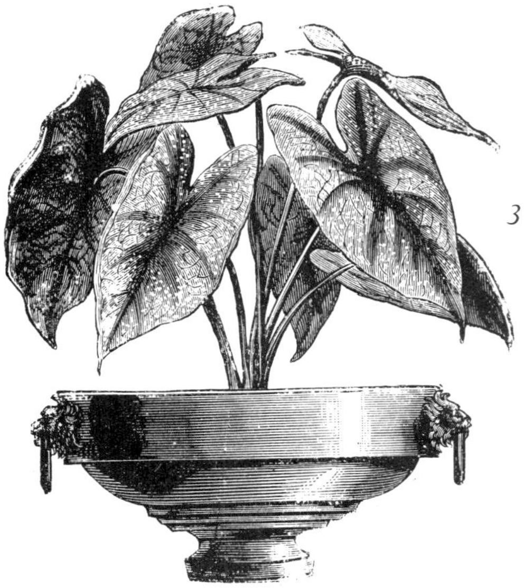
3

4

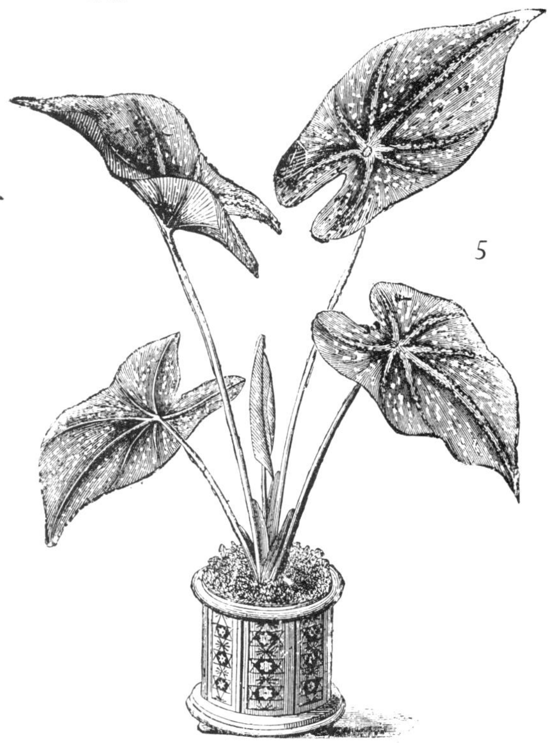
5

6

7

8

ARACEAE (Mainly Caladiums)

1

2

3

4

1

2

3
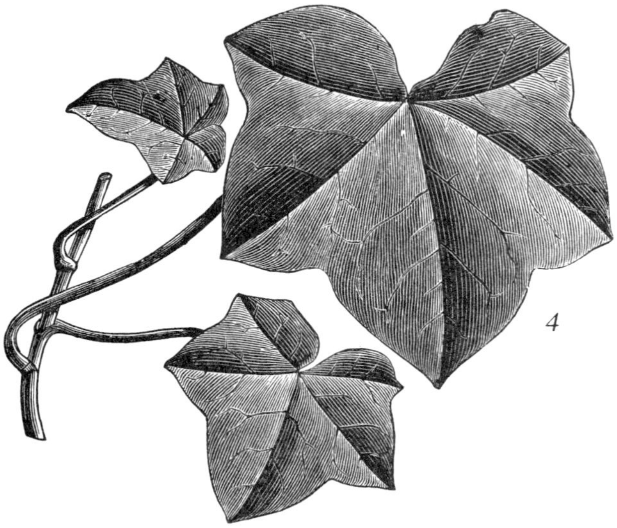
4
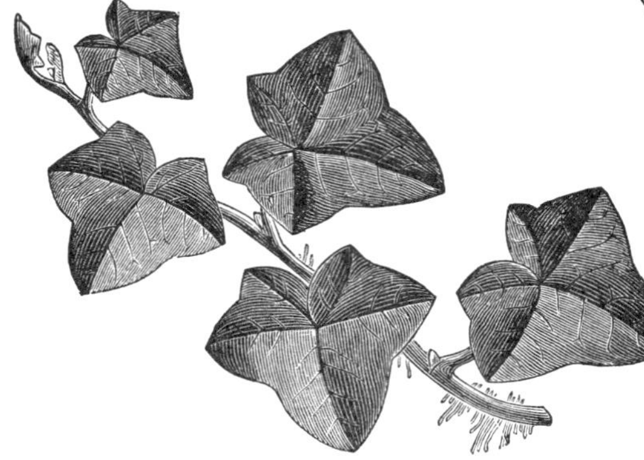
5
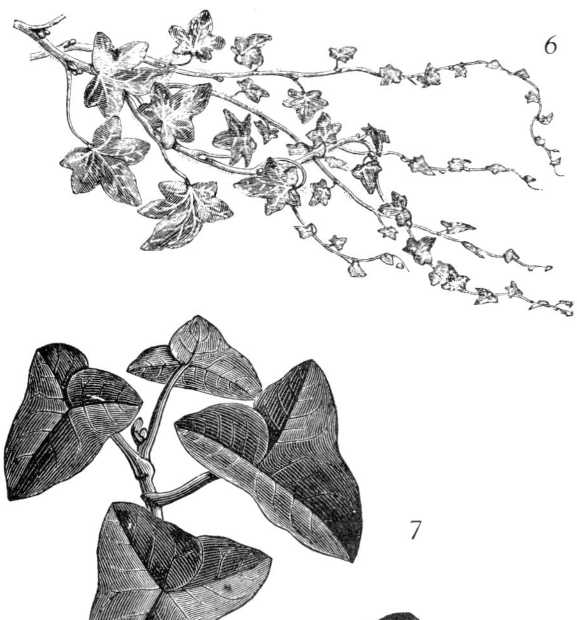
6
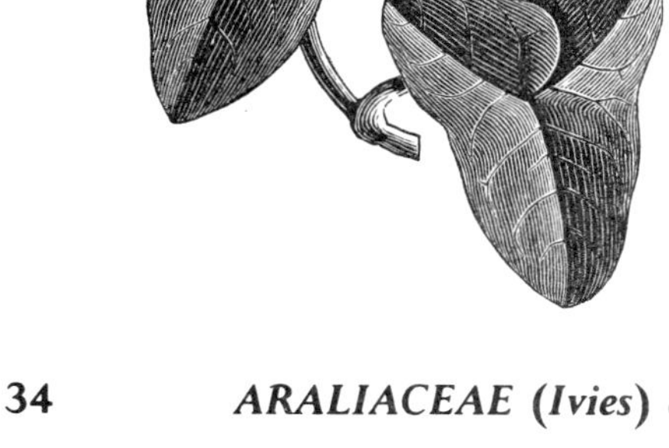
7

8

1

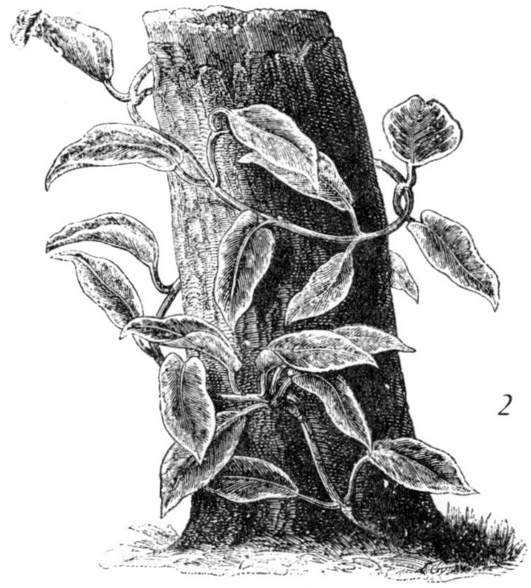

2

3

4

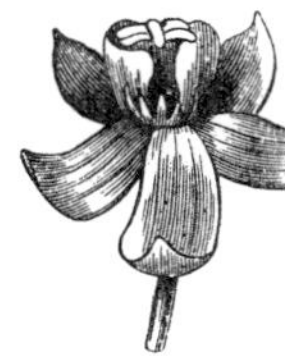

5

6

7

8

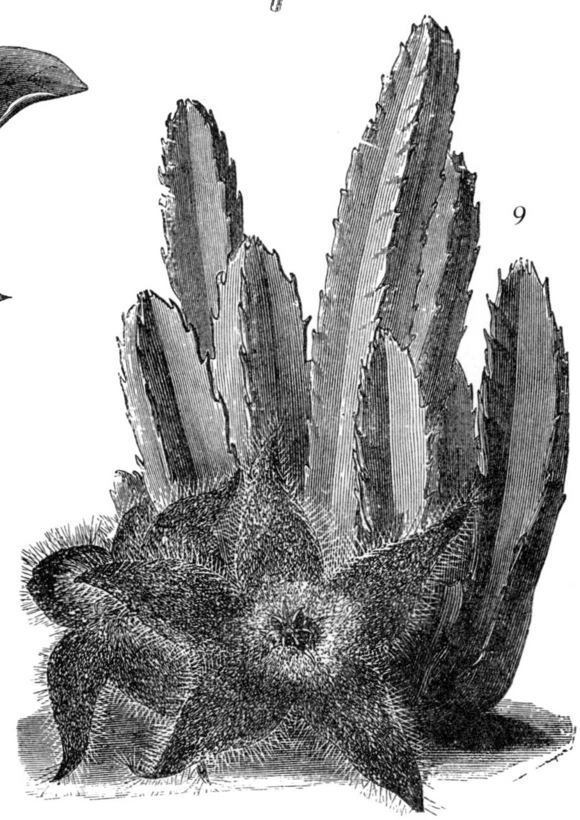

9

1

2

3

4

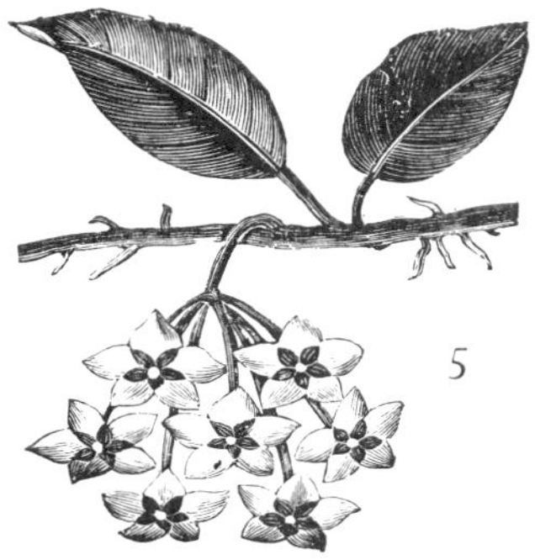

5

6

7

 ASCLEPIADACEAE (Impatiens), BALSAMINACEAE (Balsams), and BEGONIACEAE (Begonias)

1

2

3

4

5

6

7

8

9

10

11

1

2

3

4

5

6

7

8

 BEGONIACEAE (Begonias)

1

2

3

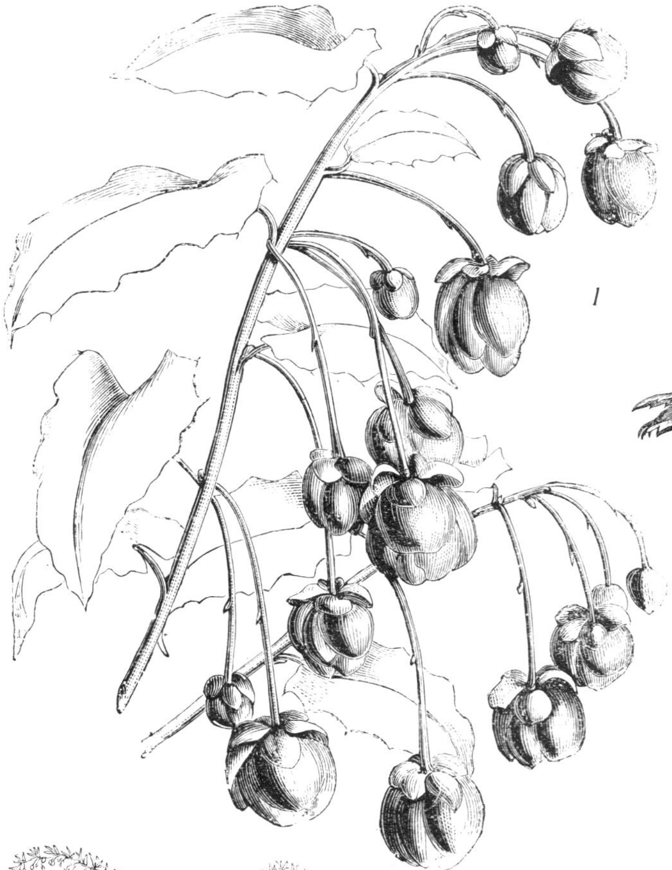

1

2

3

4

5

6

 BEGONIACEAE (Begonias) and BERBERIDACEAE (Barberries, Mayapples)

1

2

3

4

5

6

7

1

2

3

4

5

6

BORAGINACEAE (*Forget-Me-Nots, Borages*)

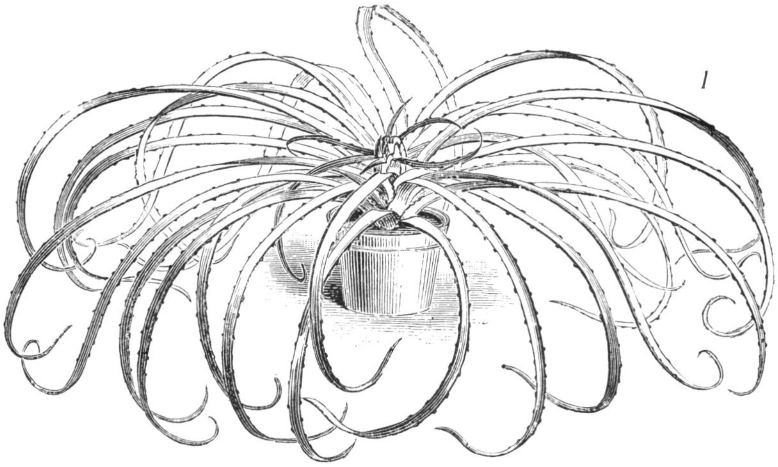
1

2

3

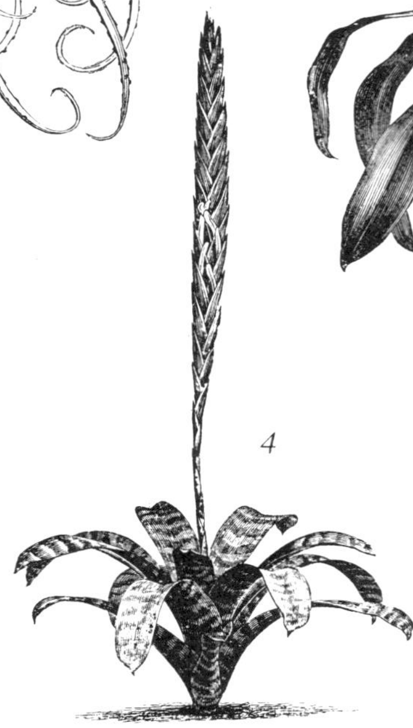
4

5

7

6

8

BROMELIACEAE (*Pineapples, Bromeliads*)

1

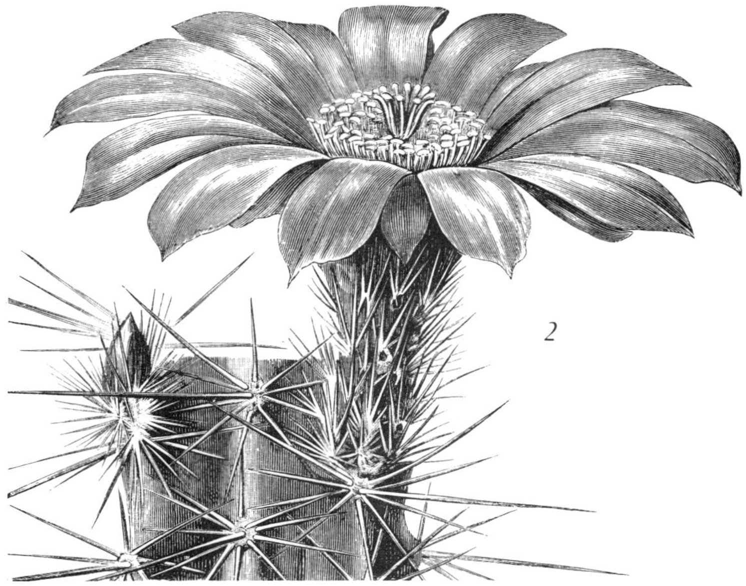

2

3

4

5

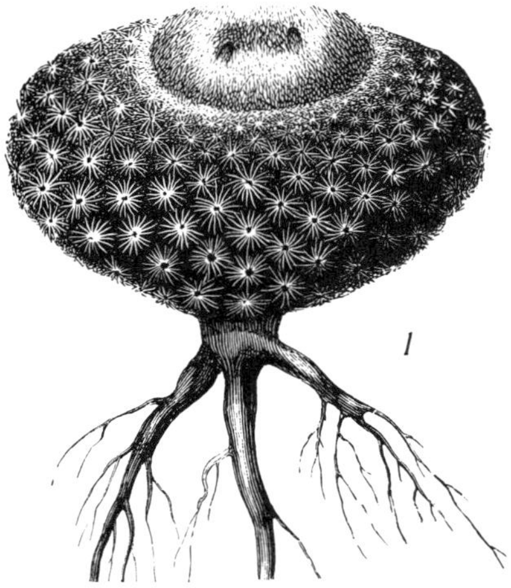

1

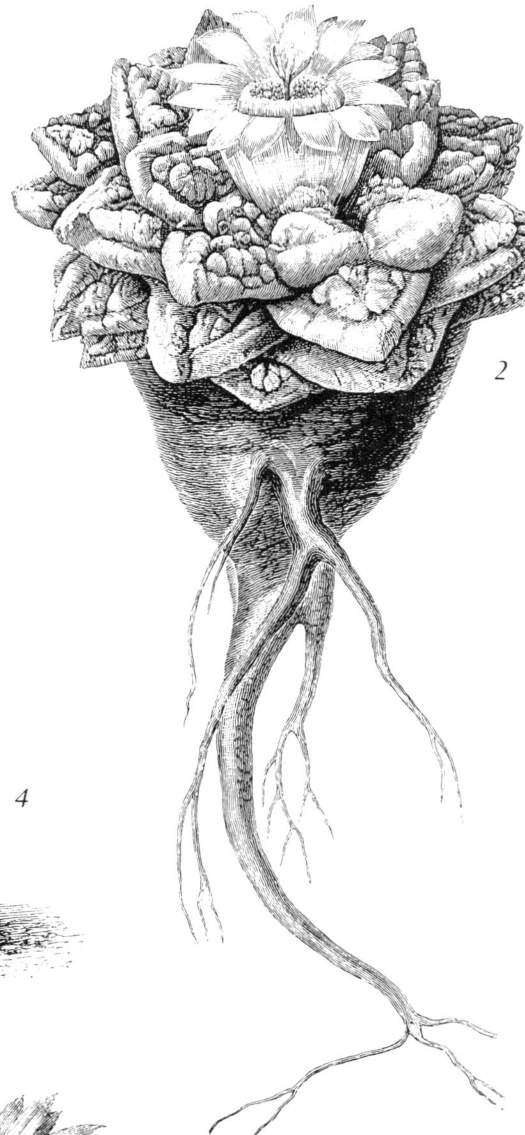

2

3

4

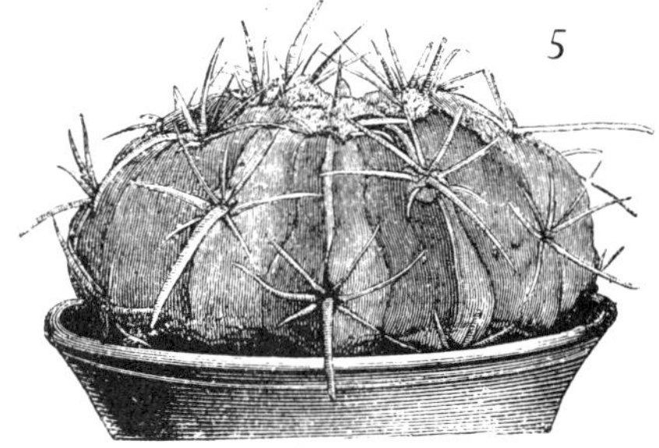

5

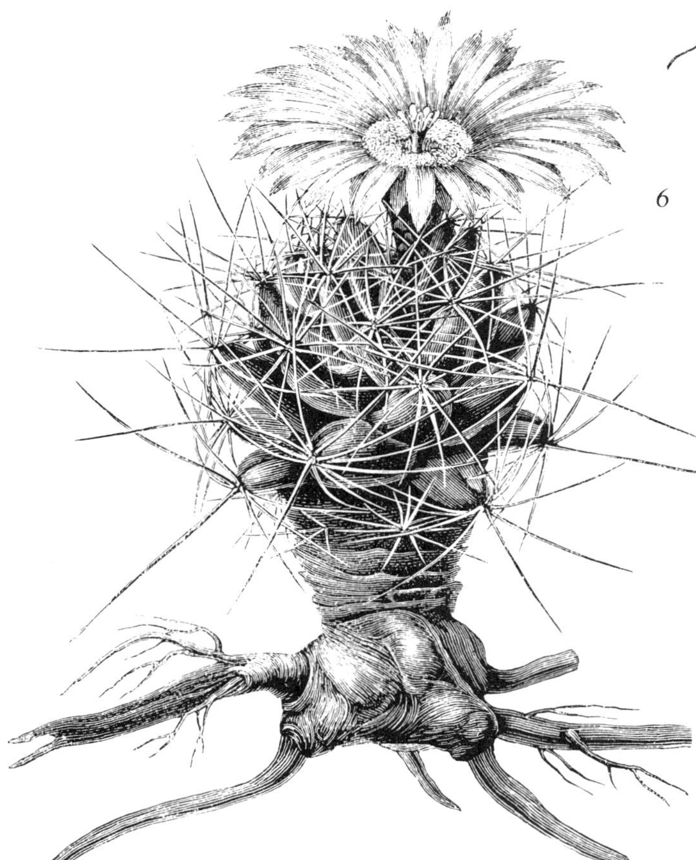

6

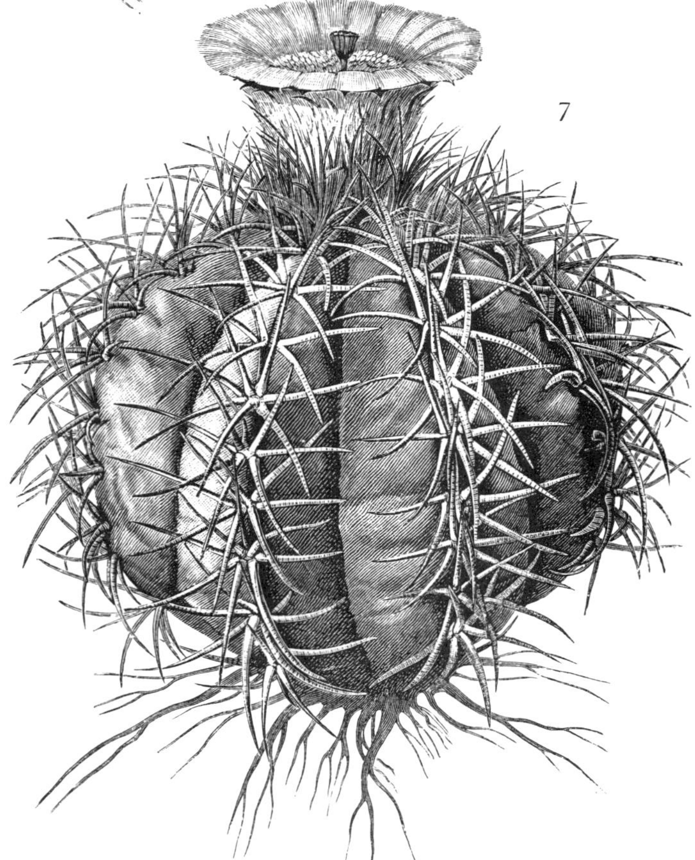

7

1
2
3
4
5
6
7
8
9

1

2

3

4

5

6

7

1

2

3

5

4

6

7

1

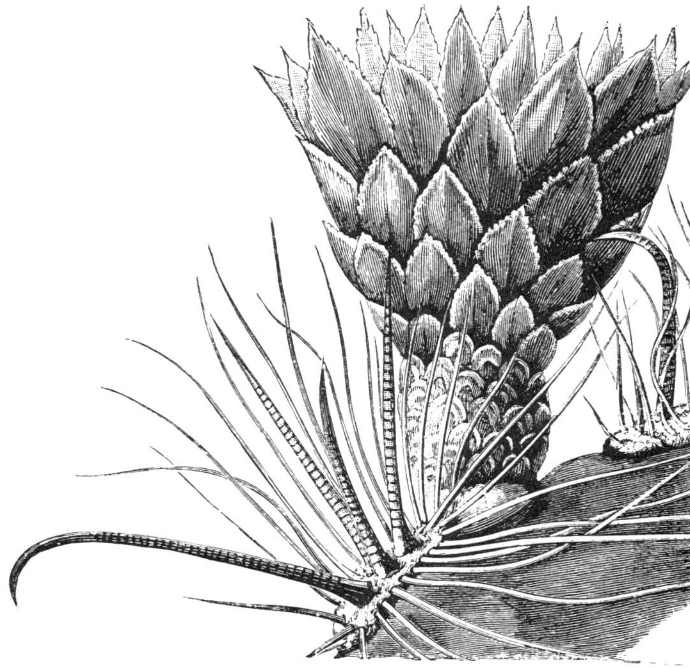

2

3

4

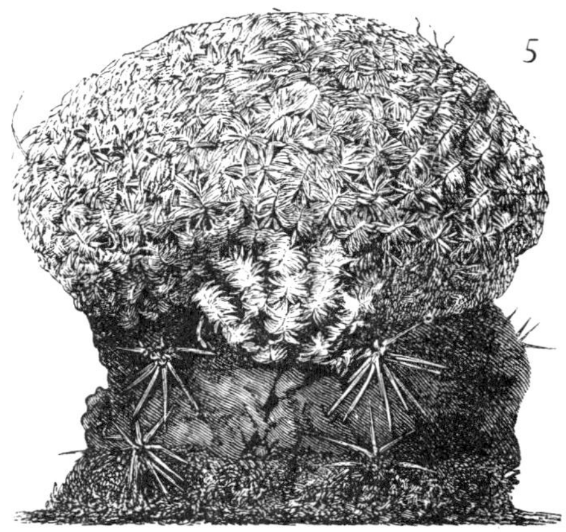

5

6

7

1

2

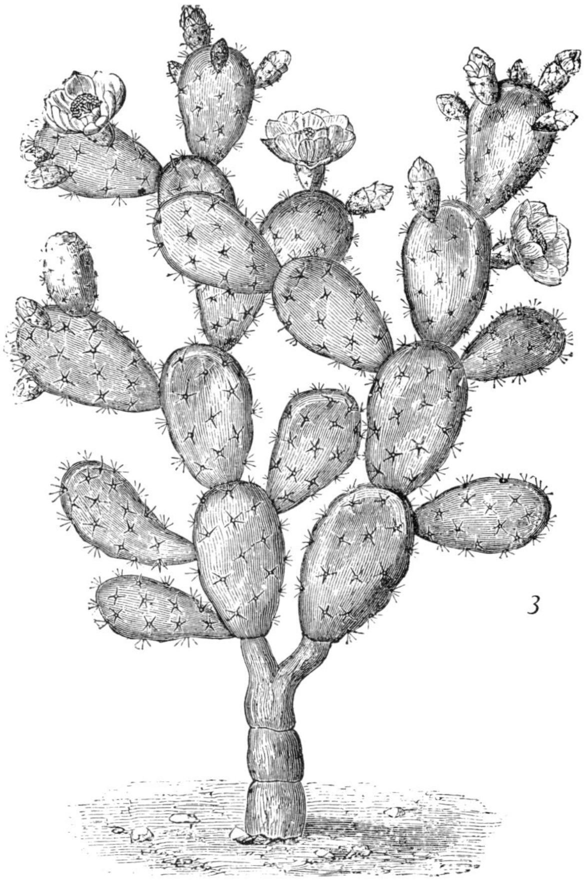

3

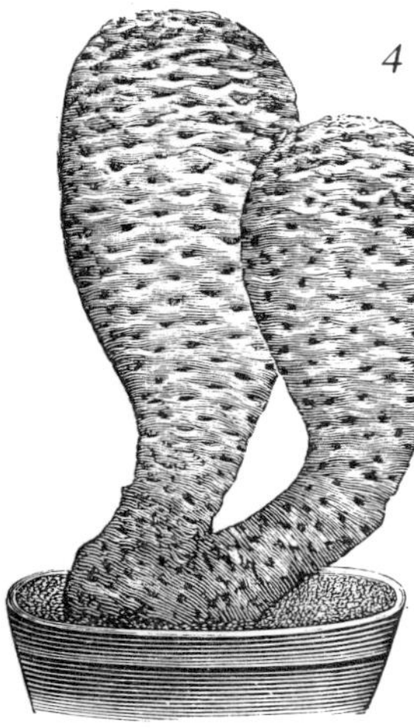

4

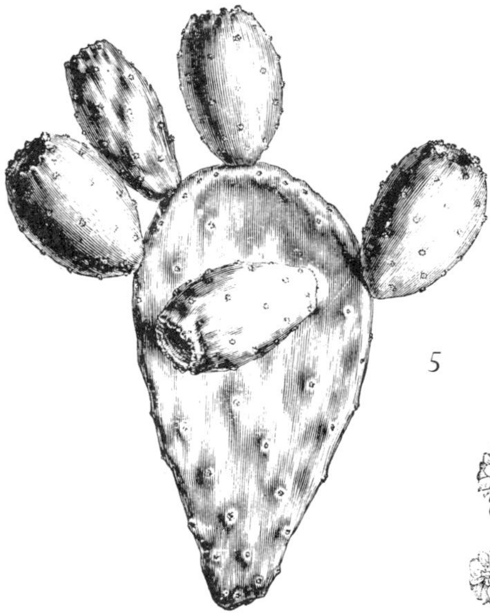

5

6

7

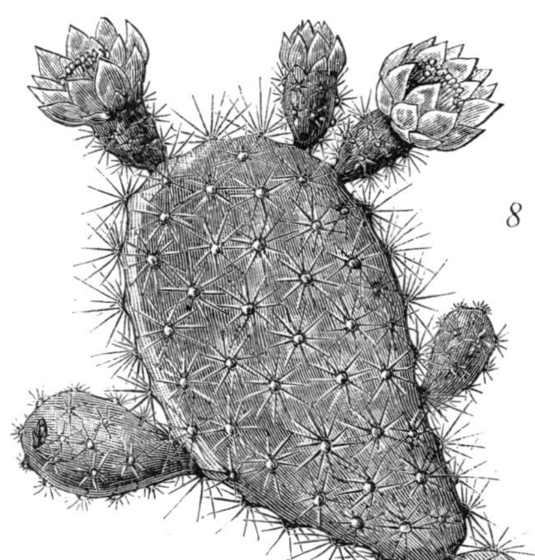

8

1

3

2

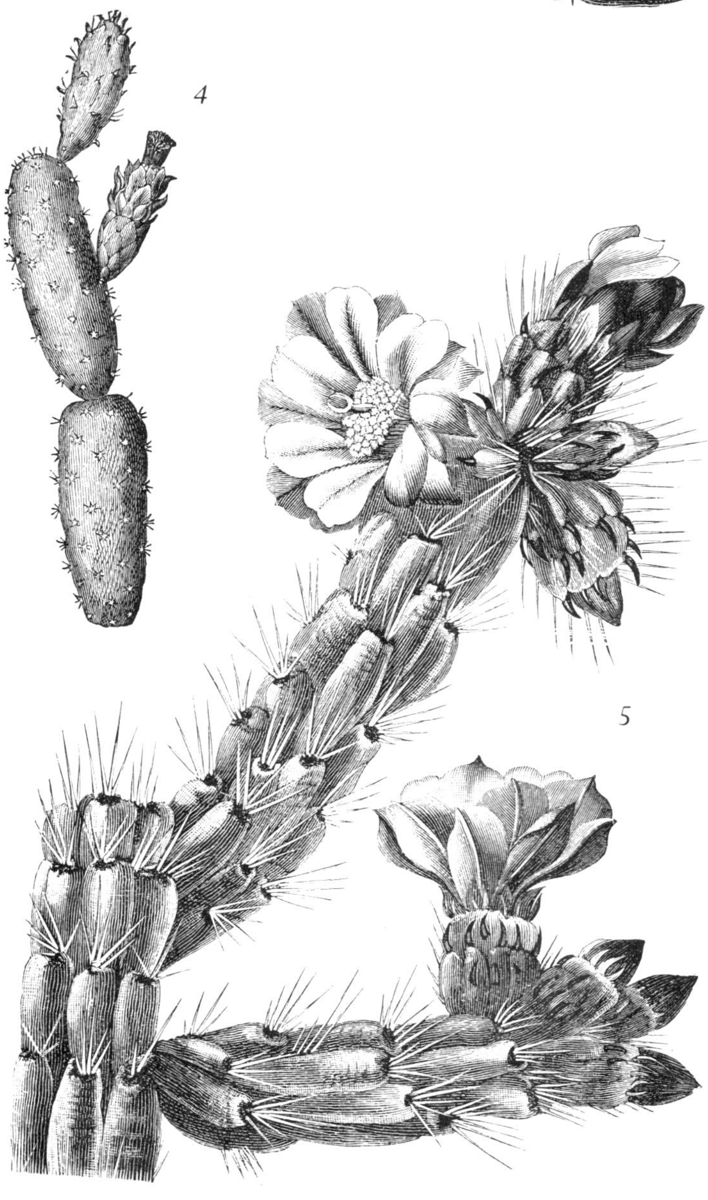

4

6

5

1

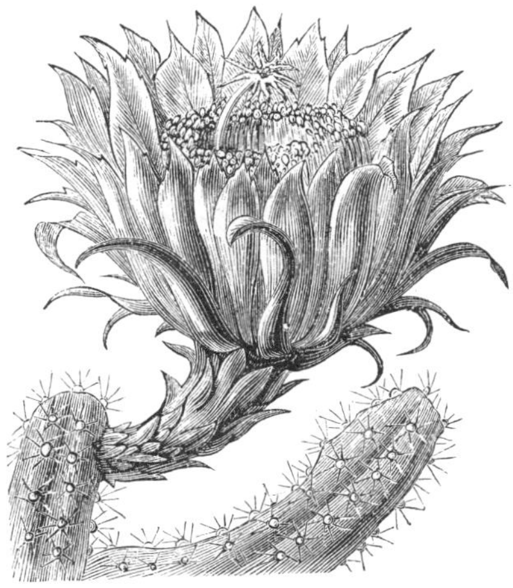

2

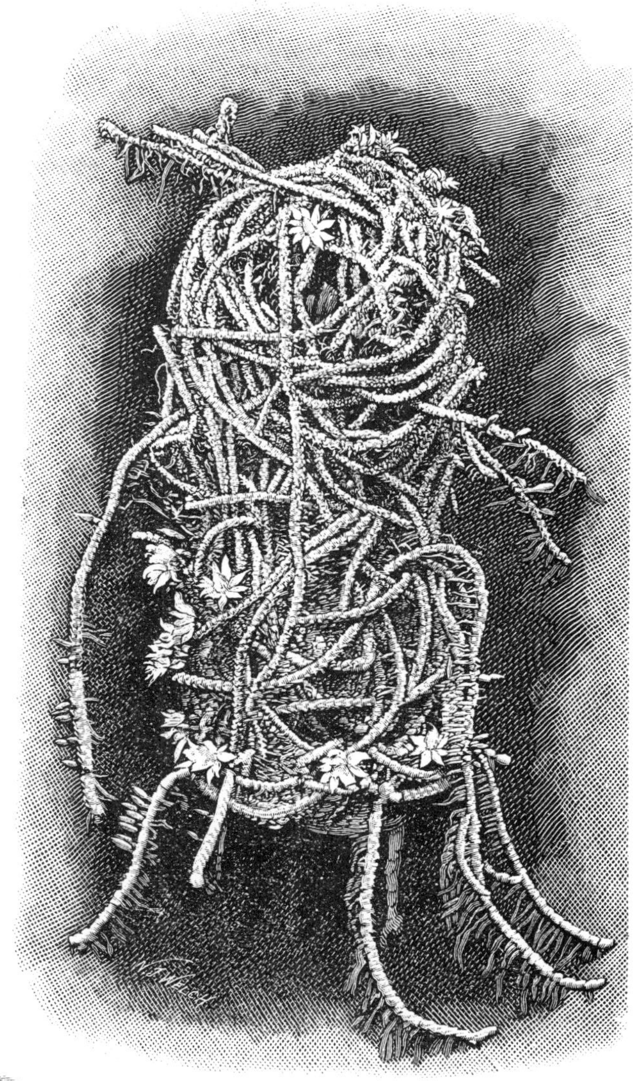

3

4

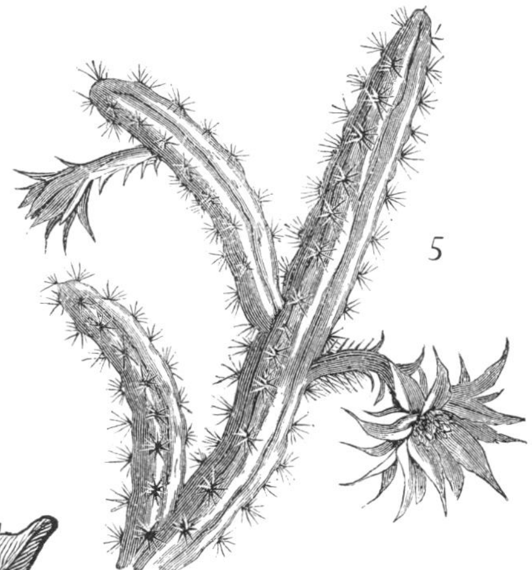

5

6

7

8

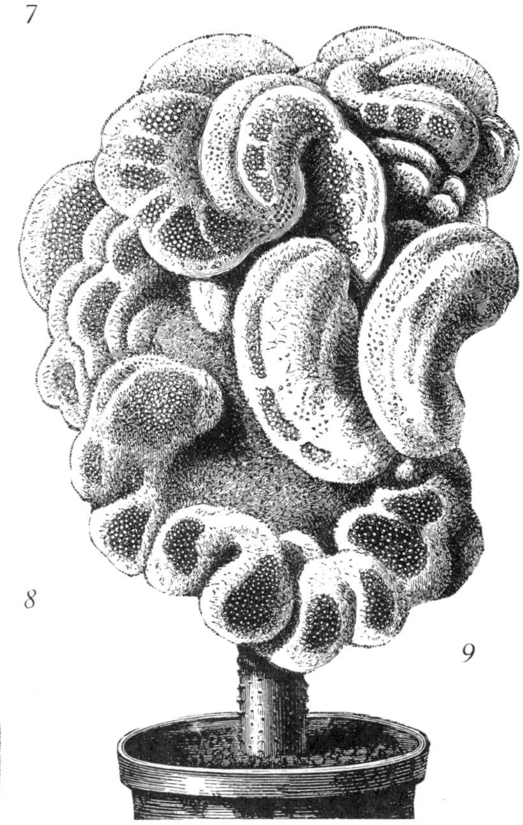

9

1

2

3

4

5

6

7

8

1

2

3

4

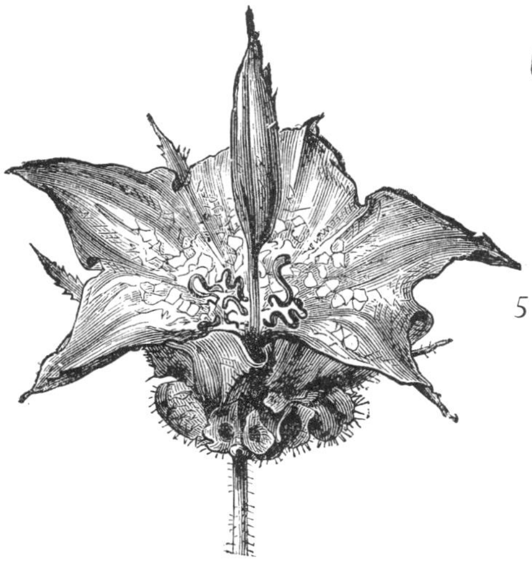

5

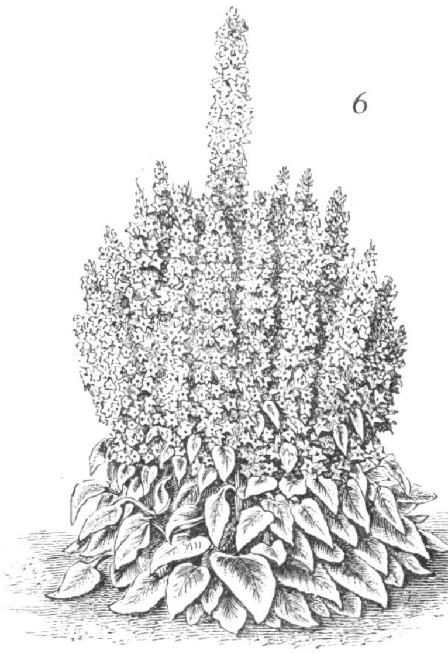

6

7

8

9

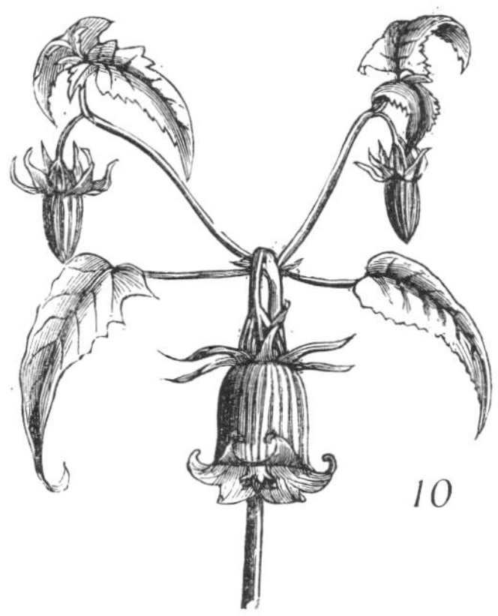

10

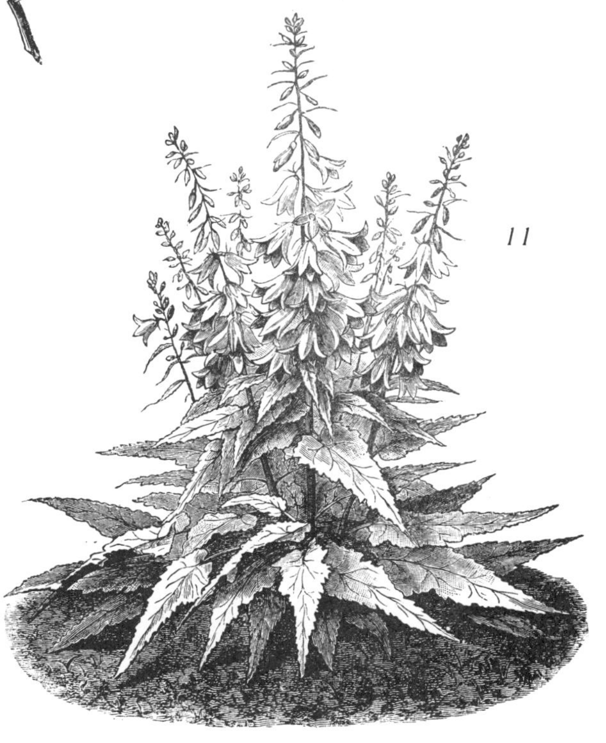

11

CAMPANULACEAE **(*Campanulas, Bellflowers*)**

CAMPANULACEAE **(*Campanula, Bellflowers*)**

1

2

3

4

5

6

7

1

2

3

4

5

6

7

8

9

10

***CARYOPHYLLACEAE* (*Carnations, Pinks*)**

1

2

3

4

5

6

7

8

9

1

2

3

4

5

6

7

8

9

10

CELASTRACEAE (Spindle Trees), CISTACEAE (Rock Roses), COMBRETACEAE (Combretums), COMMELINACEAE (Spiderworts), and COMPOSITAE (Asters, Sunflowers, Dandelions, Chrysanthemums)

1

2

3

4

5

1

2

3

4

5

6

7

8

9

10

11

1

2

3

4

5

6

7

1

2

3

5

6

4

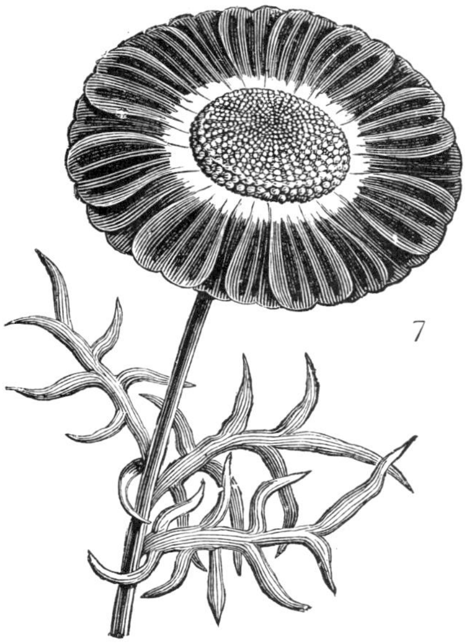

7

8

9

 COMPOSITAE (*Chrysanthemums*)

1

2

3

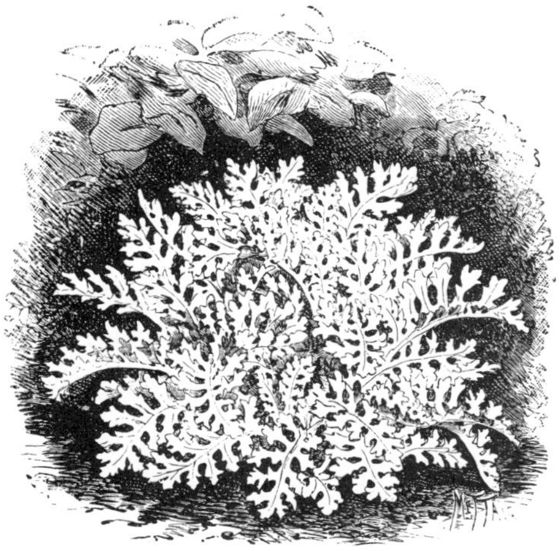

4

5

6

7

COMPOSITAE (*Chrysanthemums, Cinerarias*)

 COMPOSITAE (Chrysanthemums and others)

1

2

3

4

5

6

7

8

9

1

2

3

4

5

6

1

2

3

4

5

6

7

8

9

10

11

12

 COMPOSITAE (Helianthus, Sunflowers)

1

2

3

4

5

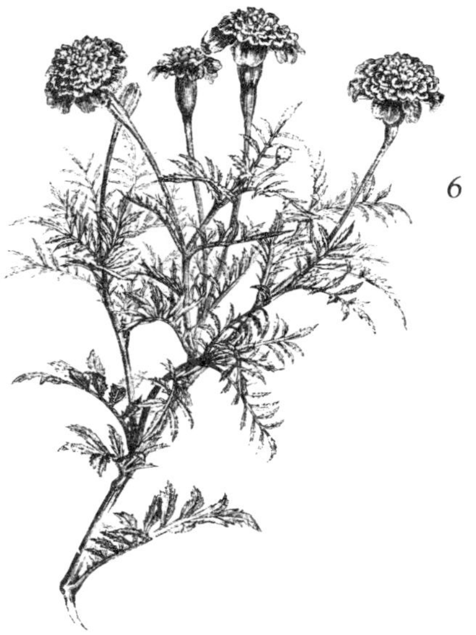
6

7

8

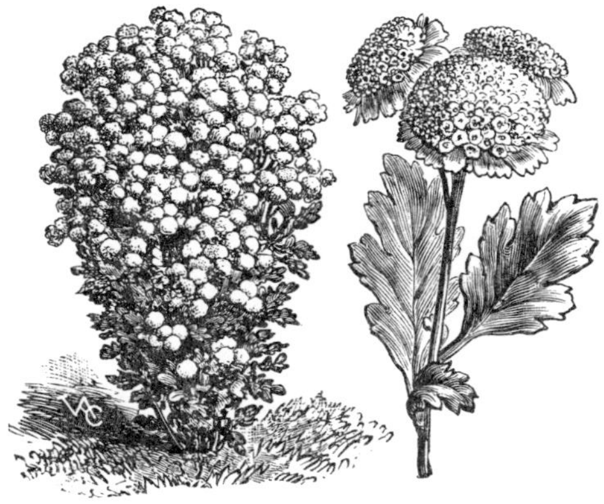
9

10

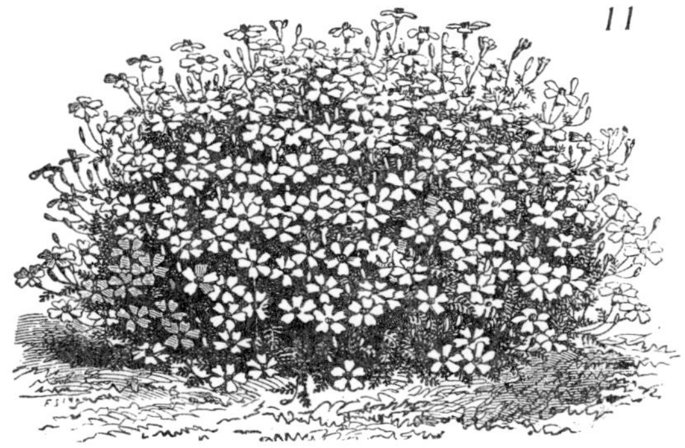
11

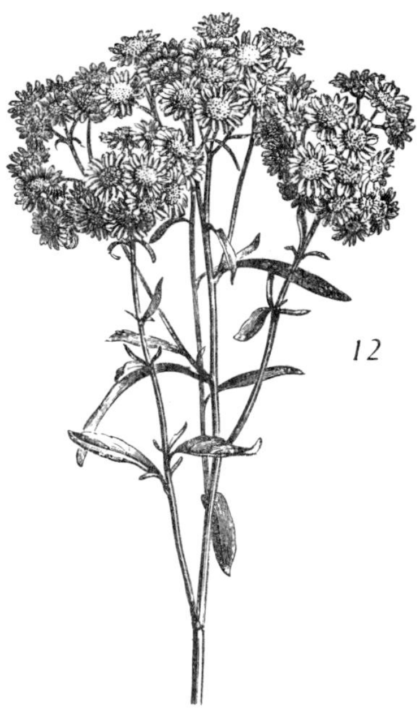
12

1

2

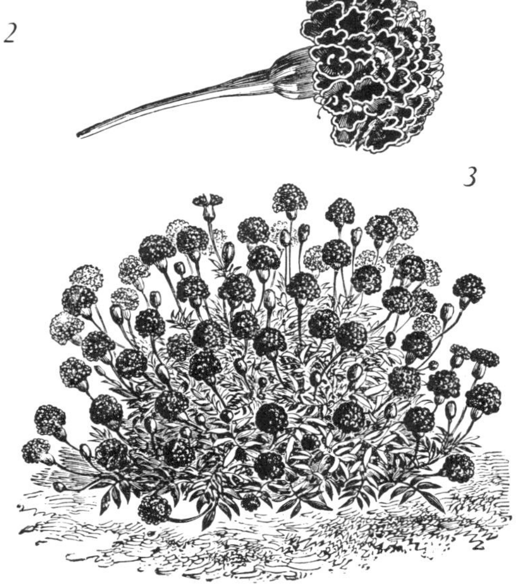

3

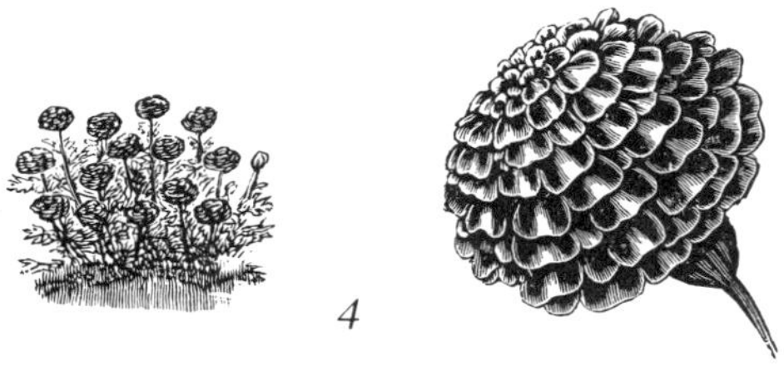

4

5

6

7

8

9

10

 COMPOSITAE (Marigolds, Zinnias, and others)

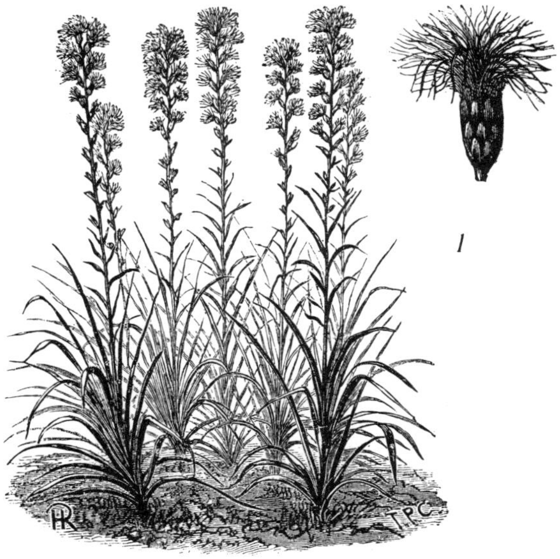

1

2

3

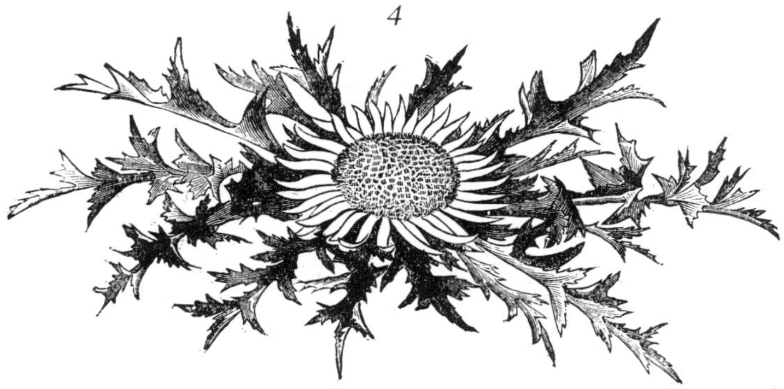

4

5

6

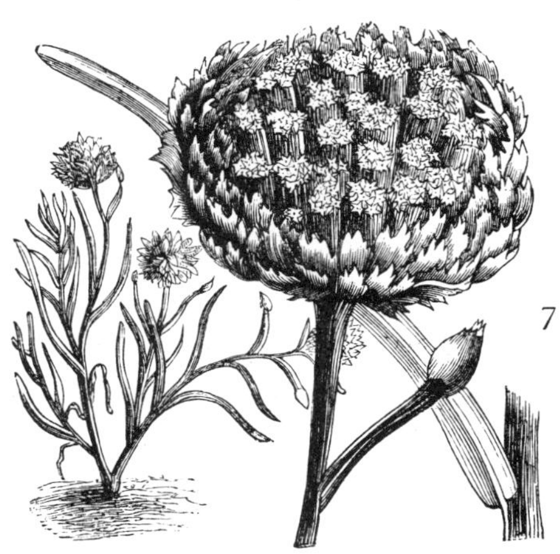

7

8

9

 COMPOSITAE (*Zinnias*)

1

2

3

4

5

6

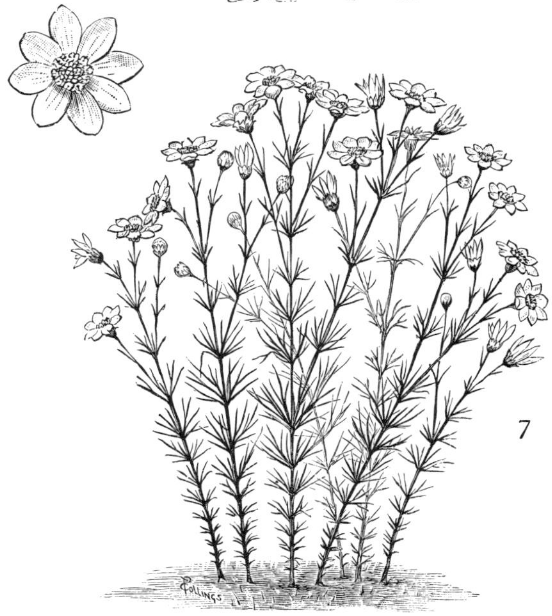

7

9

10

8

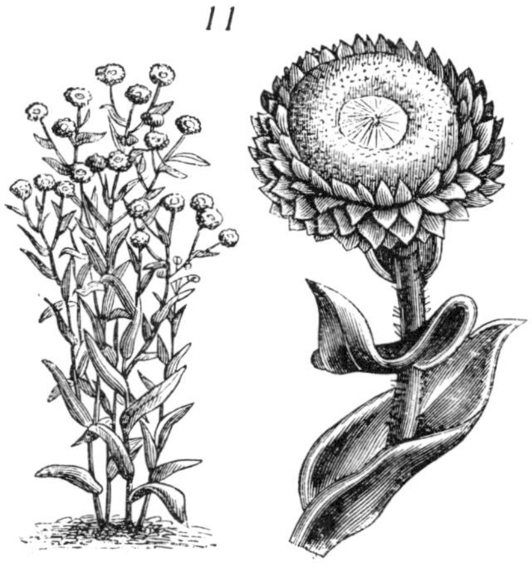

11

12

1

2

3

4

5

6

7

1

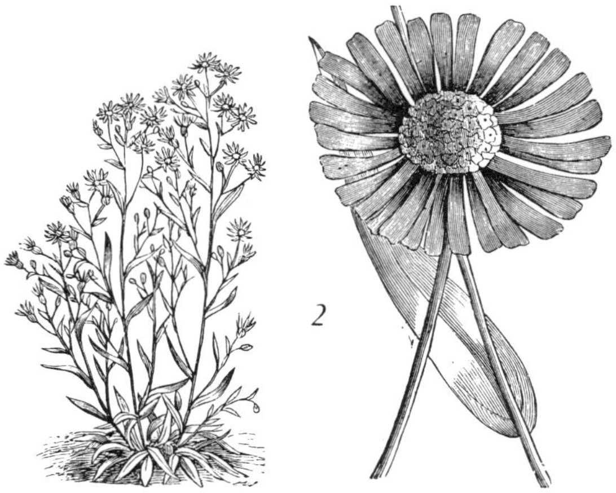

2

3

4

5

6

9

7

8

10

11

12

1

2

3

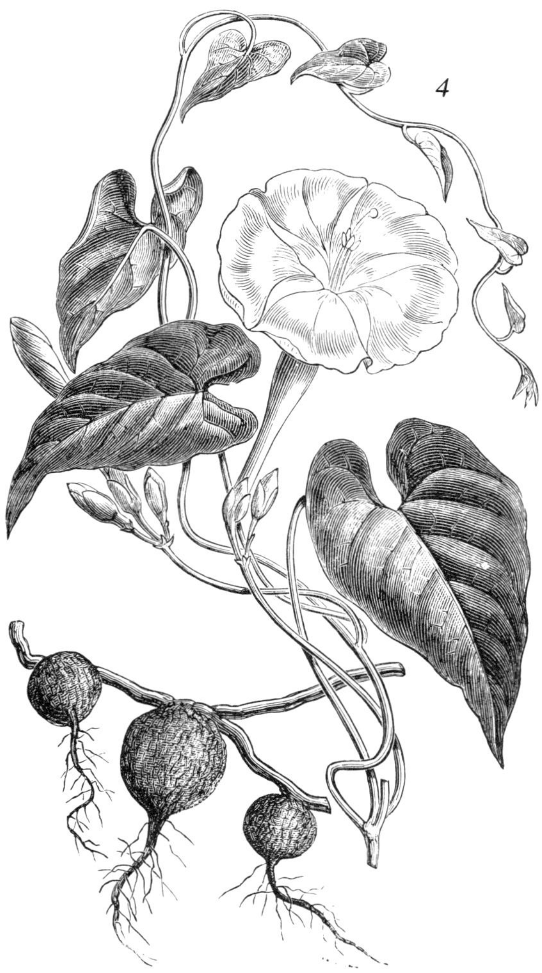

4

5

6

7

8

CONVOLVULACEAE (Morning Glories, Convolvuluses)

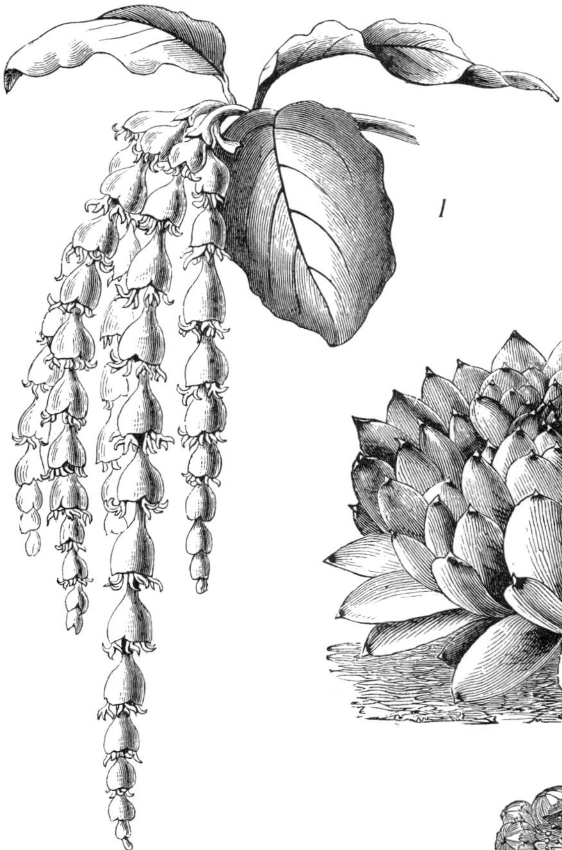

1

2

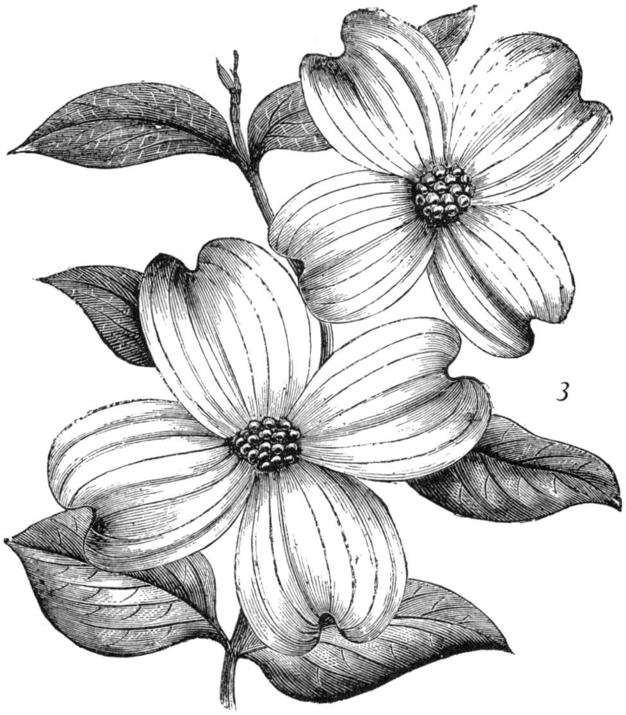

3

4

5

6

7

8

9

10

11

CONVOLVULACEAE (Morning Glories), CORNACEAE (Dogwoods), and CRASSULACEAE (Stonecrops, Houseleeks)

1

2

3

4

5

6

7

8

9

10

11

12

13

14

15

1
2
3
4
5
6
7
8
9
10
11
12
13
14
15

1

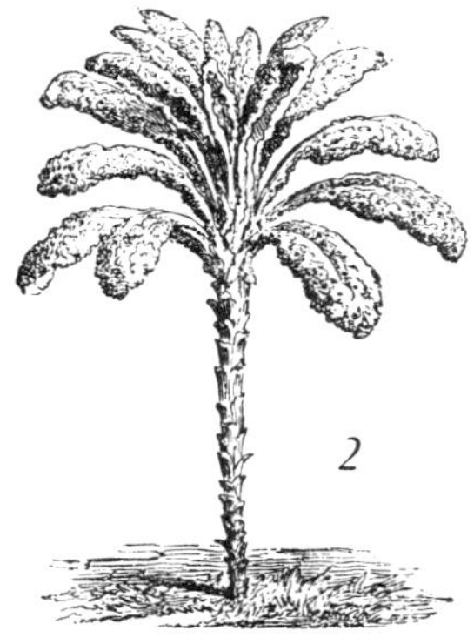
2

3

4

5

6

7

8

9

10

11

12

13

14

15

16

1

2

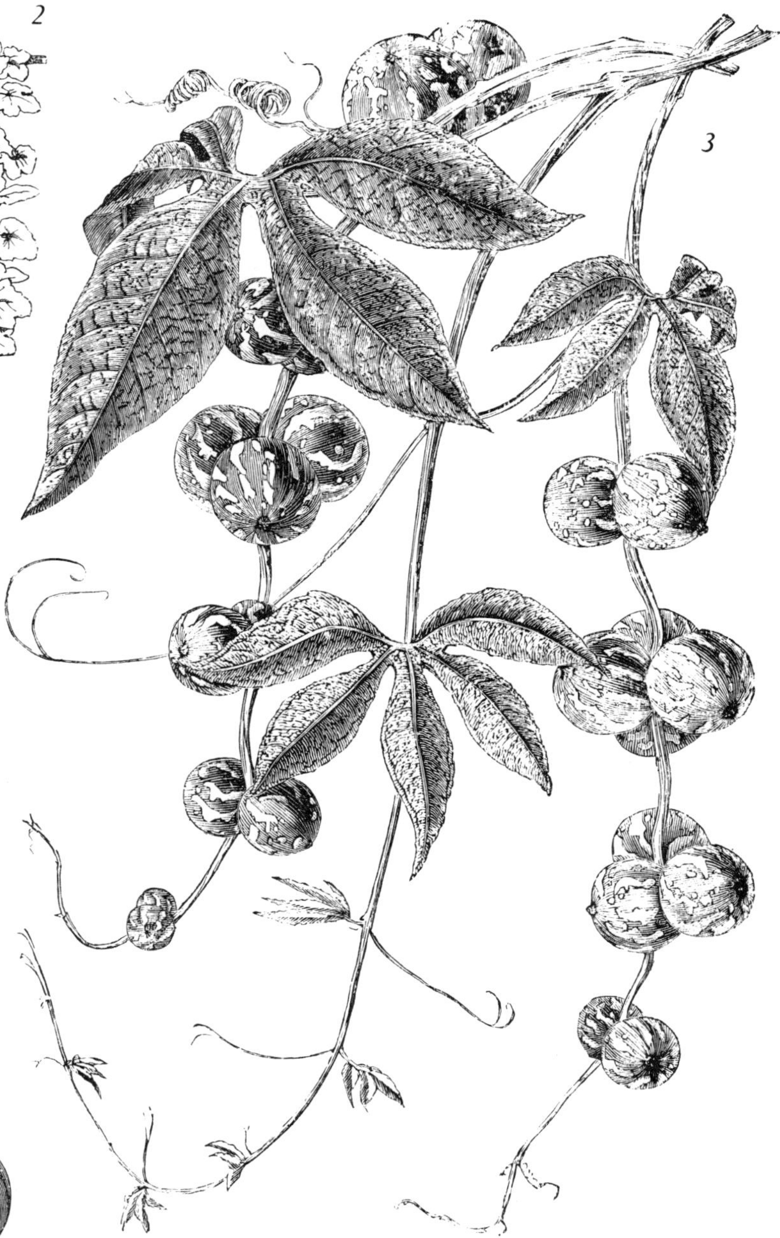

3

4

5

6

7

8

9

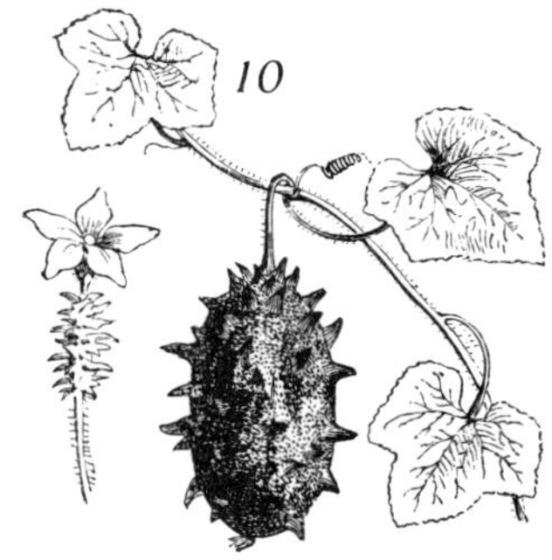

10

11

12

13

CUCURBITACEAE (Cucumbers, Squashes, Gourds)

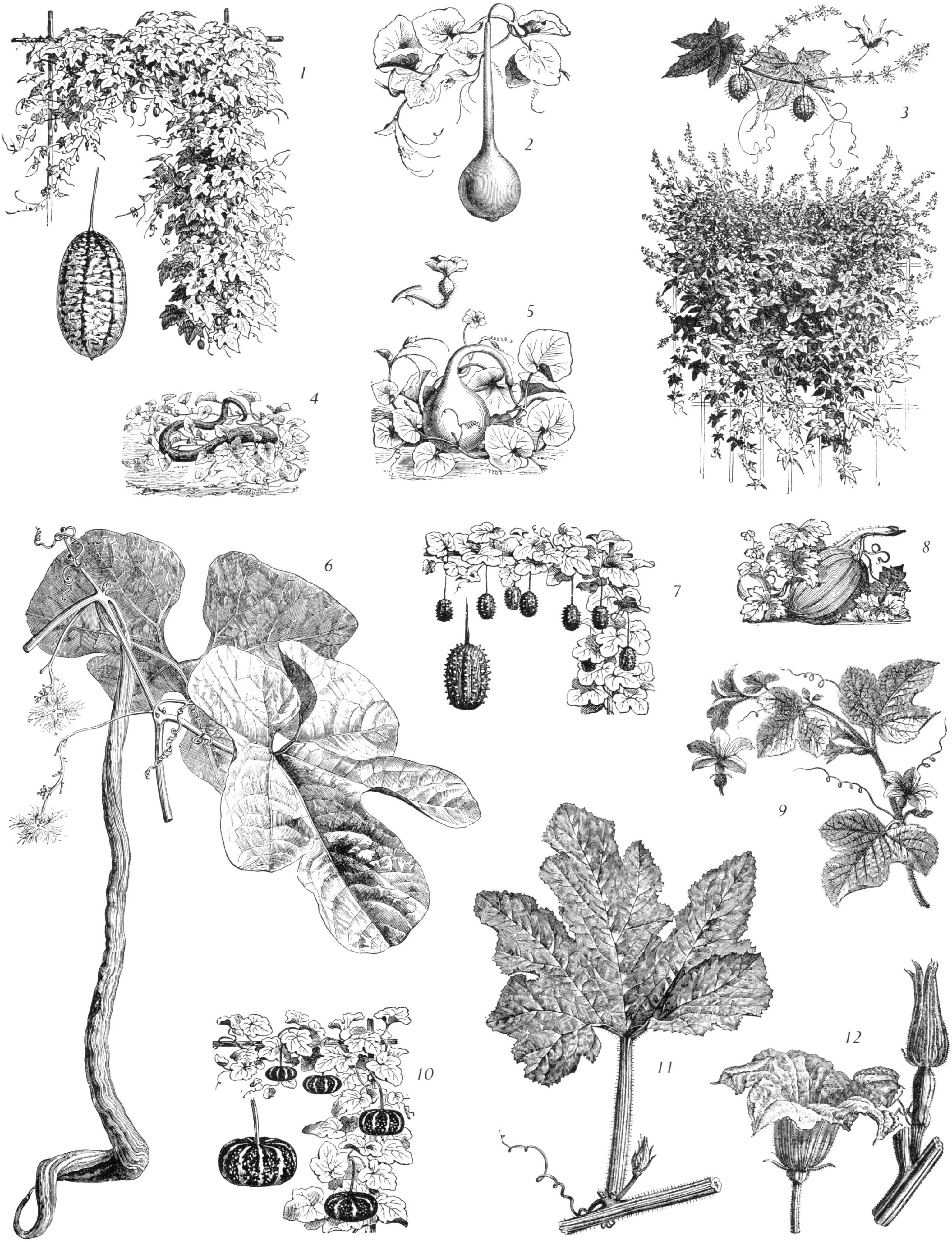

 CUCURBITACEAE **(*Cucumbers, Squashes, Gourds*)**

1

2

3

4

5

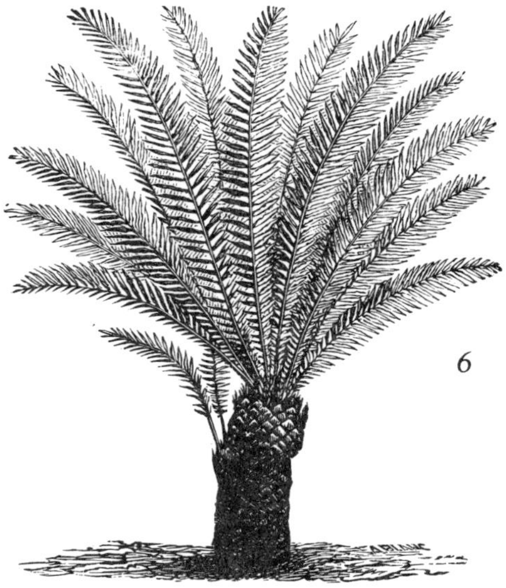

6

7

8

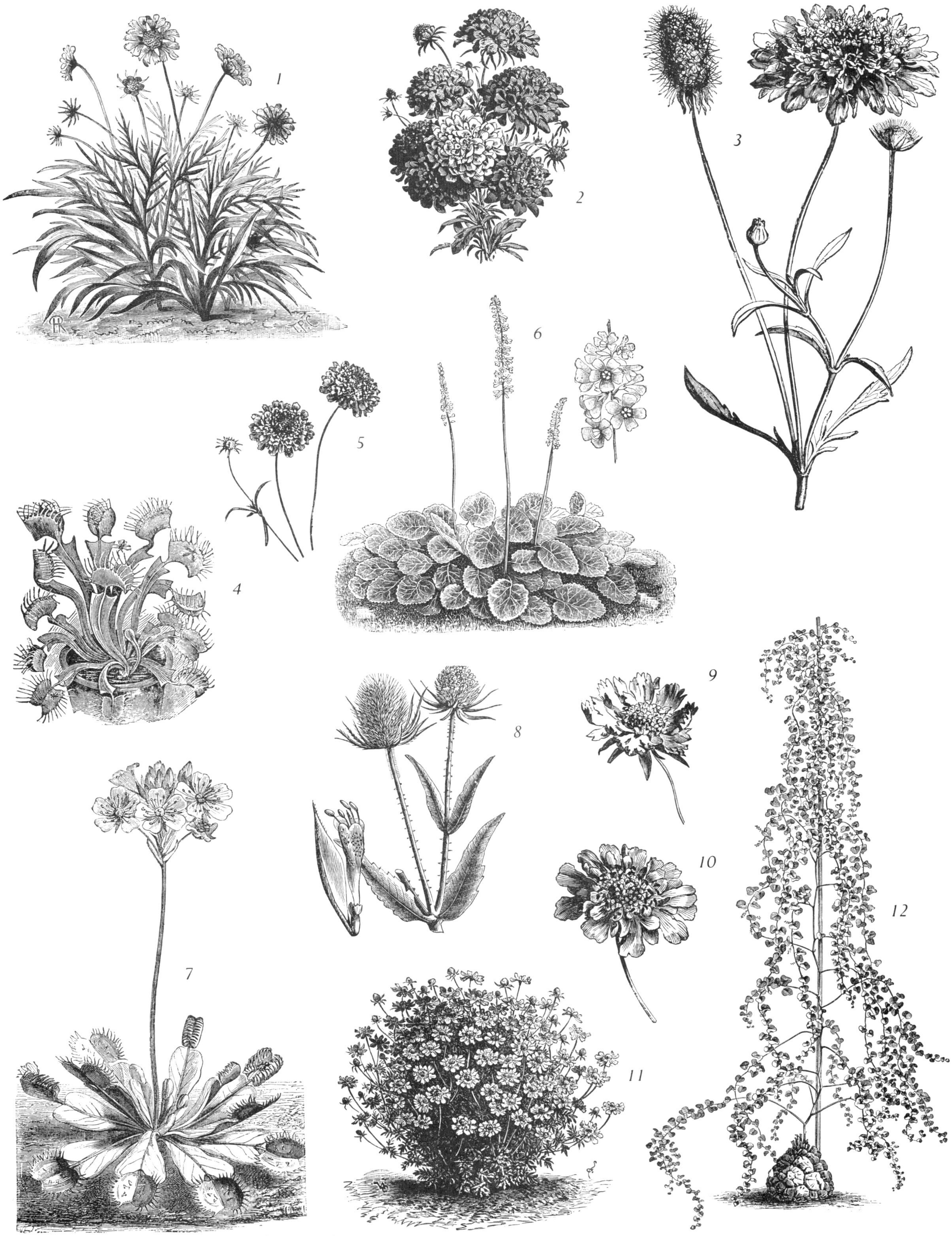

DIAPENSIACEAE (*Shortias*), *DIOSCOREACEAE* (*Yams*), *DIPSACEAE* (*Teasels, Scabiouses*), and *DROSERACEAE* (*Sundews, Venus's-flytraps*)

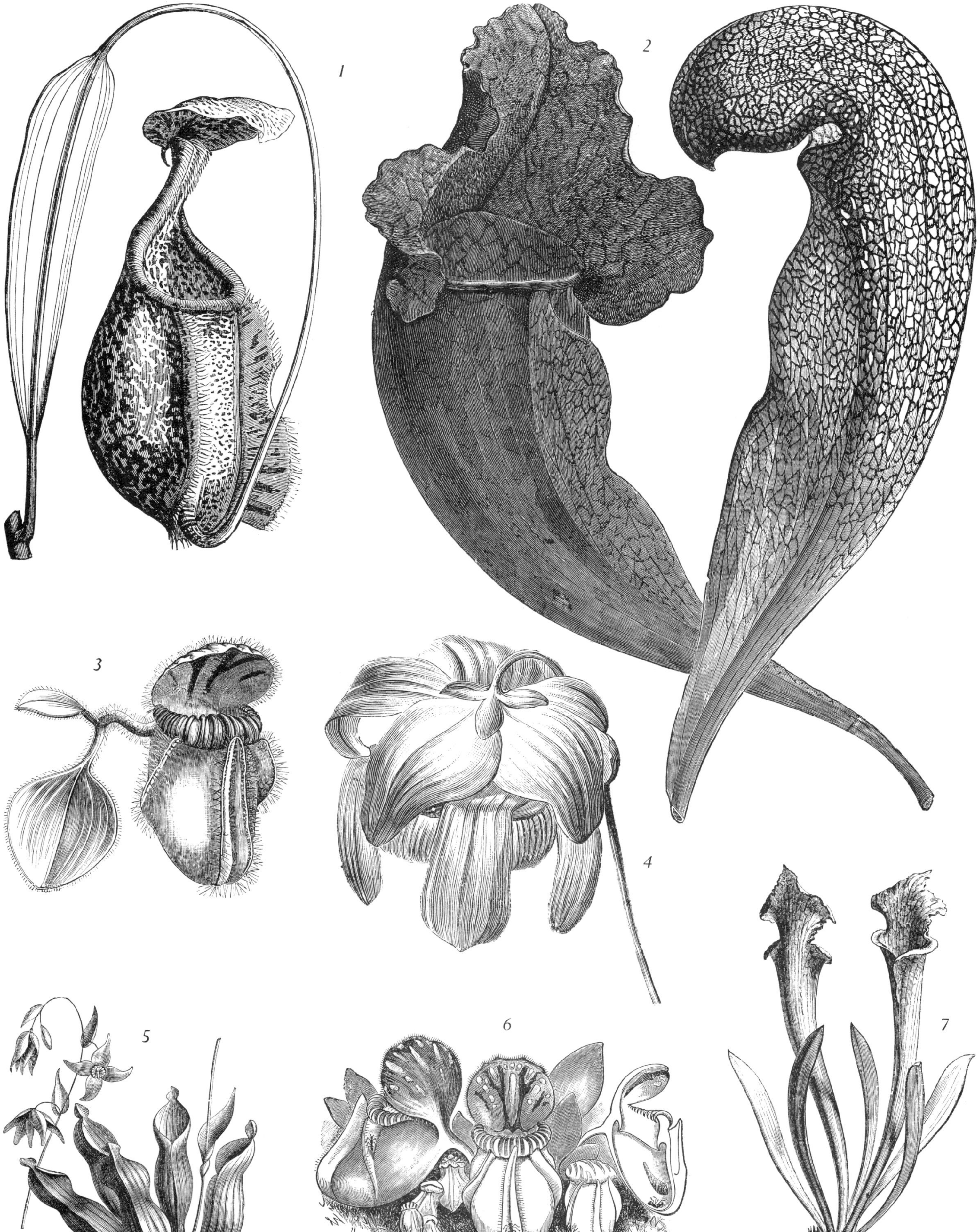

DROSERACEAE (Sundews, Venus's-flytraps) and carnivorous plants of other families

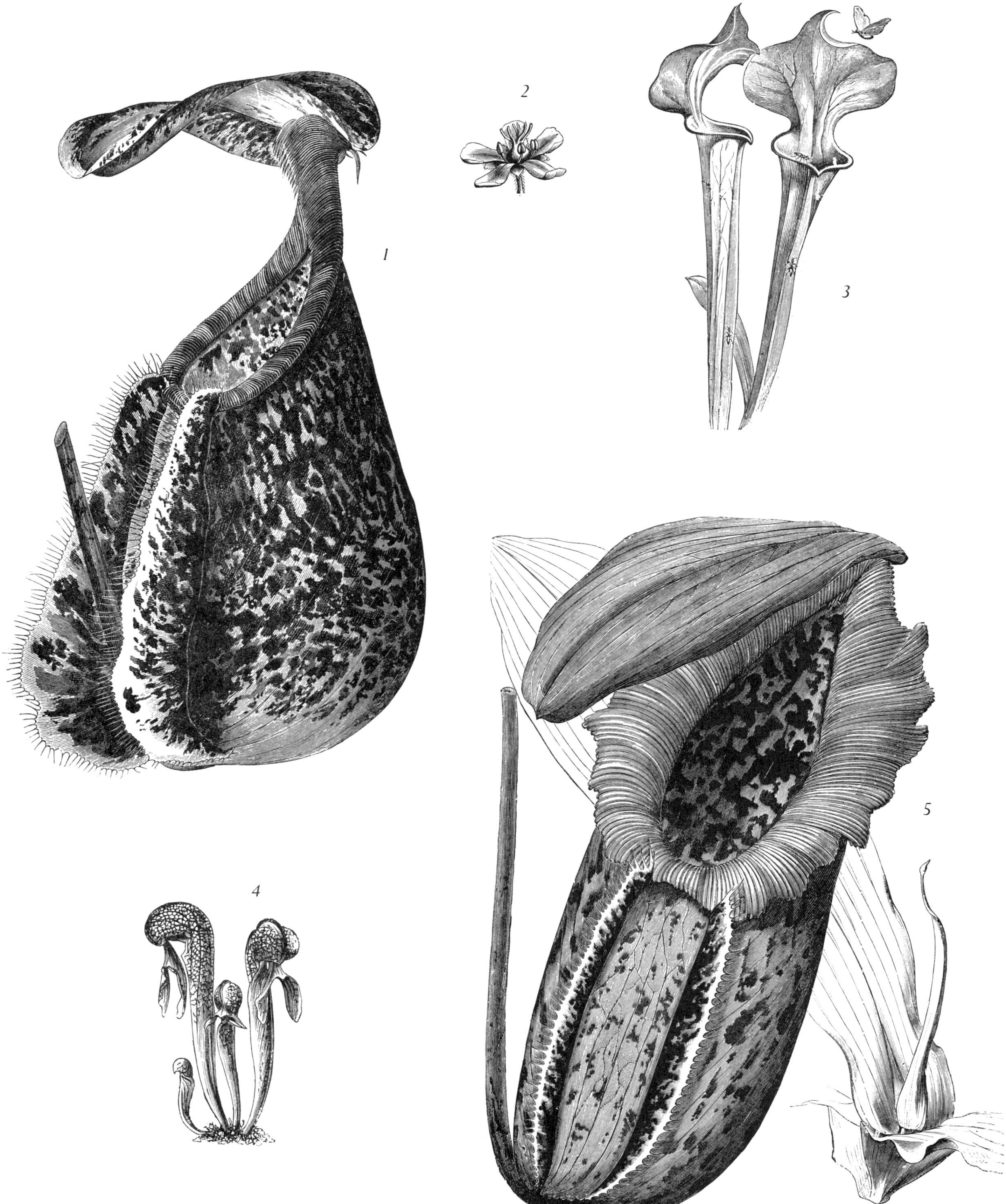

90 ***DROSERACEAE (Sundews, Venus's-flytraps) and carnivorous plants of other families***

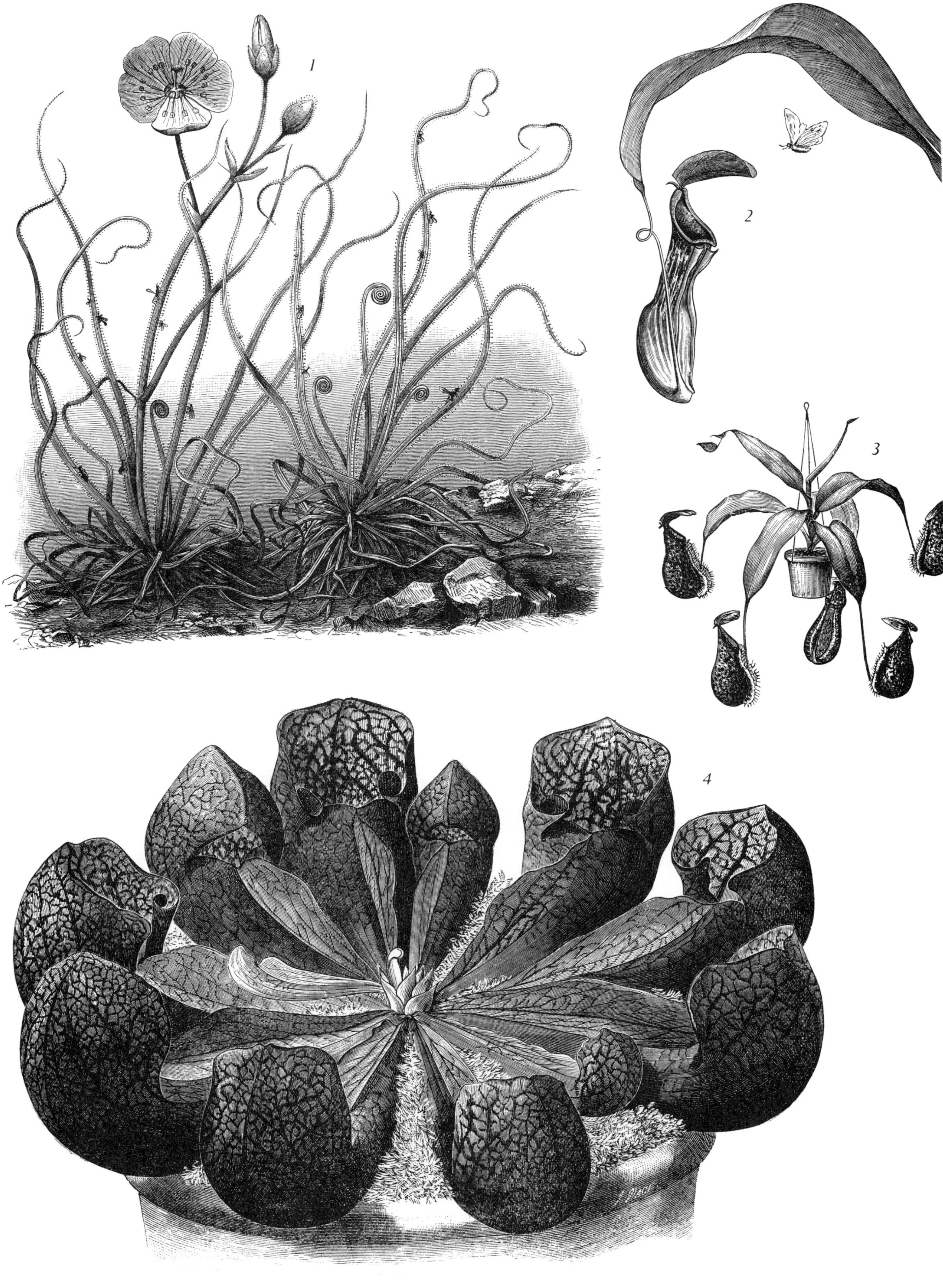

DROSERACEAE (Sundews, Venus's-flytraps) and carnivorous plants of other families

1

2

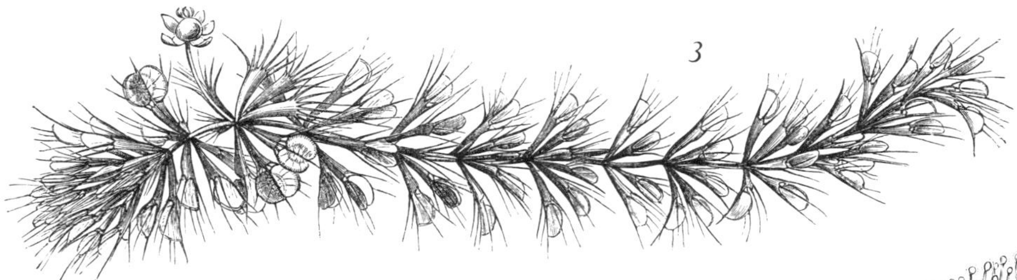

3

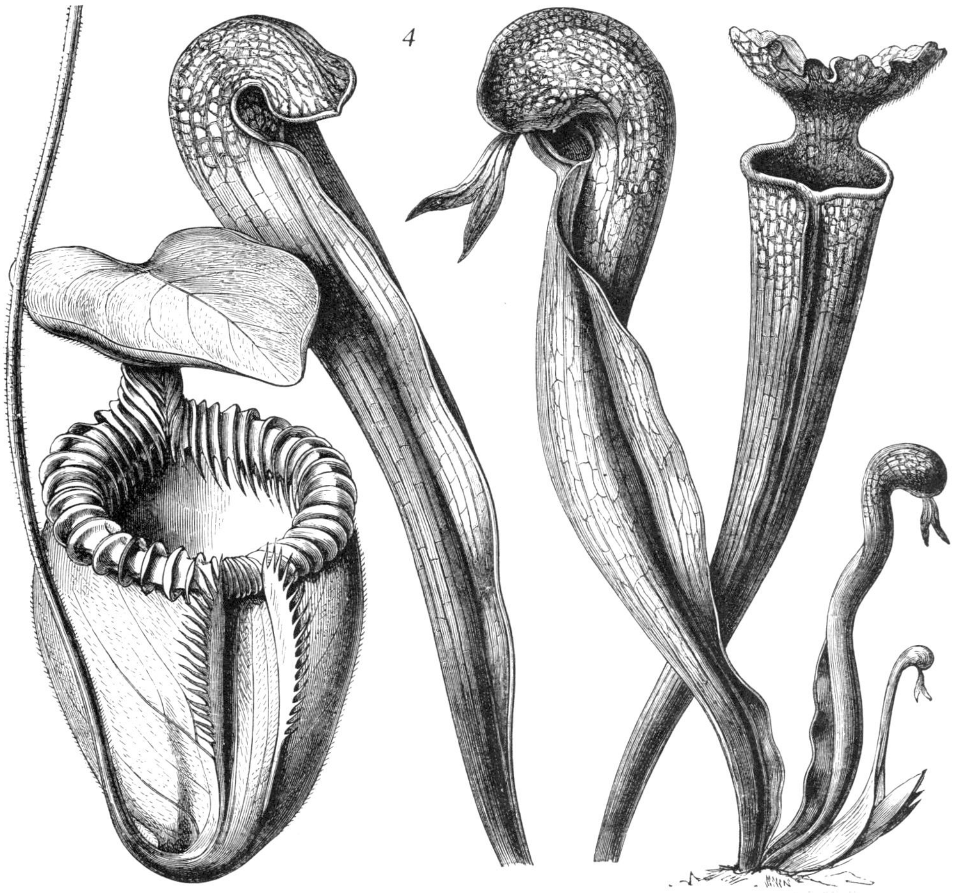

4

5

6

 DROSERACEAE (Sundews, Venus's-flytraps) and carnivorous plants of other families

1

2

3

4

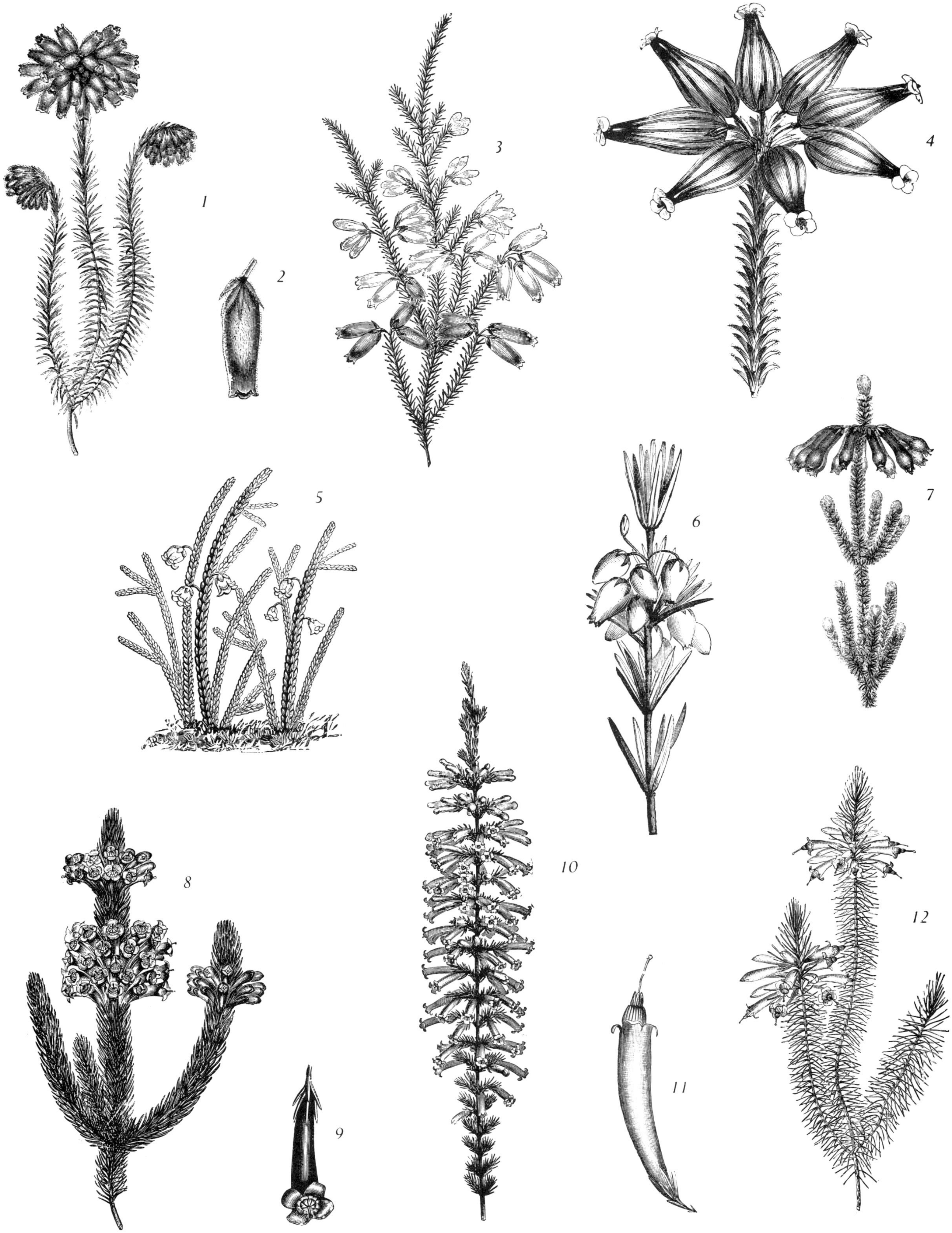

ERICACEAE (Heaths, Heathers, Rhododendrons, Azaleas)

1
2
3
4
5
6
7
8

1

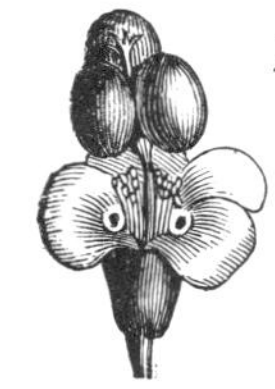

2

3

4

5

6

7

8

9

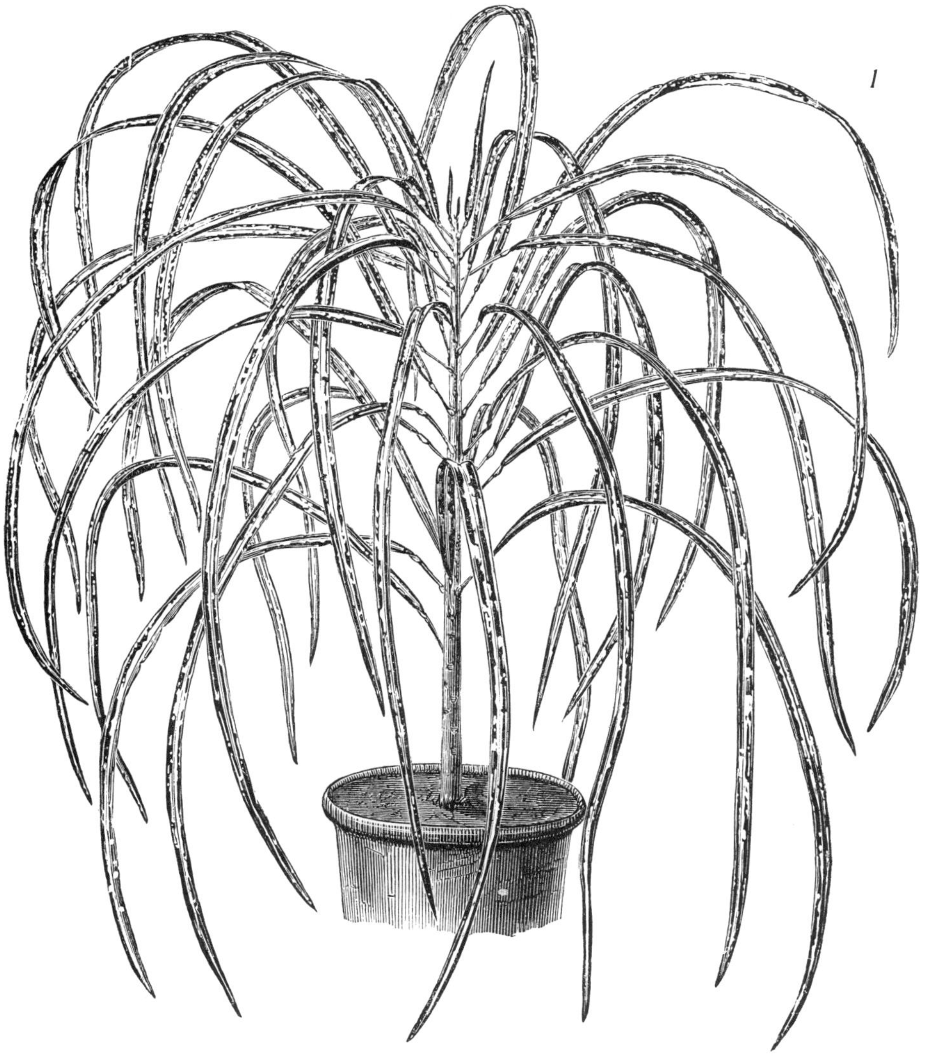

1

2

3

1

2

3

4

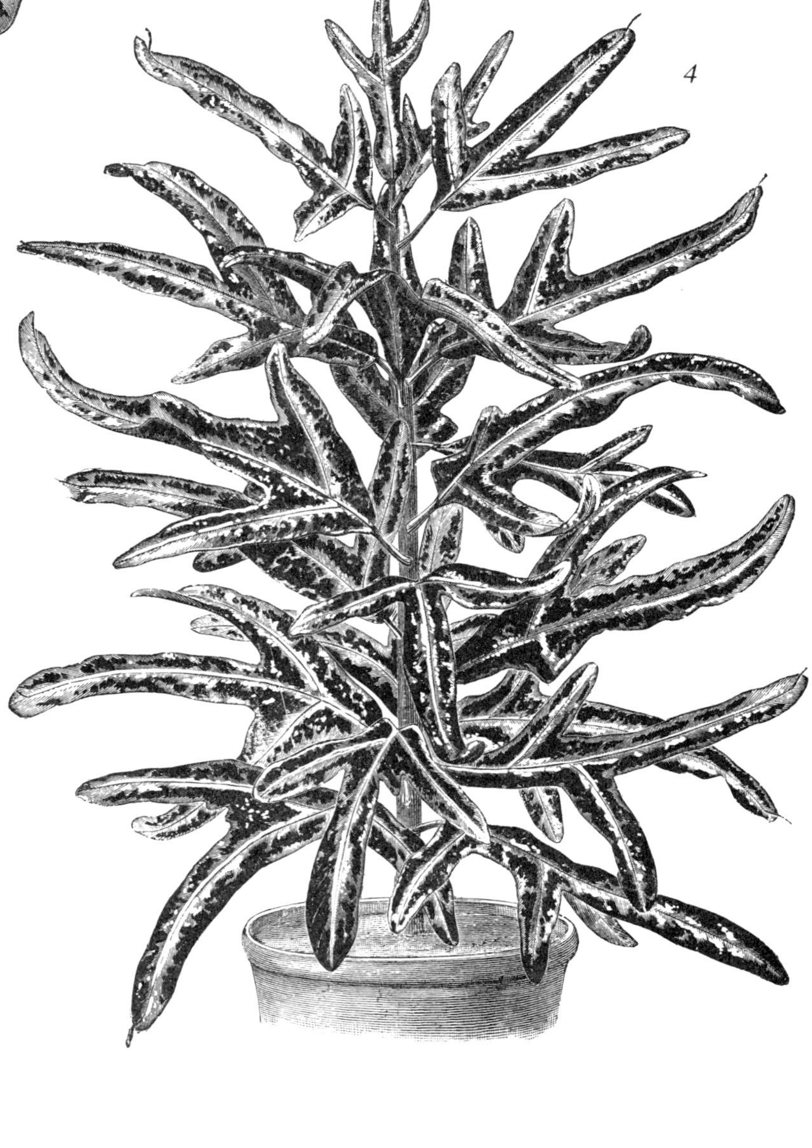

1

2

4

3

5

7

8

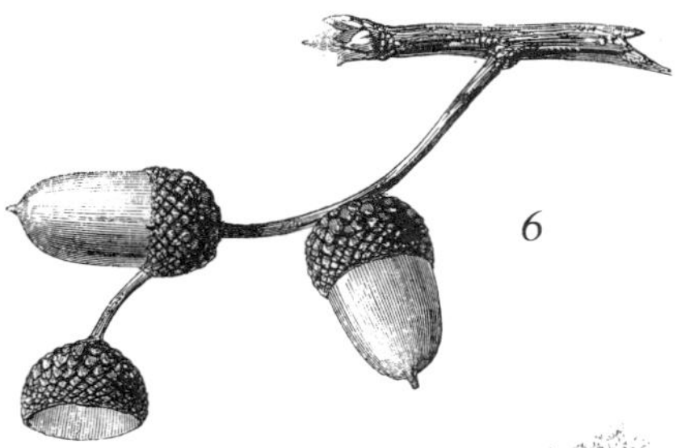

6

9

10

12

11

1

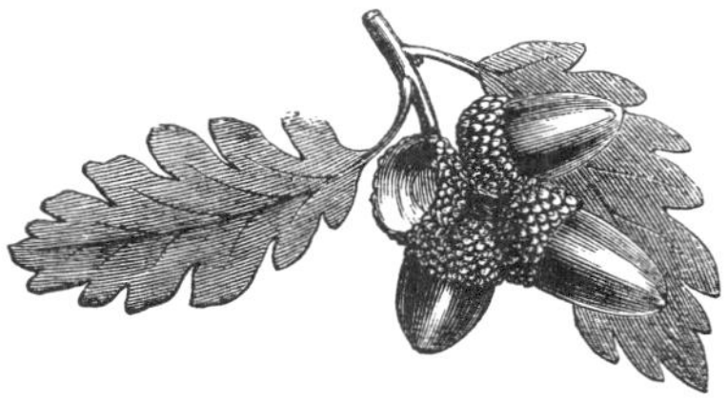

2

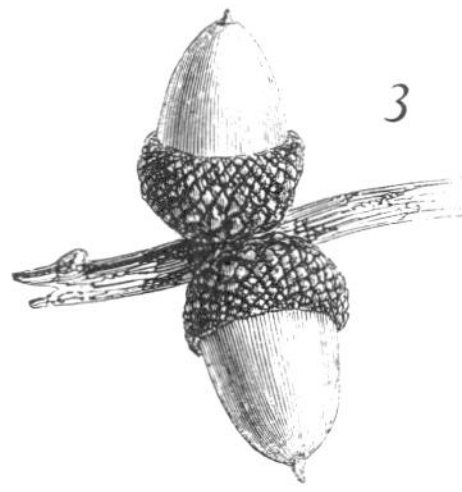

3

4

5

6

7

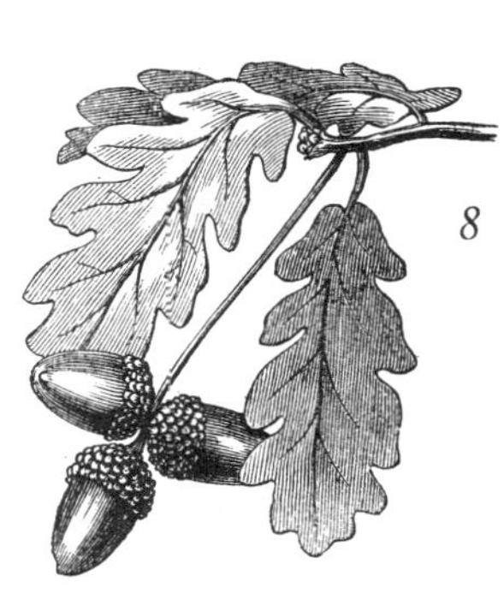

8

1

2

3

4

5

6

9

7

8

1

2

3

6

7

4

5

8

9

10

1

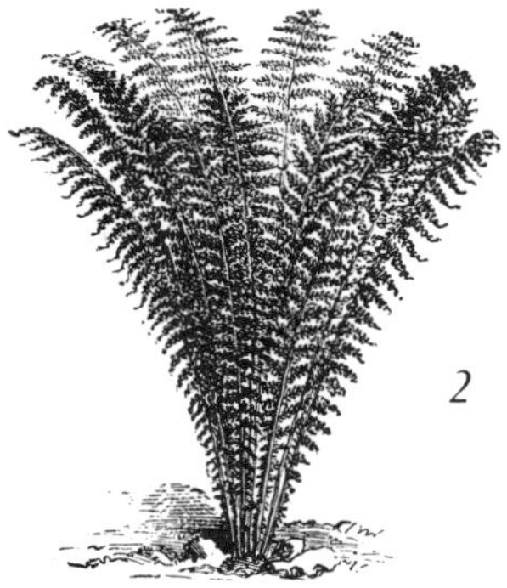

2

3

4

5

6

1
2
3
4
5
6
7
8

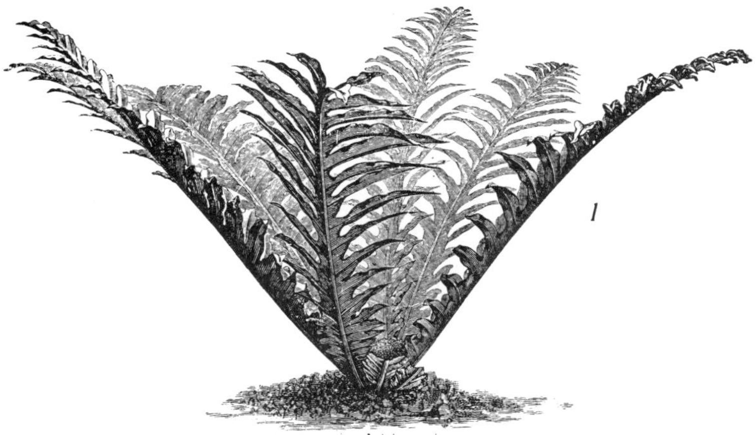

1

2

3

4

5

6

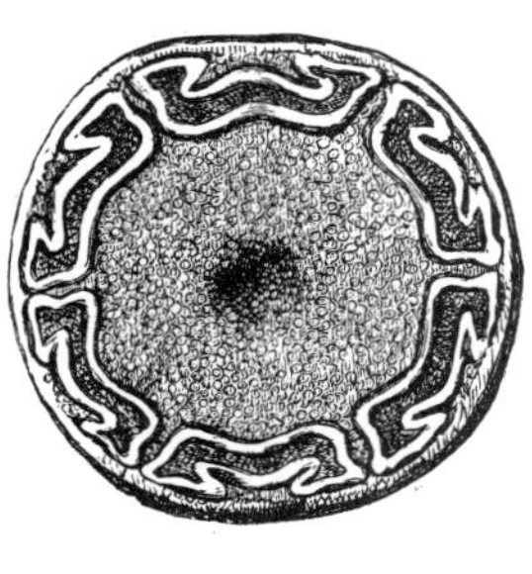

8

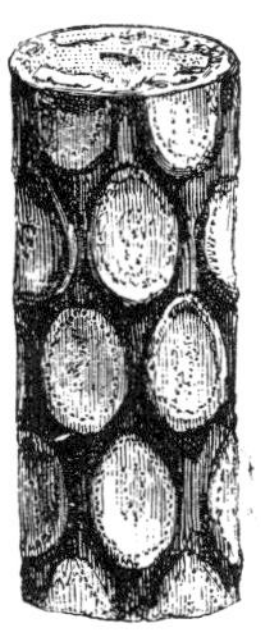

7

***FILICES* (*Ferns*)**

1

2

3

4

5

6

7

1

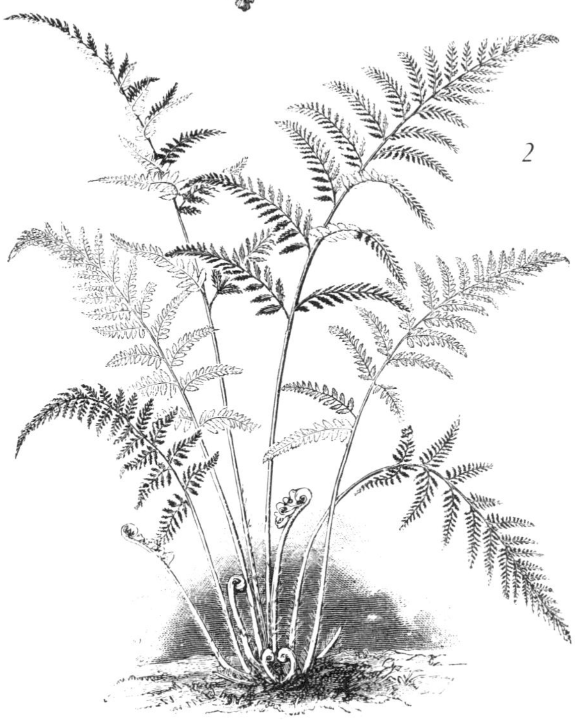

2

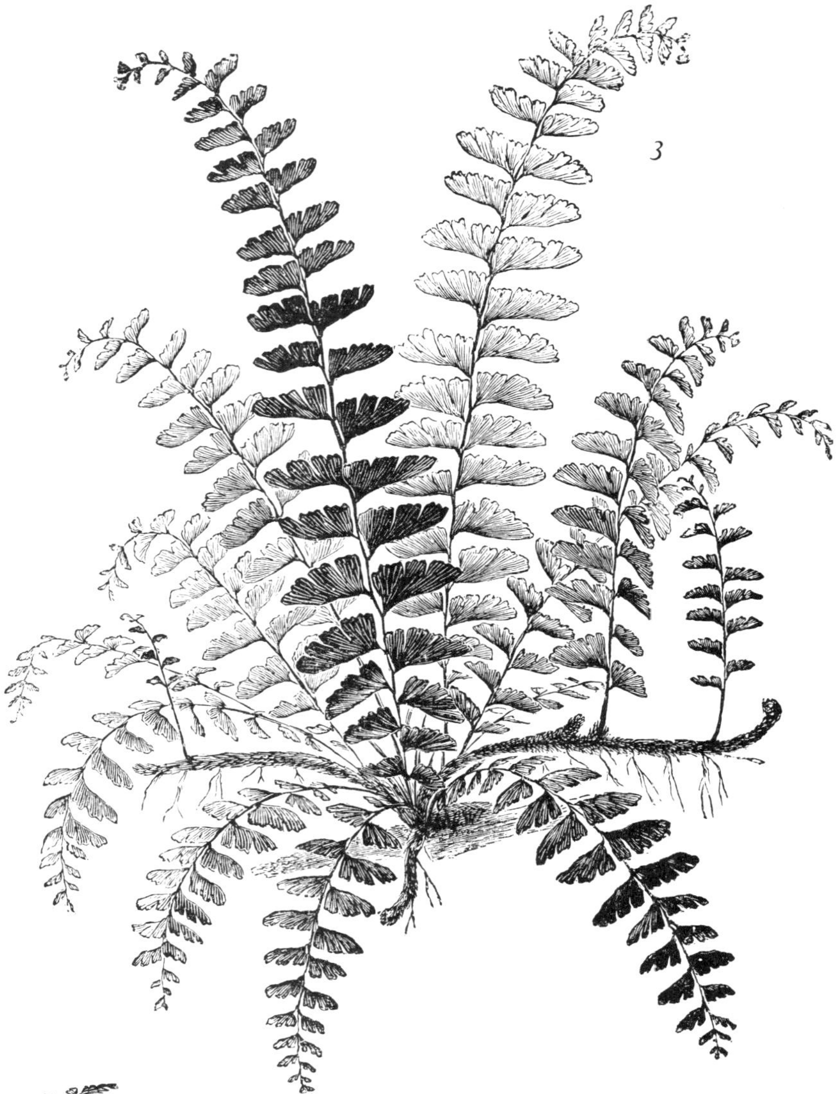

3

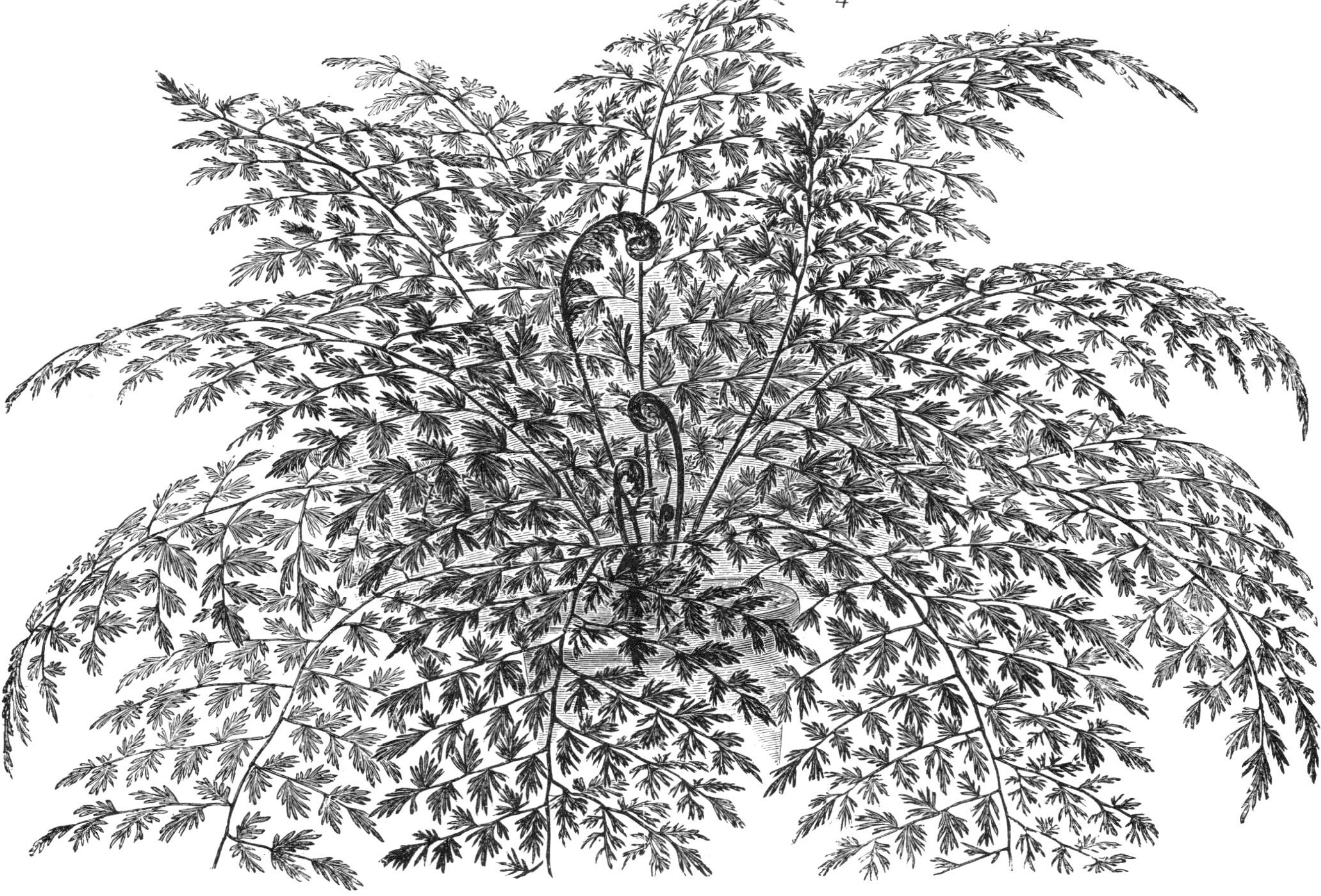

4

1

3

2

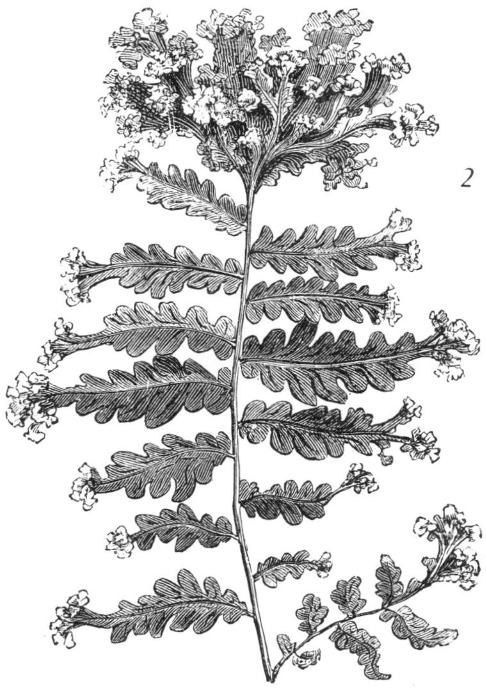

4

6

5

7

8

1

2

3

4

5

6

7

1

2

5

4

3

7

6

1

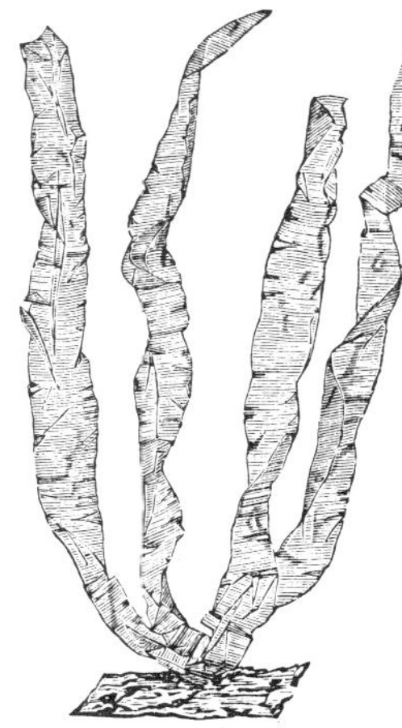

2

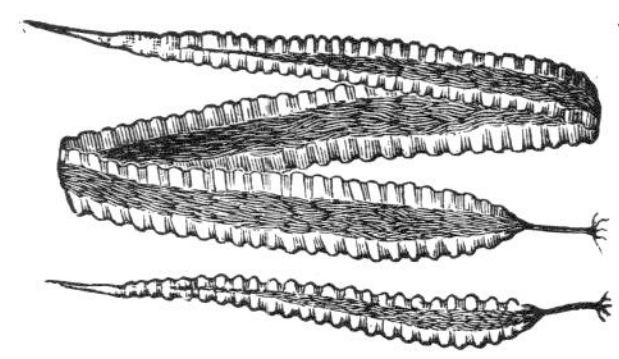

3

4

5

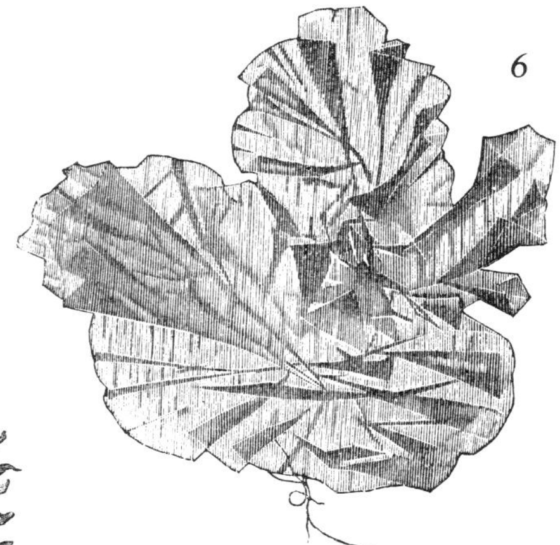

6

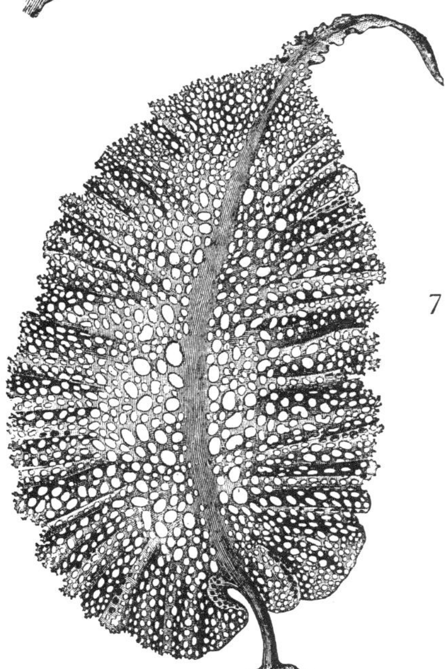

7

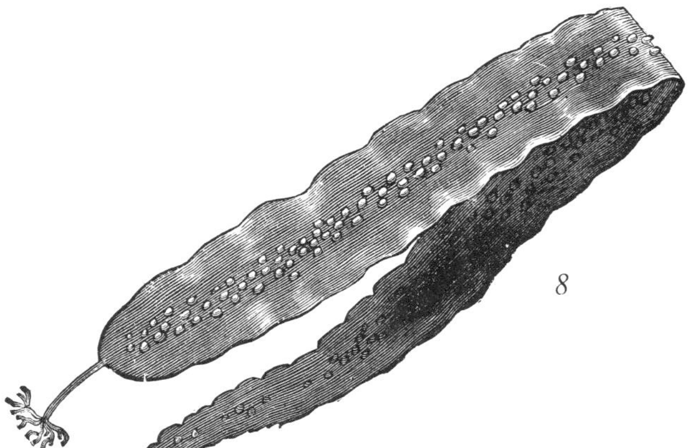

8

9

FUCACEAE (Kelps, Seaweeds) and other algae

1

2

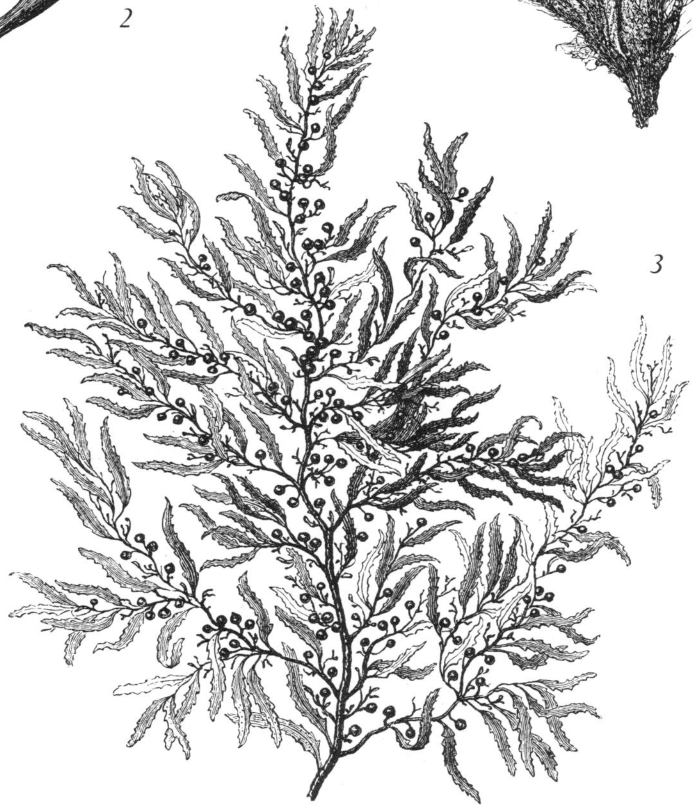

3

4

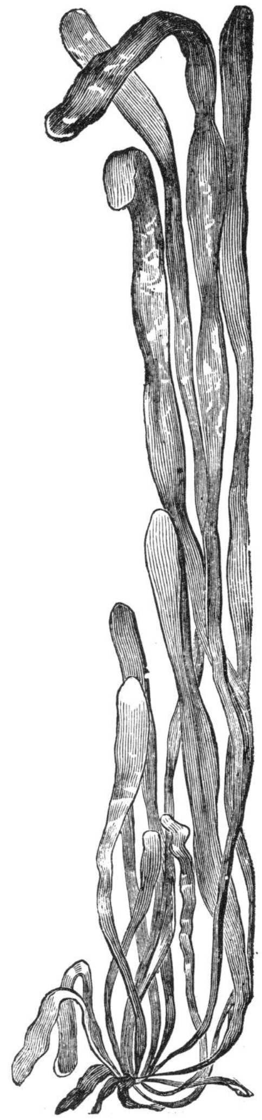

5

6

FUCACEAE (Kelps, Seaweeds) and other algae

1
2
3
4
5
6
7
8
9
10
11
12

1

2

3

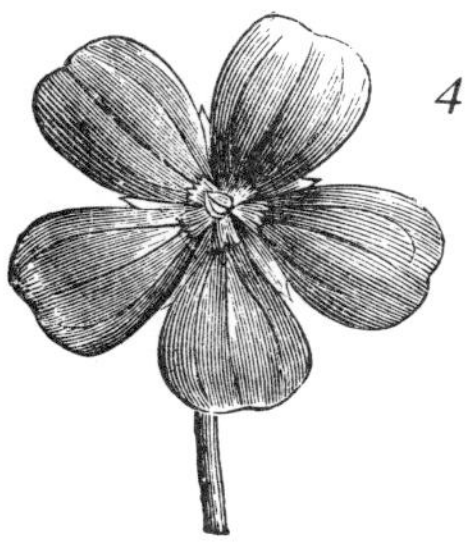
4

5

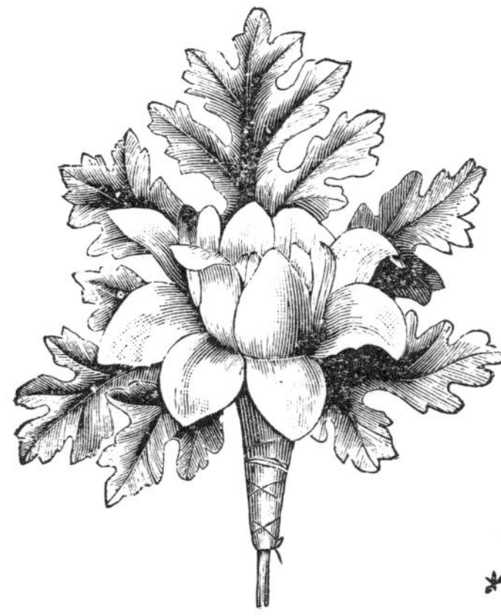
6

7

8

9

10

1

2

3

4

5

6

7

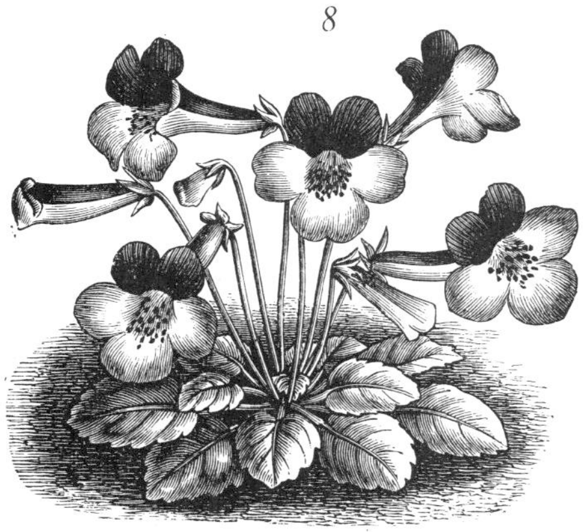
8

9

10

 GESNERIACEAE (Gloxinias, Gesneriads)

1

2

3

4

5

6

7

1

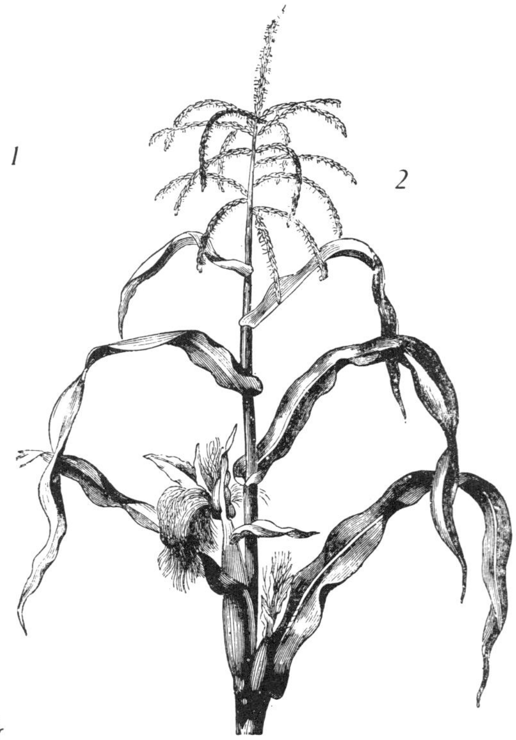

2

3

4

5

6

7

8

9

1

2

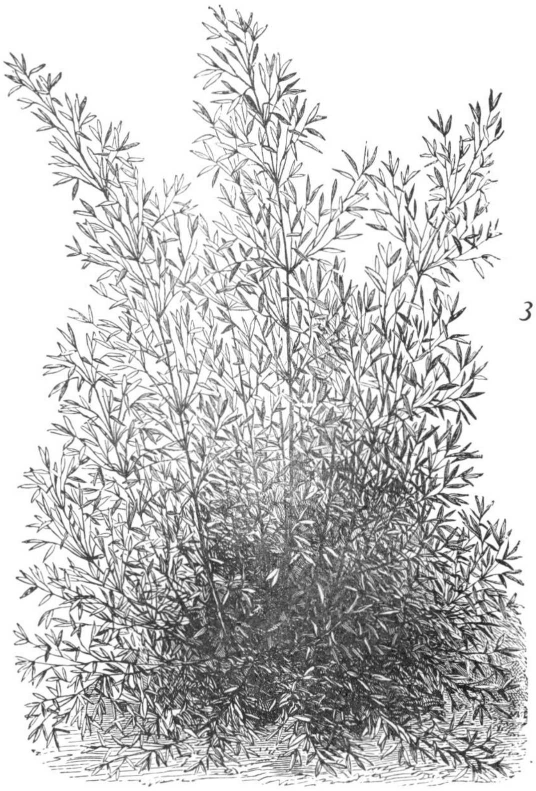
3

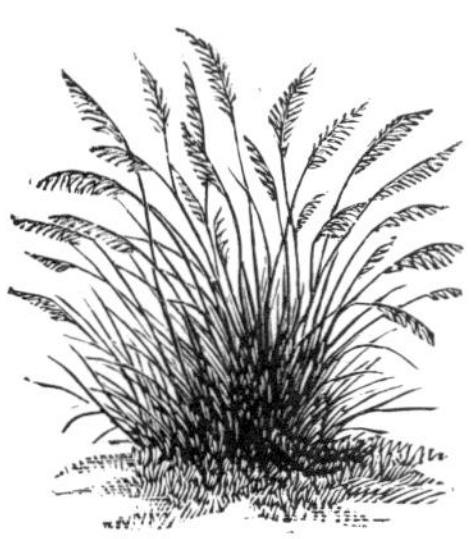
4

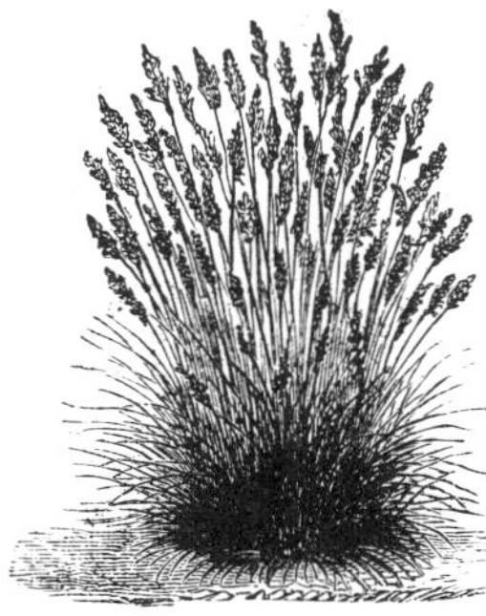
5

6

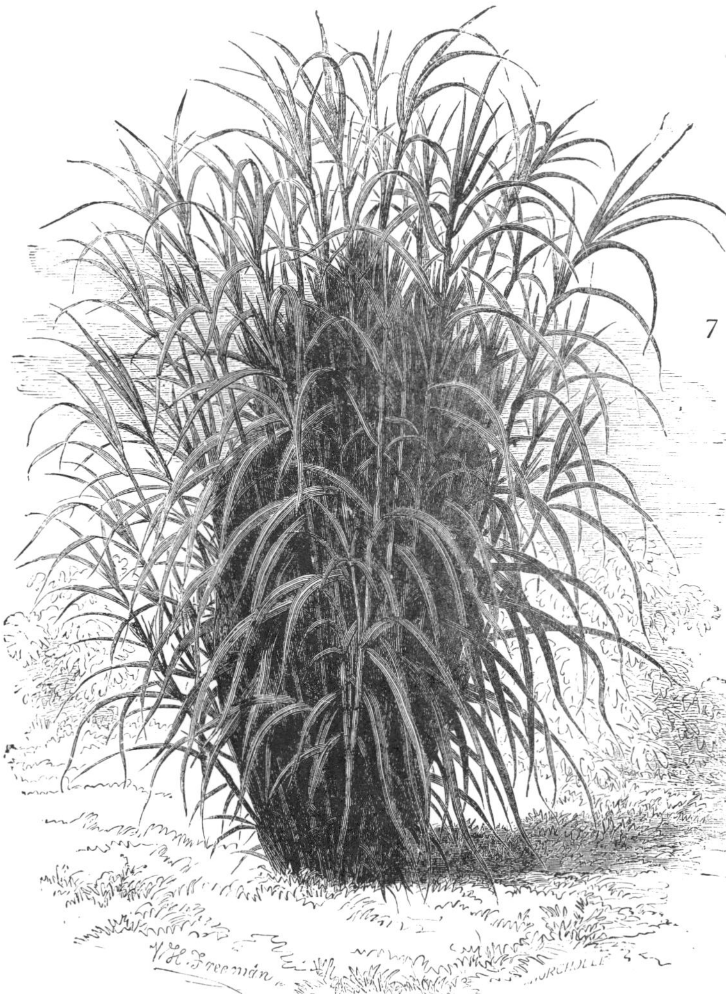
7

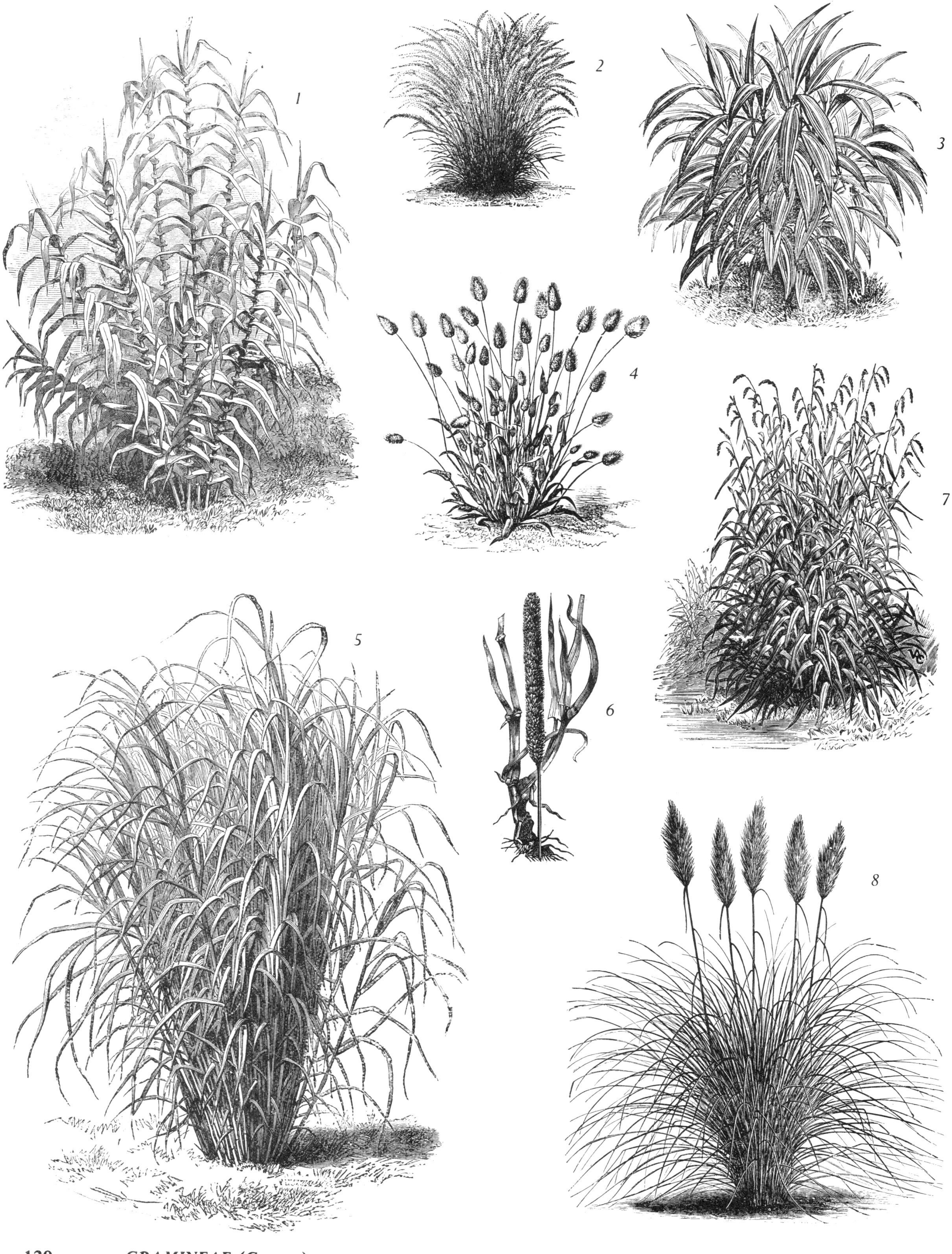

 GRAMINEAE (Grasses)

1

2

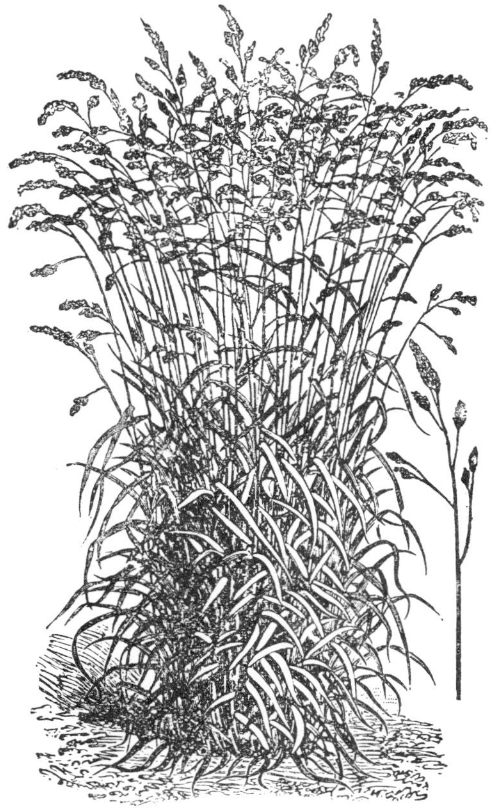
3

4

5

6

7

8

 GRAMINEAE (*Grasses*)

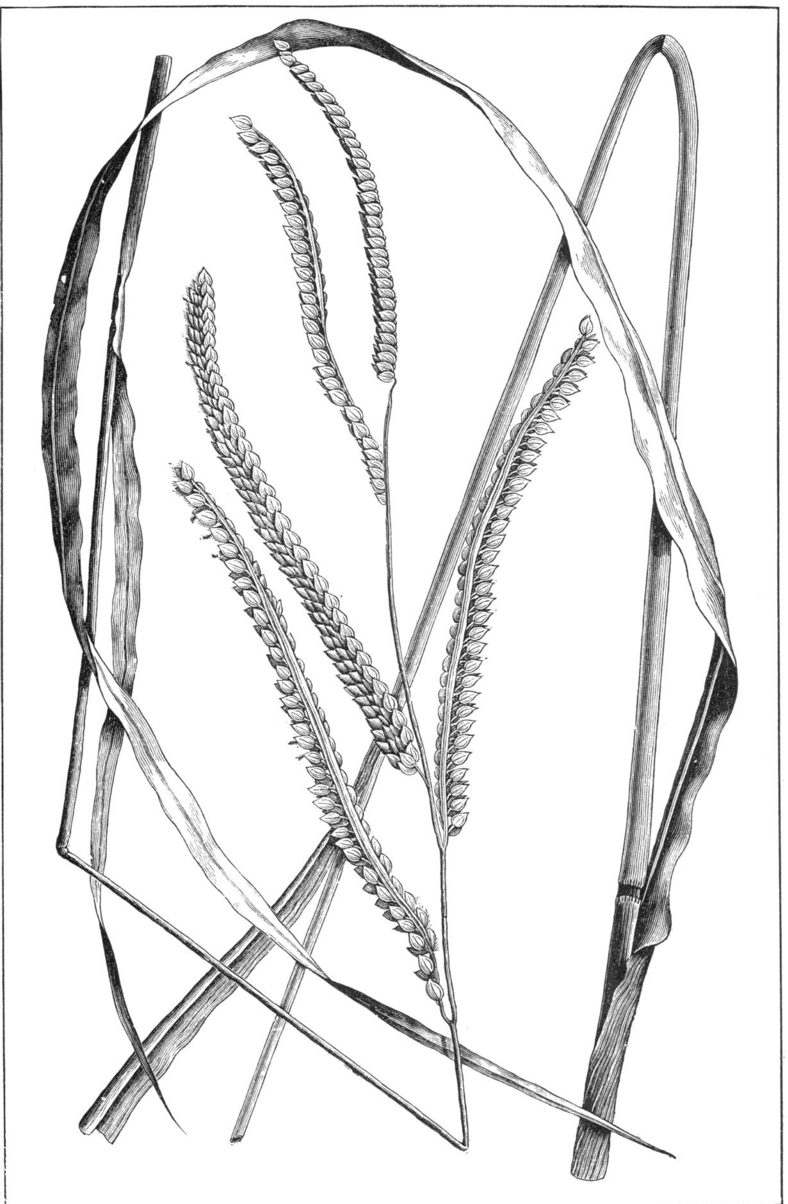

1

2

1

2

3

4

5
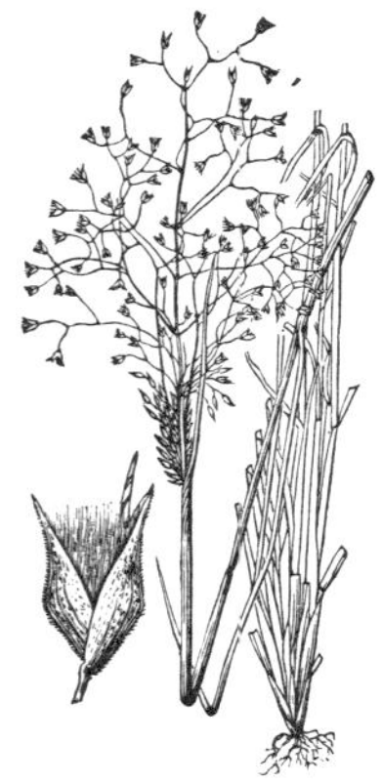
6

7

8

9

10

11

12

13

14

15

16

17

18

19

20

21

22

23
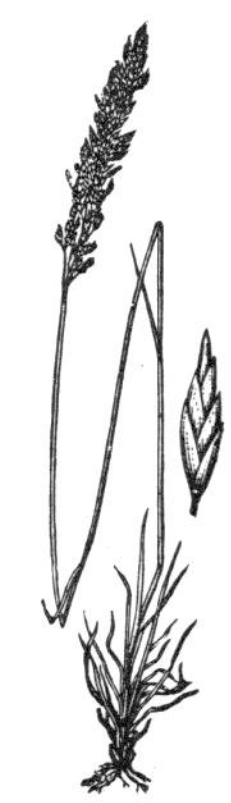
24

25

26

27

28

29

30

31
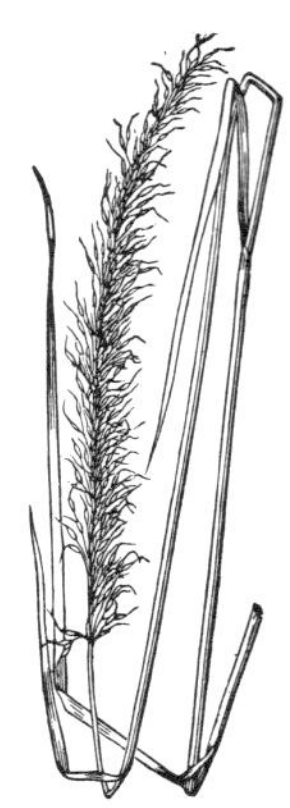
32

1

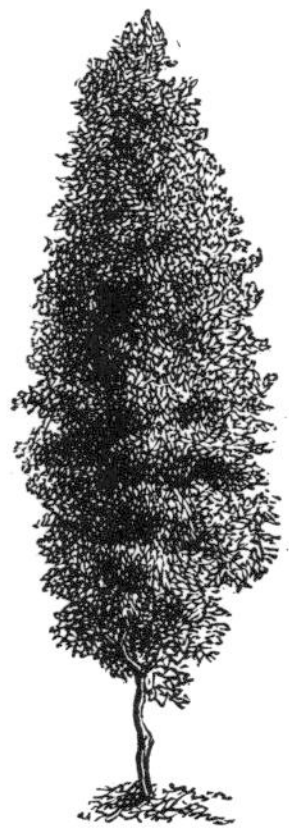

2

3

4

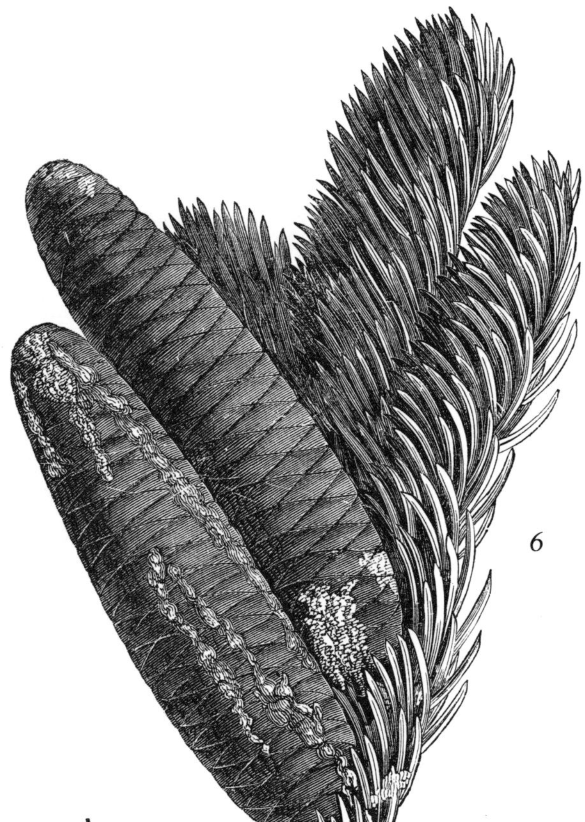

6

5

GYMNOSPERMAE: Cupressaceae (Junipers, Cypress, Cedars) and Pinaceae

1

2

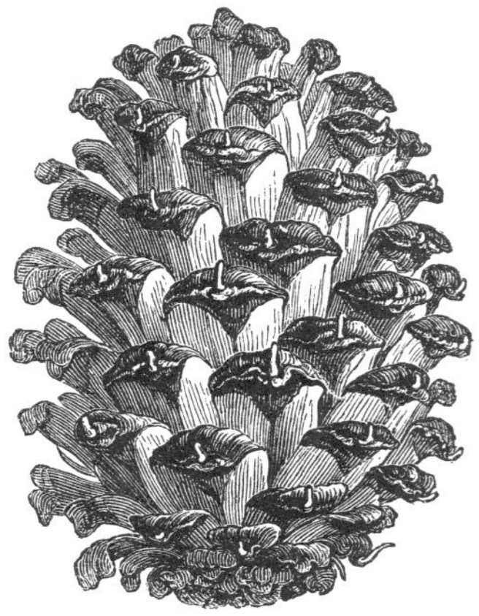

3

4

5

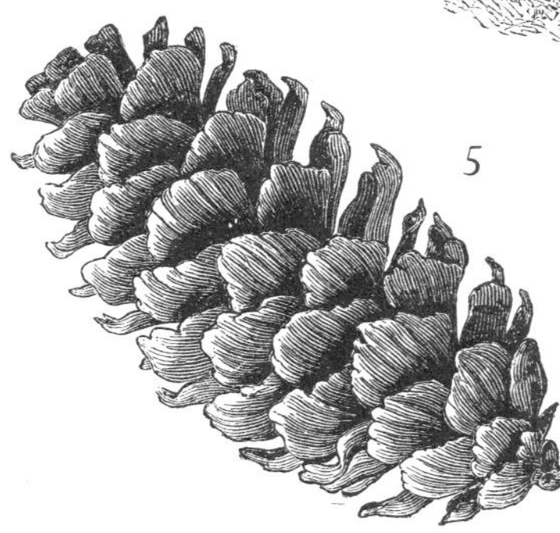

6

 GYMNOSPERMAE: Pinaceae (Pines, Spruces) and Cupressaceae (Cedars)

1

2

3

4

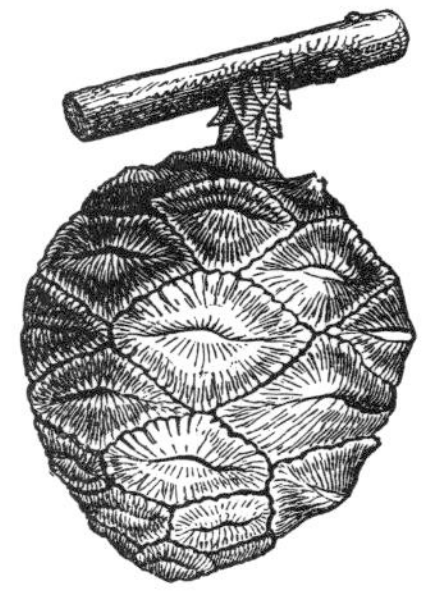

5

6

7

GYMNOSPERMAE: Pinaceae (Pines, Spruces, Firs), Taxaceae (Yews), and Taxodiacene (Cypress)

GYMNOSPERMAE: Pinaceae (*Spruces, Pines*), *Cupressaceae* (*Arborvitae, Cedars*), *and Taxodiaceae* (*Cryptomeria*)

GYMNOSPERMAE: Pinaceae (Pines), Cupressaceae (Cypress), Taxaceae (Torreya), and Taxodiaceae

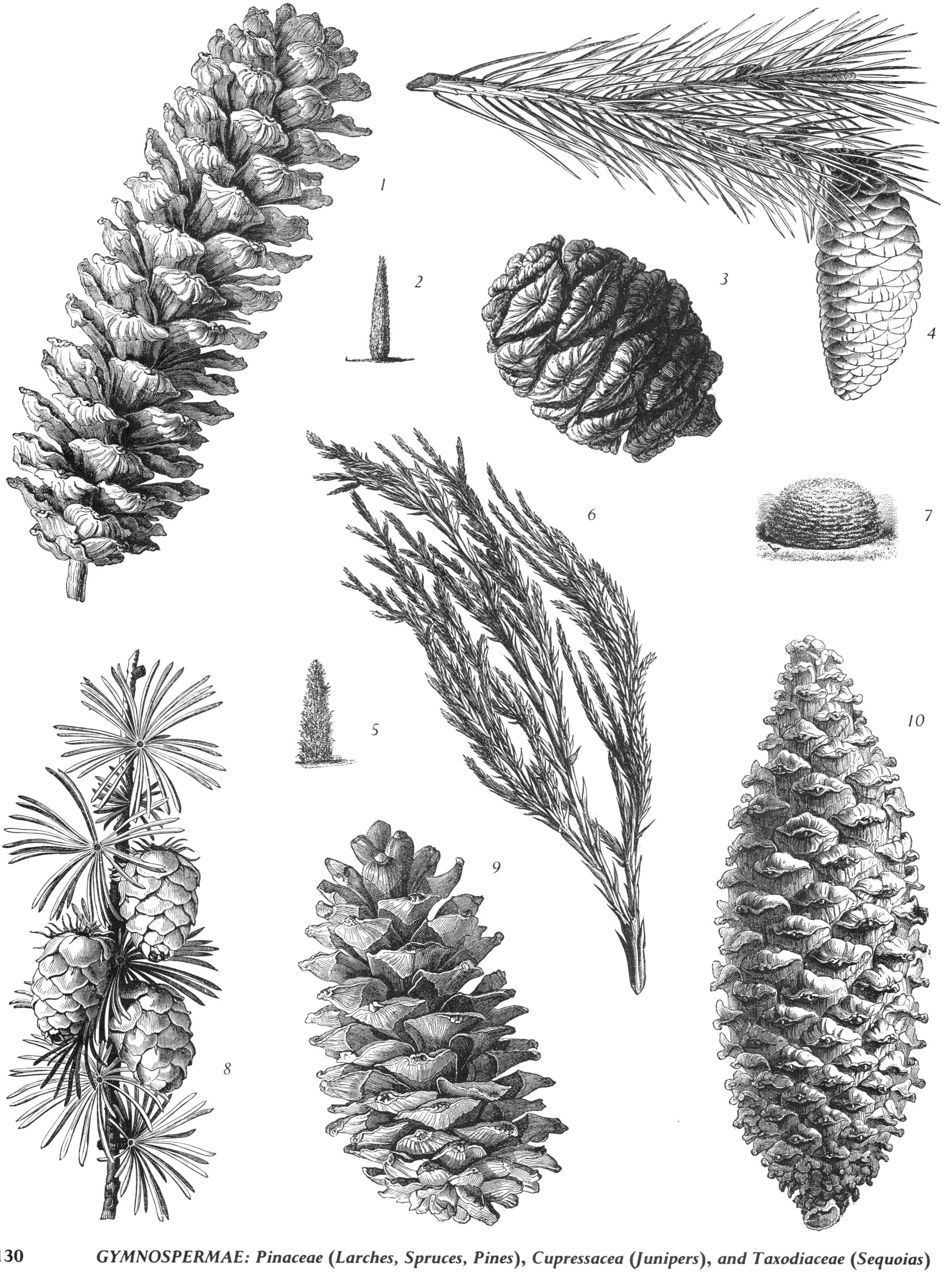

 GYMNOSPERMAE: Pinaceae (Larches, Spruces, Pines), Cupressacea (Junipers), and Taxodiaceae (Sequoias)

1

3

2

6

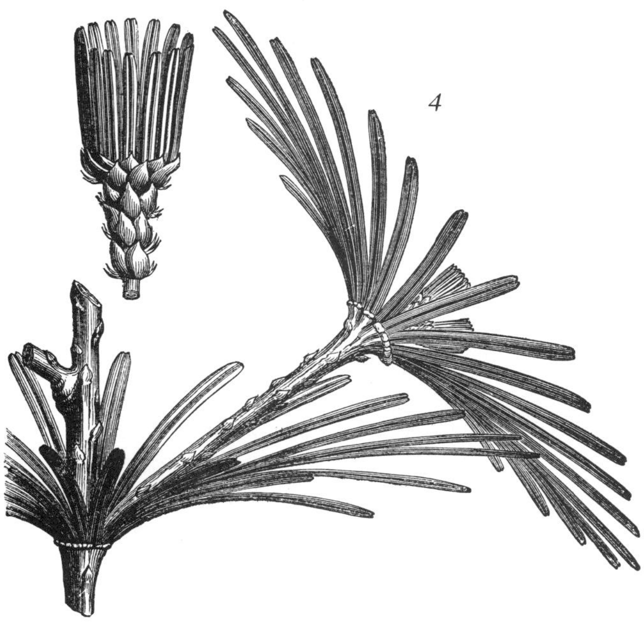

4

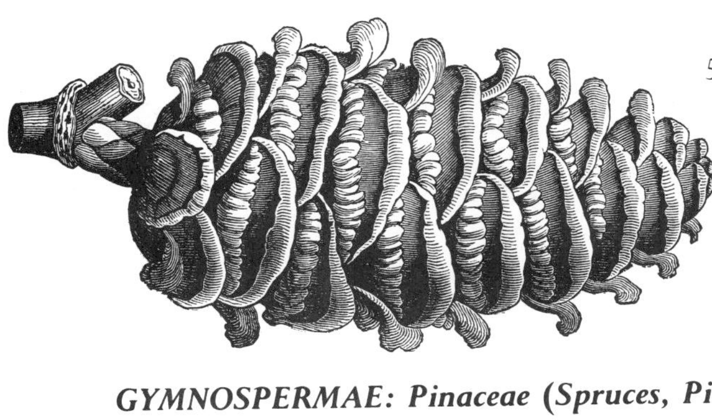

5

GYMNOSPERMAE: Pinaceae (*Spruces, Pines*), *Cupressaceae* (*Arborvitae, Cedars*), *and Taxodiaceae* (*Cryptomeria*)

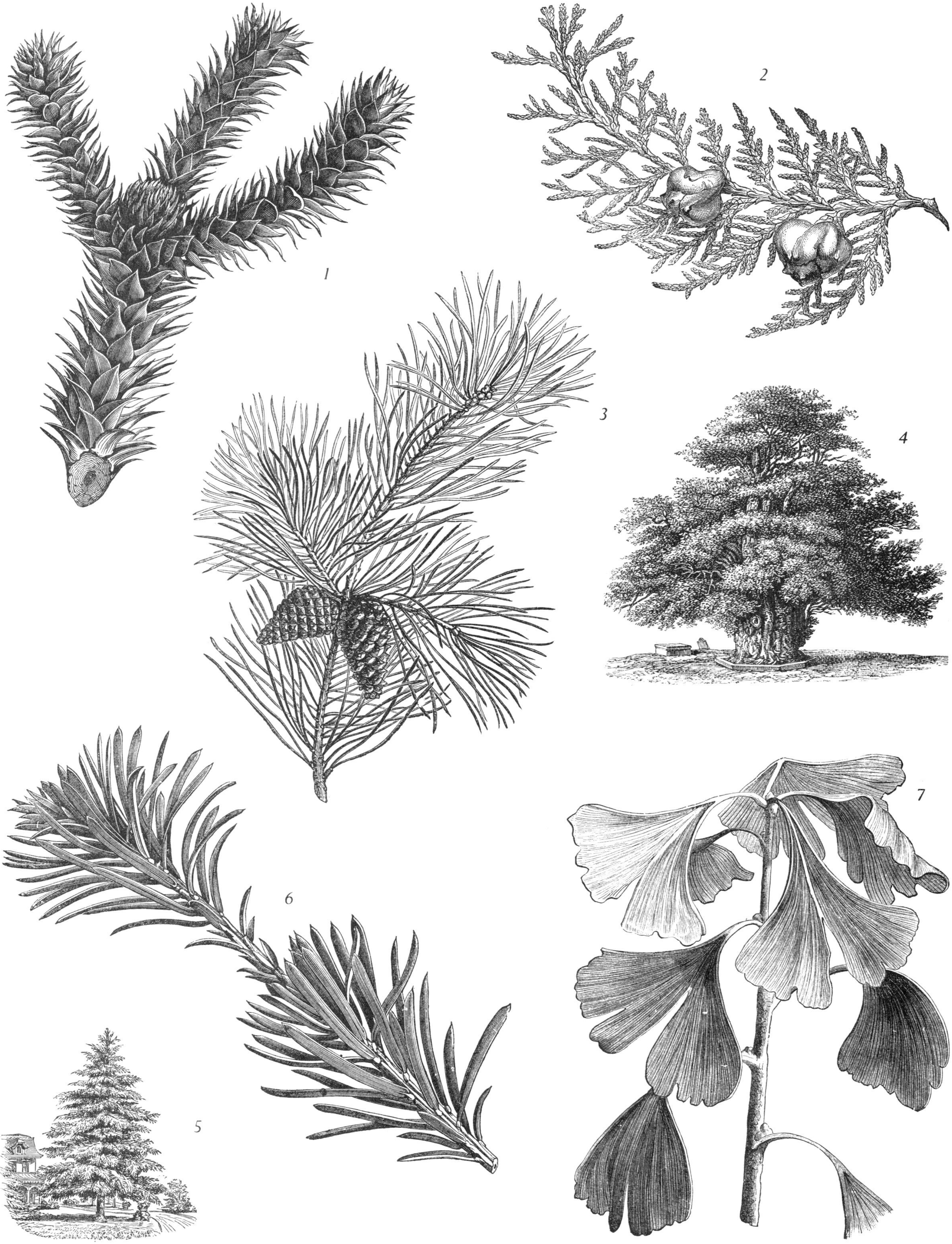

GYMNOSPERMAE: Pinaceae (*Pines, Firs*), *Araucariaceae* (*Chili Pines*), *Taxaceae* (*Yews*), *Cupressaceae* (*Arborvitae*), *and Ginkgoales* (*Ginkos*)

1

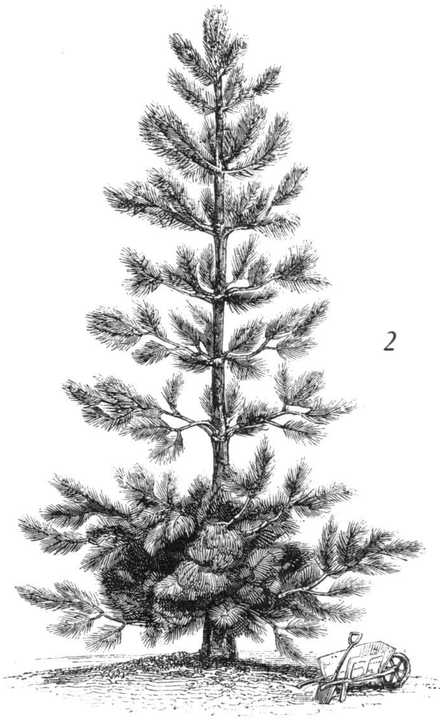

2

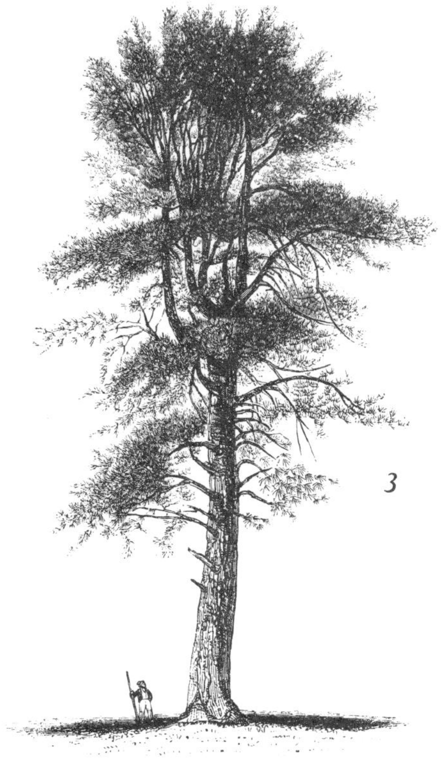

3

4

5

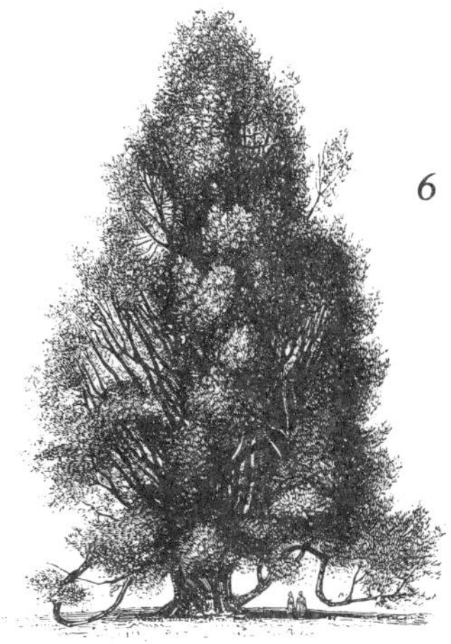

6

7

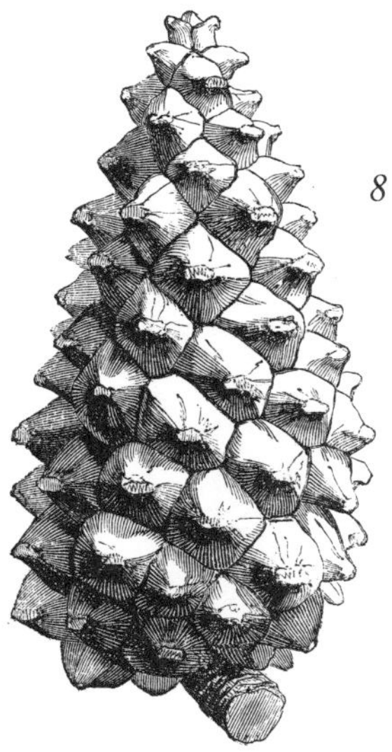

8

9

GYMNOSPERMAE: Pinaceae (Pines) and Taxaceae (Yews)

1

2

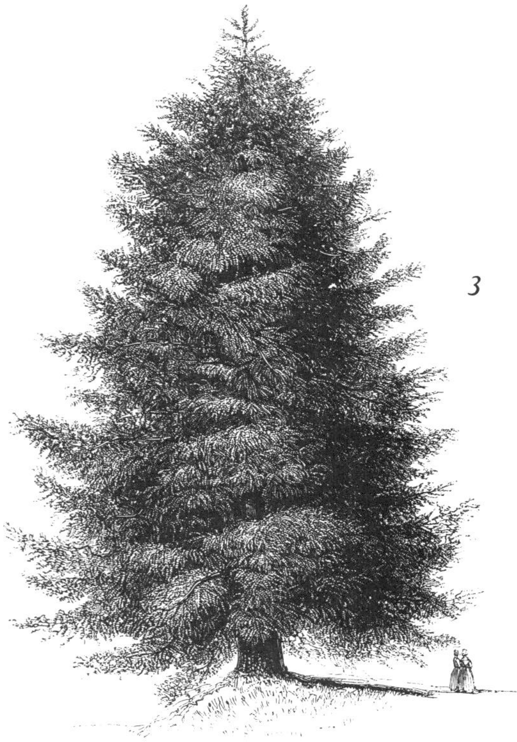

3

4

5

6

7

8

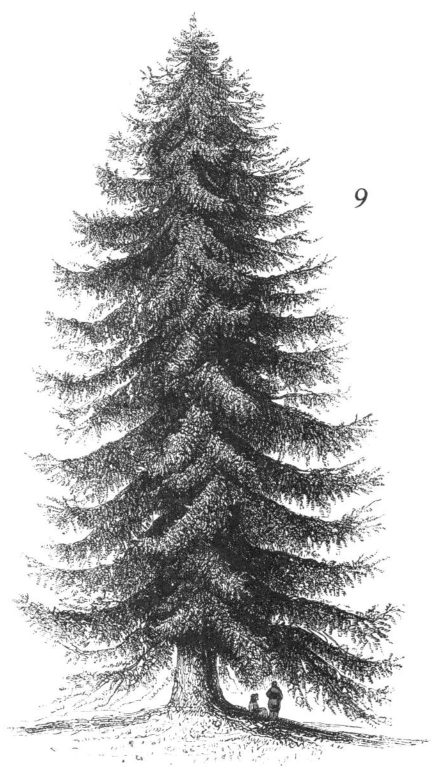

9

 GYMNOSPERMAE: Pinaceae (Pines, Larches, Firs, Spruces)

1

2

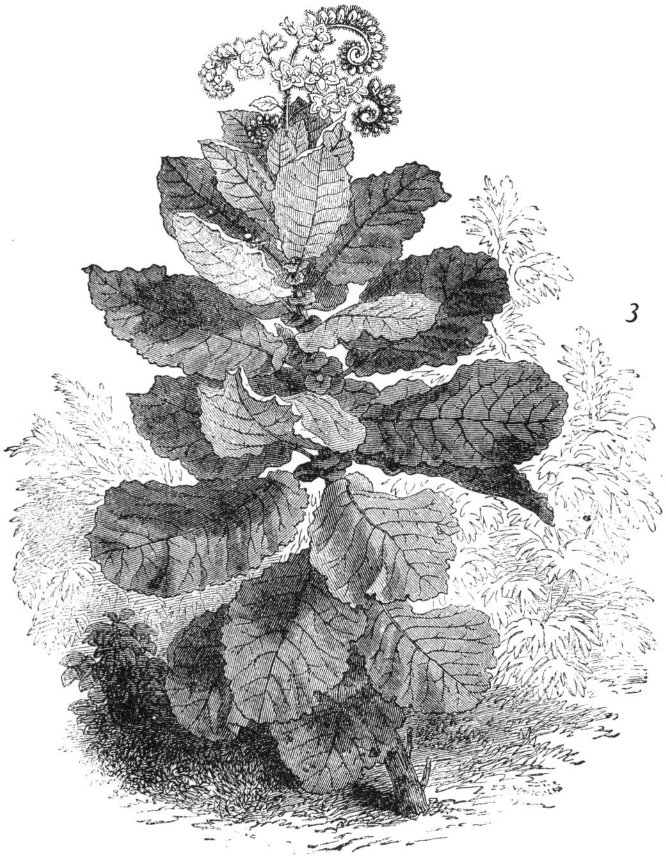

3

4

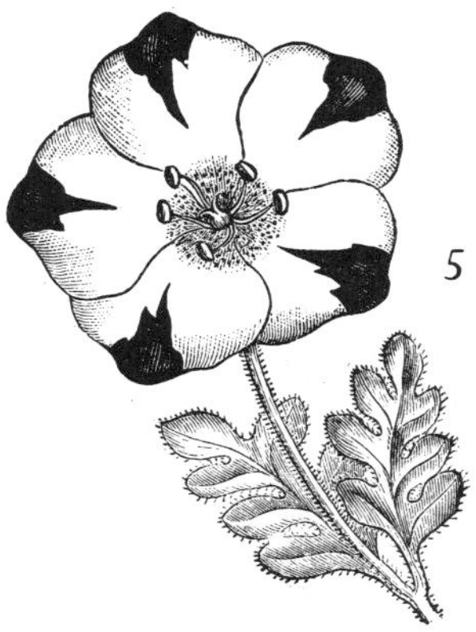

5

6

7

8

1

2

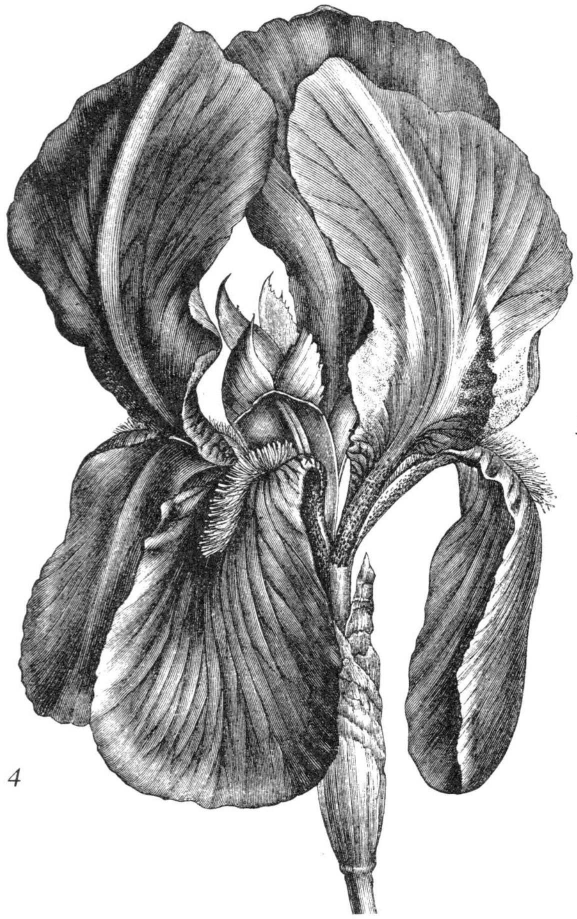

3

4

5

6

7

1

2

3

4

5

6

7

8

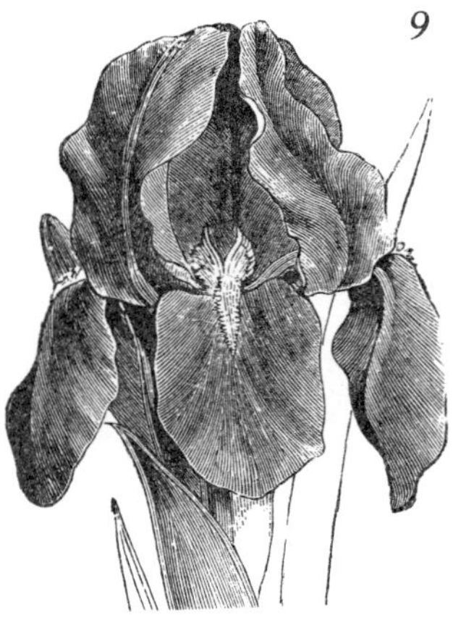

9

10

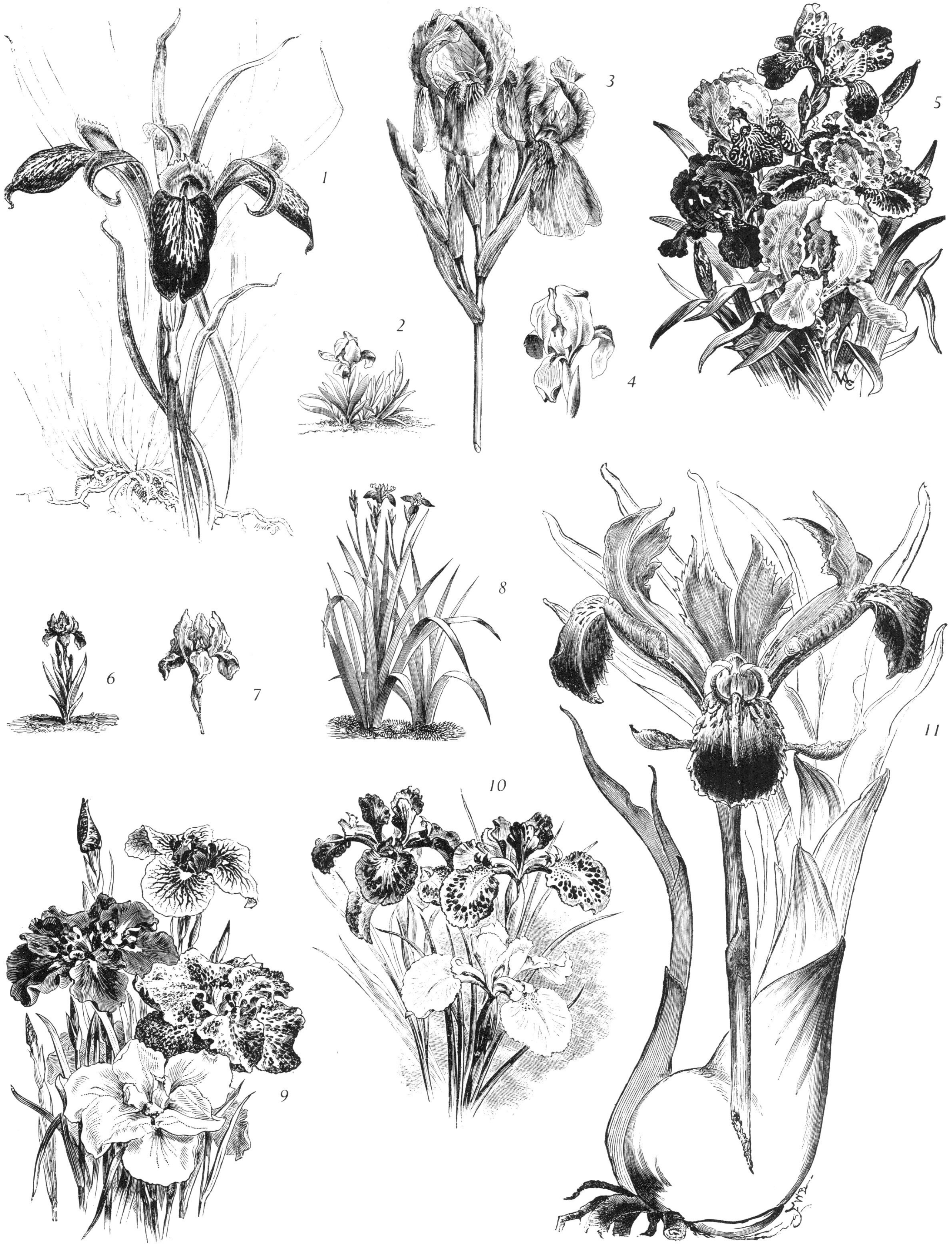
1
2
3
4
5
6
7
8
9
10
11

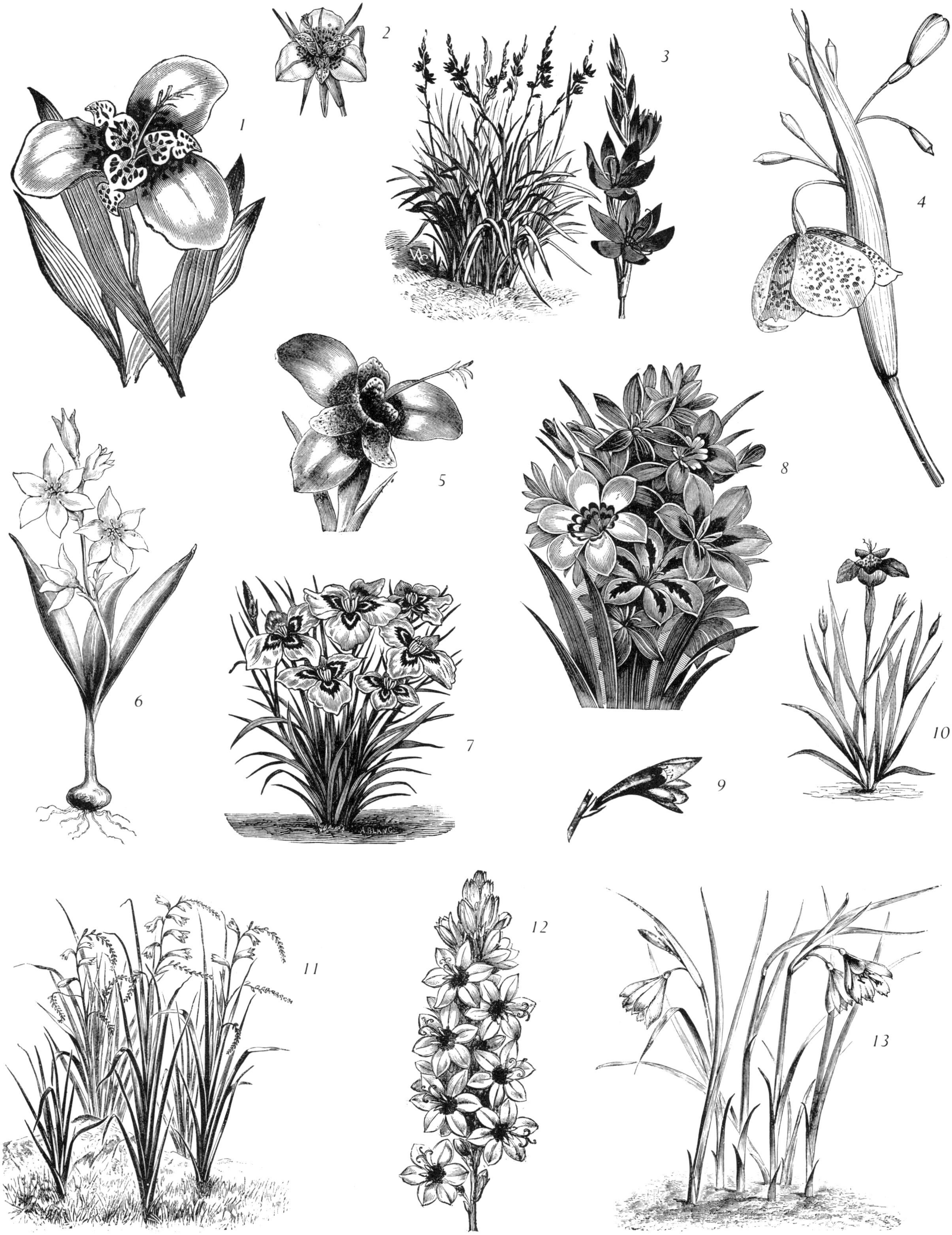
1
2
3
4
5
6
7
8
9
10
11
12
13

1

2

3

4

5

6

7

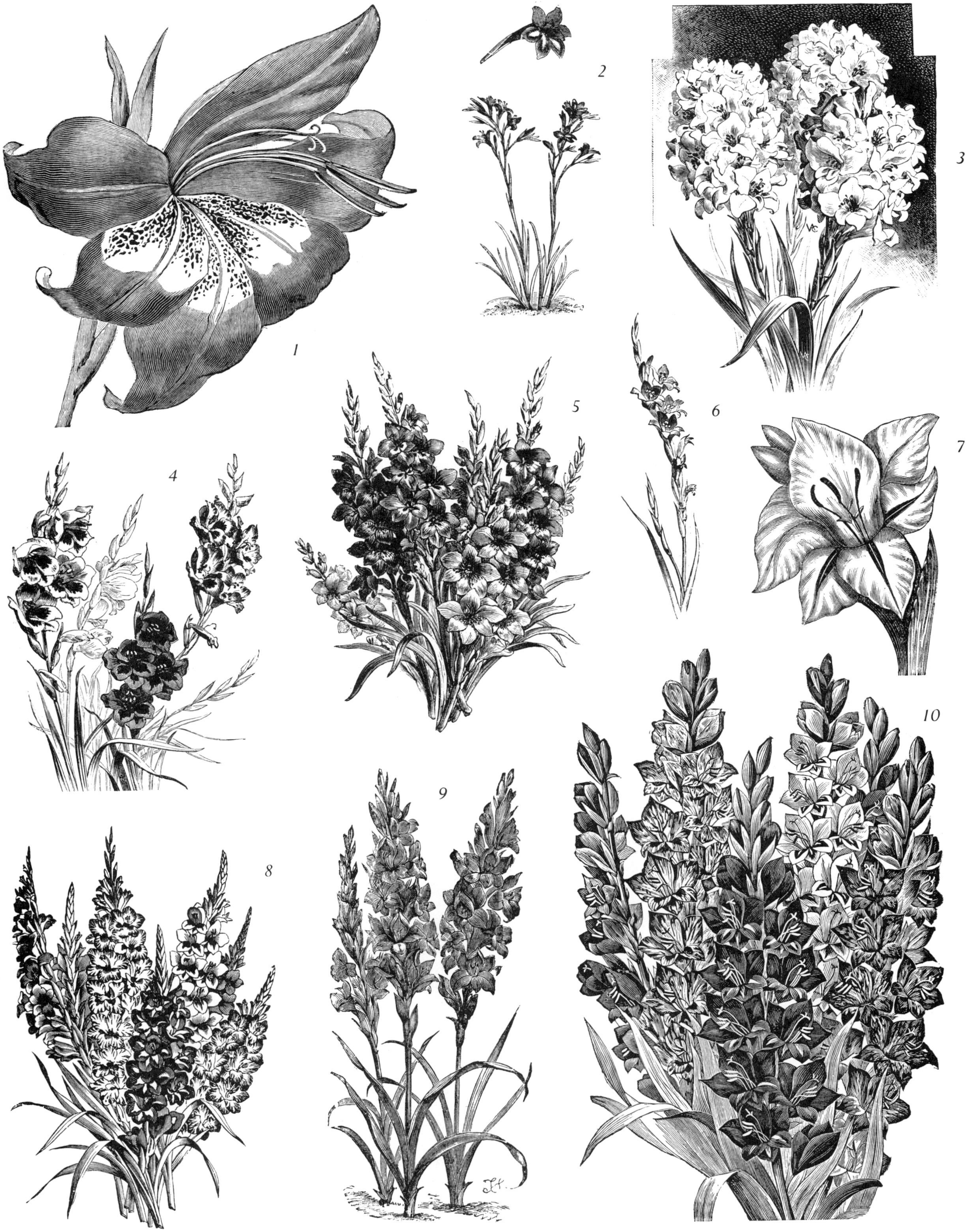
1
2
3
4
5
6
7
8
9
10

1

2

3

4

5

6

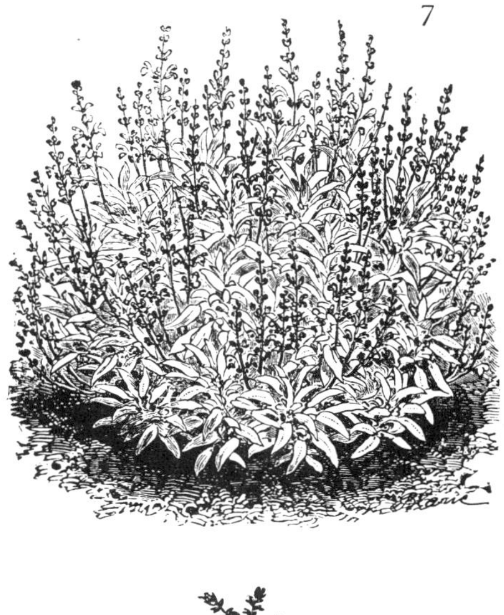

7

8

9

10

1

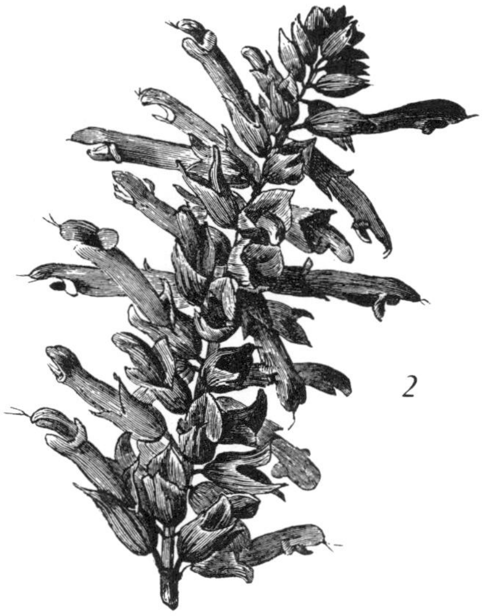

2

3

4

5

6

7

8

9

10

11

12

13

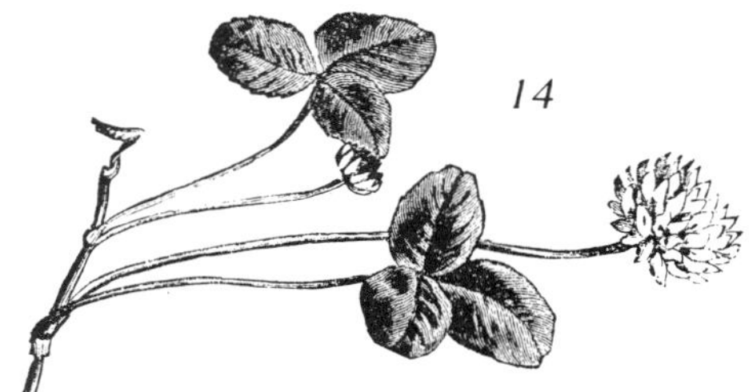

14

15

1
2
3
4
5
6
7
8

1

2

3

4

5

6

7

8

1

2

3

4

5

6

1

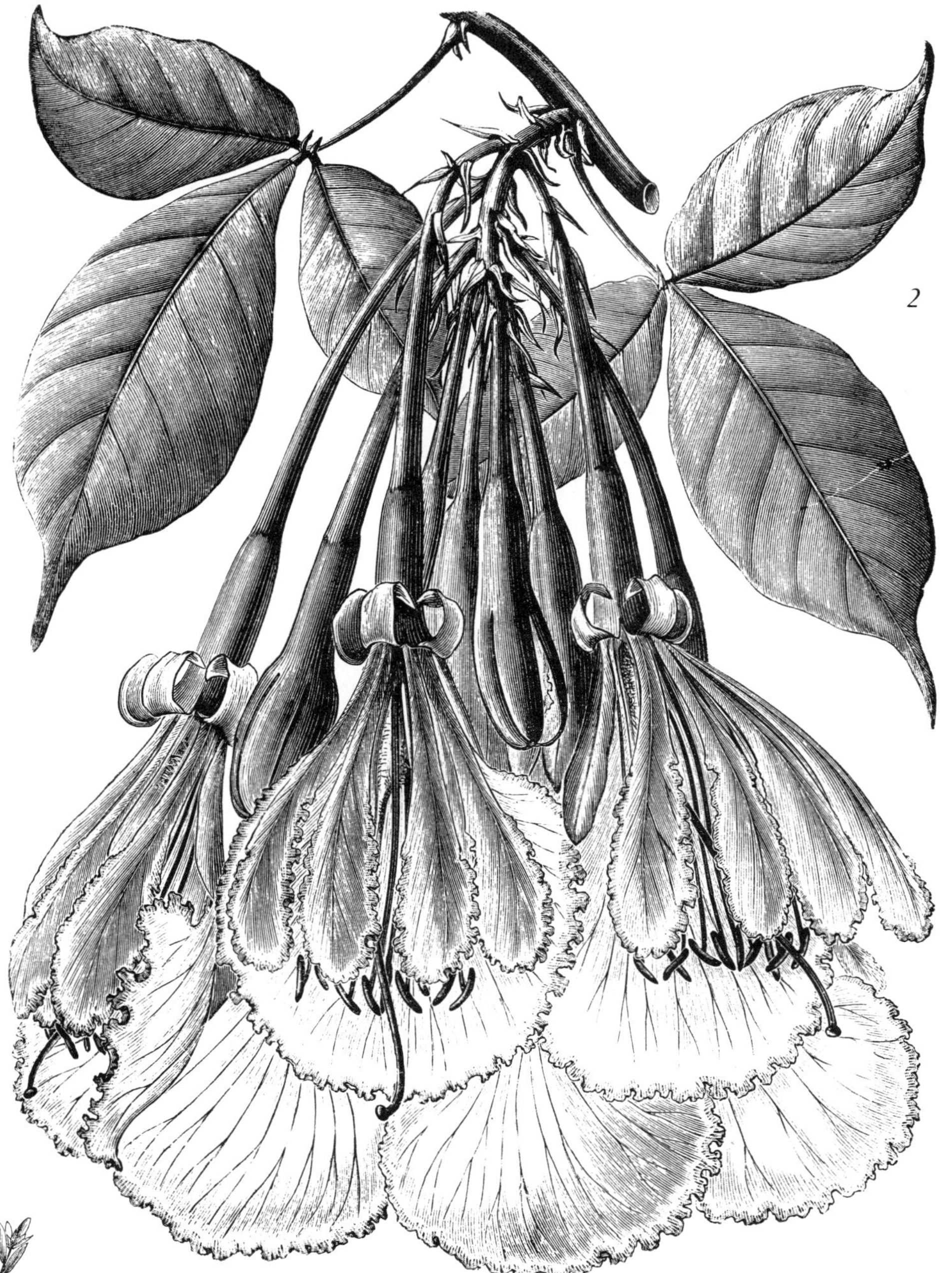

2

3

4

5

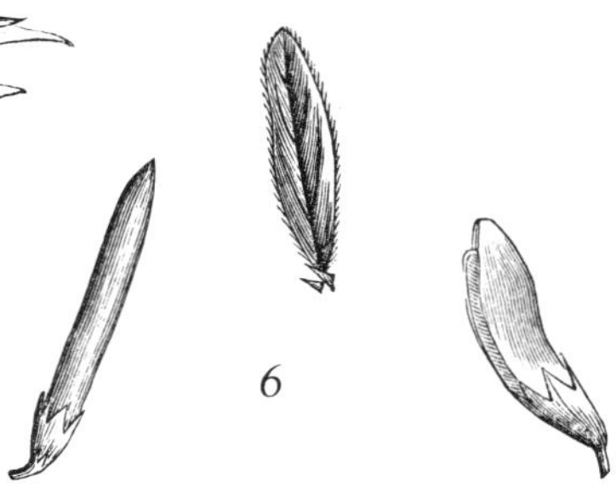

6

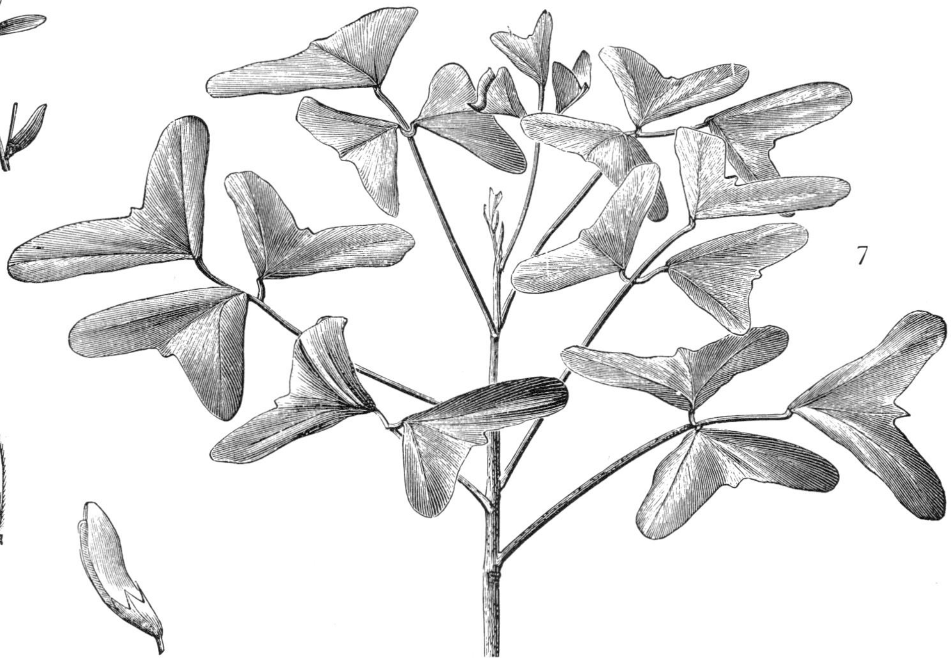

7

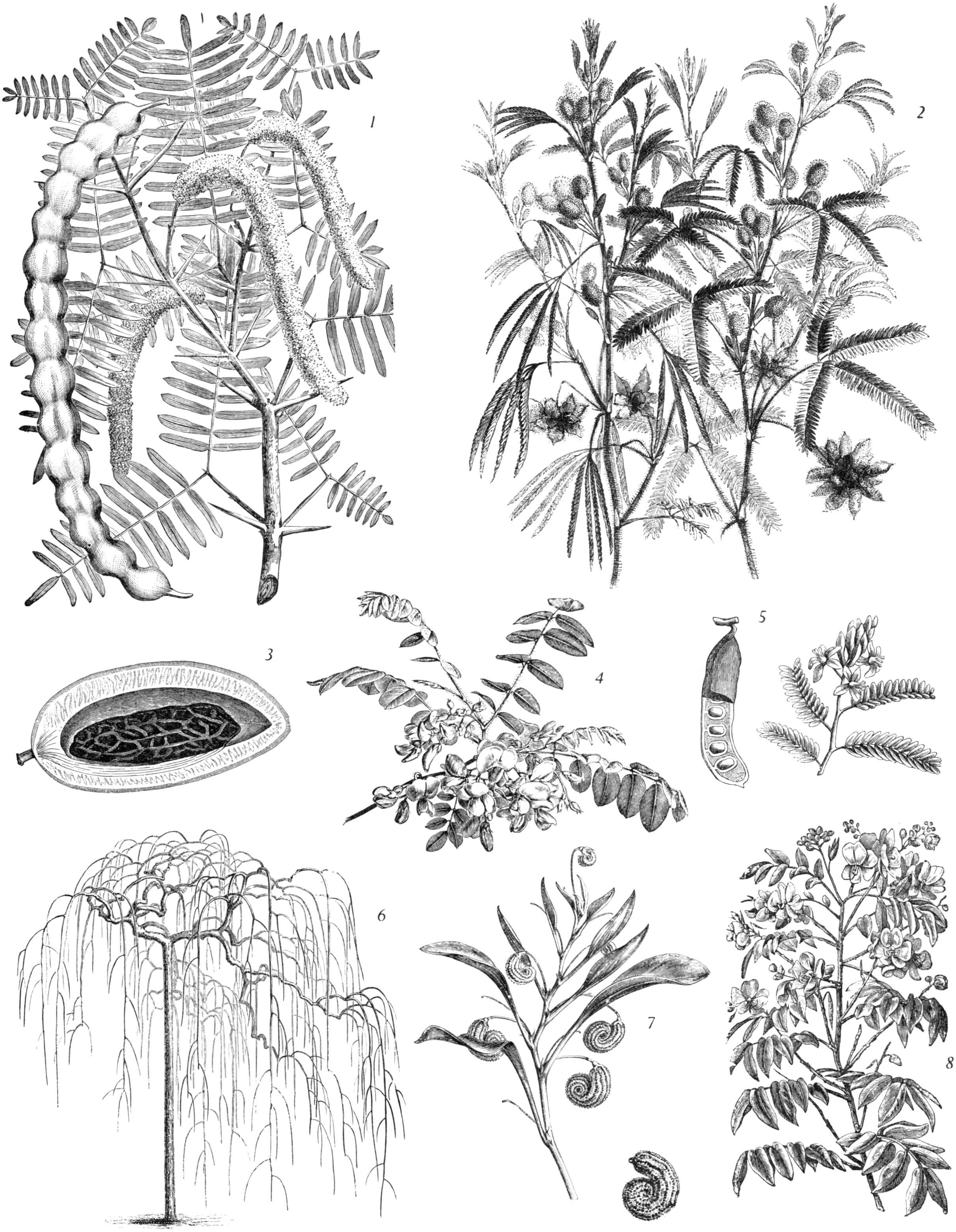
1
2
3
4
5
6
7
8

1

2

3

4

5

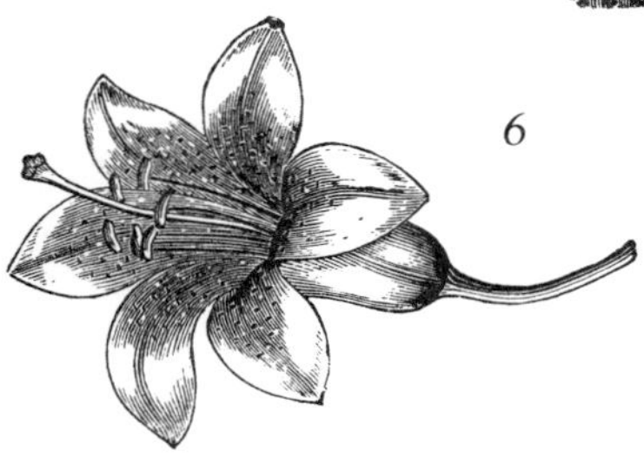

6

7

8

1

2

3

4

5

6

7

8

9

10

1

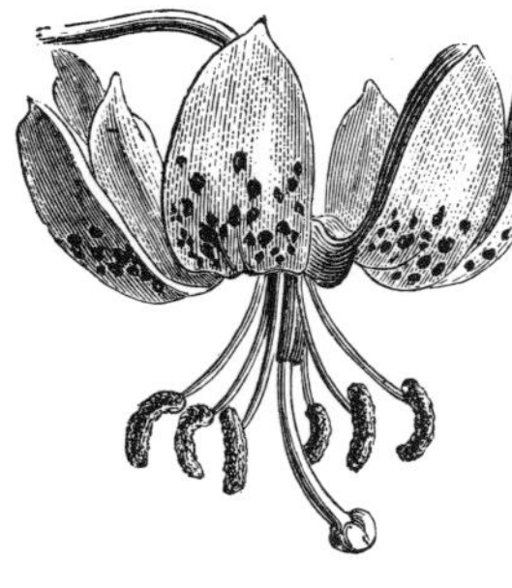

2

3

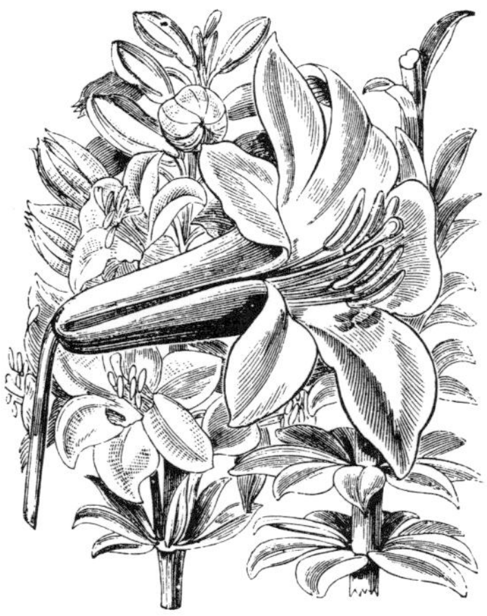

4

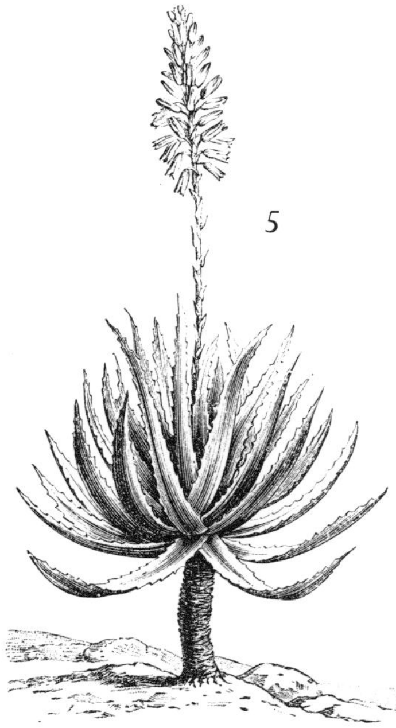

5

6

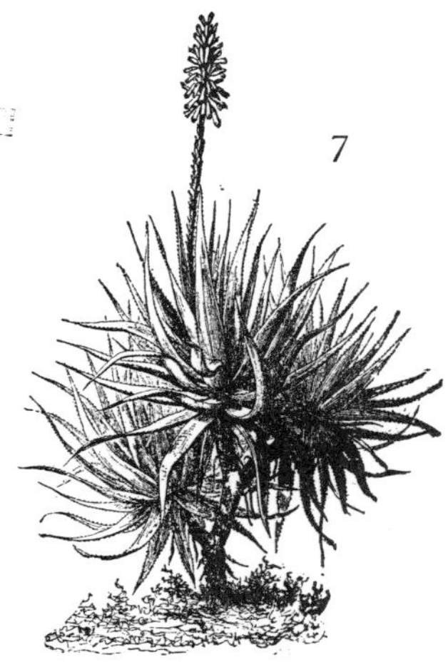

7

8

9

10

1

2

3

4

5

6

7

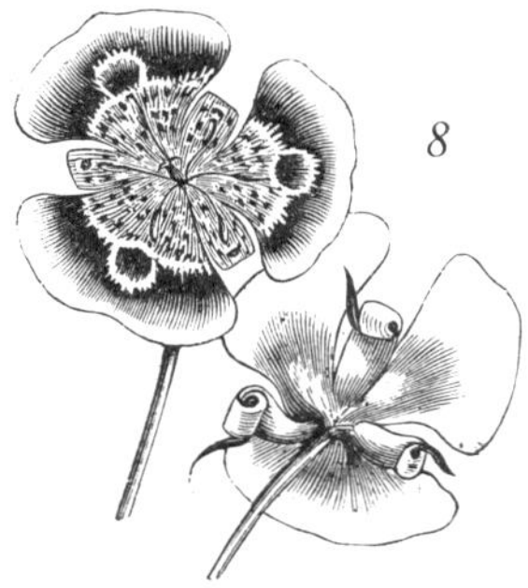

8

9

1

2

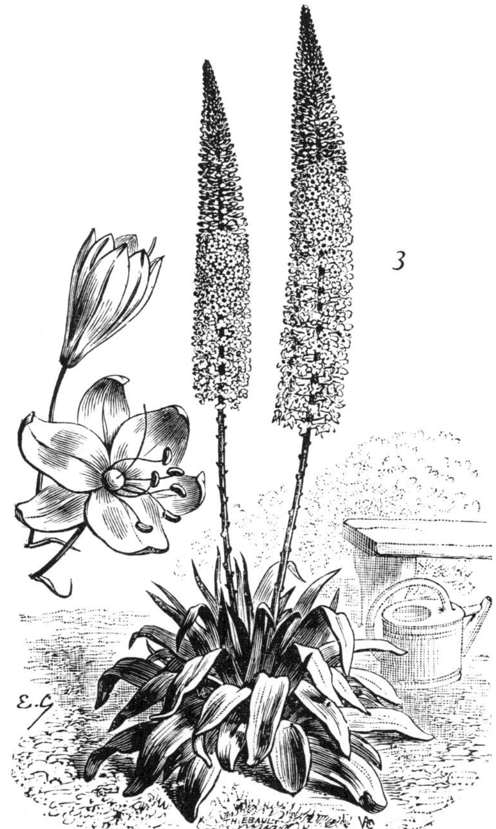

3

4

5

6

7

8

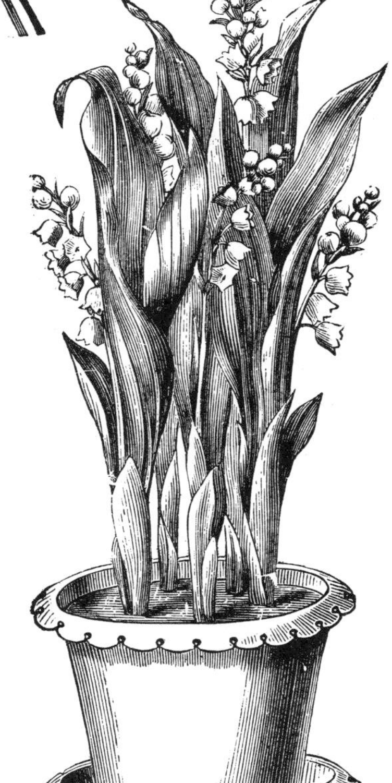

9

1

2

3

4

5

6

7

8

9

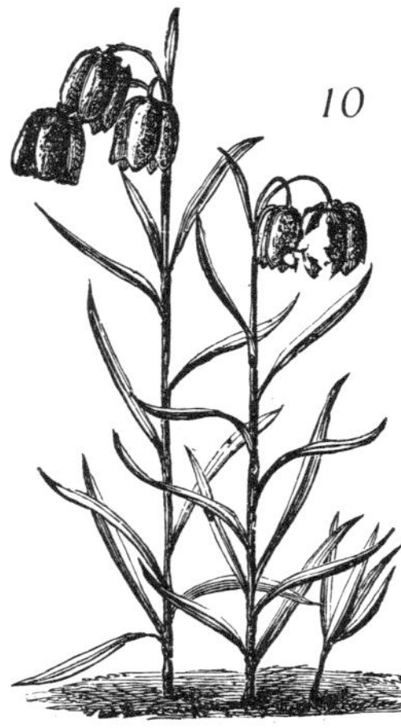

10

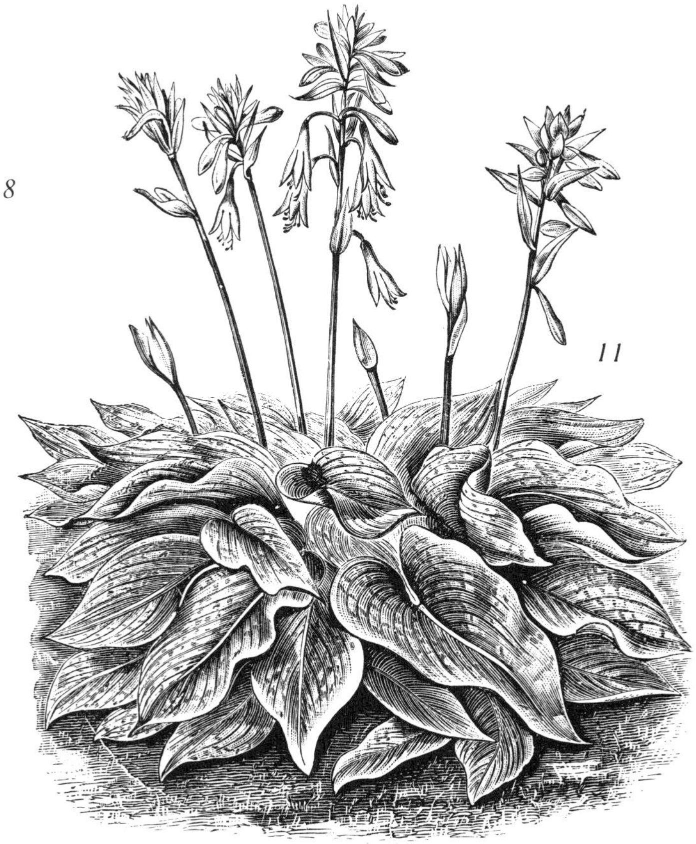

11

1

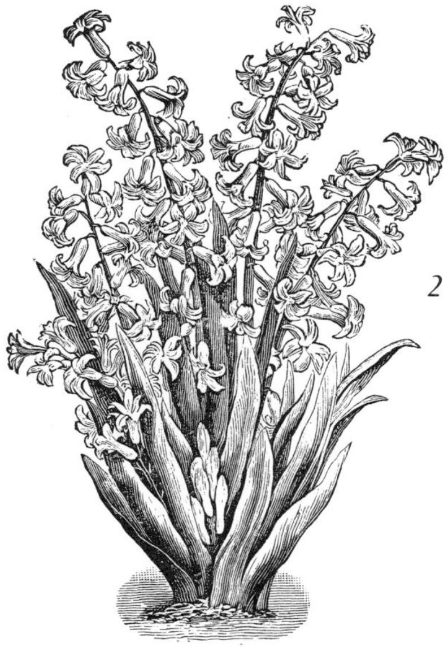

2

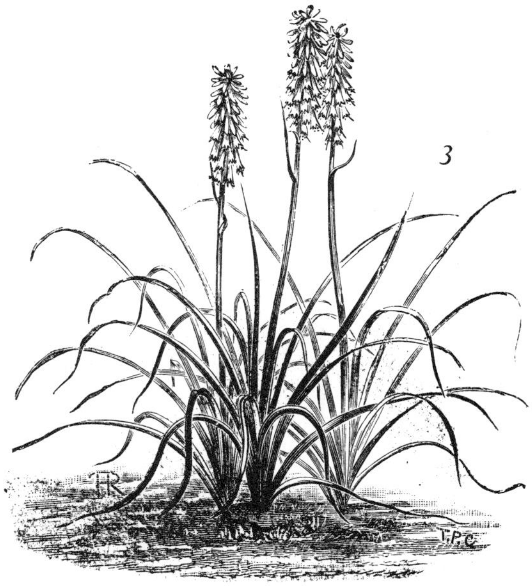

3

4

5

6

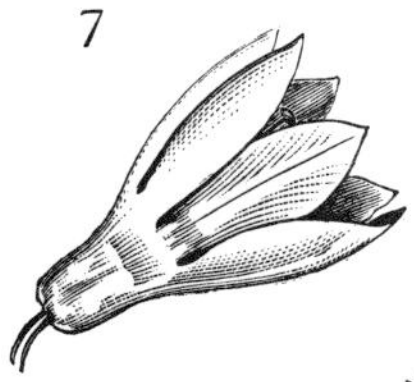

7

8

9

10

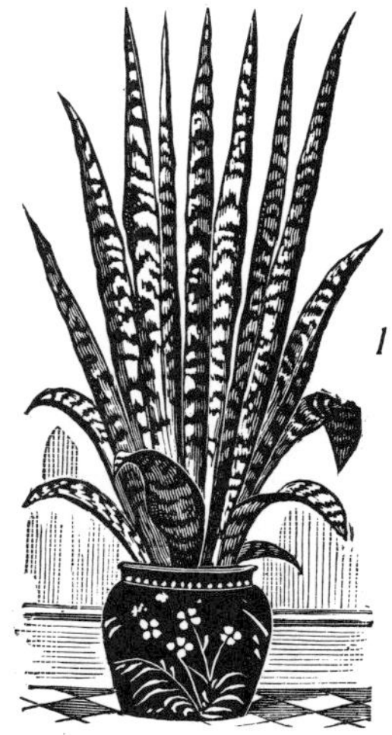

11

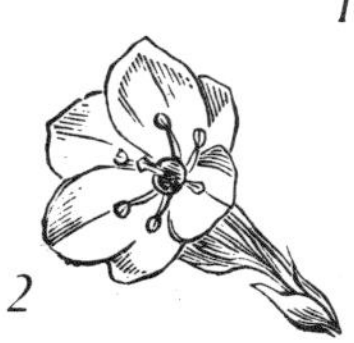

12

13

14

15

16

17

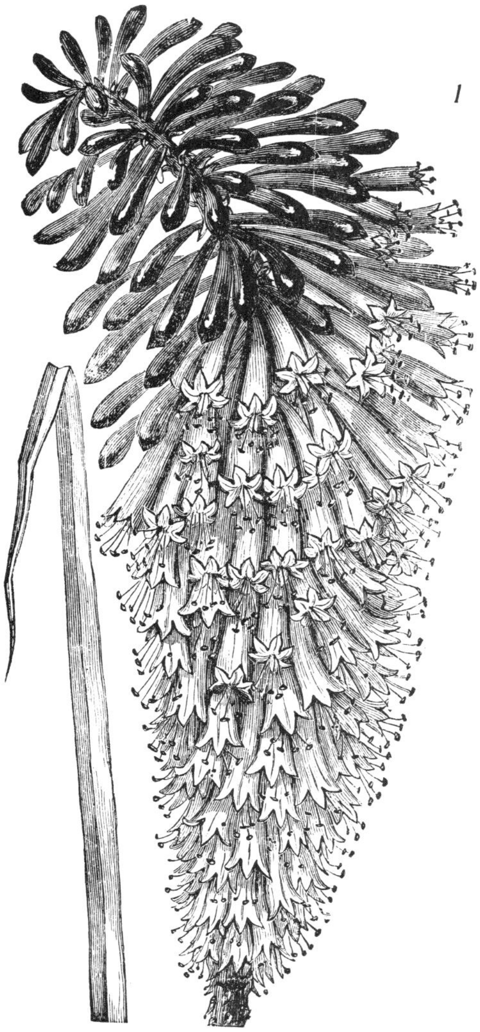

1

2

3

4

5

6

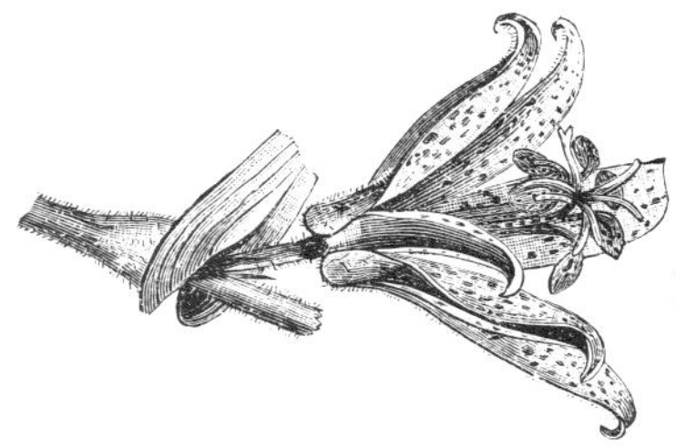

7

8

9

10

1

2

3

4

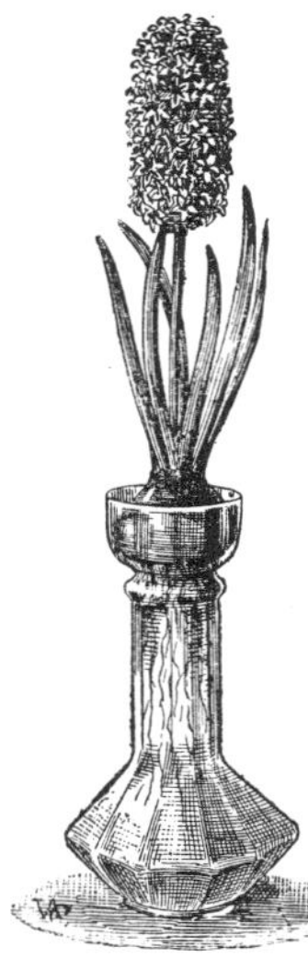
5

6

7

8

LILIACEAE (Tulips)

1

2

3

4

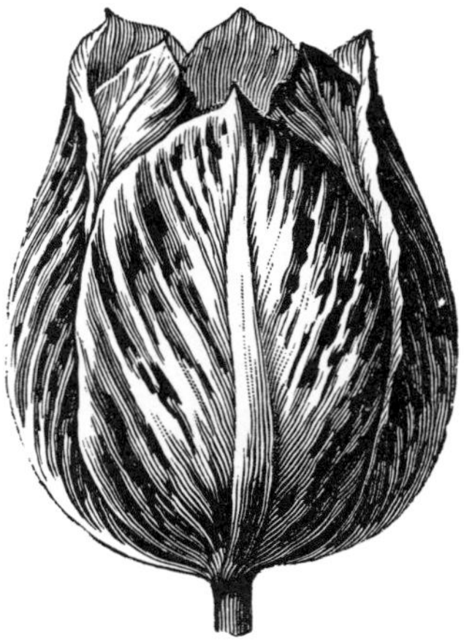

5

6

7

8

9

10

11

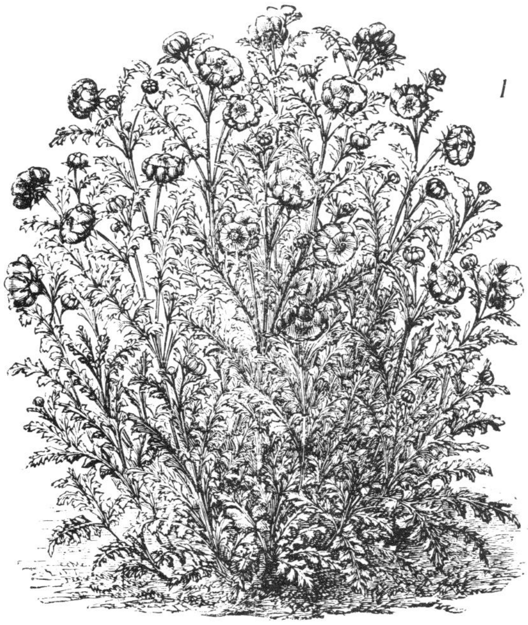

1

2

3

4

5

6

7

1

2

3

4

5

6

7

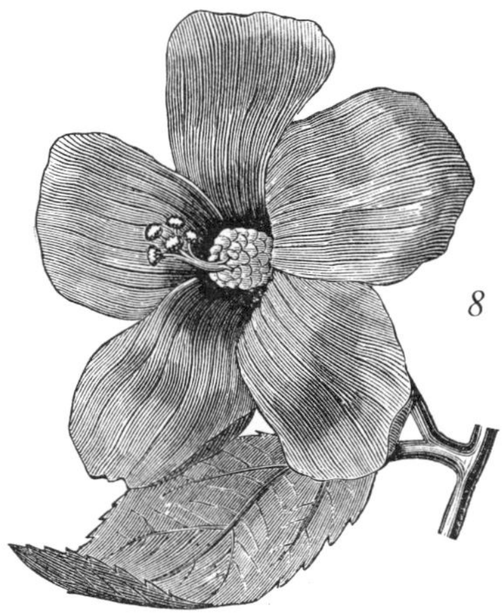
8

9

10

11

12

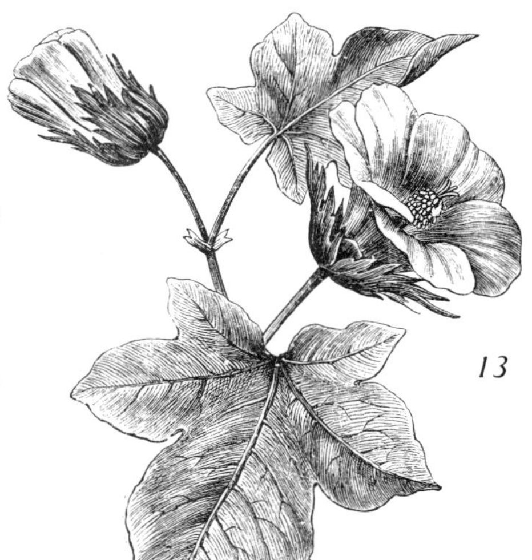
13

MAGNOLIACEAE (Magnolias) and MALVACEAE (Mallows)

1

2

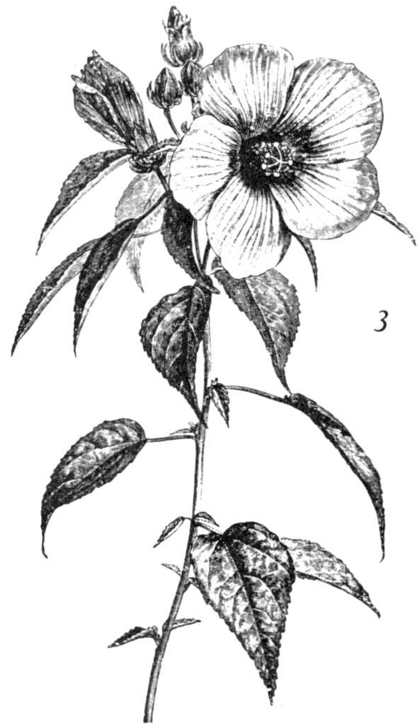

3

4

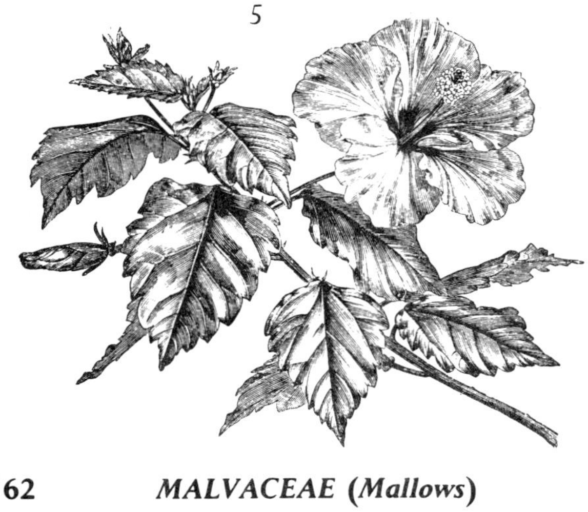

5

6

1
2
3
4
5
6
7

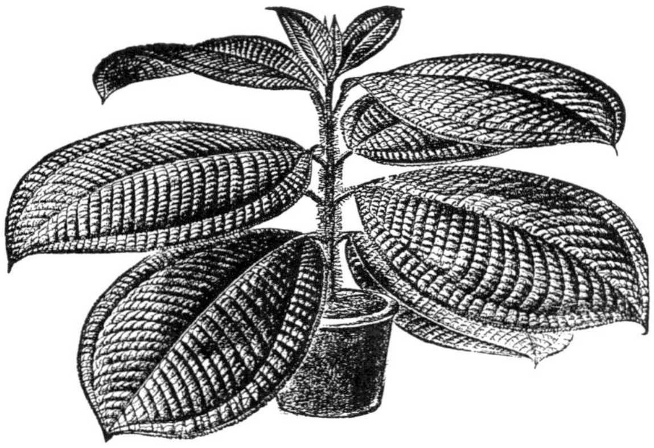

1

2

4

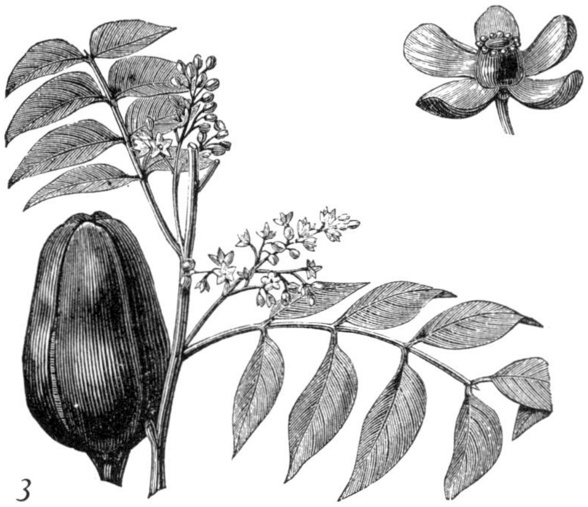

3

5

6

7

8

MARANTACEAE (Arrowroots), *MELASTOMATACEAE (Melastomas)*, *MELIACEAE (Mahoganies)*, ***and*** *MORACEAE (Figs, Mulberries)*

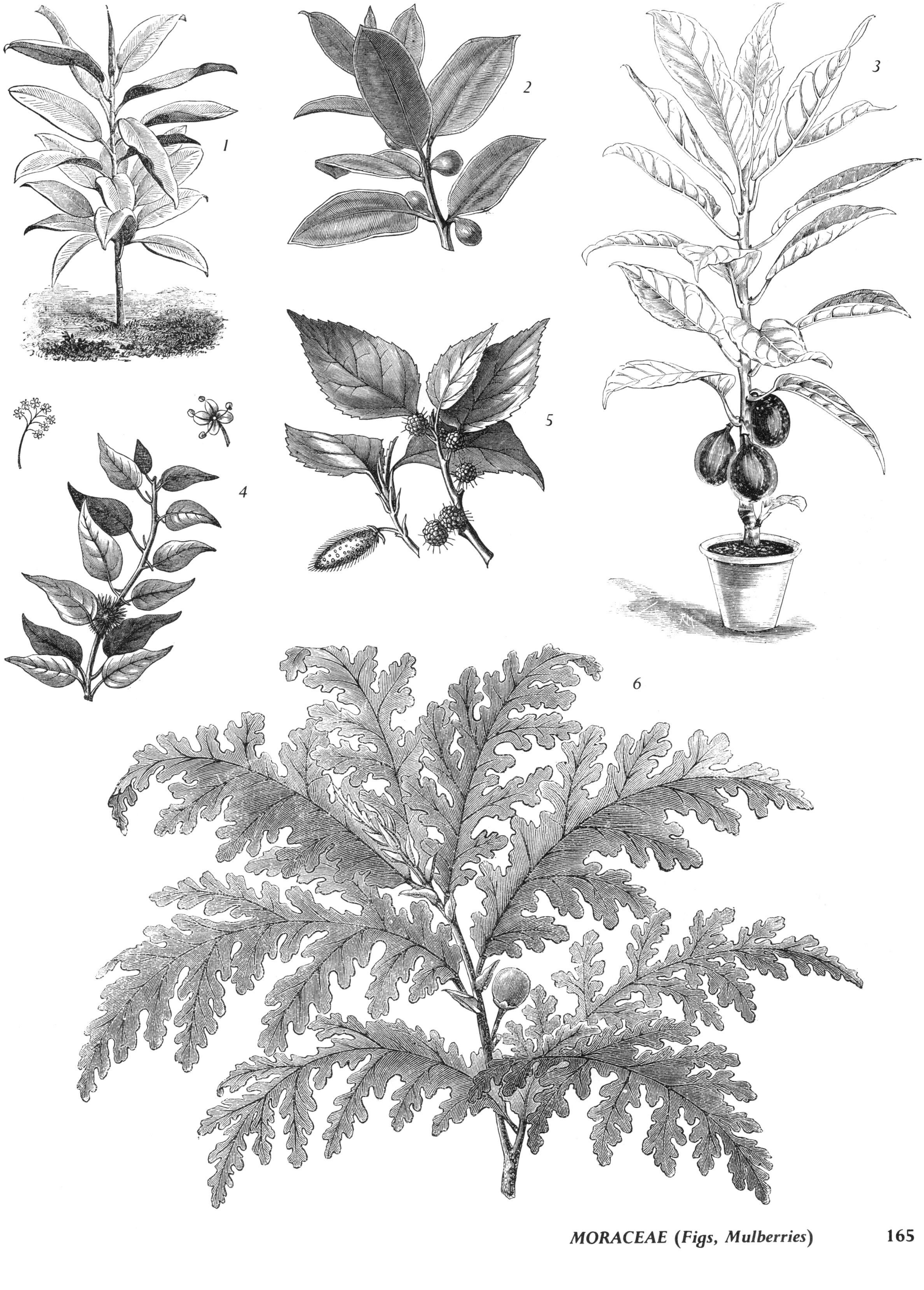
1
2
3
4
5
6

1
2
3
4
5
6
7
8
9

MYRSINACEAE (Ardisias) and MYRTACEAE (Myrtles, Eucalyptuses)

1

2

3

5

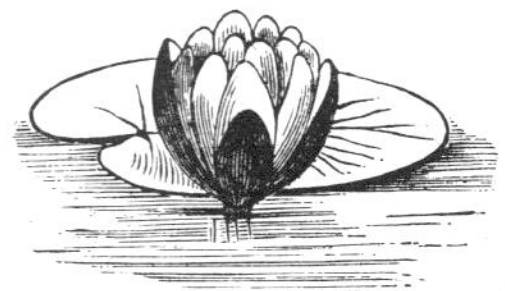
6

4

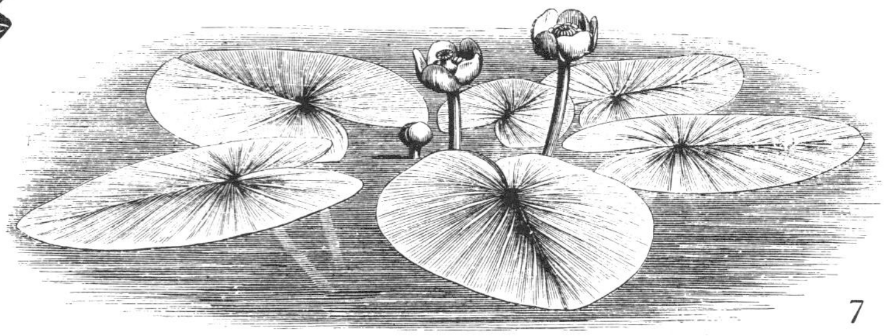
7

8

 NYMPHAEACEAE* (*Water Lilies*) *and water plants and water grasses of other families

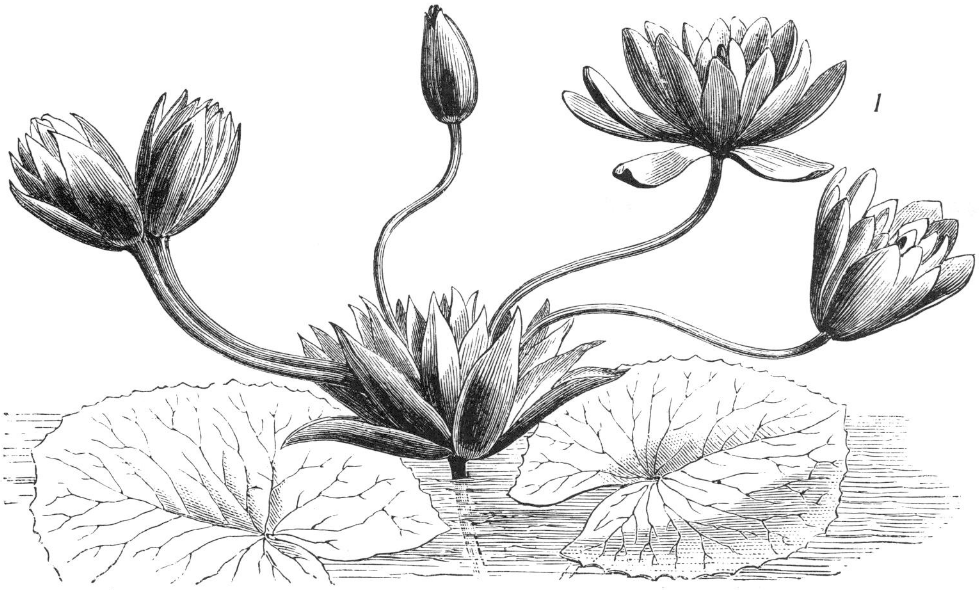
1

2

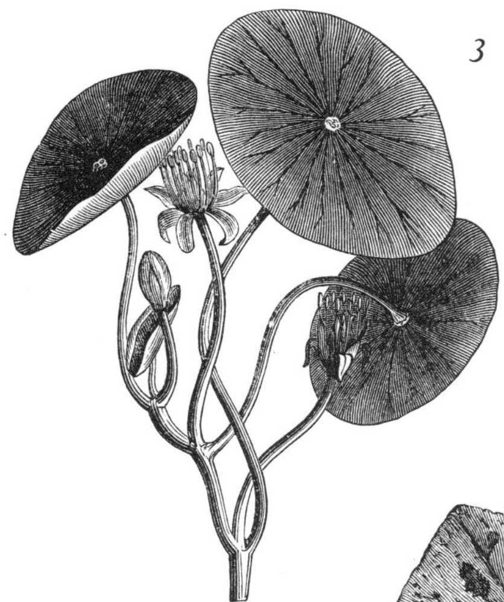
3

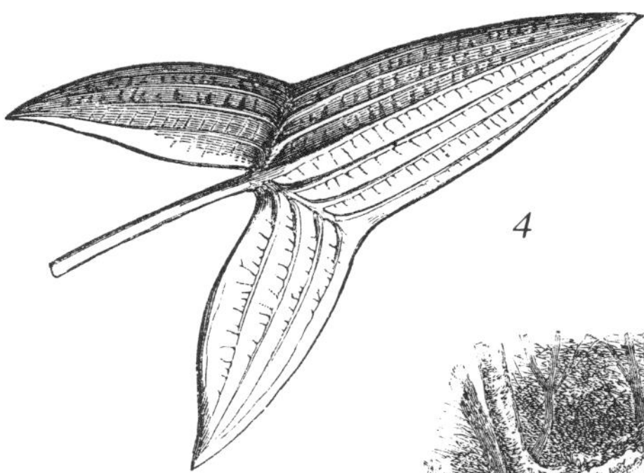
4

9

6

5

7

8

NYMPHAEACEAE* (*Water Lilies*) *and water plants and water grasses of other families

1

2

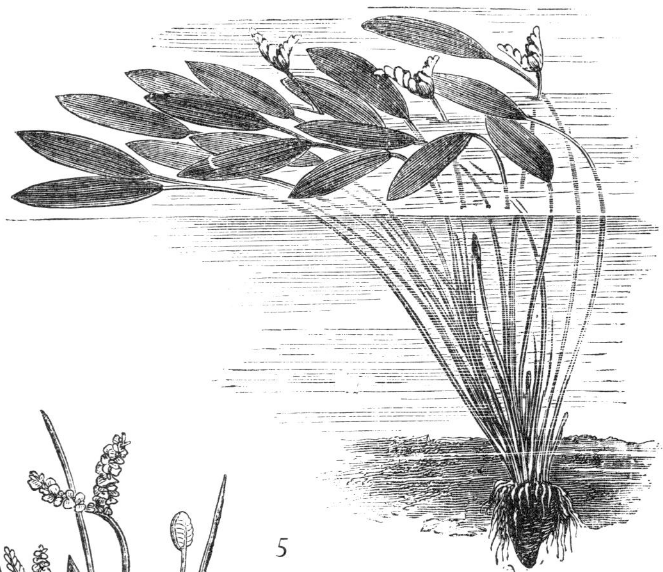

3

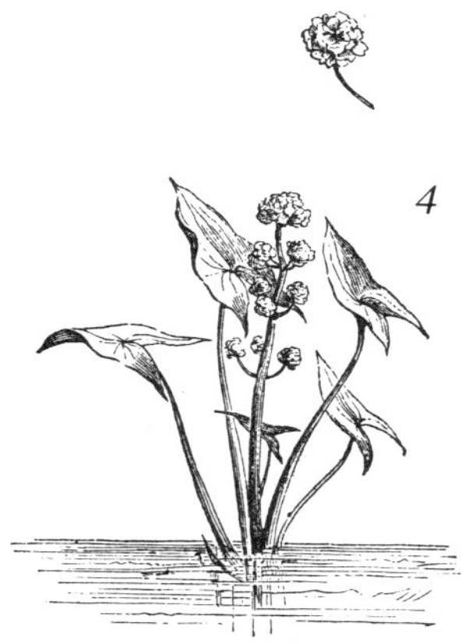

4

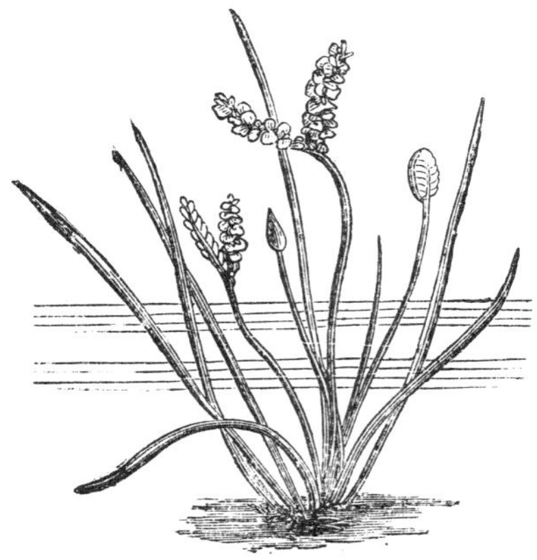

5

6

7

8

9

NYMPHAEACEAE (Water Lilies) and water plants and water grasses of other families

1

2

3

4

5

6

7

NYMPHAEACEAE (Water Lilies) and water plants and water grasses of other families

1

2

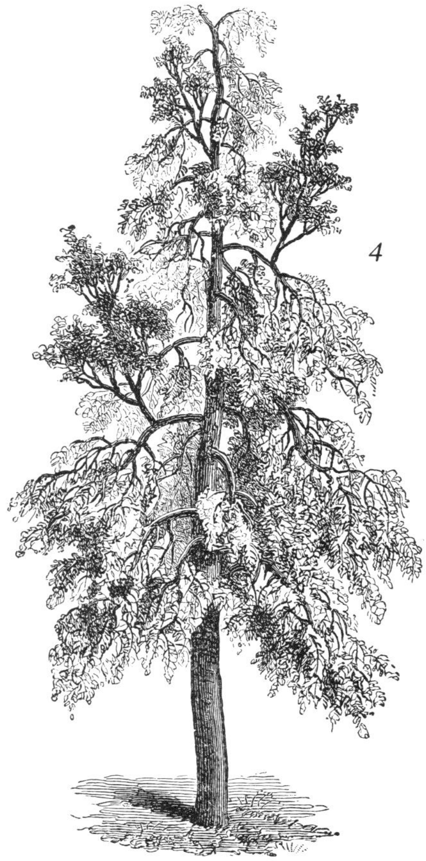
4

3

5

8

6

7

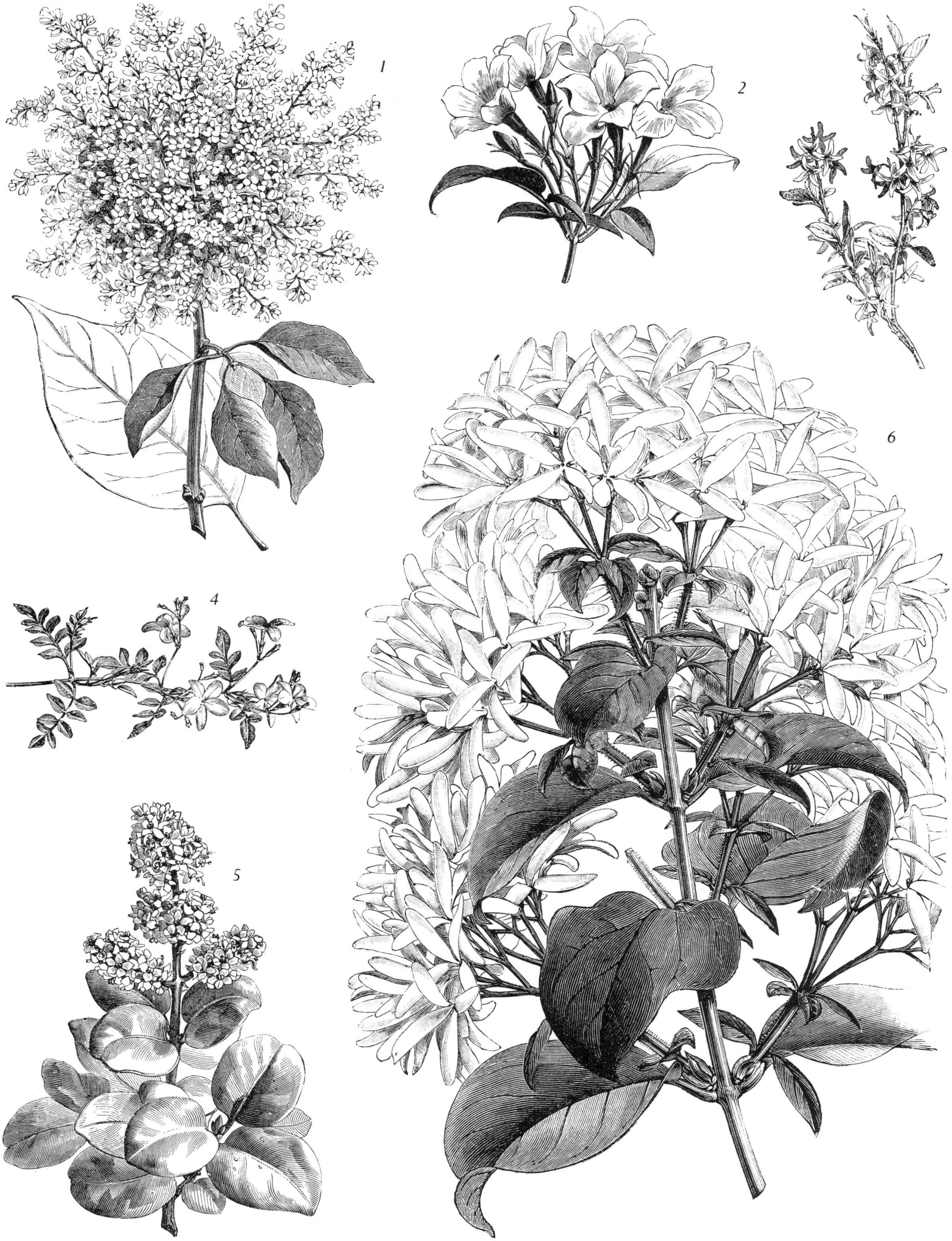
1
2
3
4
5
6

 OLEACEAE (Olives) and ONAGRACEAE (Evening Primroses)

1
2
3
4
5
6
7
8
9
10
11
12

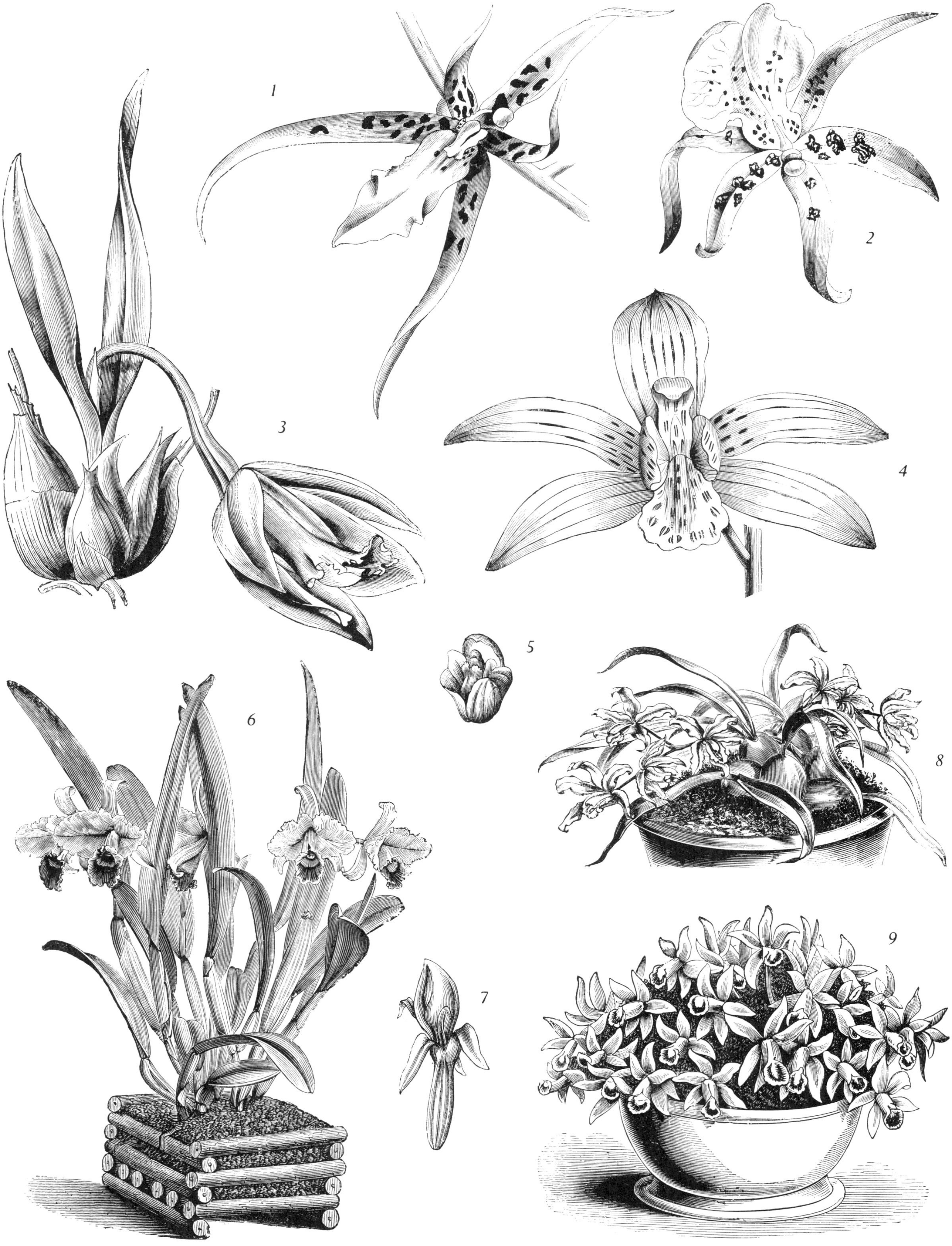
1
2
3
4
5
6
7
8
9

1

2

4

3

5

6

7

8

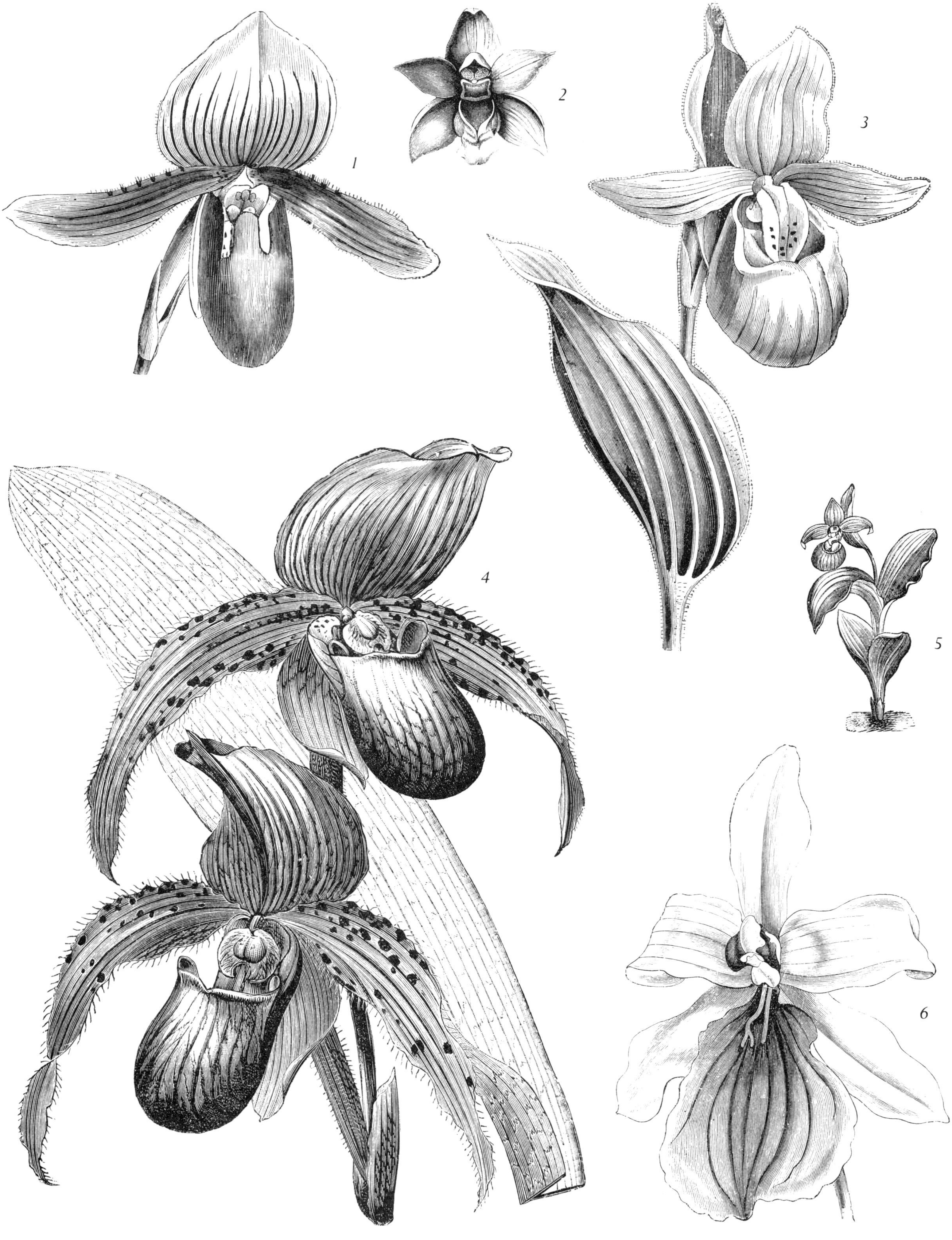
1
2
3
4
5
6

1

3

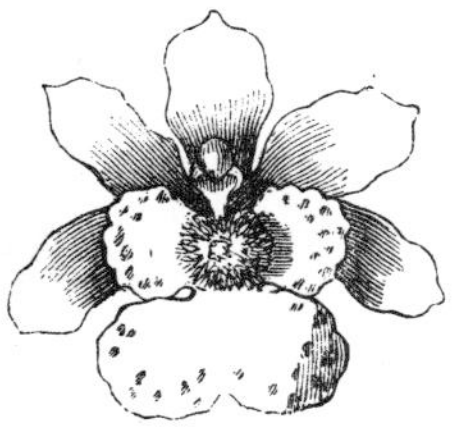

2

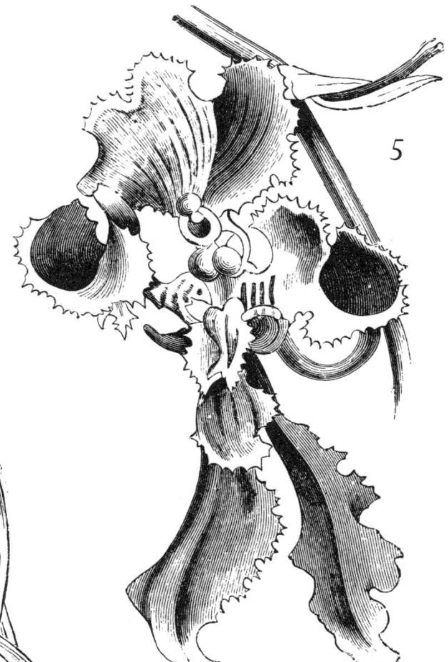

5

4

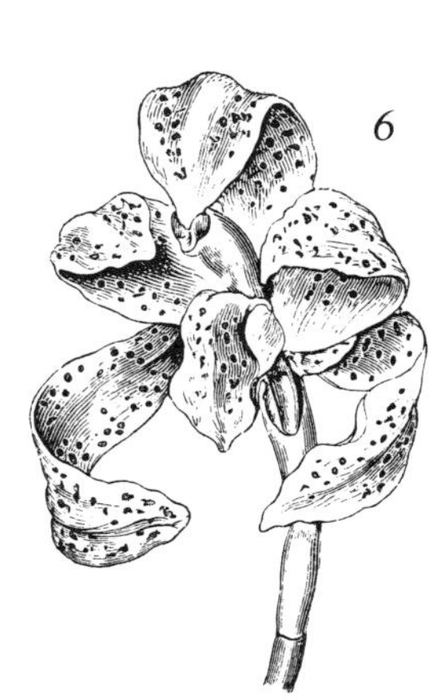

6

1

2

1
2
3
4
5
6
7

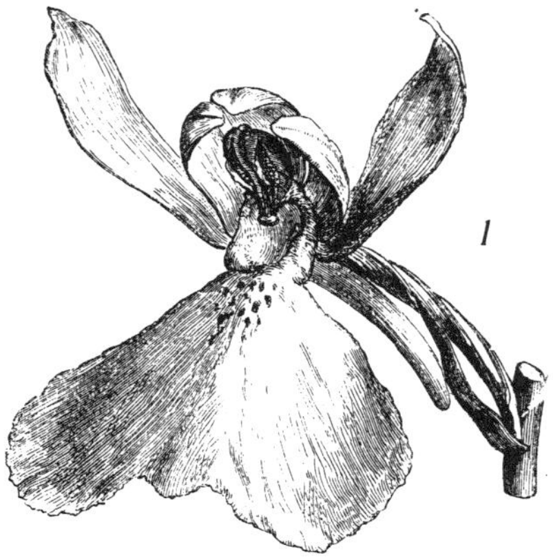

1

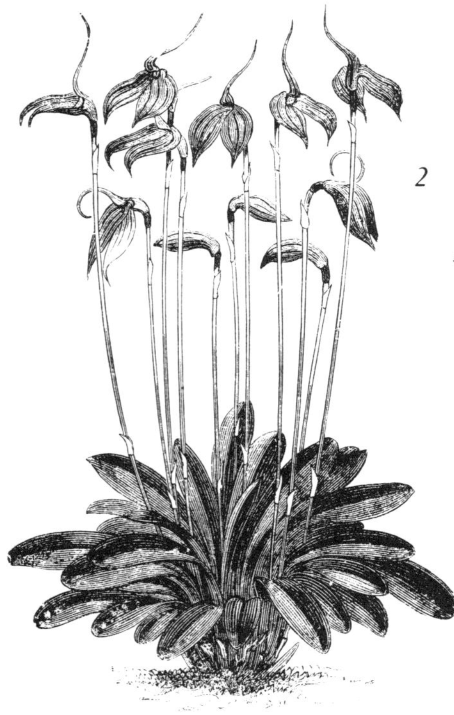

2

3

4

5

6

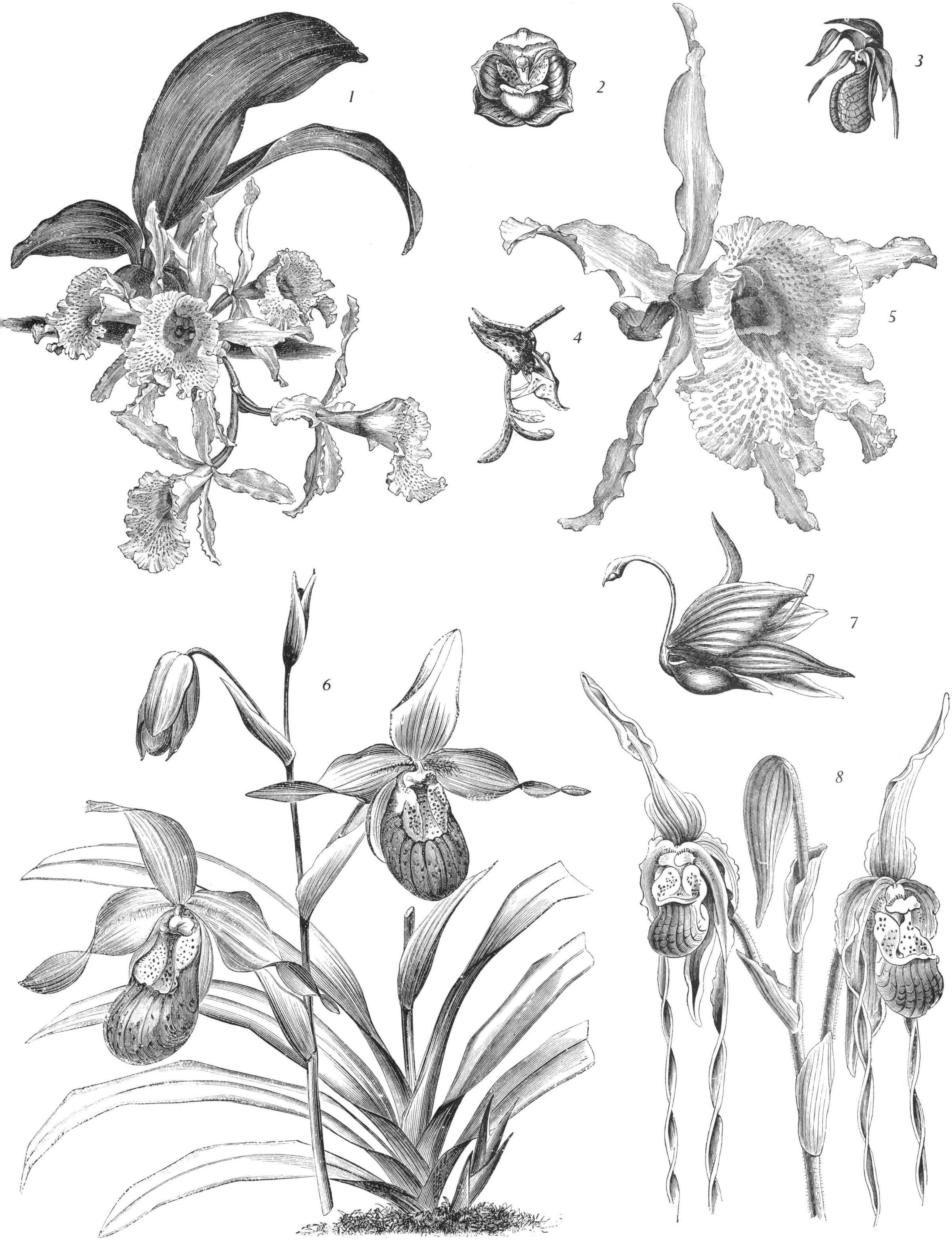
1
2
3
4
5
6
7
8

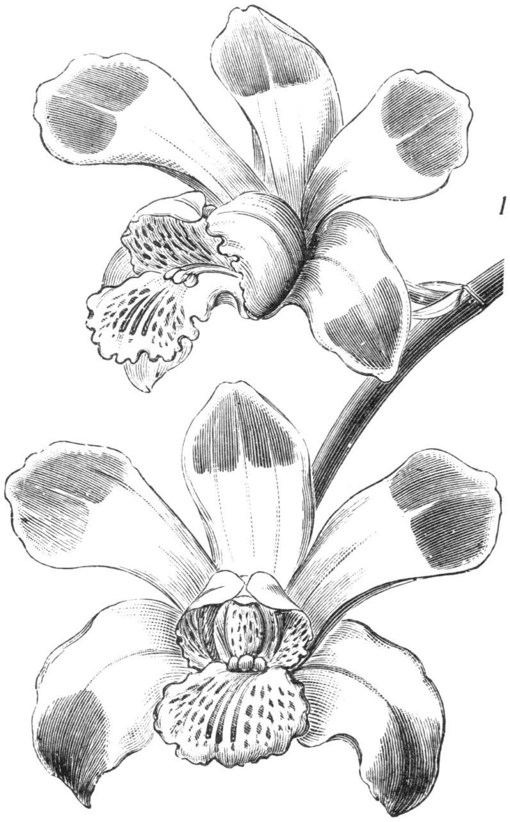

1

2

3

4

5

6

1

2

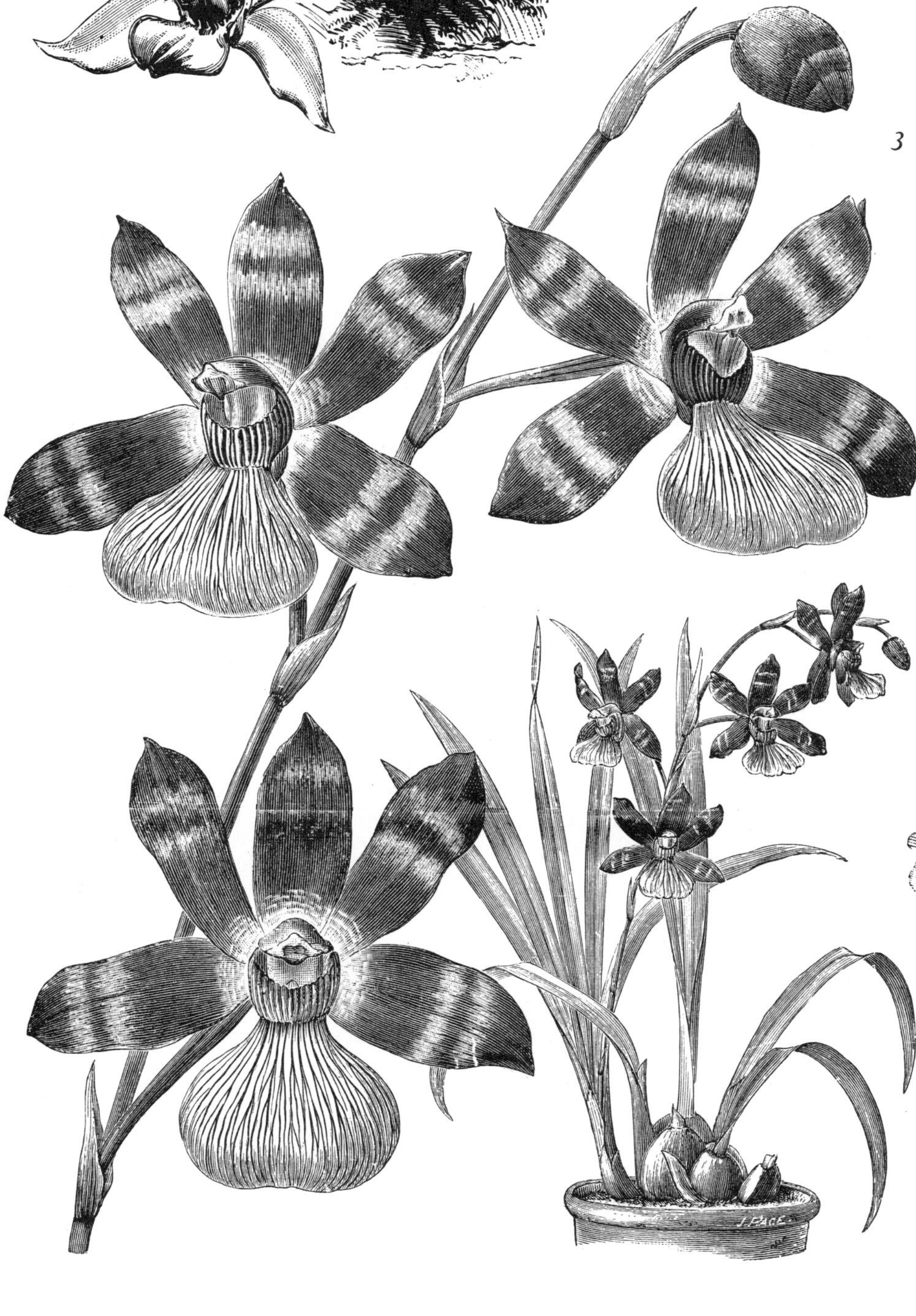
3

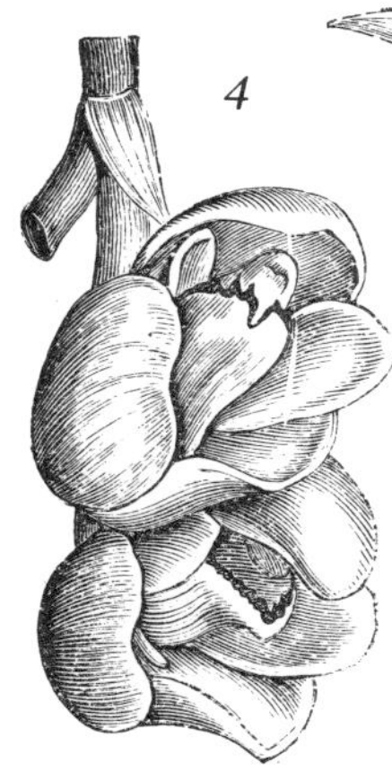
4

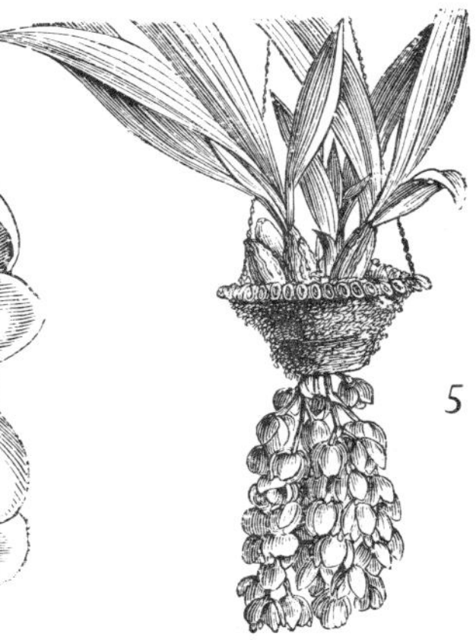
5

6

1

2

6

5

3

4

7

8

9

OXALIDACEAE (Oxalis) and PAEONIACEAE (Peonies)

1

2

3

4

5

6

1

2

3

4

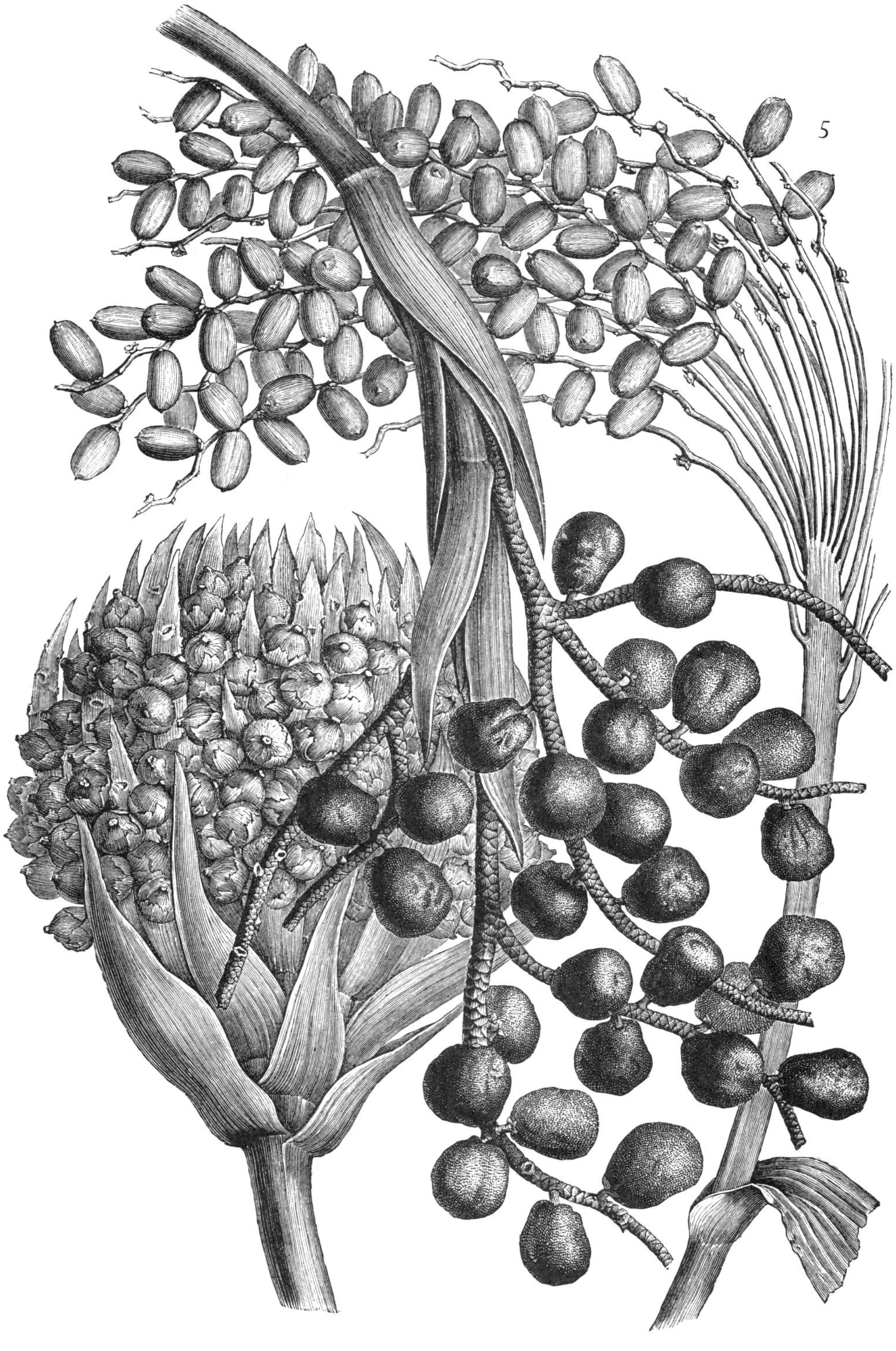

5

***PALMACEAE** (**Palms**)*

1

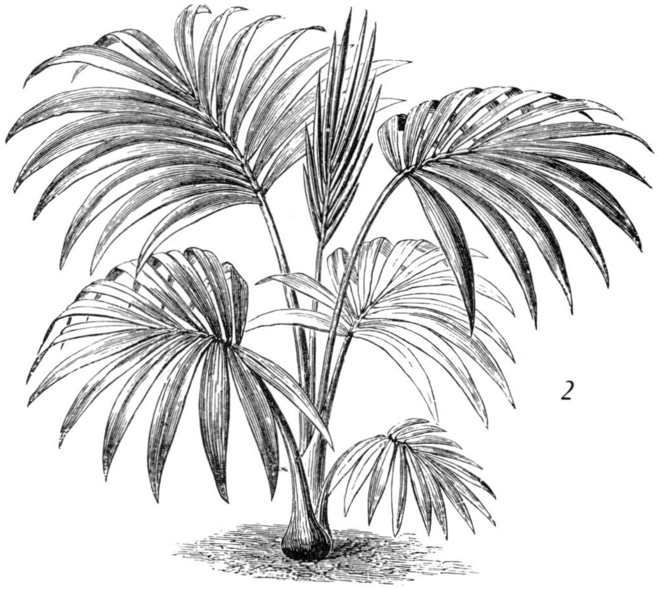

2

3

4

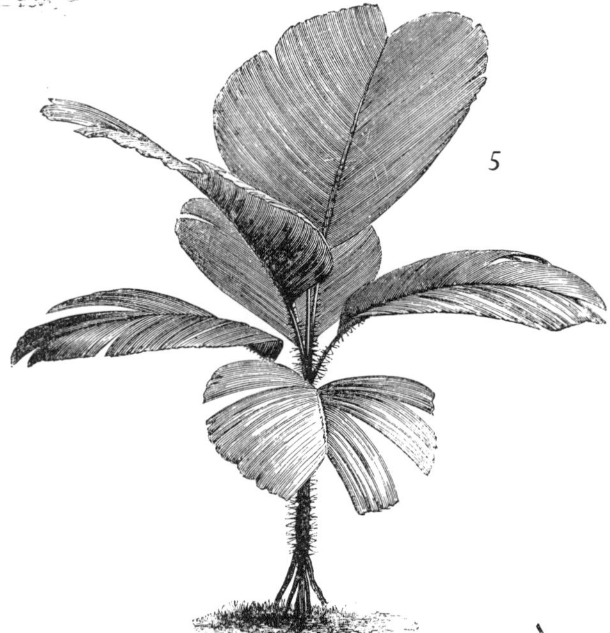

5

6

7

8

PALMACEAE (Palms)

1

2

3

4

6

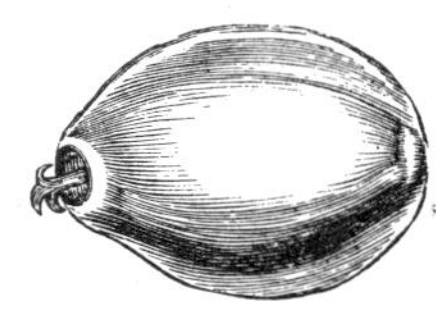
7

5

8

9

10

1

2

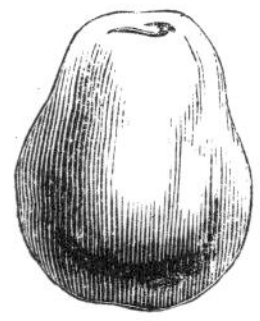
3

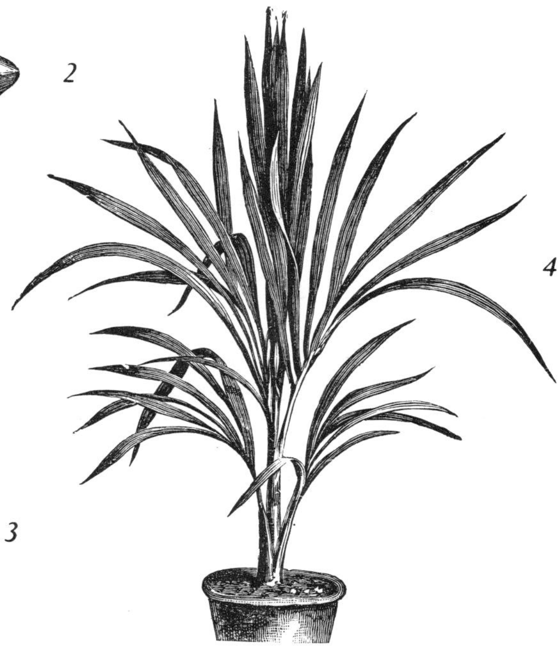
4

5

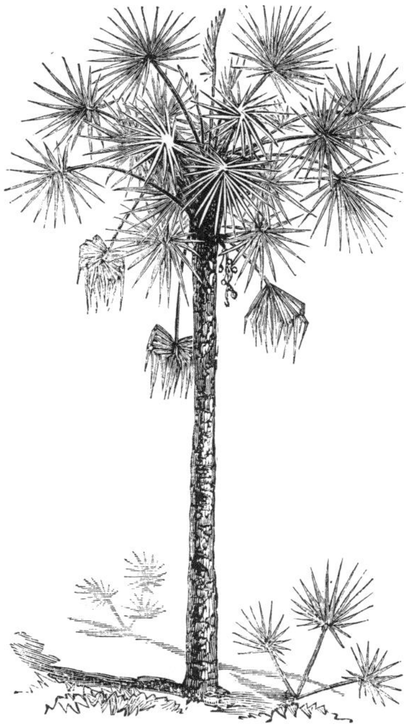
6

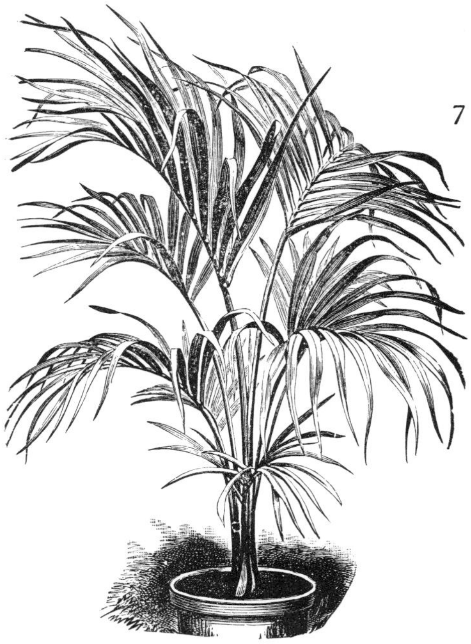
7

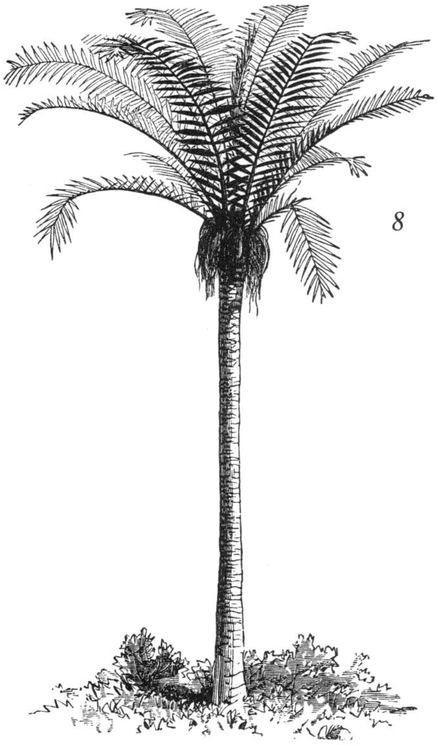
8

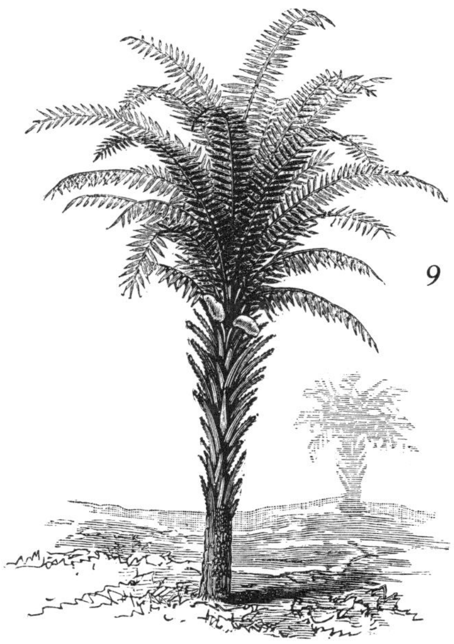
9

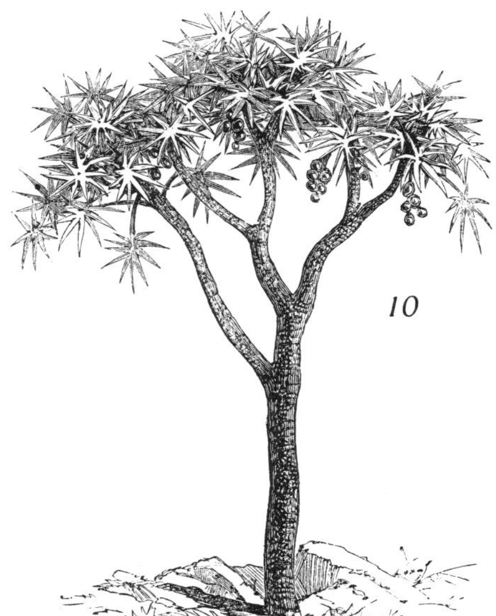
10

1

2

1

4

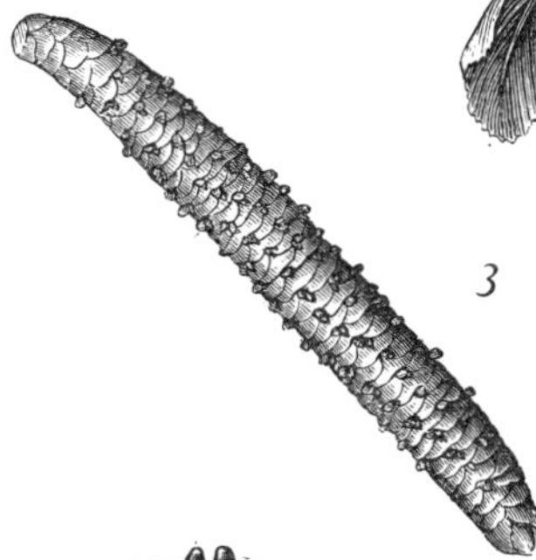

3

2

6

5

1

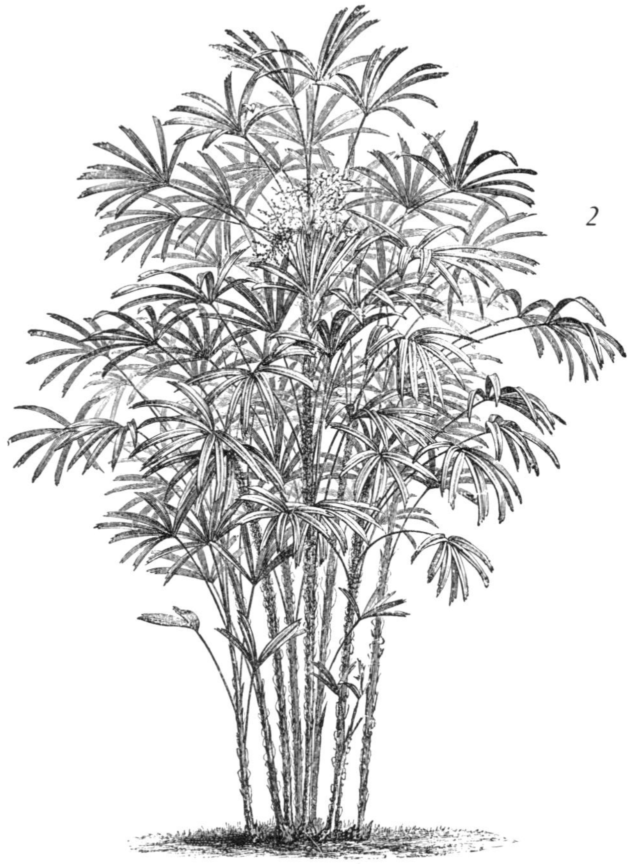
2

3

4

5

6

1

2

3

4

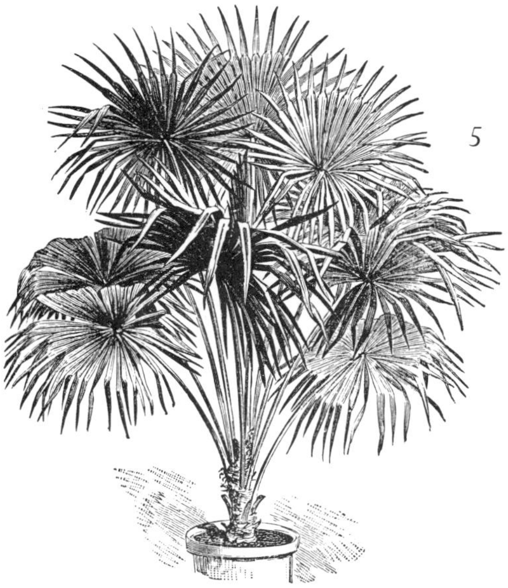
5

6

 PALMACEAE (Palms) and PANDANACEAE (Screw Pines)

1

2

3

4

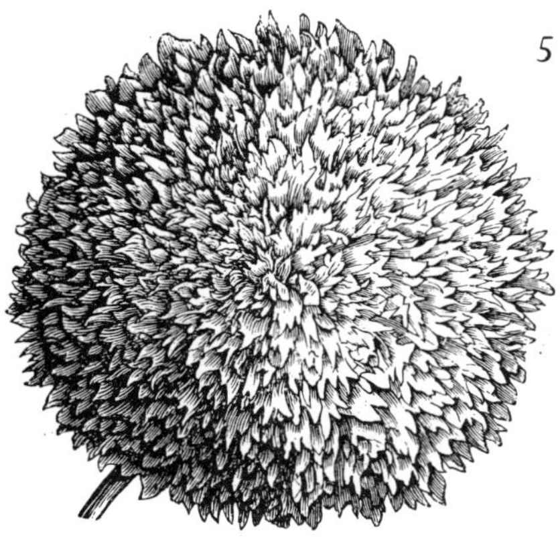

5

6

7

8

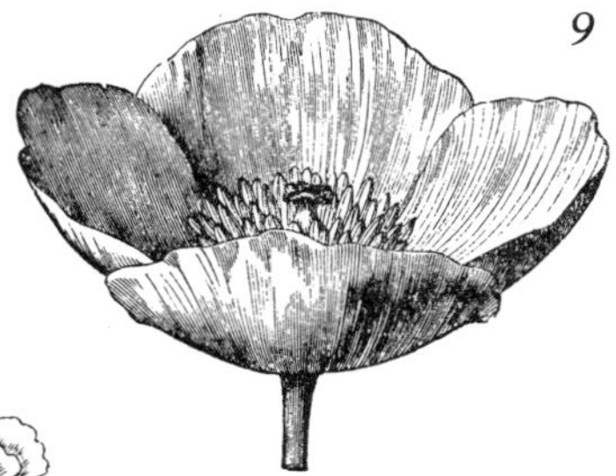

9

10

11

1

2

4

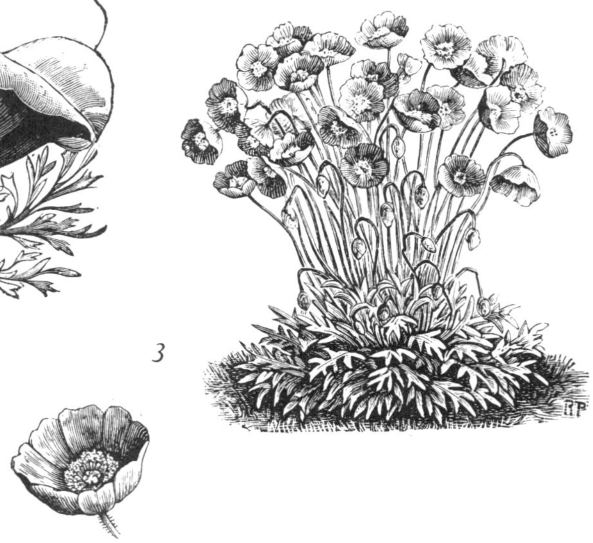
3

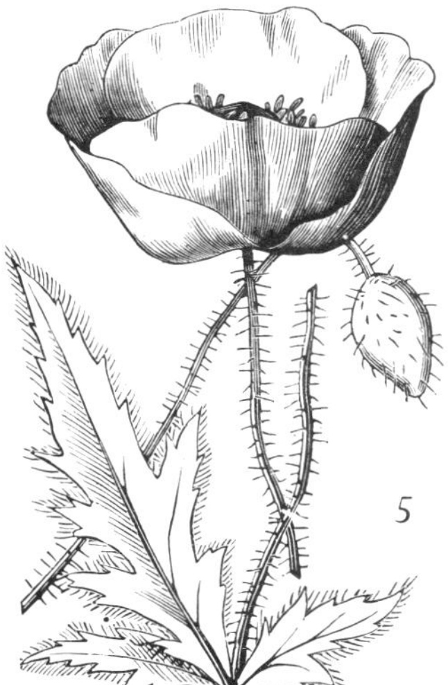
5

6

7

8

9

10

1

2

3

4

5

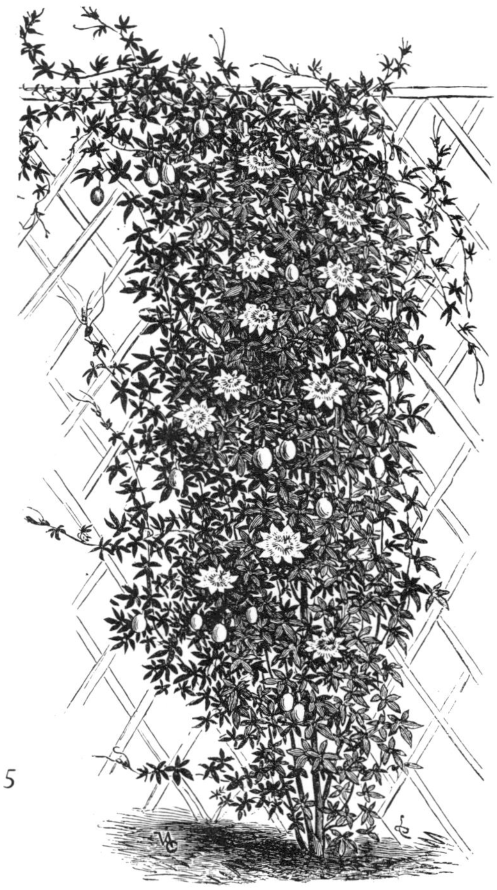

6

1
2
3
4
5
6
7
8
9
10
11

***PLUMBAGINACEAE* (*Plumago, Sea Lavender*), *POLYGALACEAE* (*Milkworts*), *POLYGONACEAE* (*Buckwheats*), and *PHYTOLACCACEAE* (*Pokeweeds*)**

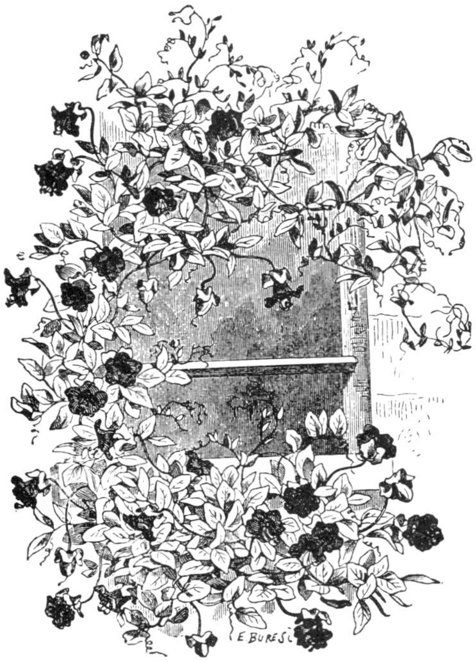
1

2

3

4

5

6

7

8

9

10

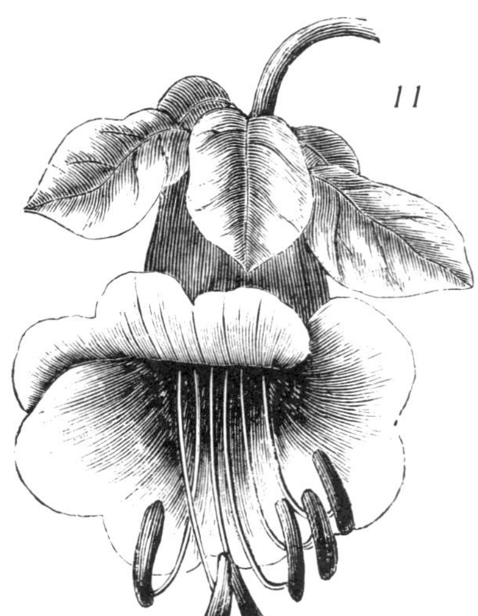
11

12

POLYGONACEAE (Buckwheats), PONTEDERIACEAE (Water Hyacinths), and PORTULACACEAE (Portulacas)

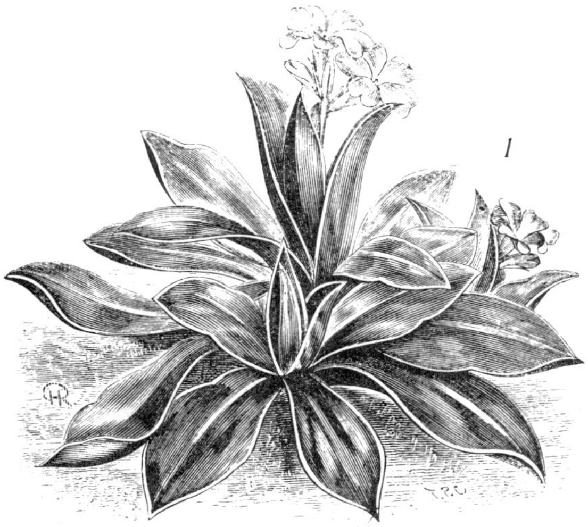

1

2

3

4

5

6

7

8

9

1

2

3

4

7

5

6

8

9

10

11

PRIMULACEAE (Primroses)

1

2

3

4

5

6

7

8

1

2

3

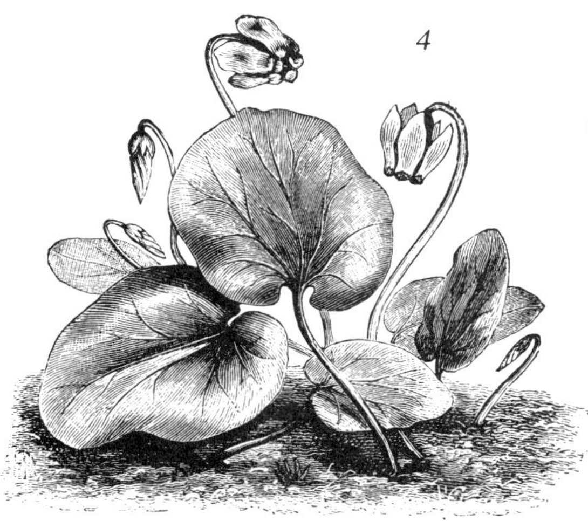

4

5

 ***PRIMULACEAE* (*Primroses, Cyclamens*)**

1

2

3

4

5

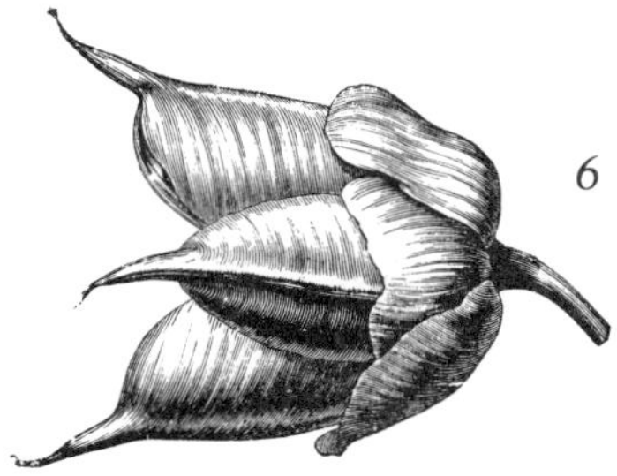

6

7

8

9

10

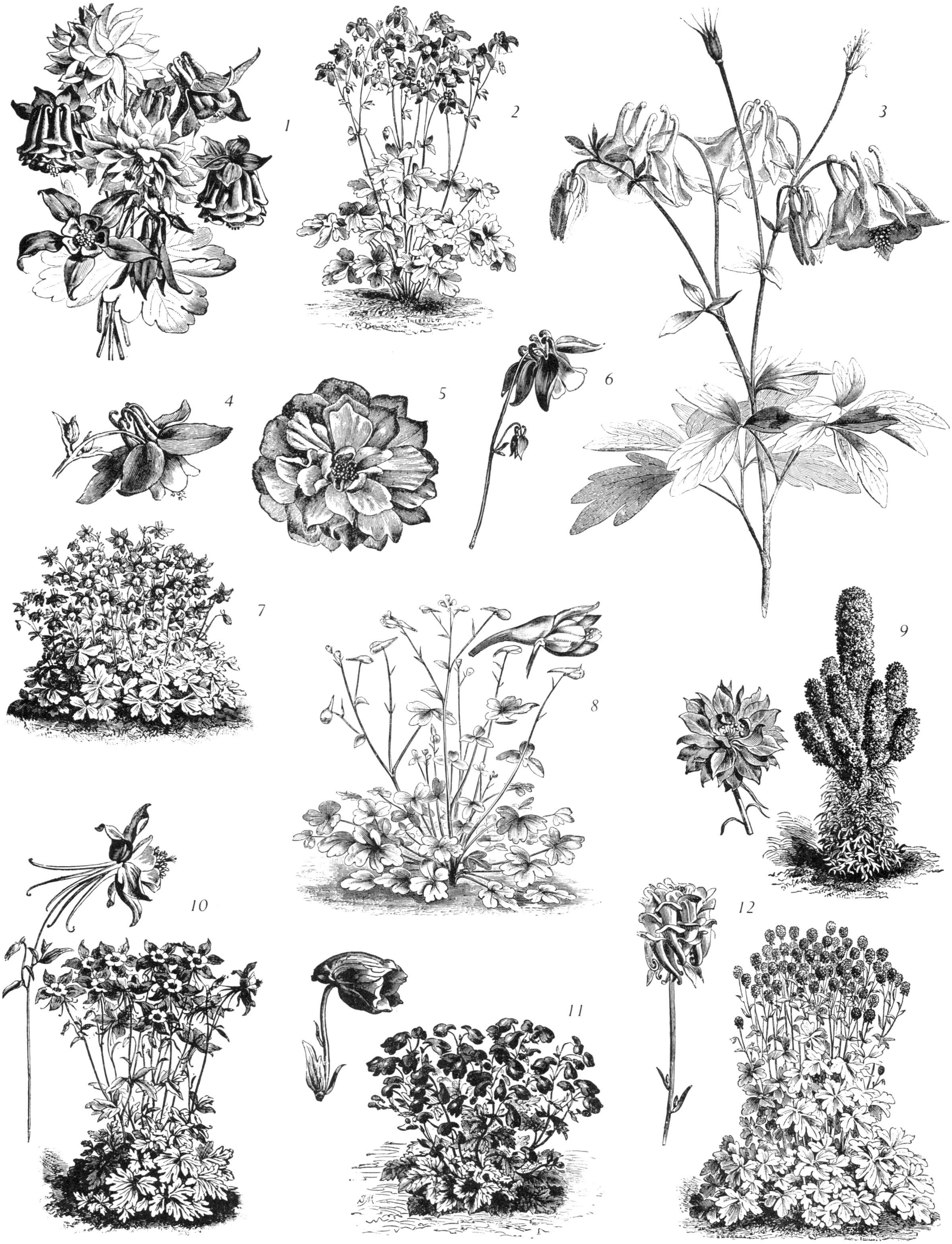
1
2
3
4
5
6
7
8
9
10
11
12

1

2

3

4

5

6

7

8

9

10

1

2

3

4

5

6

7

8

1

2

3

4

5

6

7

8

9

RESEDACEAE (Mignaneltes), RHAMNACEAE (Buckthorns), and ROSACEAE (Roses)

1

2

3

4

5

6

7

1

2

3

4

5

6

7

1

2

3

4

5

6

7

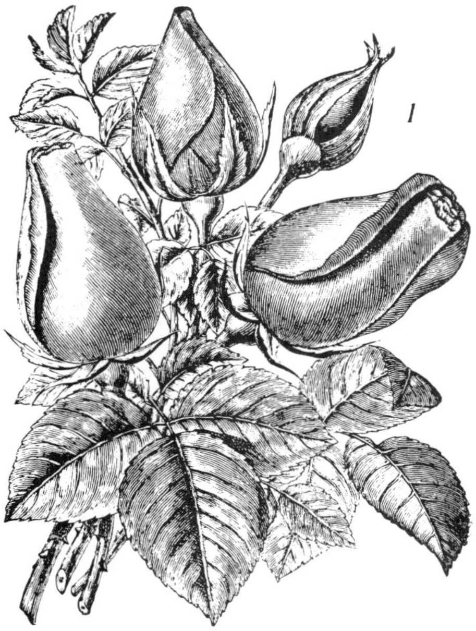

1

2

3

4

5

6

7

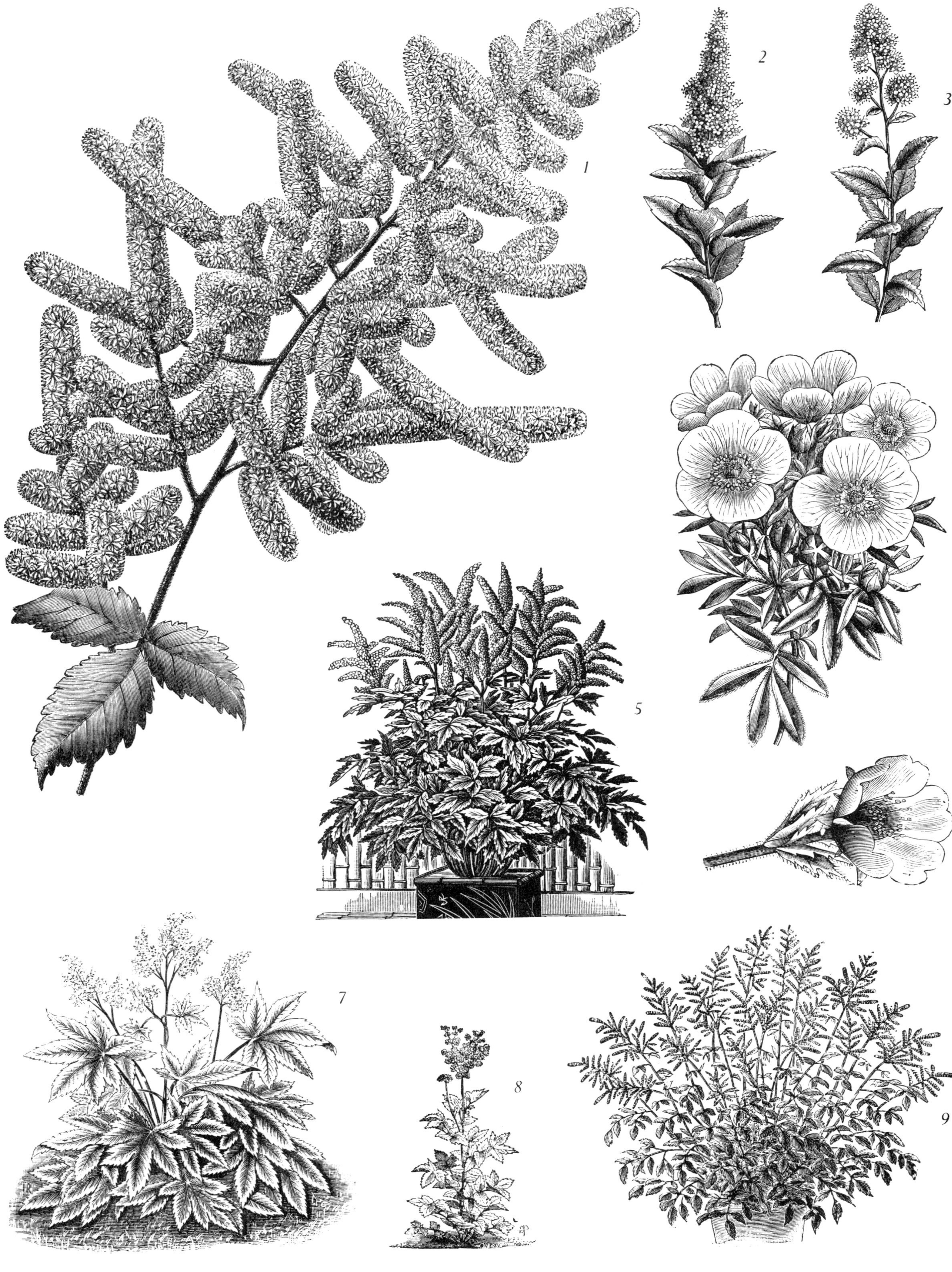
1
2
3
4
5
6
7
8
9

1

2

3

4

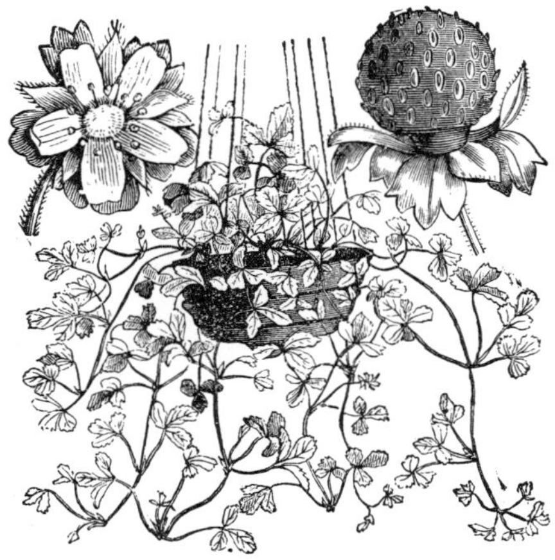

5

6

7

8

9

10

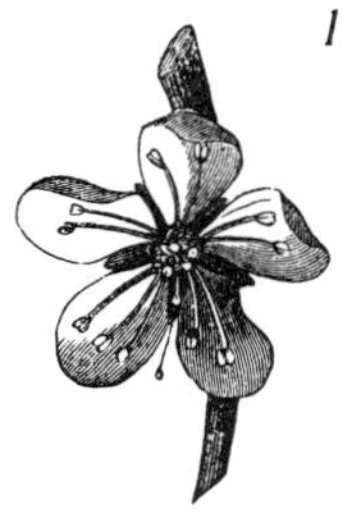

11

12

1

2

3

4

5

6

8

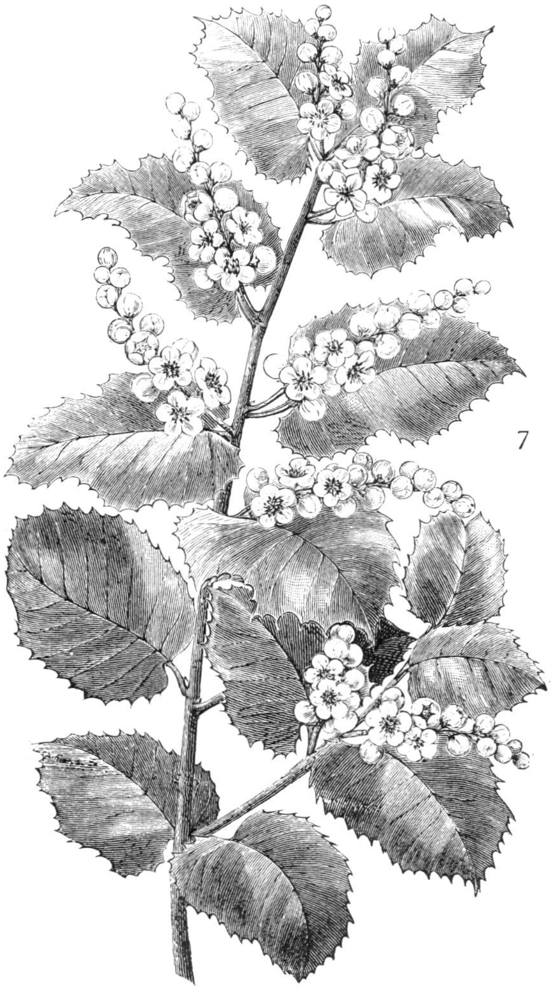

7

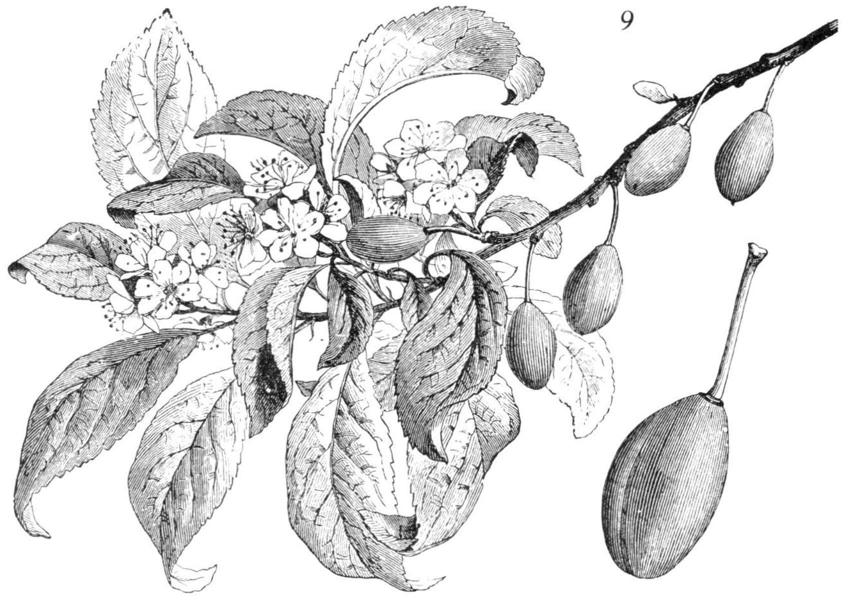

9

1

2

3

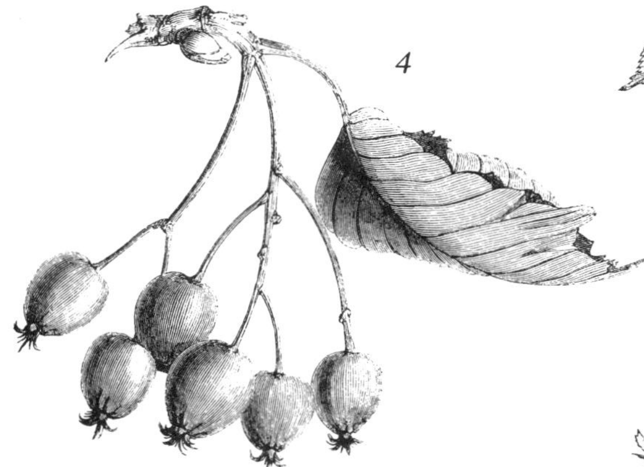
4

7

5

6

8

9

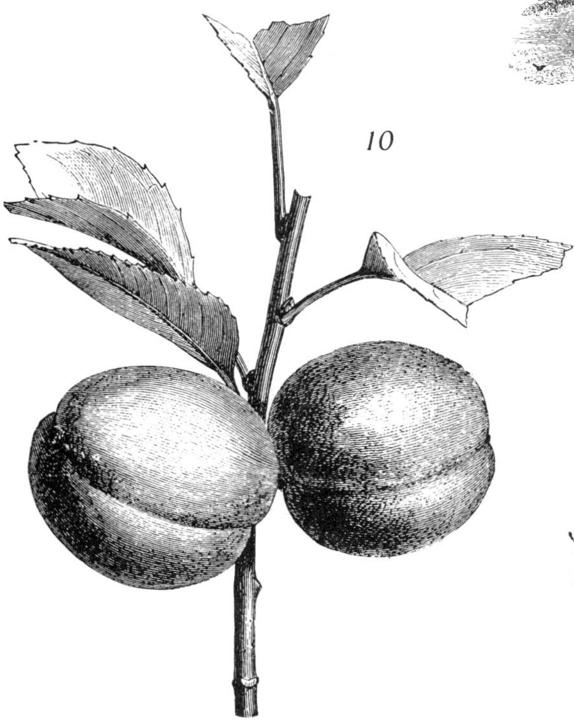
10

11

12

1

2

3

4

5

6

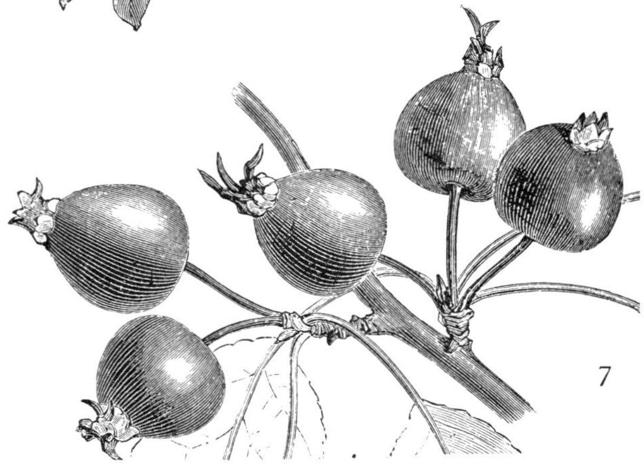

7

8

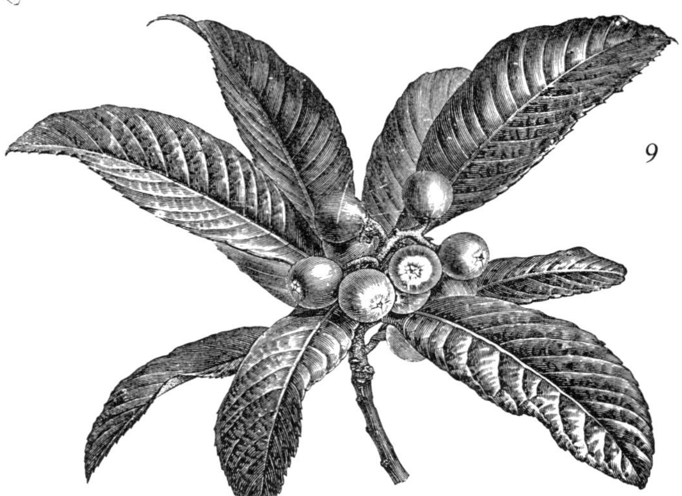

9

10

1

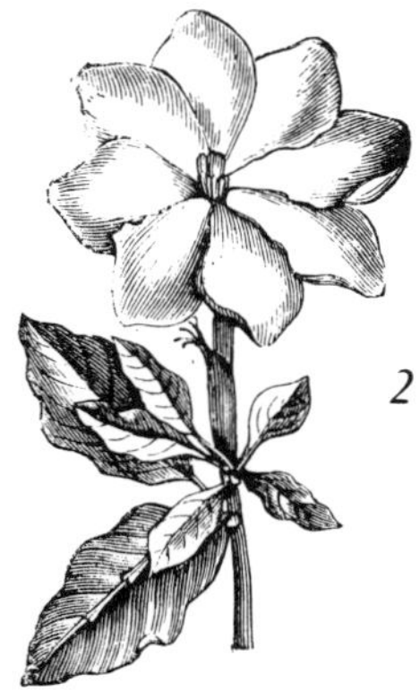
2

3

4

5

6

7

8

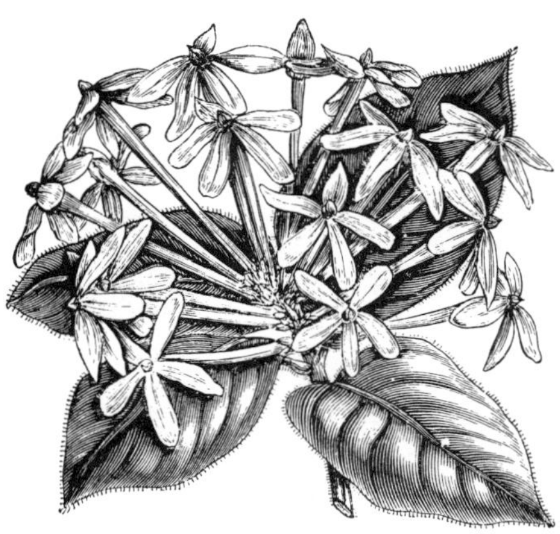
9

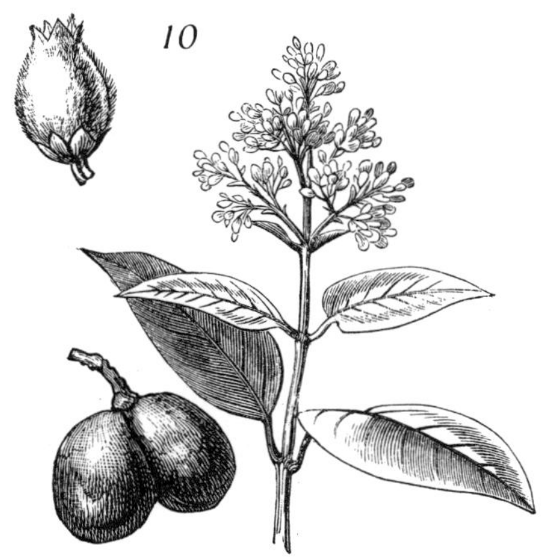
10

11

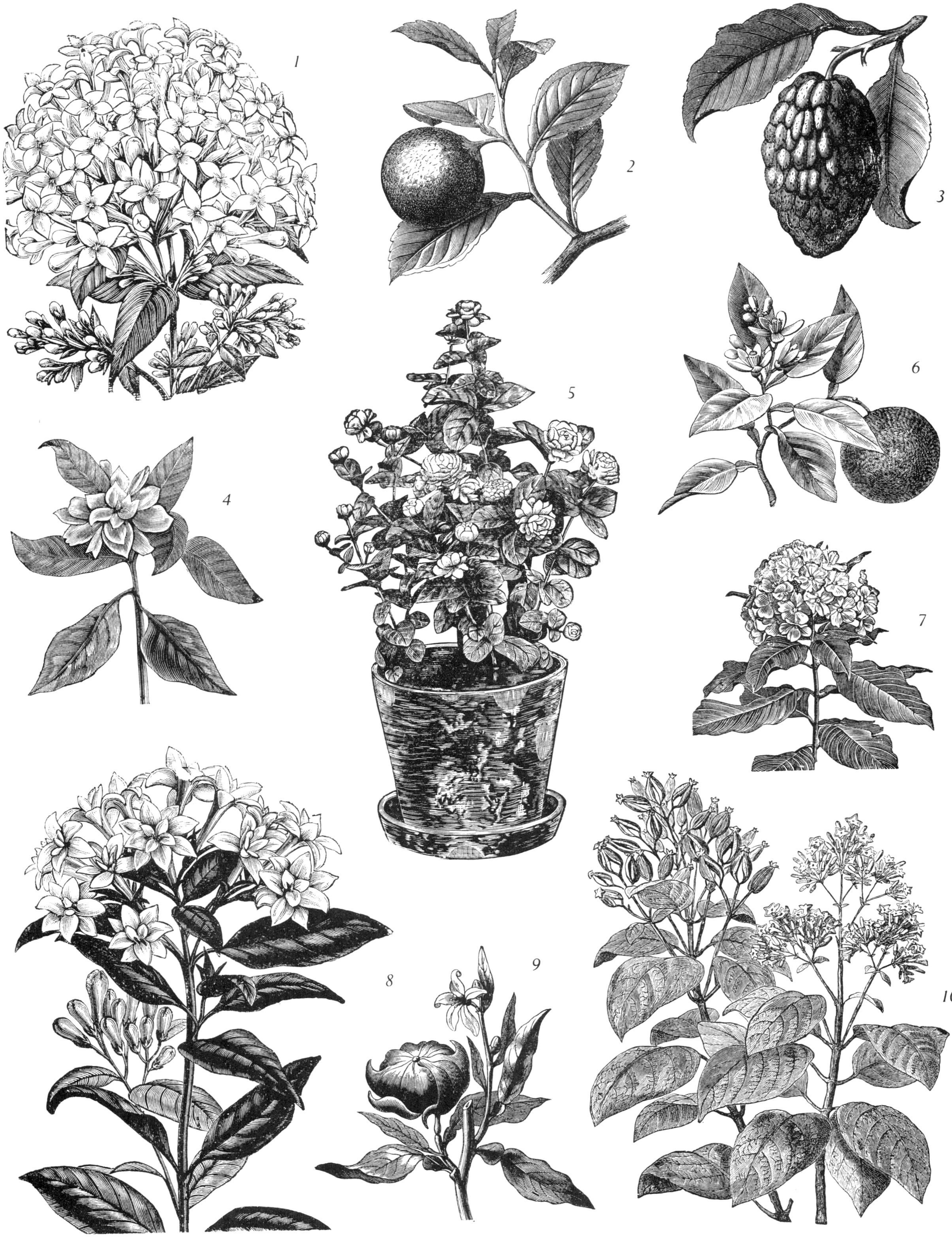

 RUBIACEAE (Gardenias) and RUTACEAE (Oranges, Lemons)

1

2

3

4

5

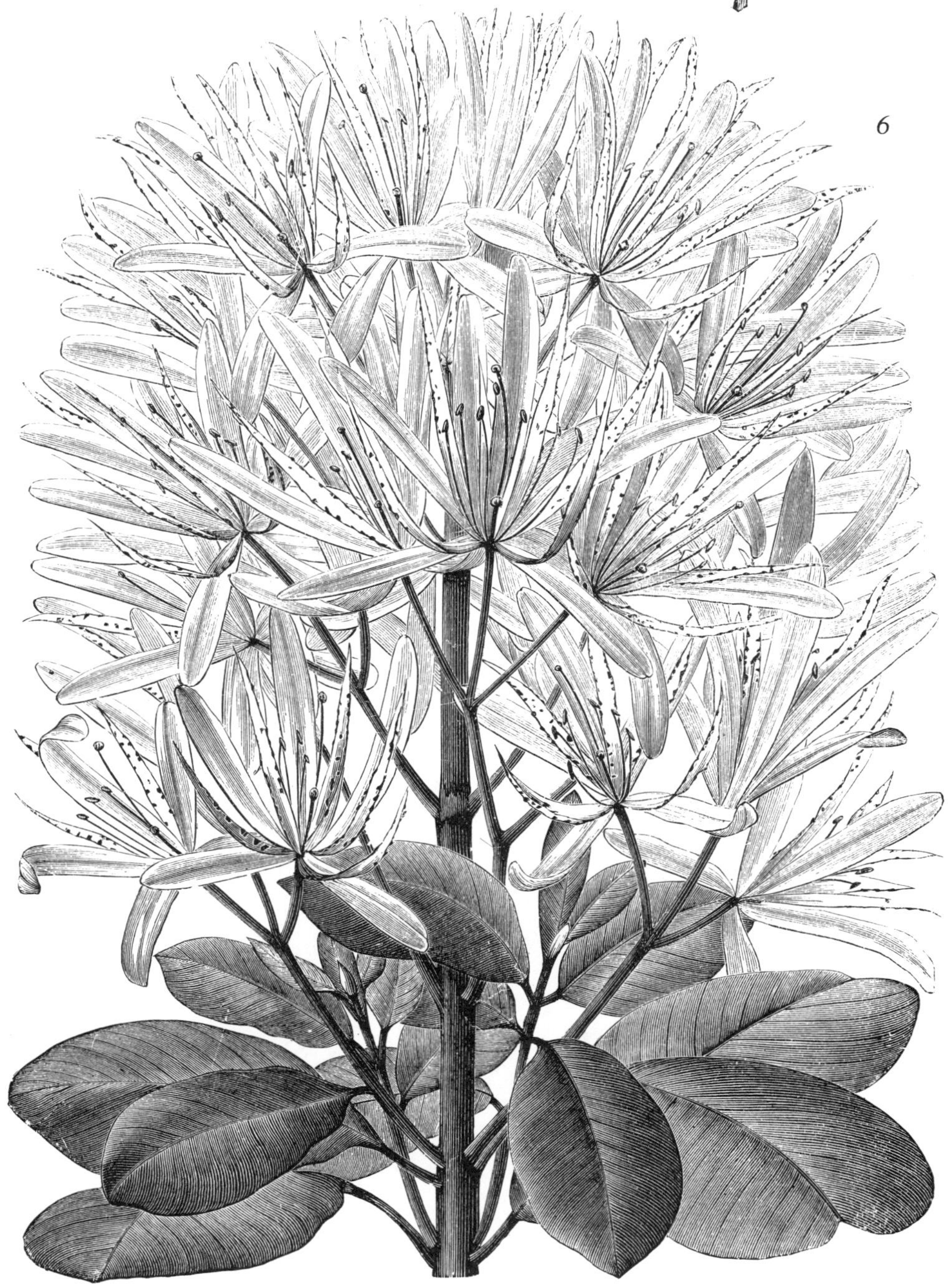
6

RUTACEAE (Oranges, Lemons)

1

2

3

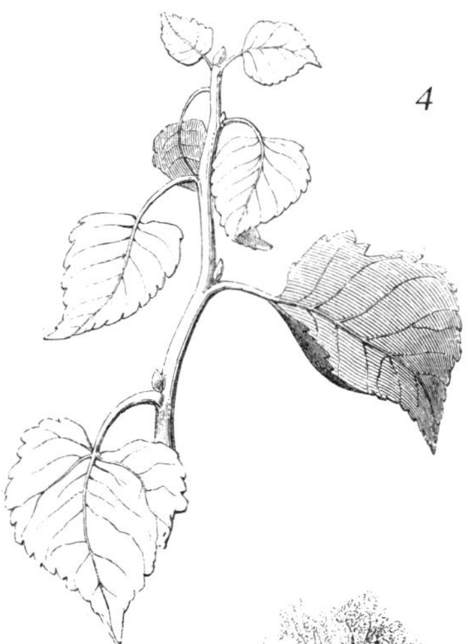

4

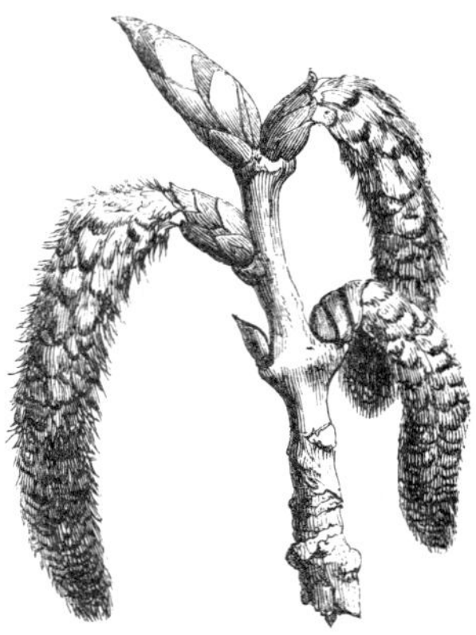

5

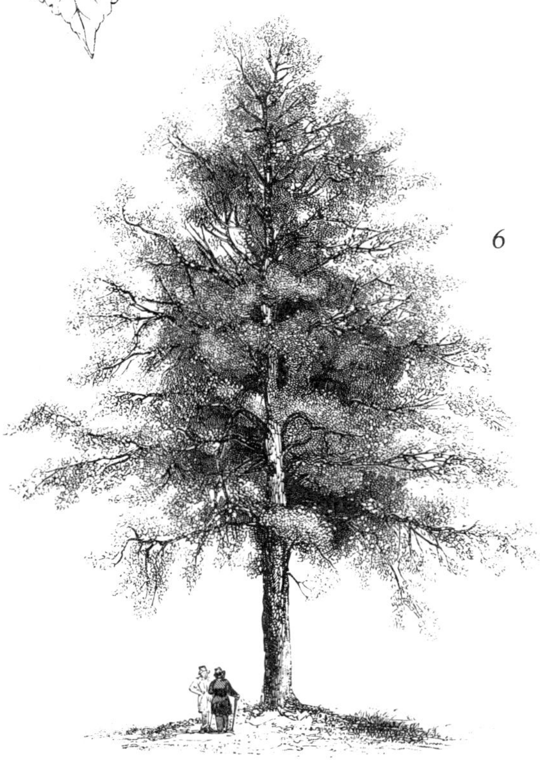

6

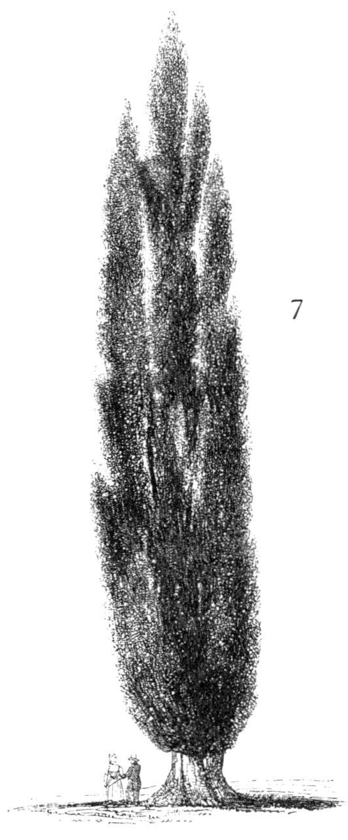

7

8

1

2

3

4

5

6

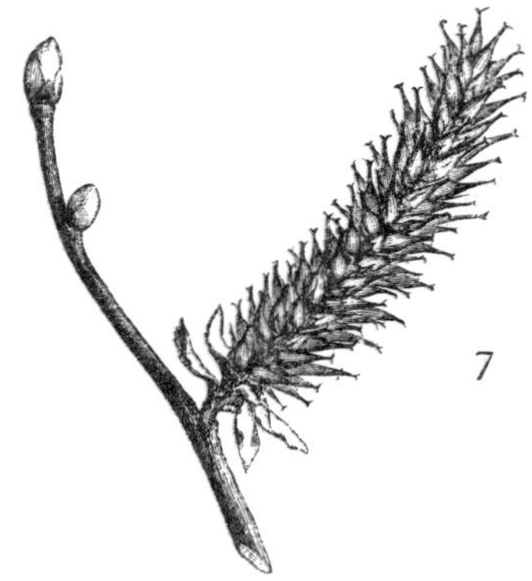

7

8

9

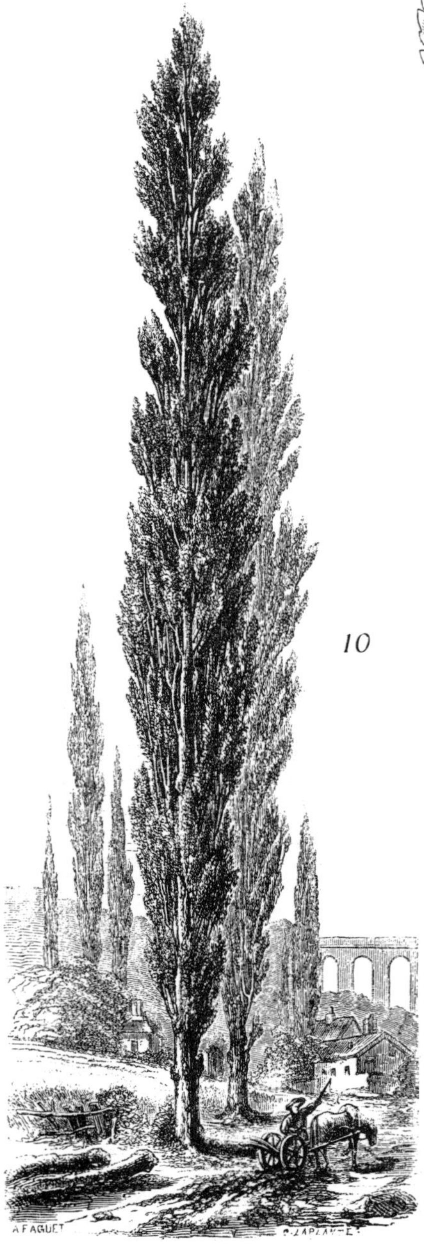

10

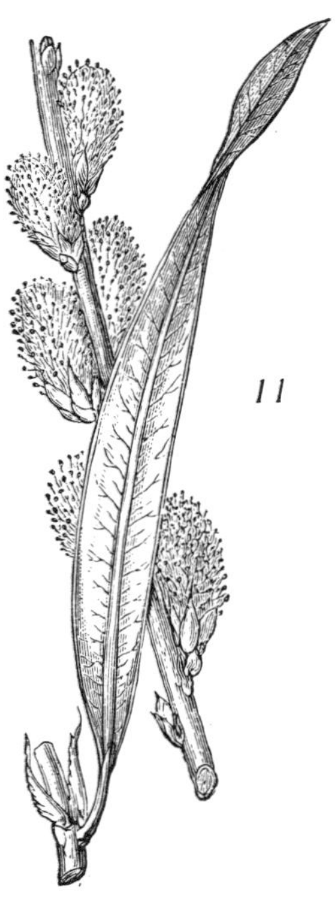

11

12

1

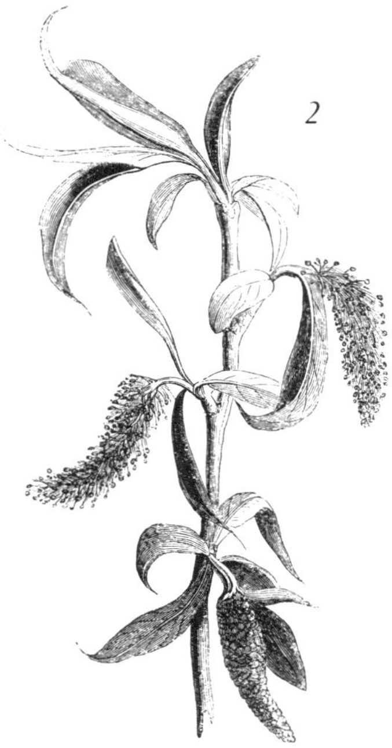
2

3

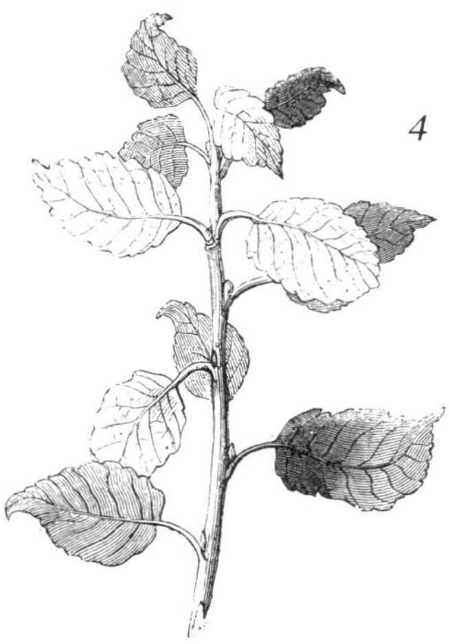
4

5

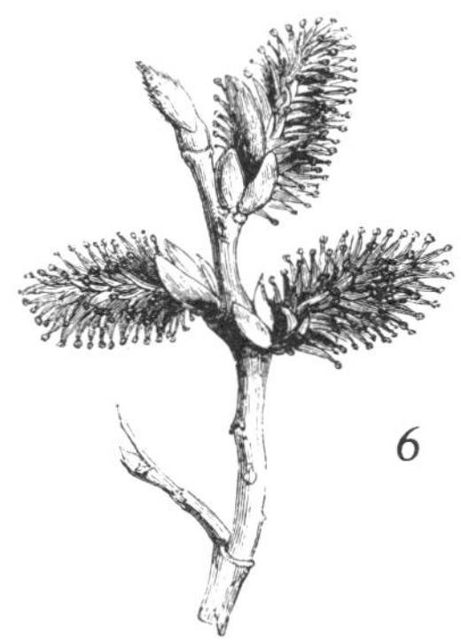
6

7

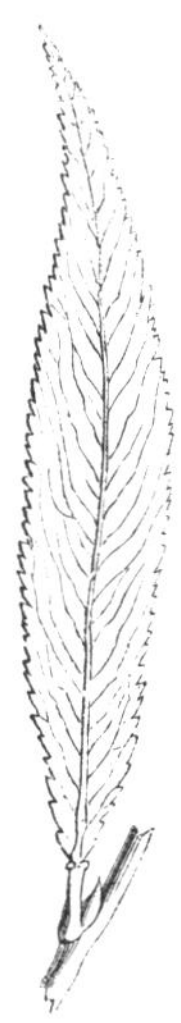
8

9

SAXIFRAGACEAE (Saxifrages, Hydrangeas)

1

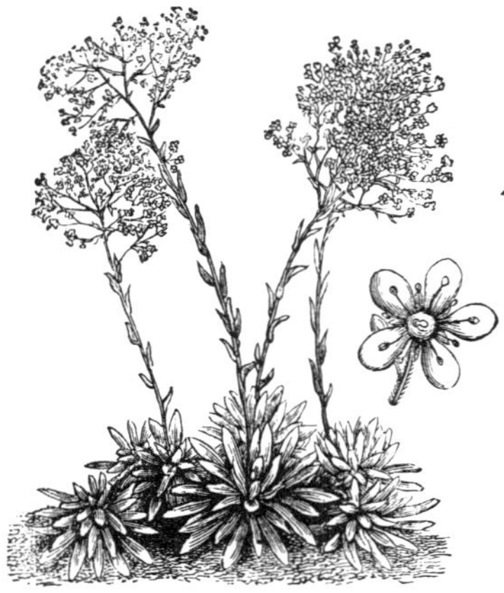
2

3

4

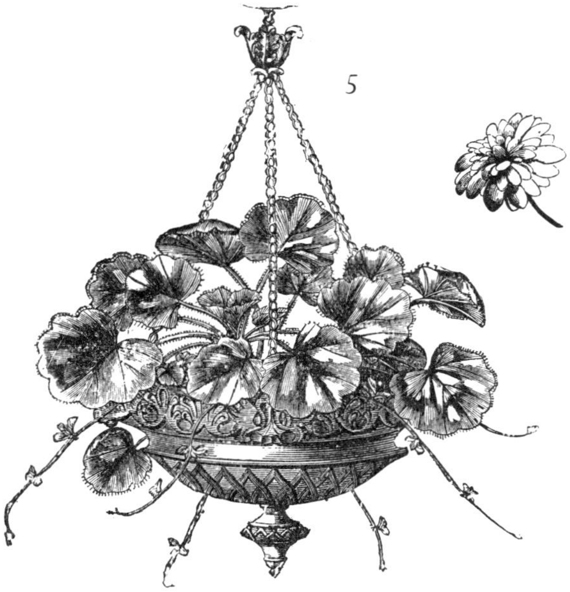
5

6

7

9

10

8

12

11

1

2

3

4

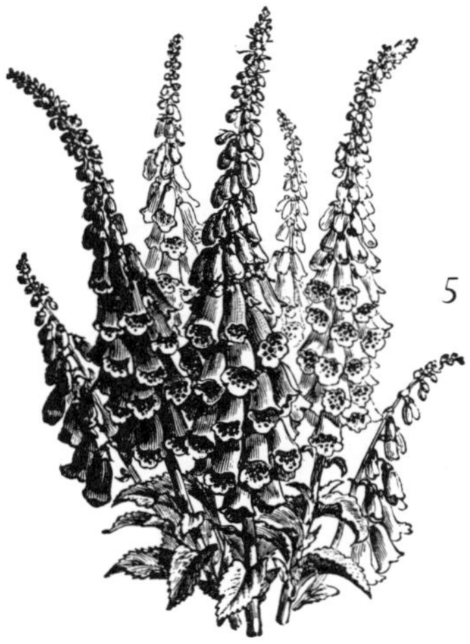

5

6

7

8

1

2

3

4

5

6

7

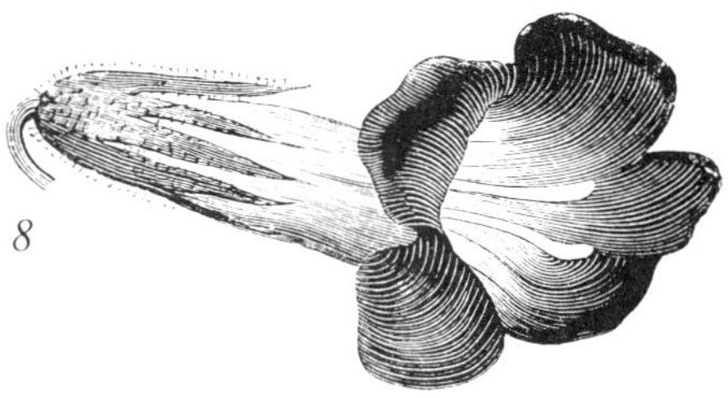

8

9

10

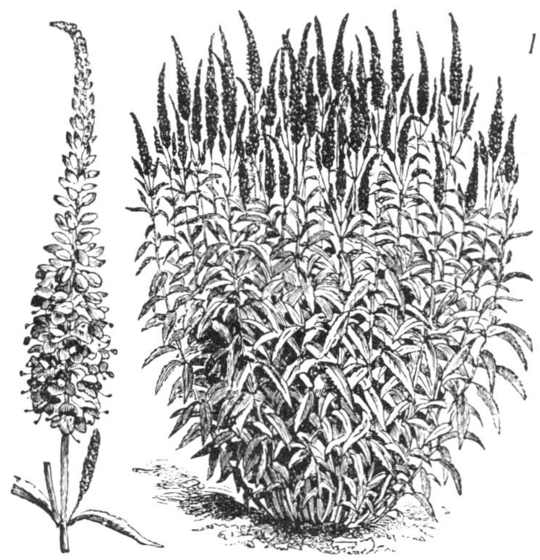

11

12

1

2

3

4

5

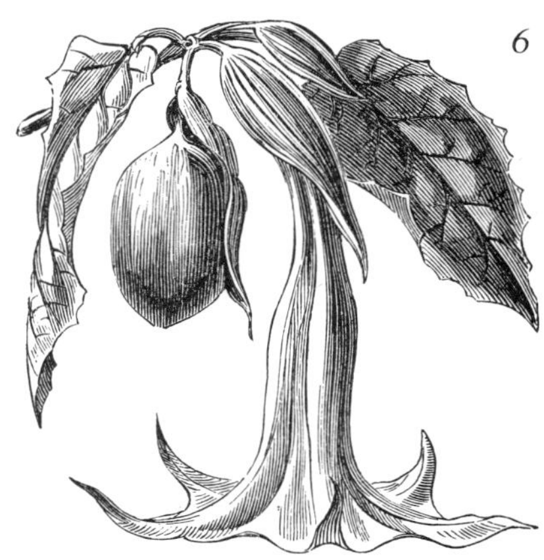

6

7

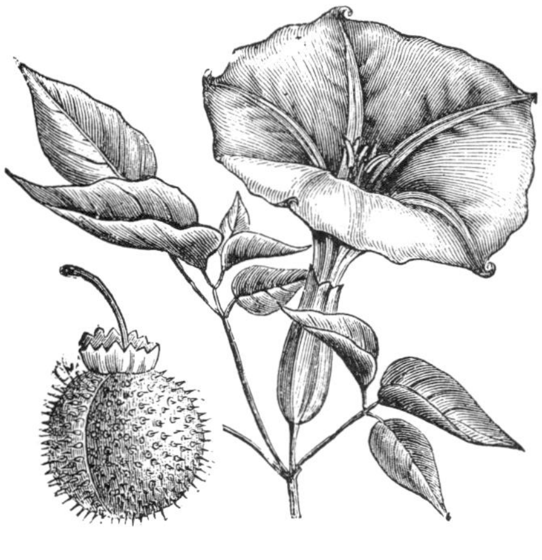

8

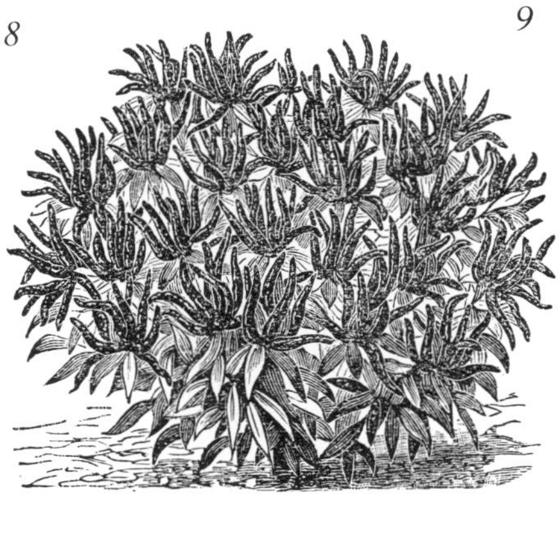

9

10

SMILACACEAE (Smilax) and SOLANACEAE (Nightshades, Tomatoes, Potatoes)

1

2

3

4

5

6

7

8

9

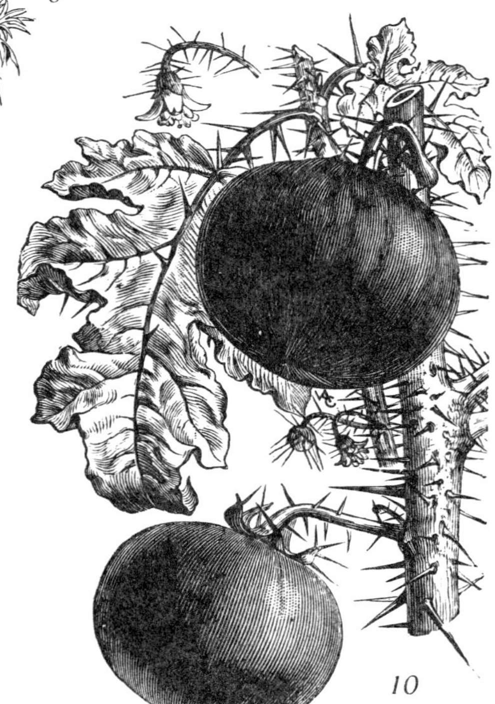
10

1

2

3

4

5

6

7

8

9

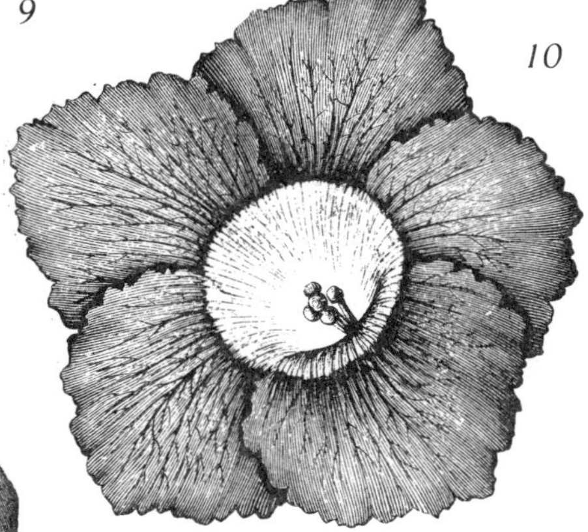

10

11

1

2

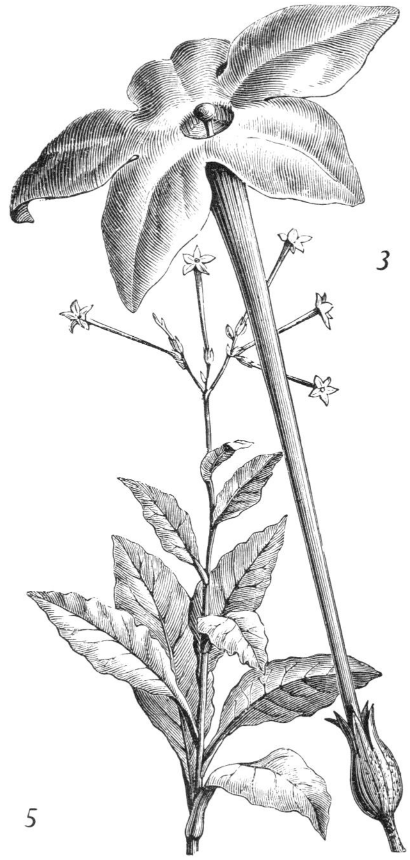
3

4

5

6

7

8

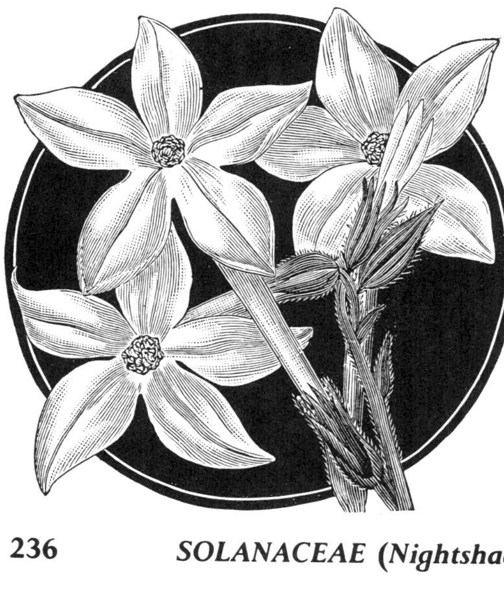
9

10

1

2

3

4

5

6

7

8

1

2

3

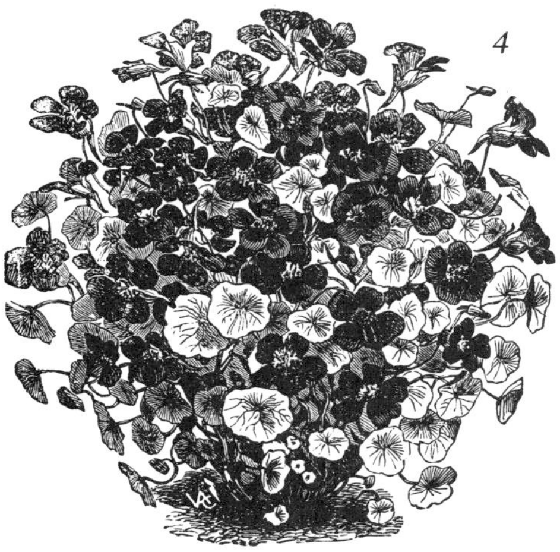

4

5

6

7

8

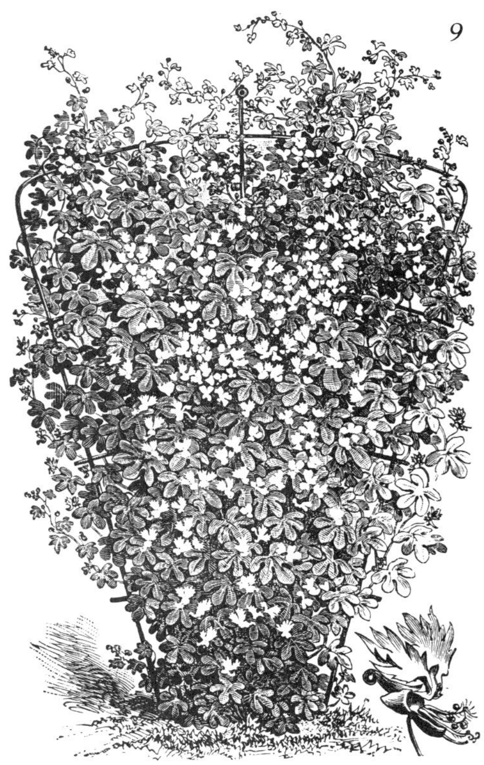

9

 TRILLIACEAE (Trilliums) and TROPAEOLACEAE (Nasturtiums)

1

2

3

4

5

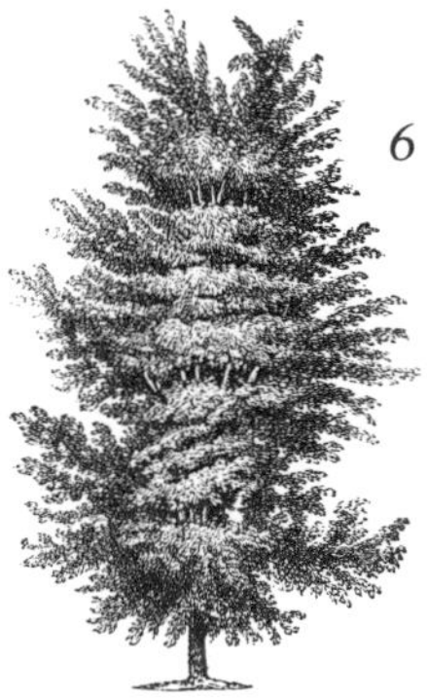

6

7

8

1

2

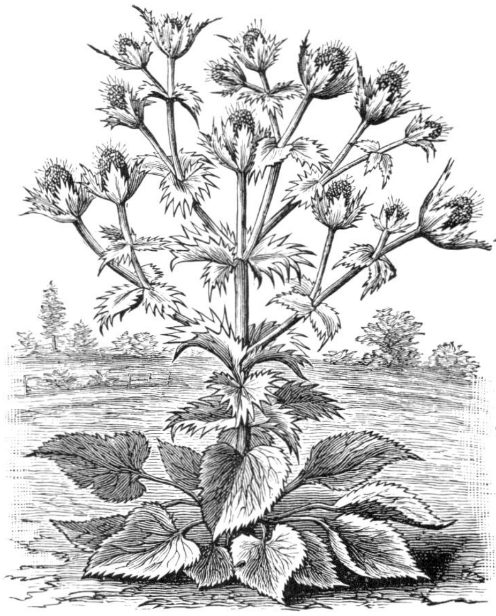

3

4

5

6

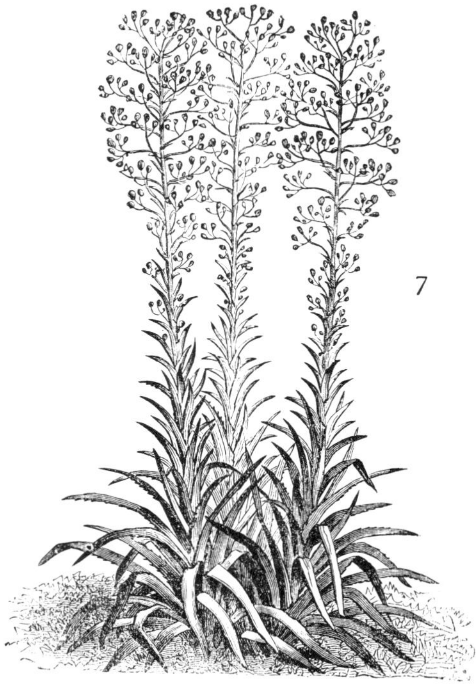

7

8

9

10

1
2
3
4
5
6
7
F.S.

1

2

3

6

4

5

7

8

1

2

3

5

4

7

6

8

VIOLACEAE (Violets, Pansies)

1

2

3

4

7

5
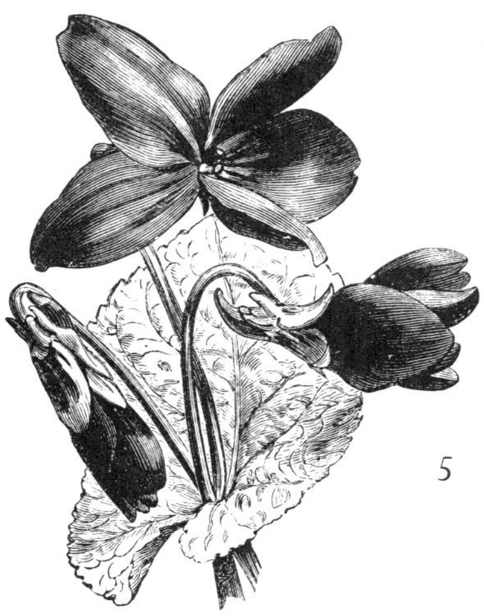

6

9

8
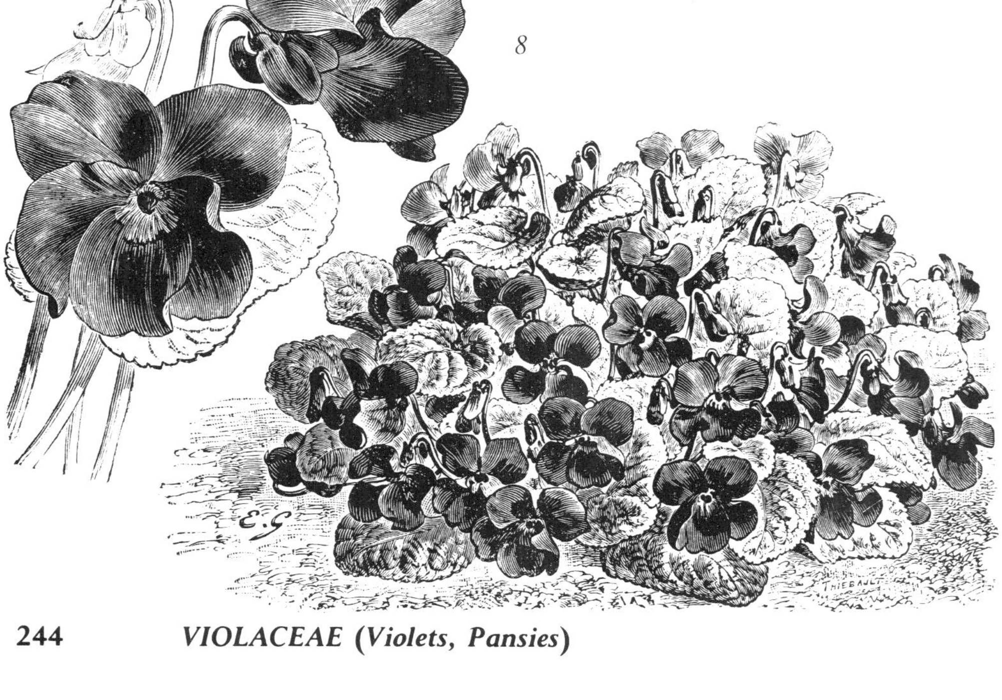

10

1

2

3

4

5

6

7

8

VIOLACEAE (Violets), VITACEAE (Virginia Creepers), and ZINGIBERACEAE (Gingers)

SECTION 2

Appendices of Botanical Images

APPENDIX A

Additional Trees

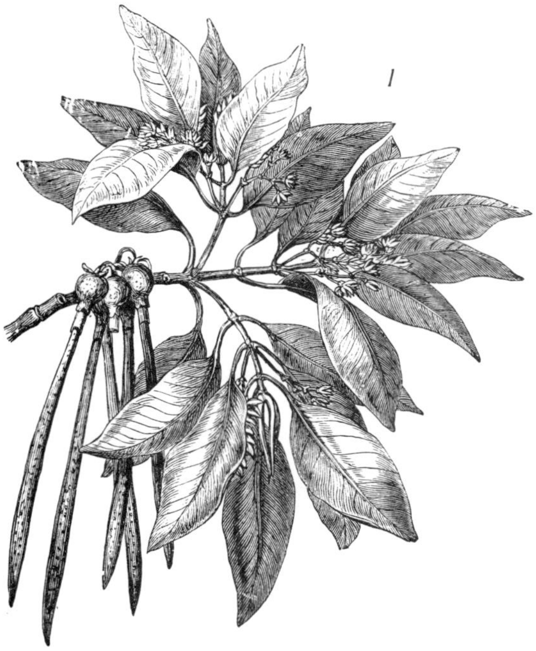

1

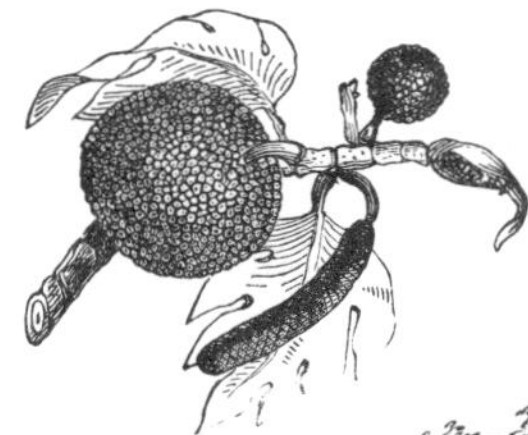

2

3

4

5

6

7

1

2

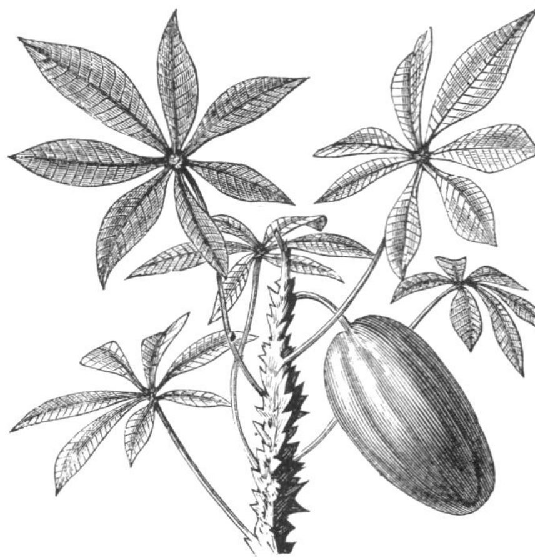

3

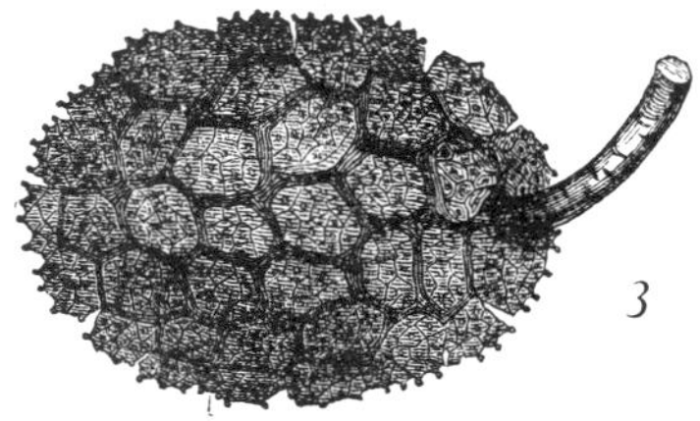

4

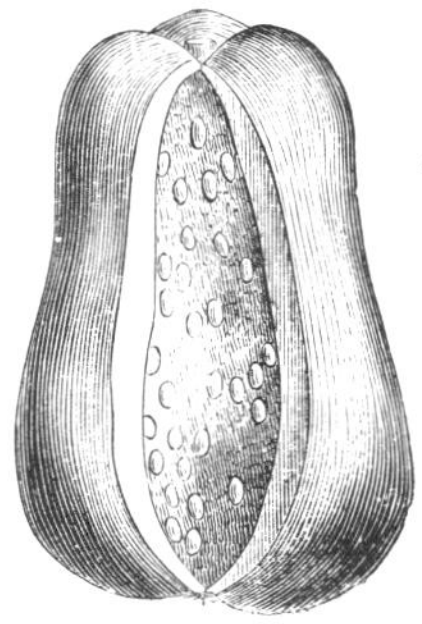

5

6

7

1

2

3

4

5

6

1

2

3

1

2

3

4

5

6

1

2

3

4

5

6

1

2

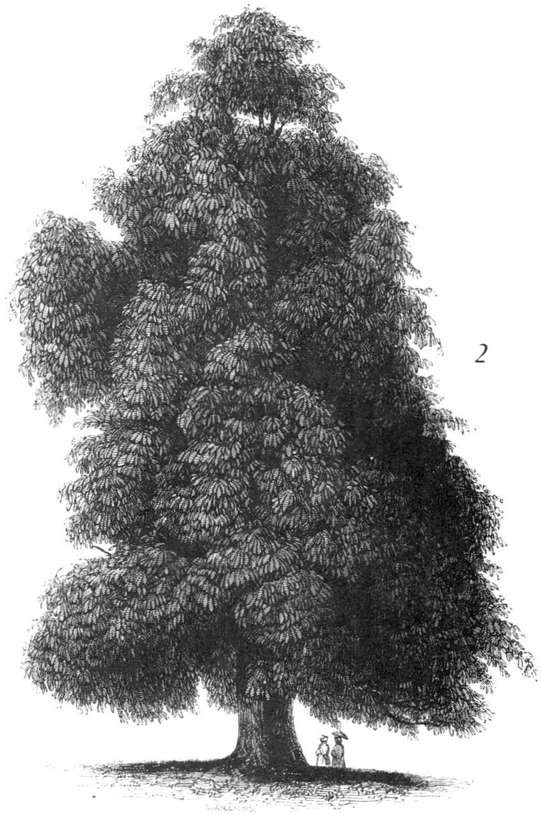

3

4

5

1

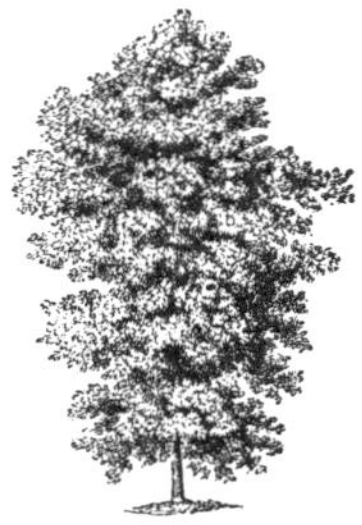
2

3

4

5

6

7

8

9

10

1

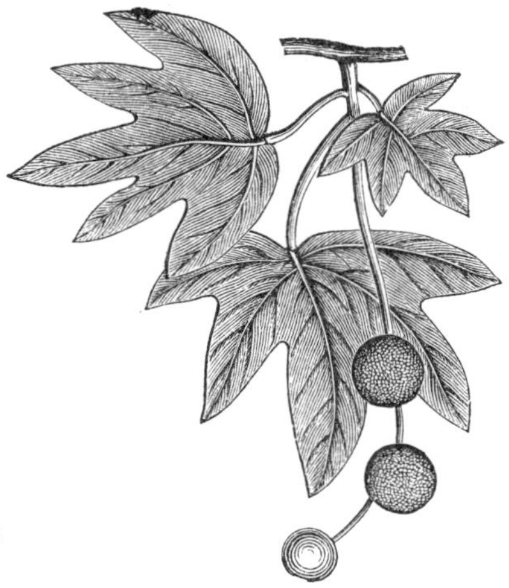

2

3

4

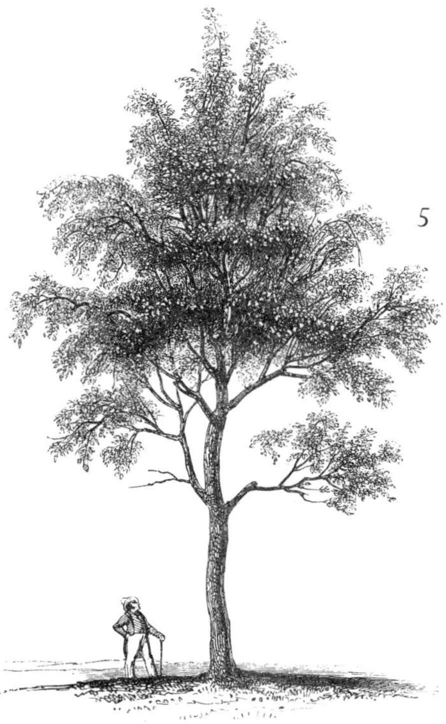

5

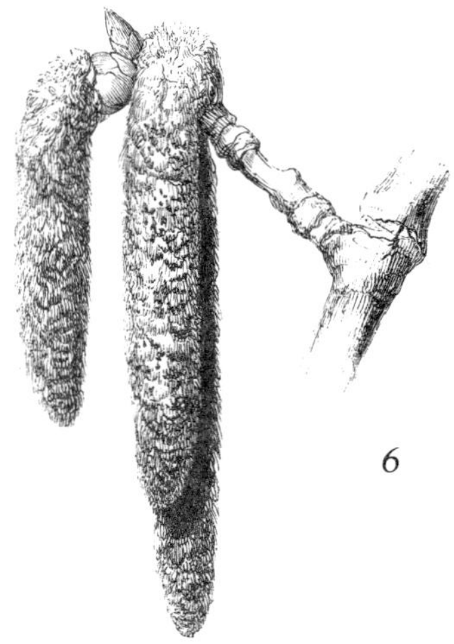

6

7

8

9

1

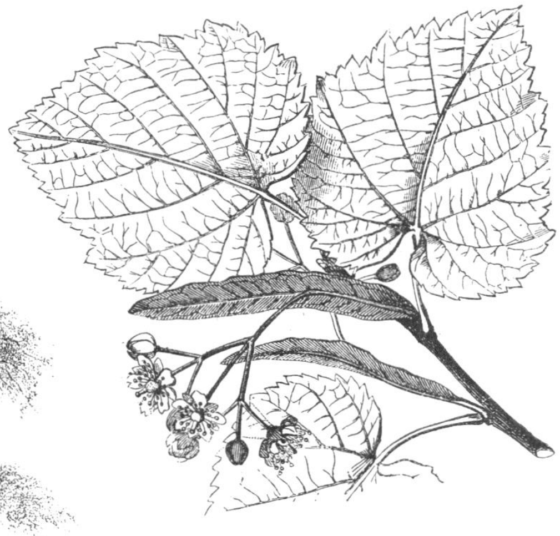

2

3

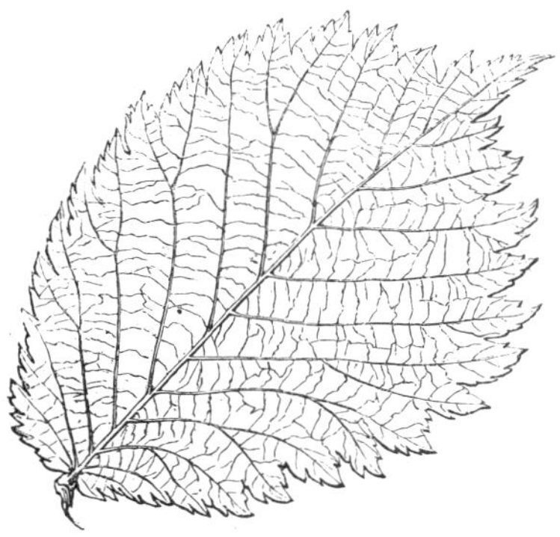

4

5

6

7

8

9

1

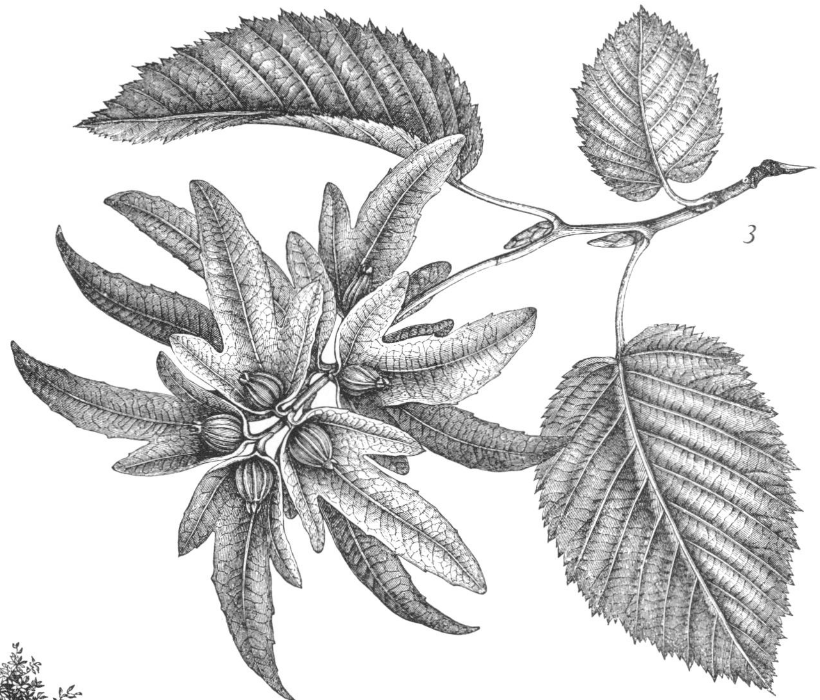

3

2

4

5

6

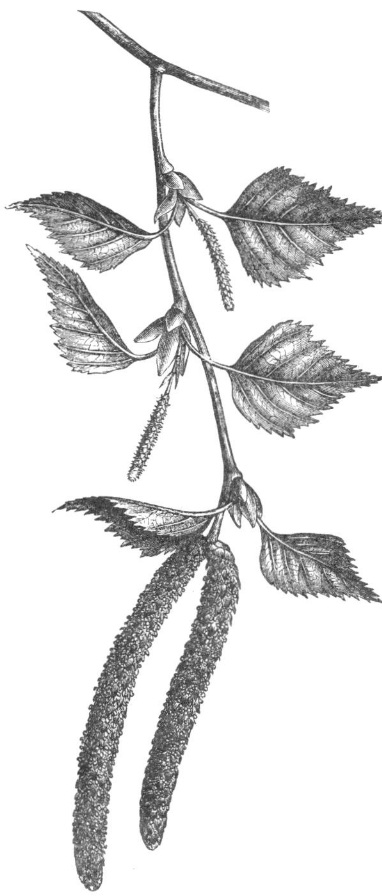

7

1

2

1

2

1

2

1

2

1

2

1

2

1

2

1

2

1

2

1

2

1

2

1

2

1

2

1

2

APPENDIX B

Edible Foods, Nuts, Fruits, Vegetables, Legumes, Grains, Beverages, Herbs and Spices

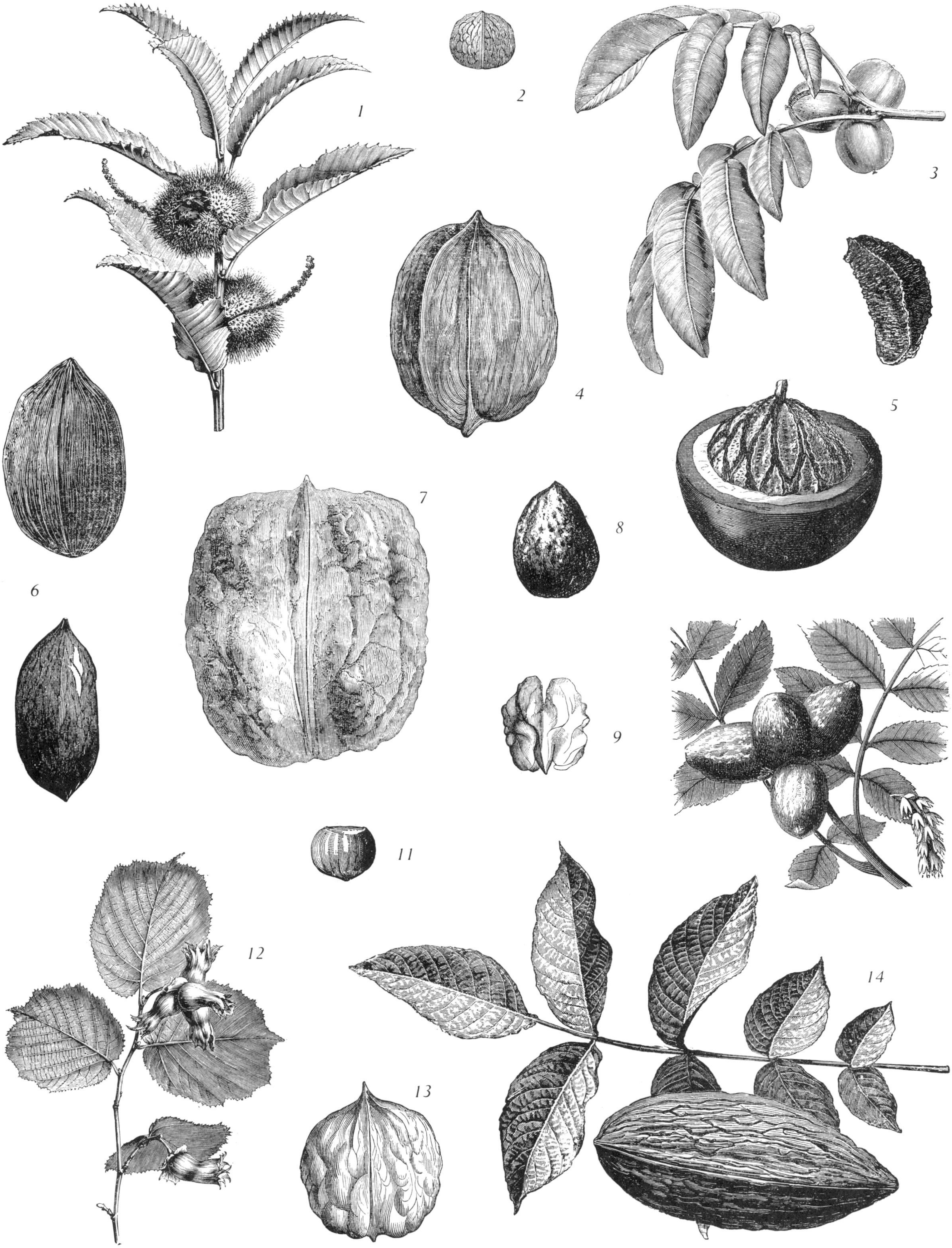
1
2
3
4
5
6
7
8
9
10
11
12
13
14

1

2

3

4

5

6

7

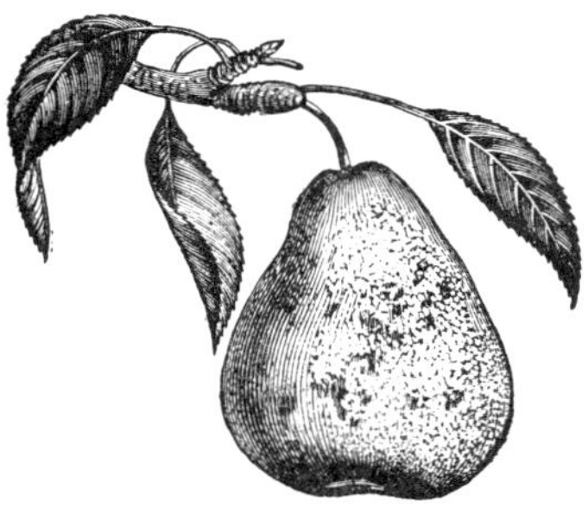
8

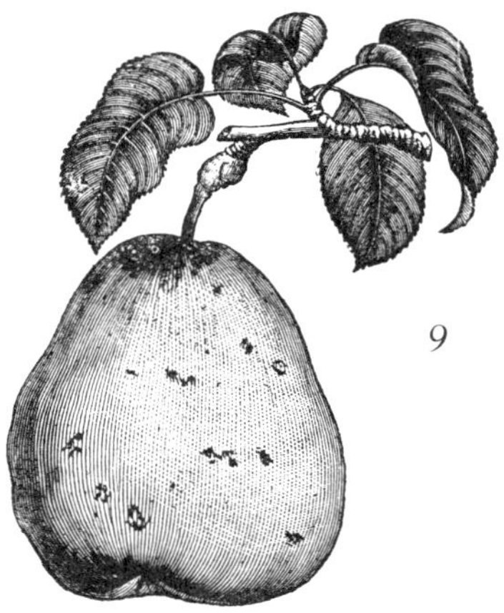
9

10

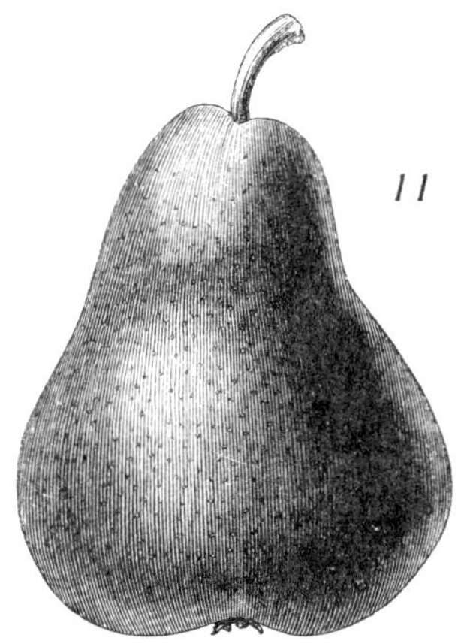
11

12

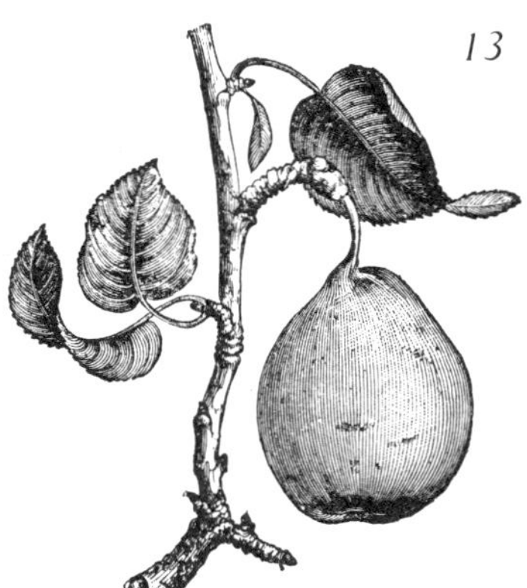
13

14

1
2
3
4
5
6
7
8
9
10
11
12
13
14

1

2

3

4

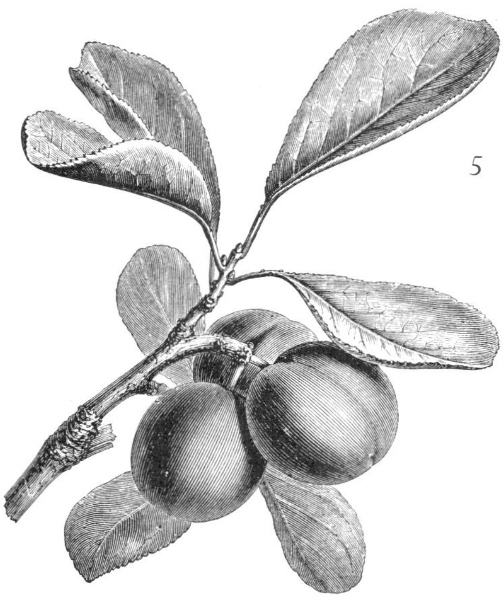

5

6

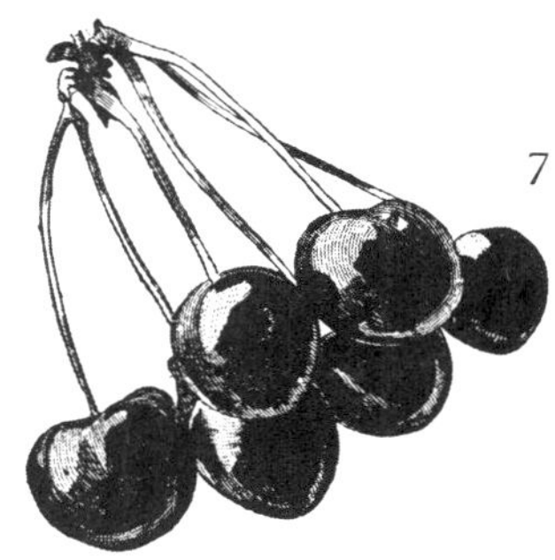

7

8

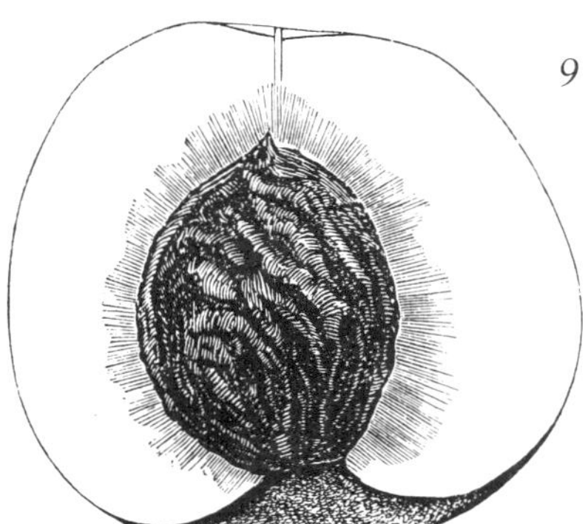

9

10

1

2

3

4

5

6

7

8

9

10

11

1

2

3

4

5

6

7

8

9

1

2

3

4

5

6

7

8

9

1
2
3
4
5
6
7

1

2

3

4

5

6

7

8

9

10

1

2

3

4

5

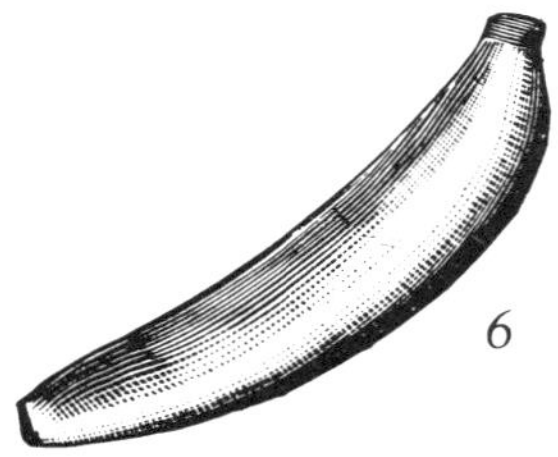
6

7

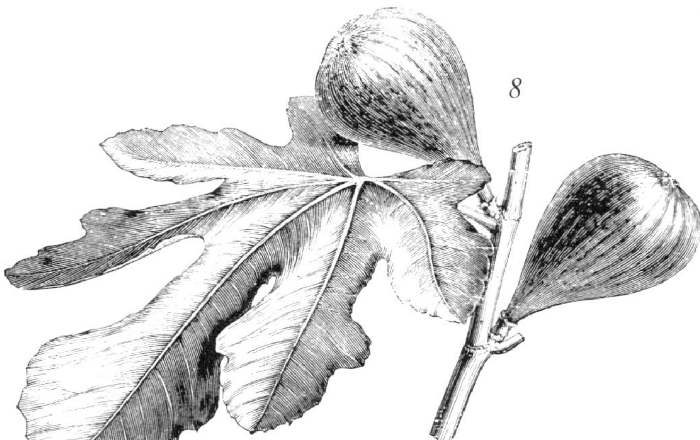
8

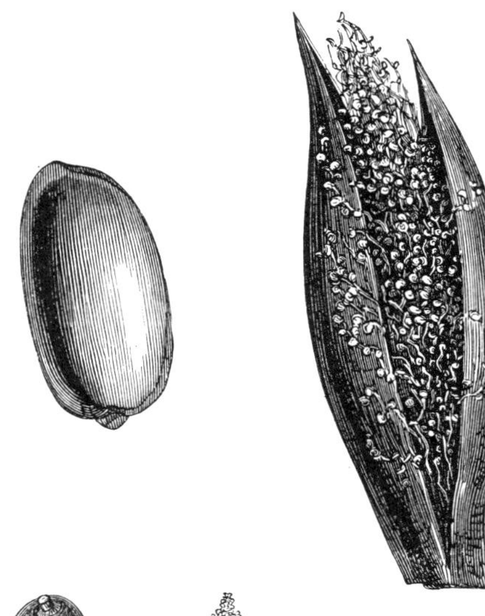
9

10

11

1
2
3
4
5
6
7
8

1

2

3

4

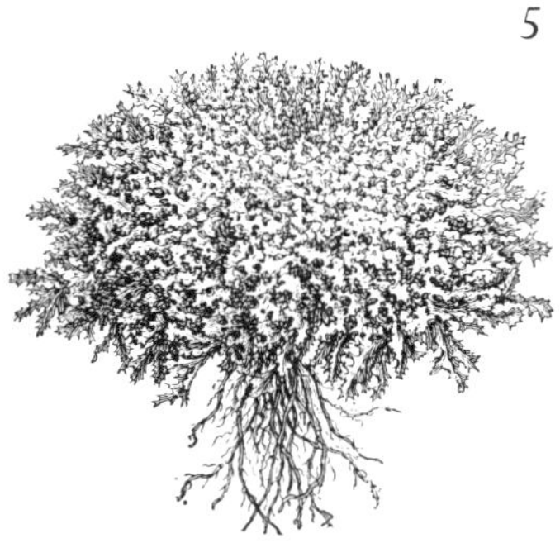

5

6

8

7

9

11

10

12

1

2

3

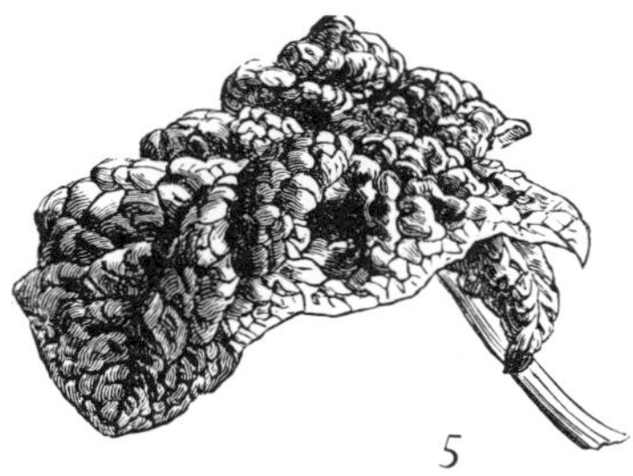
5

4

6

7

8

9

10

11

12

1

2

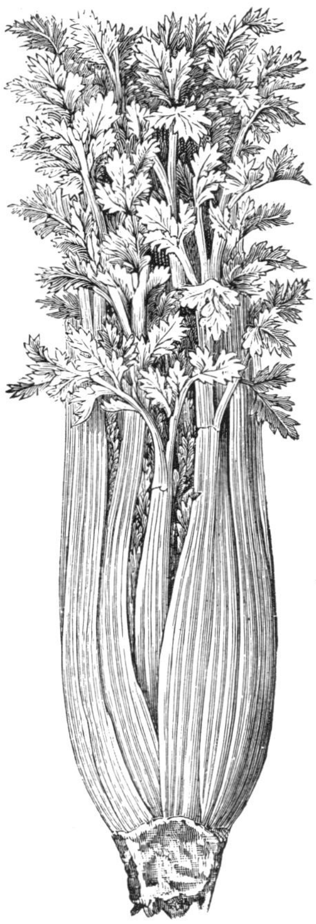

3

4

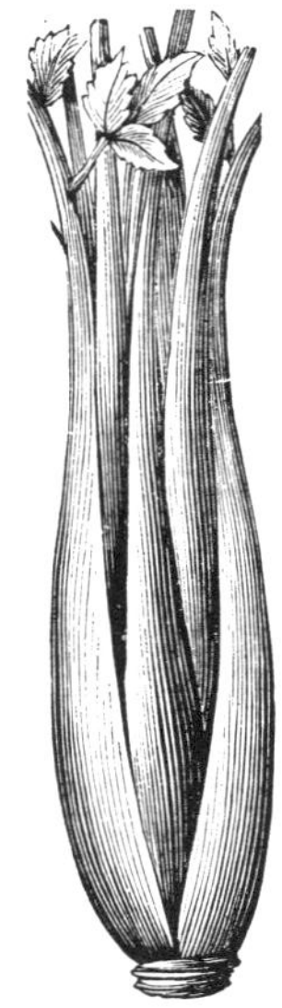

5

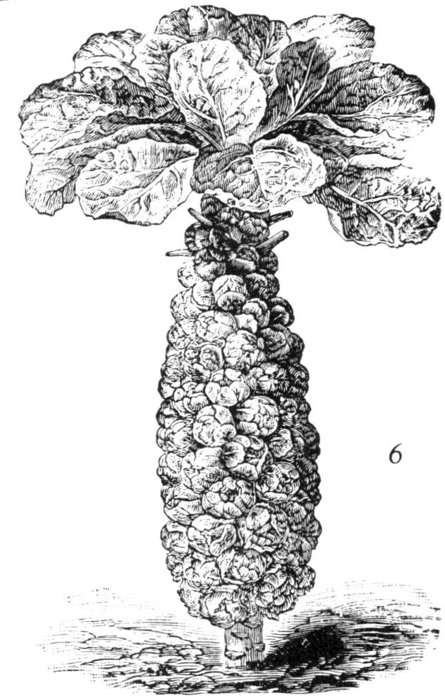

6

8

7

9

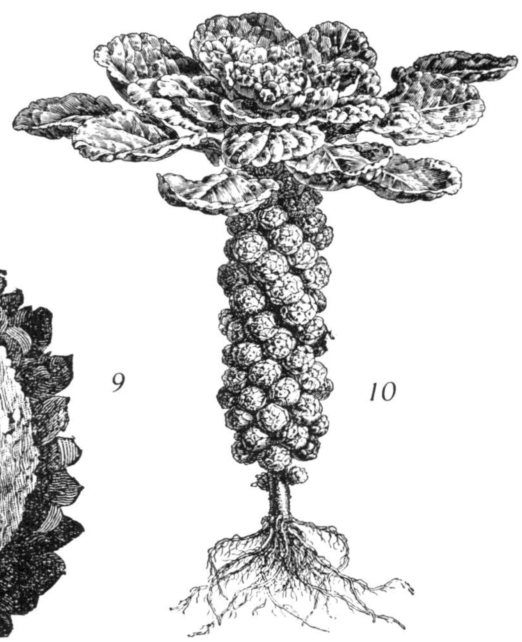

10

1
2
3
4
5
6
7
8
9
10
11
12
13

1
2
GOLDEN DAWN
SWEET SPANISH
MONSTROUS
CAYENNE
3
4
5
6
7
8
9
10
11
12
13
14
15

1

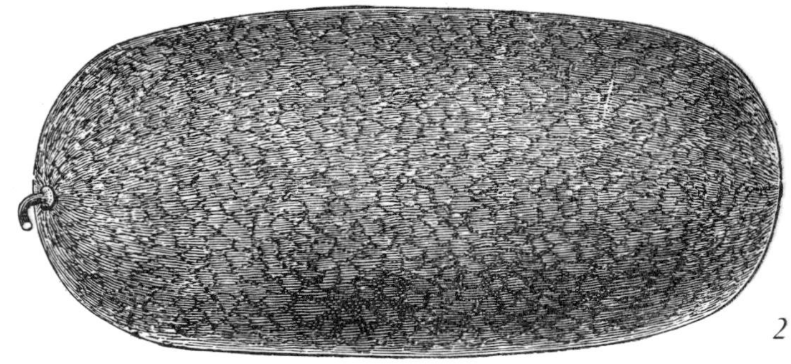

2

3

4

5

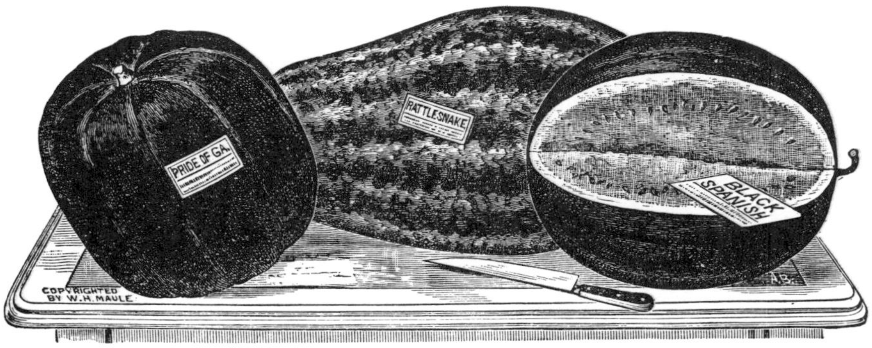

6

7

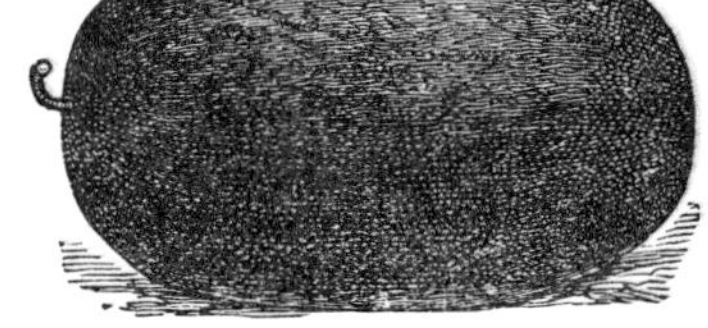

8

9

10

1
2
3
4
5
6
7
8
9
10
11
12
13
14
15
16
17

1

2

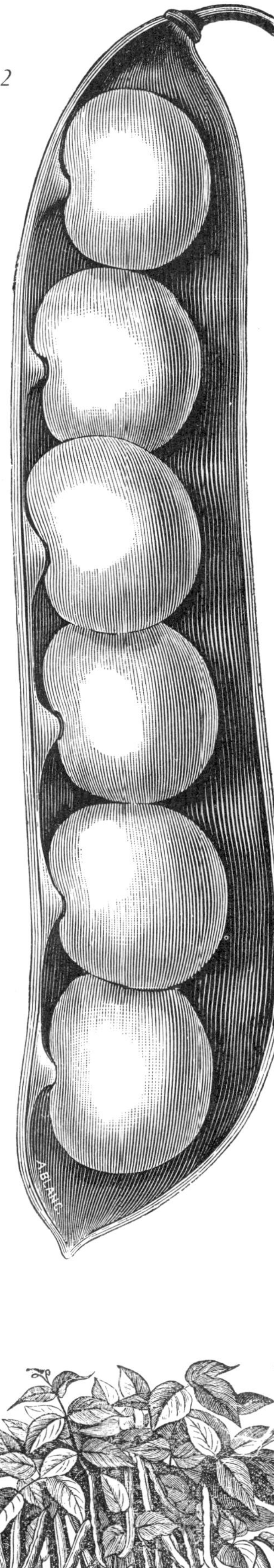

6

5

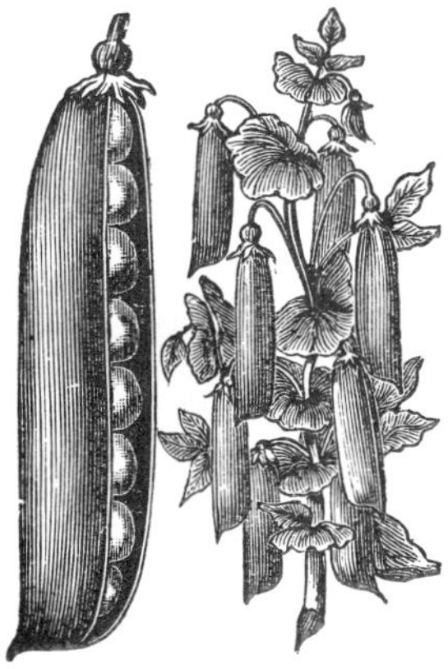

3

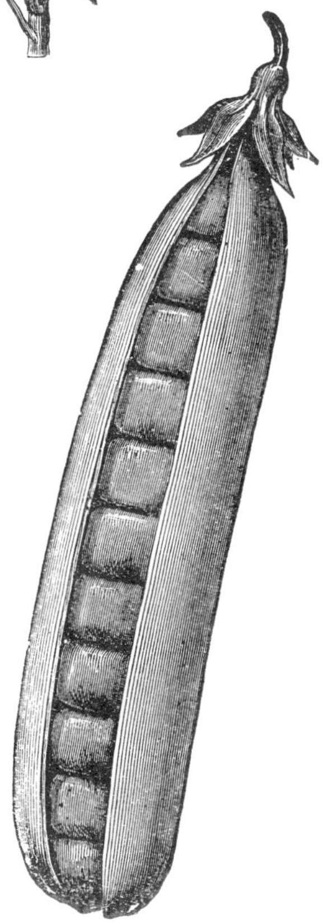

4

7

8

9

10

1
2
3
4
5
6
7
8

1
2
3
4
5
6
7
8
9
10
11
12

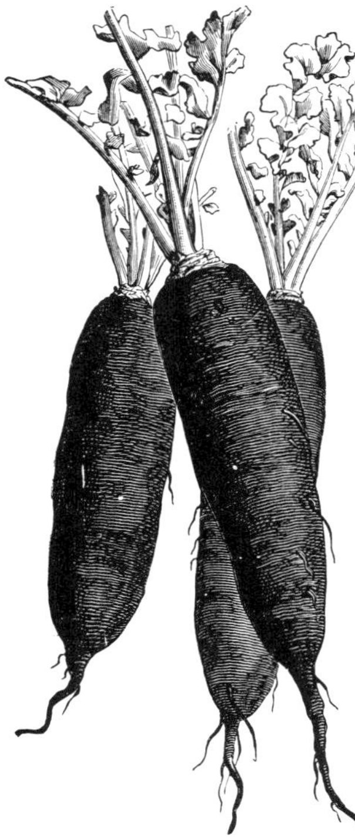
1

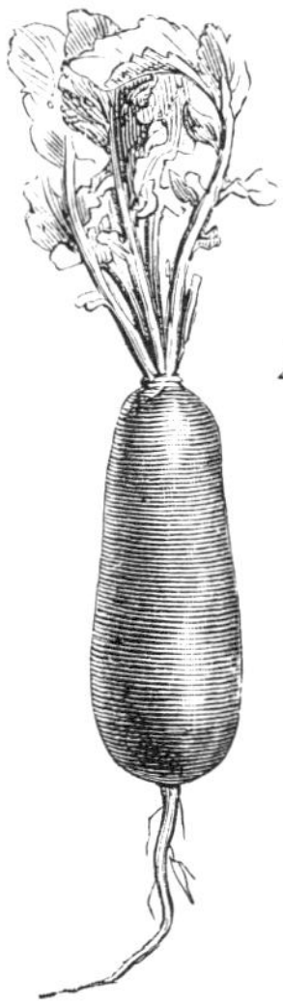
2

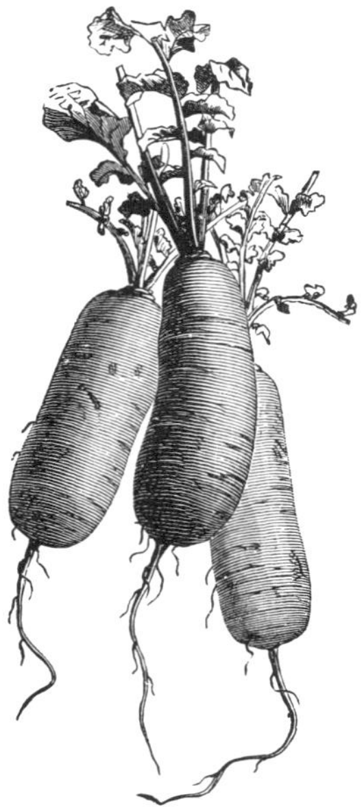
3

4

5

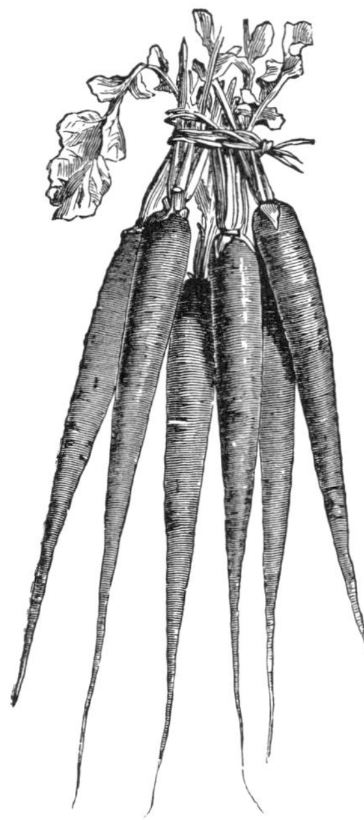
6

7

8

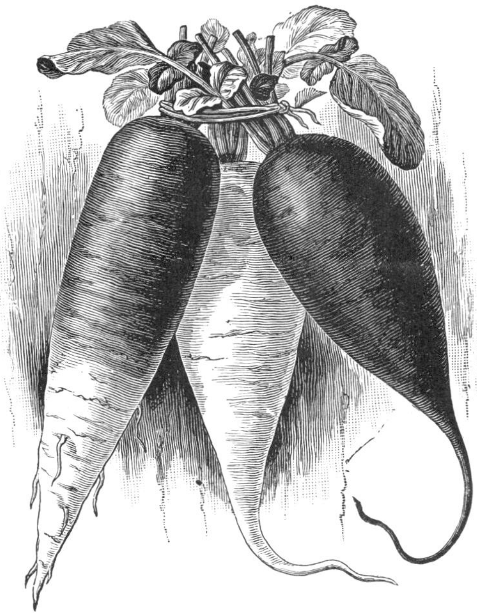
9

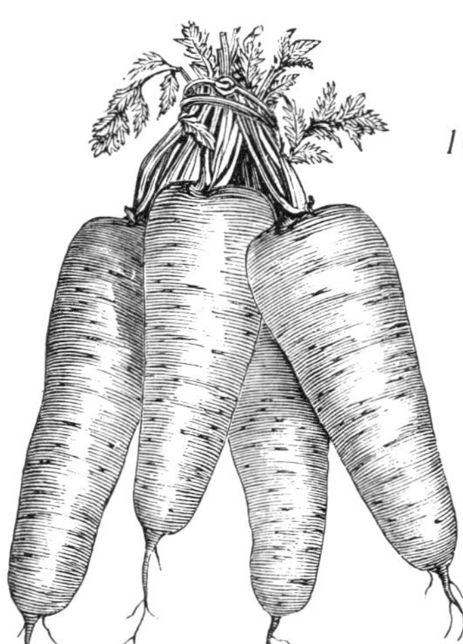
10

11

12

13

14

1

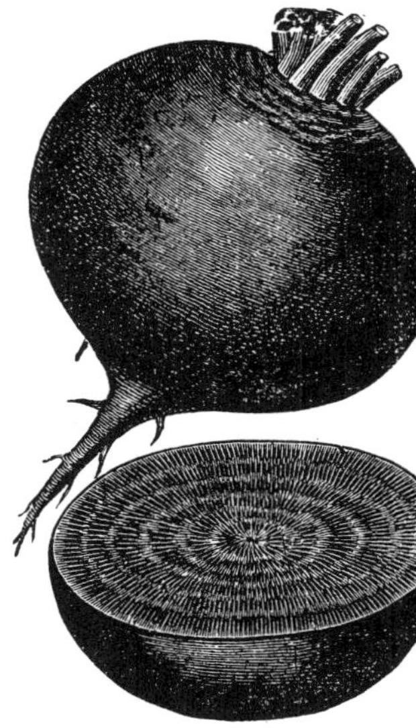

2

3

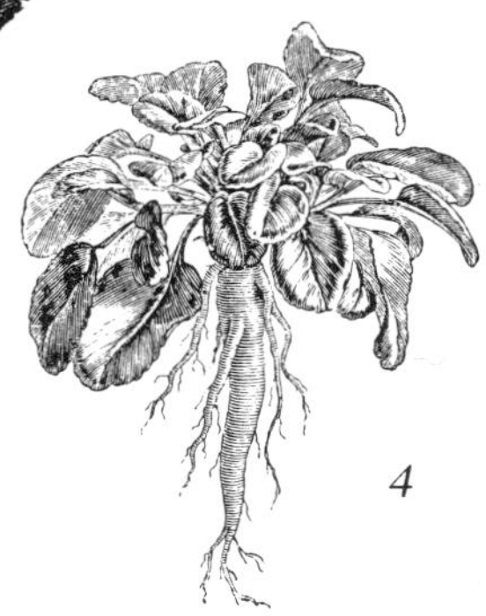

4

5

6

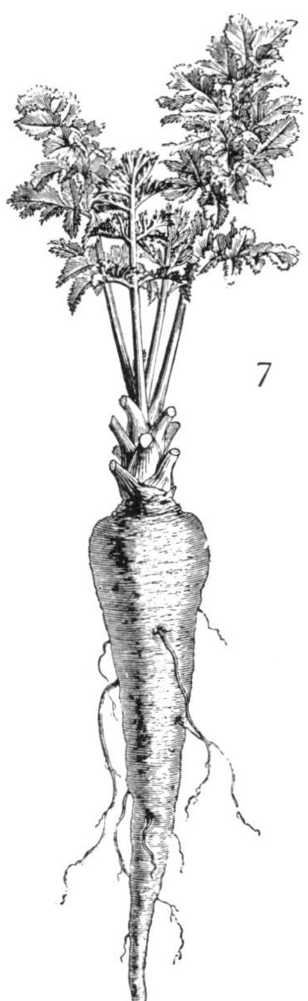

7

8

9

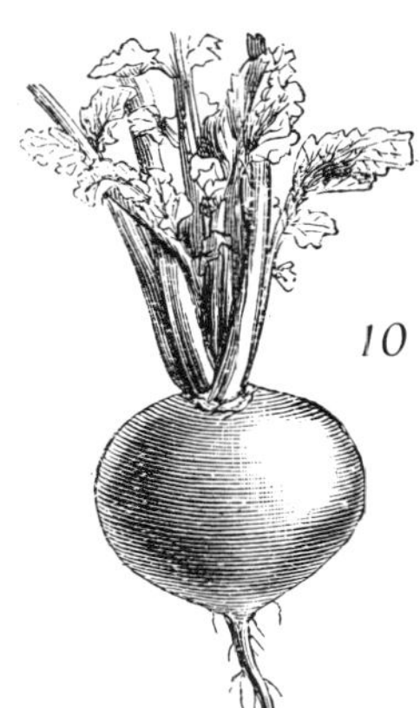

10

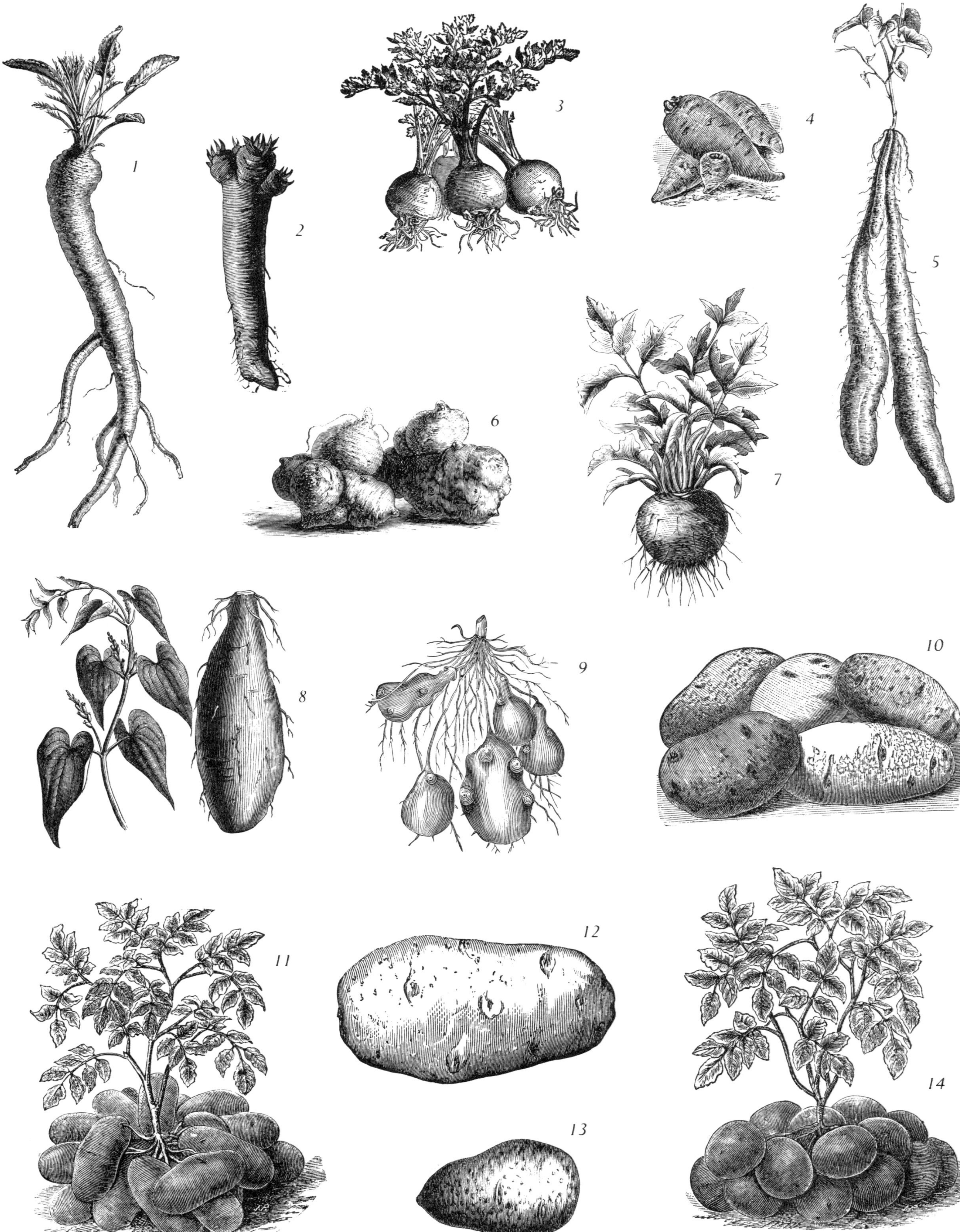
1
2
3
4
5
6
7
8
9
10
11
12
13
14

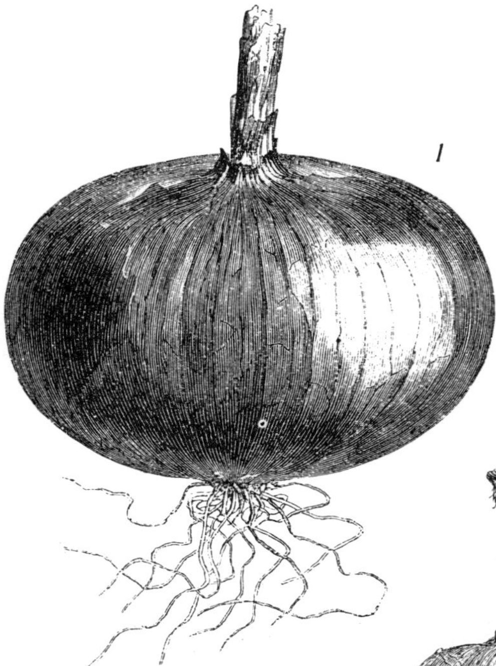

1

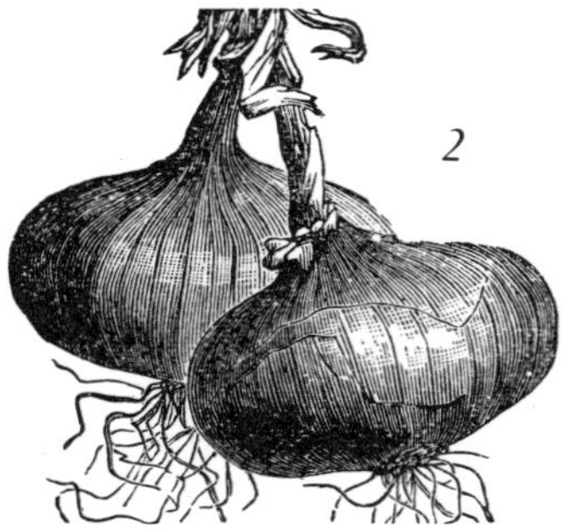

2

3

4

6

7

5

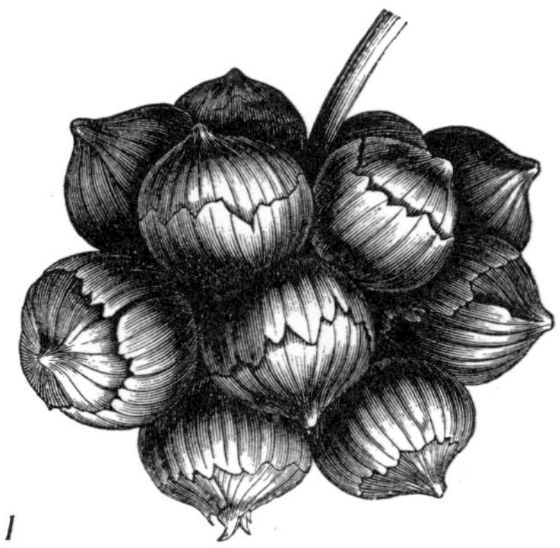

8

9

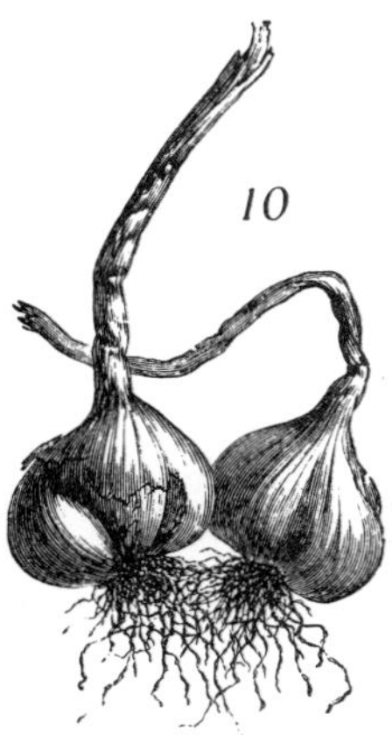

10

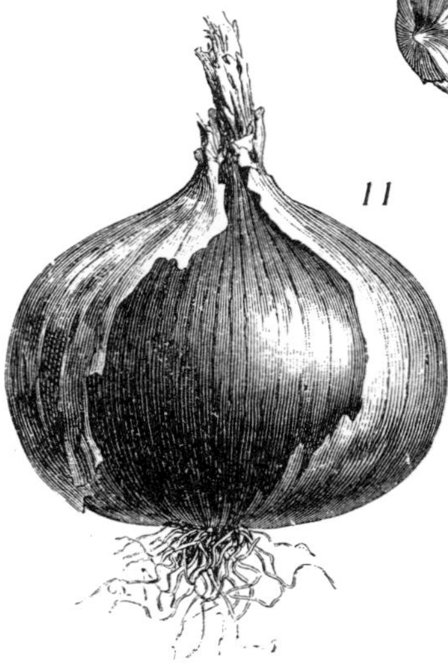

11

13

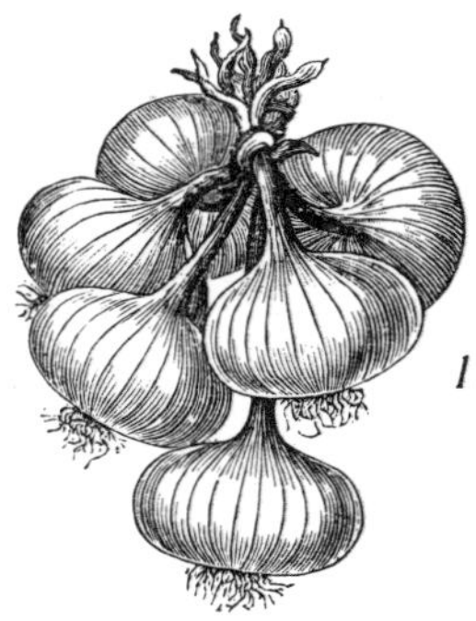

12

14

15

16

1

2

3

4

5

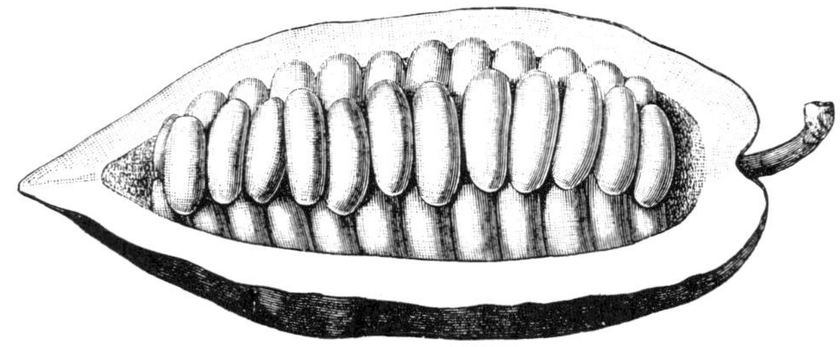
6

7

8

9

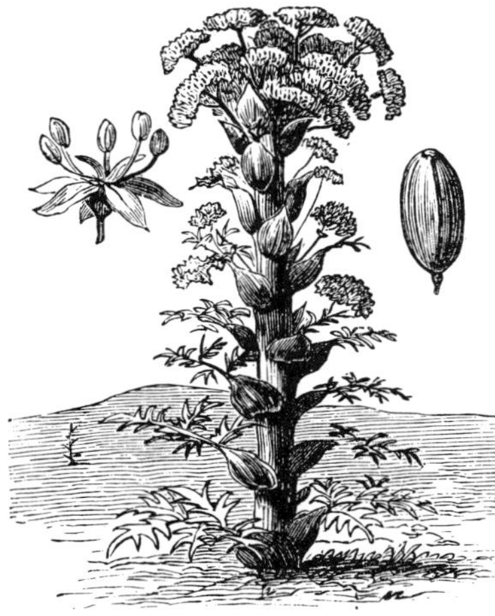
1

2

3

4

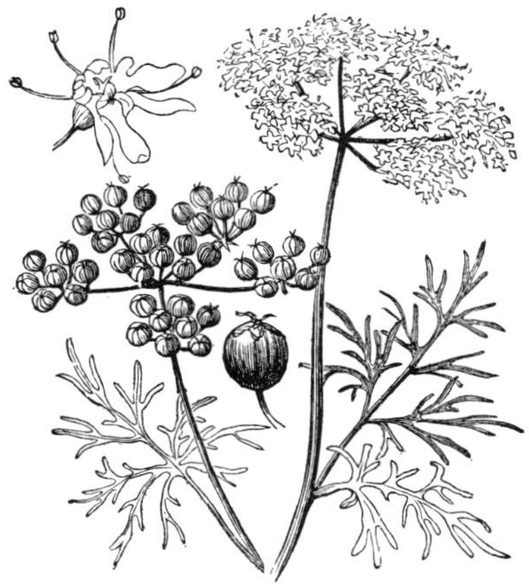
5

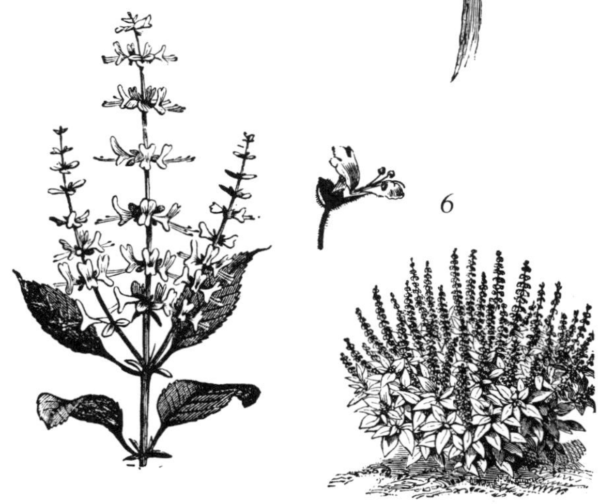
6

7

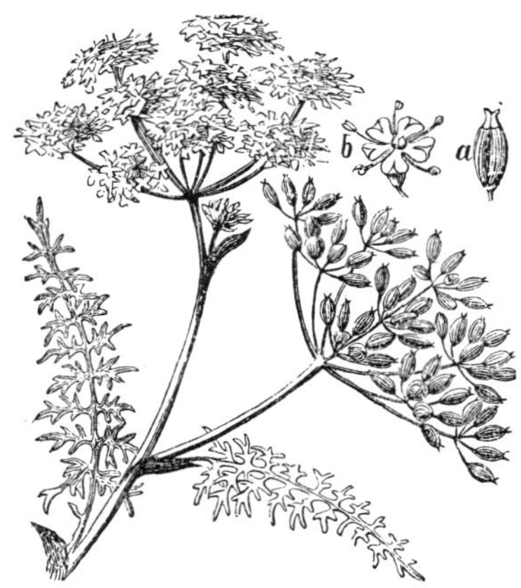

8

9

10

11

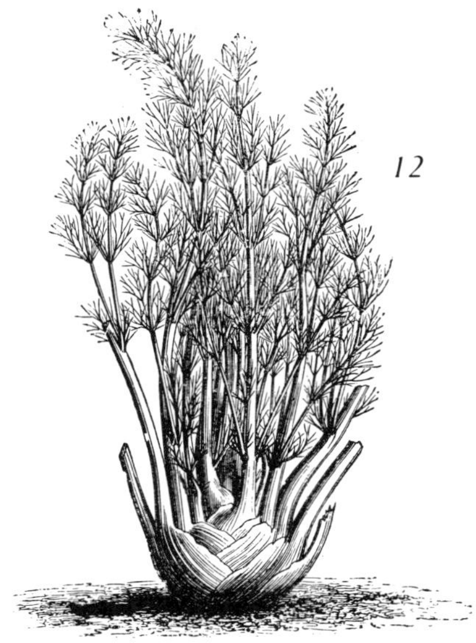
12

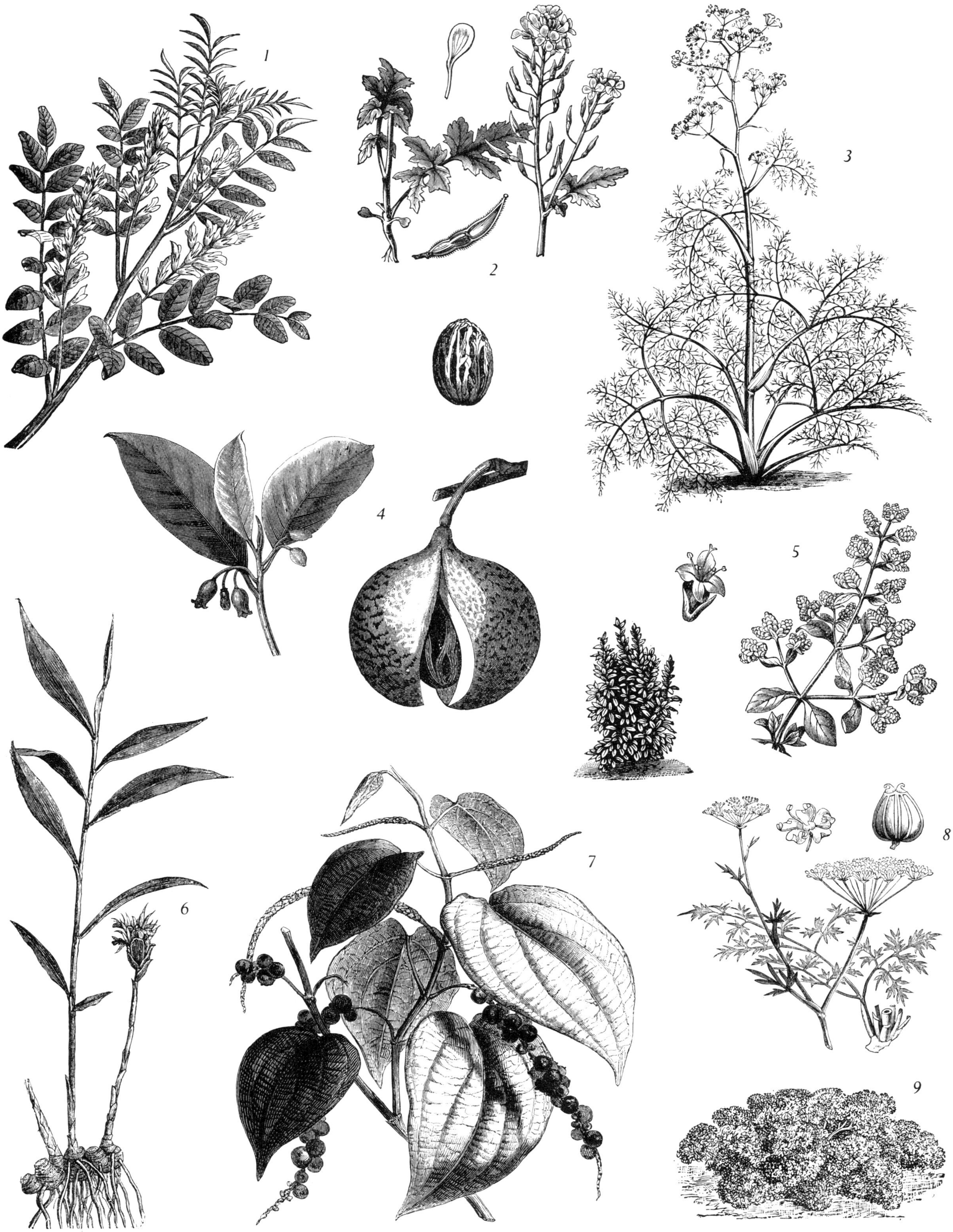
1
2
3
4
5
6
7
8
9

1
2
3
4
5
6
7
8
9
10
11
12
13

APPENDIX C

Medicinal Herbs, Narcotic and Psychotropic Plants, Plants with Miscellaneous Uses

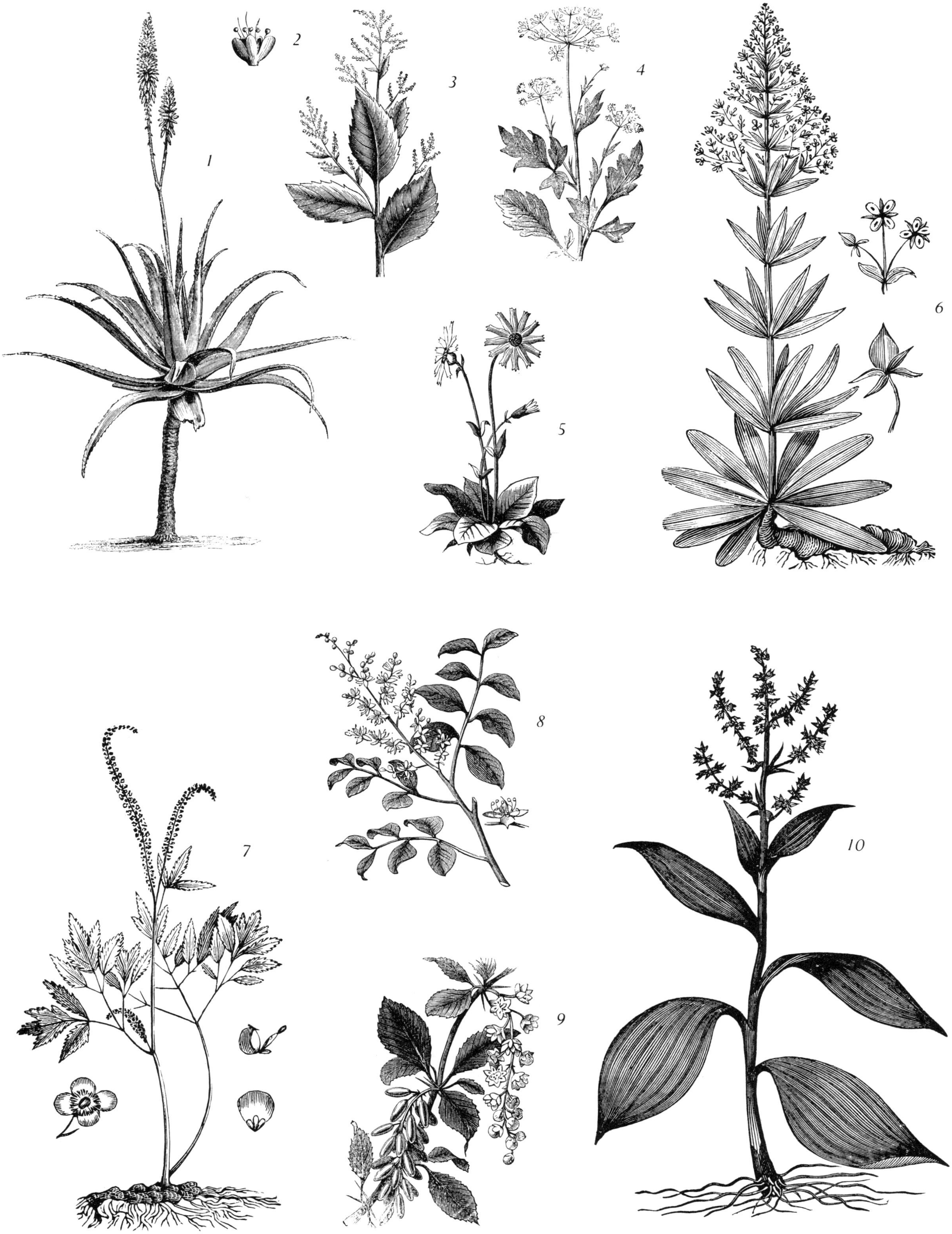
1
2
3
4
5
6
7
8
9
10

1
2
3
4
5
6
7
8
9
10
11
12

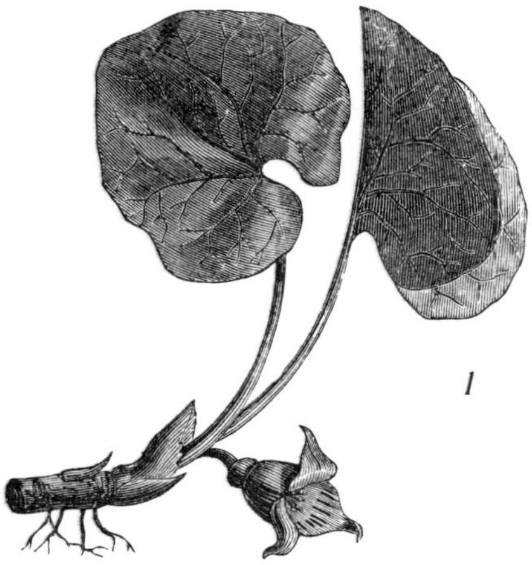

1

2

3

4

5

6

7

8

9

10

1
2
3
4
5
6
7
8
9
10
11

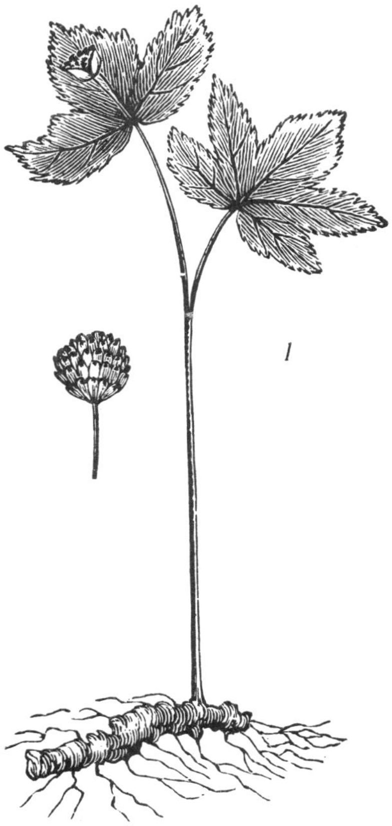

1

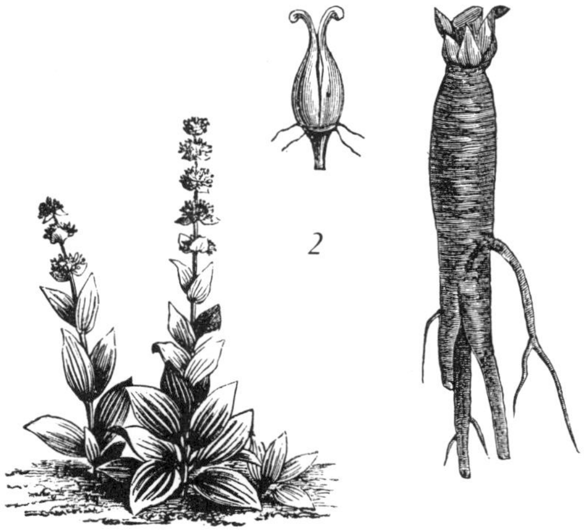

2

3

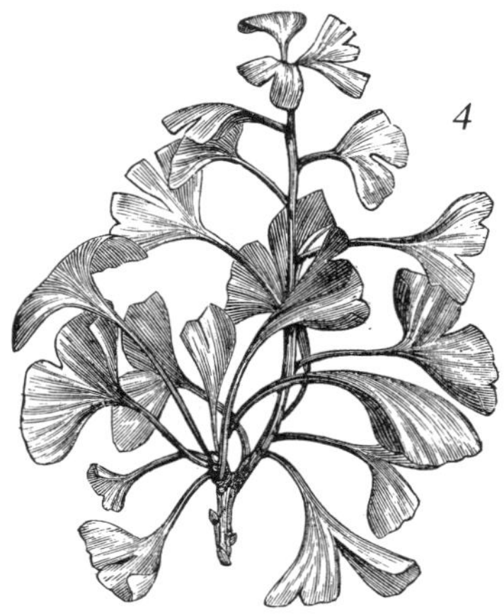

4

5

6

7

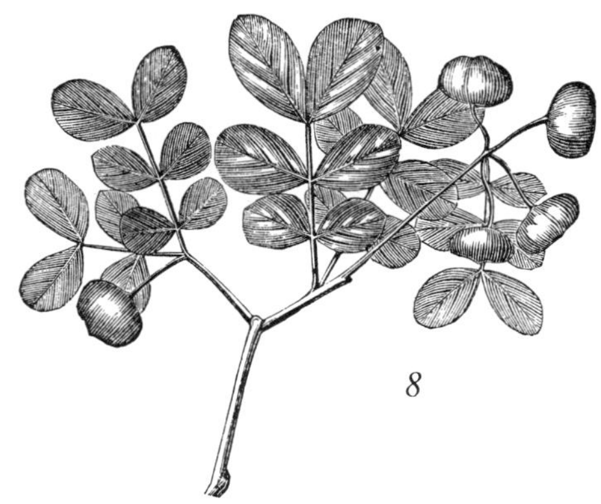

8

9

10

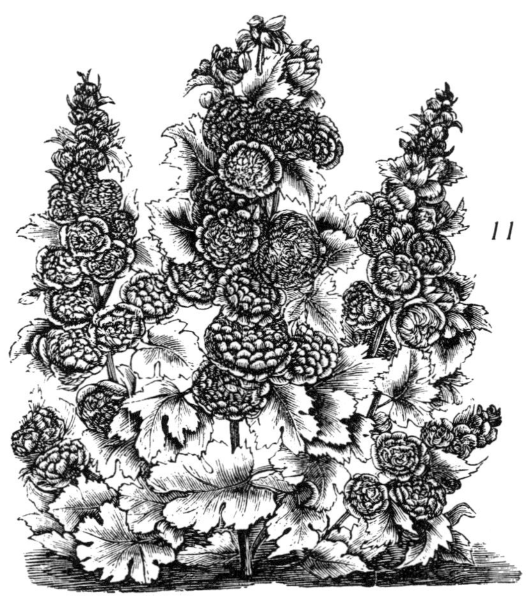

11

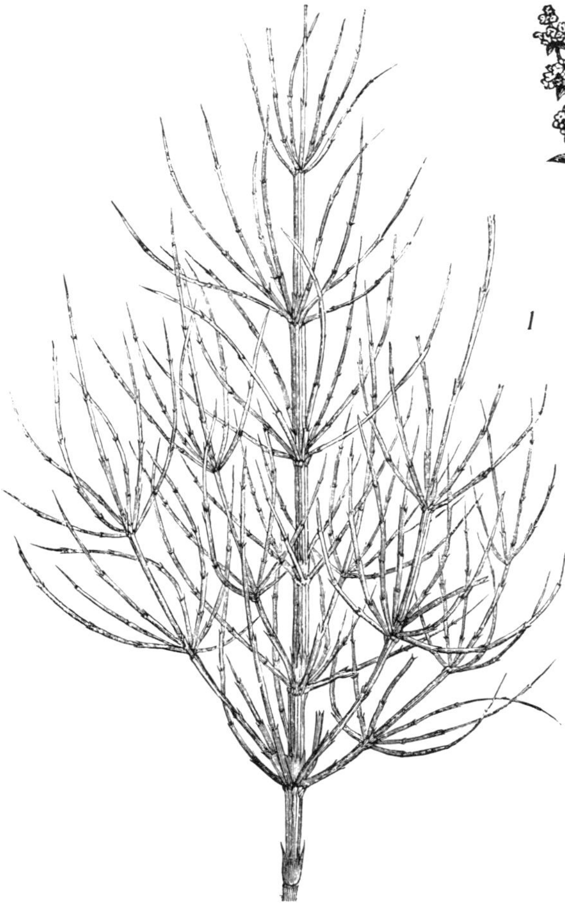
1

2

3

4

5

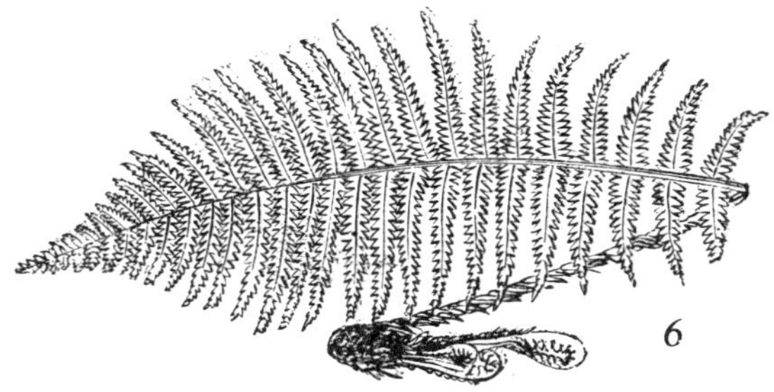
6

7

8

9

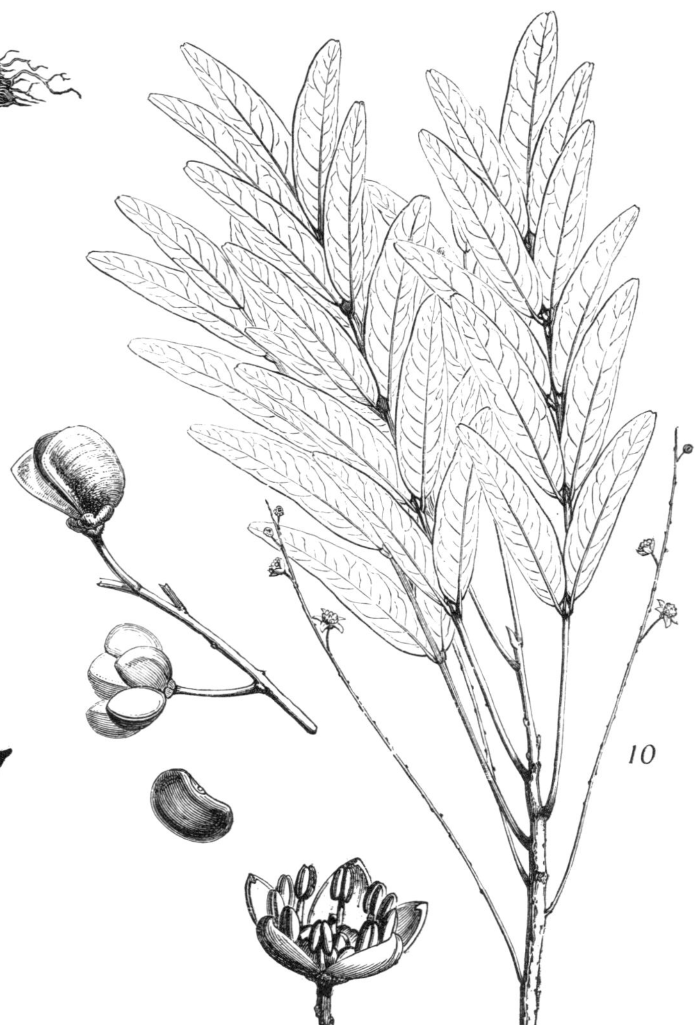
10

1
2
3
4
5
6
7
8
9
10
11

1

2

3

4

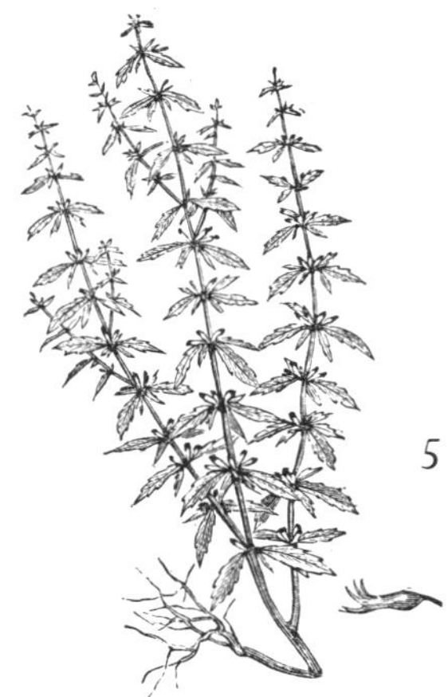

5

6

7

8

1

2

3

4

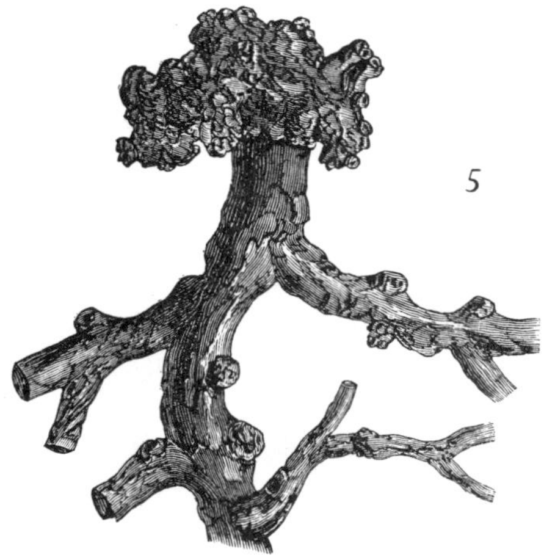

5

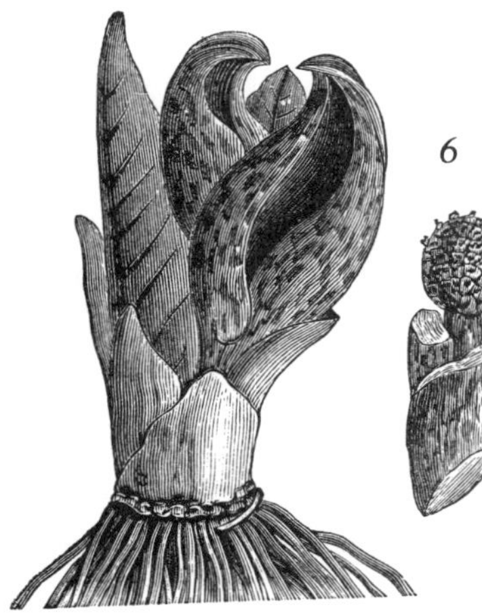

6

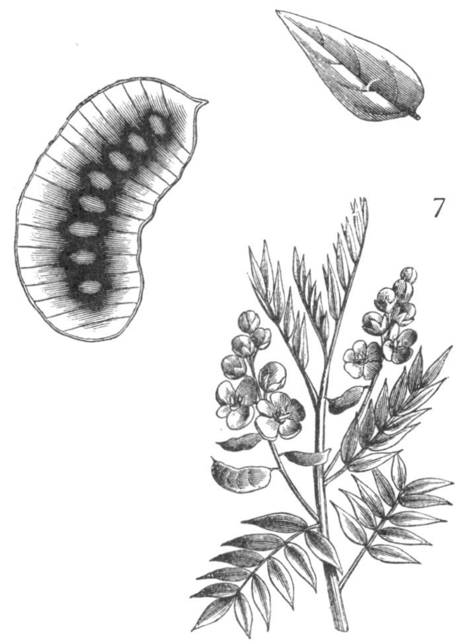

7

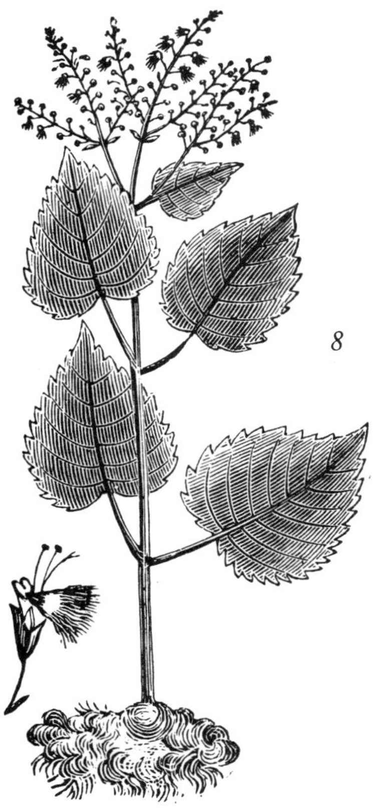

8

9

10

1
2
3
4
5
6
7
8
9
10
11
12

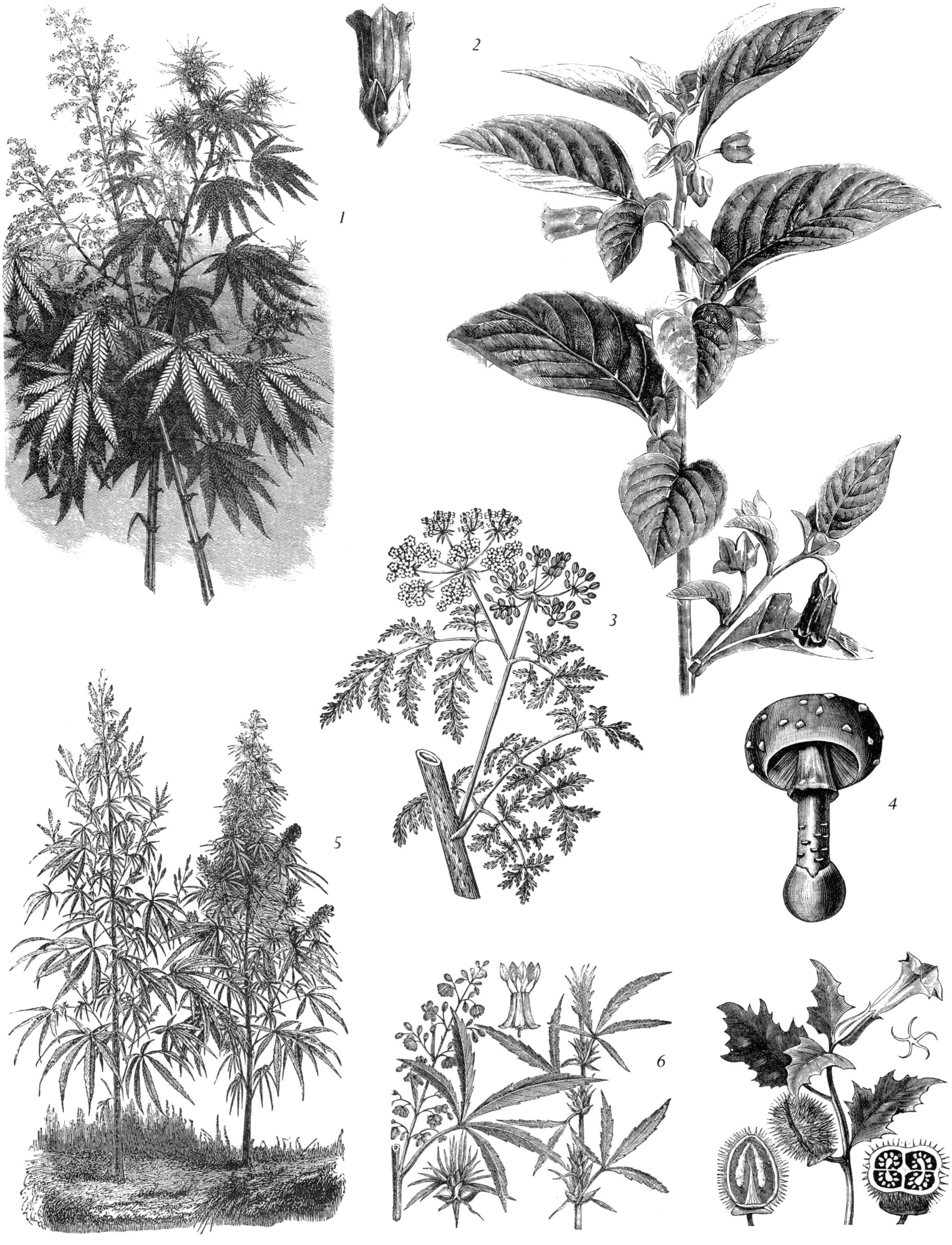
1
2
3
4
5
6
7

1

2

3

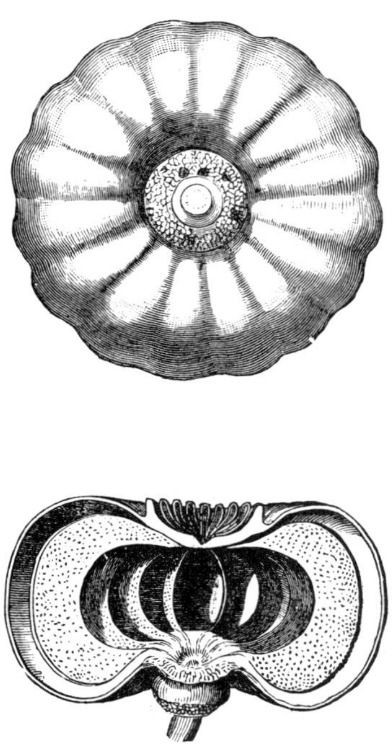

4

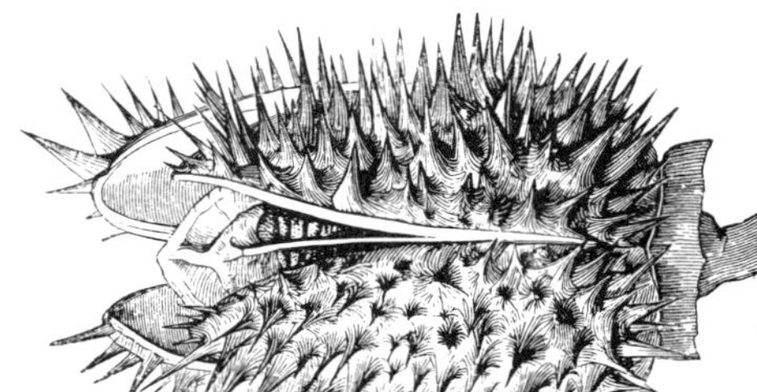

5

6

7

8

1

2

3

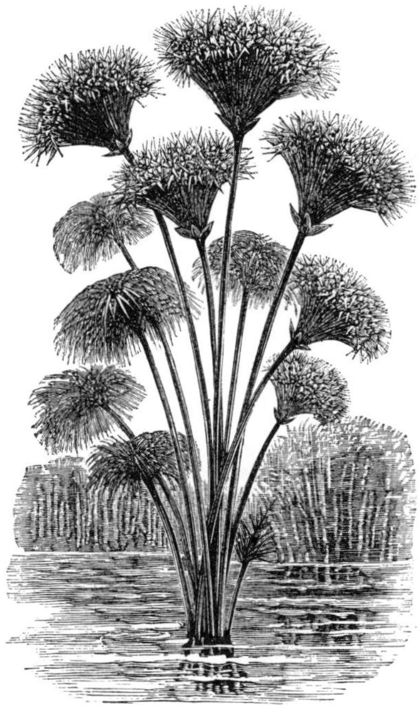
5

6

7

4

8

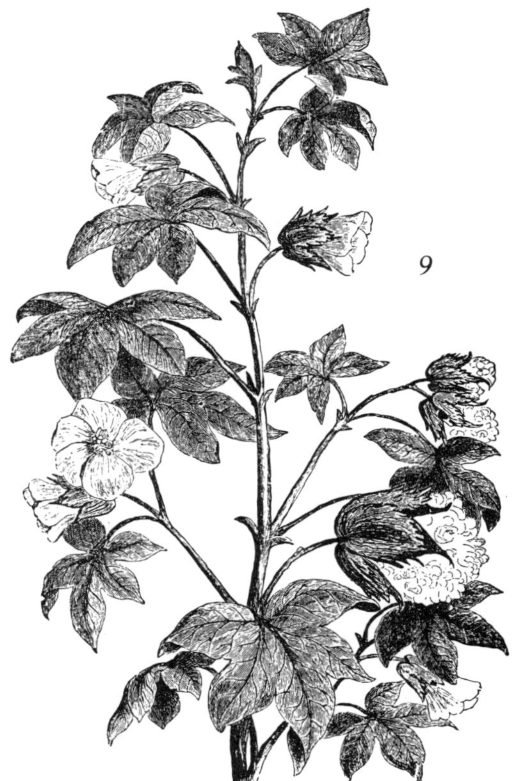
9

1

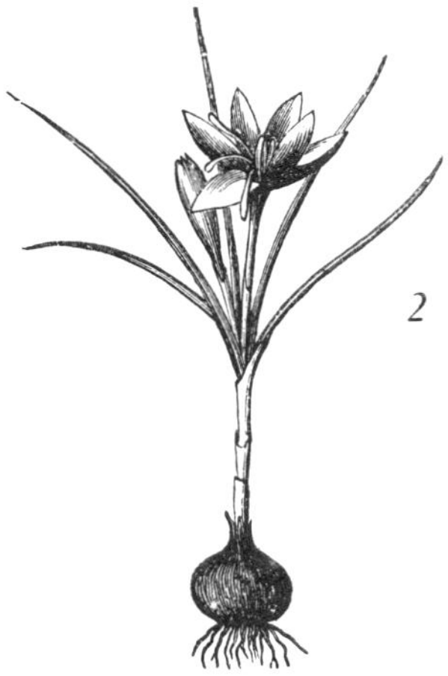

2

3

4

5

6

7

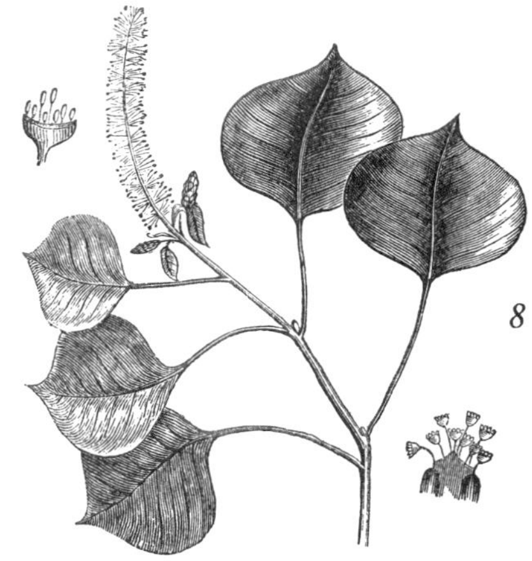

8

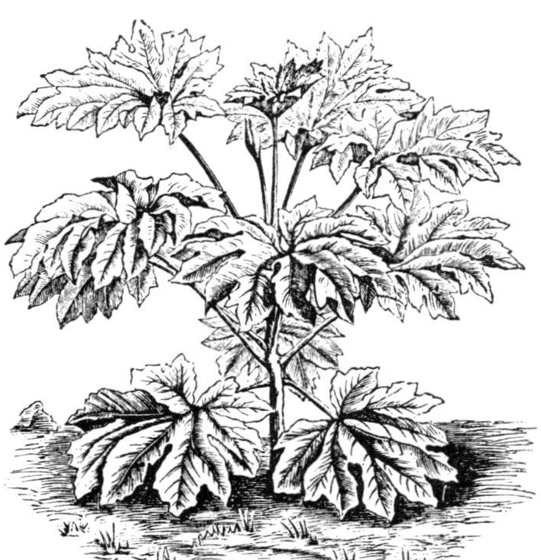

9

10

11

APPENDIX D

Vases and Urns, Decorative Flowers and Plants, Window Gardens, Greenhouses, Gardening, and Gardening Tools

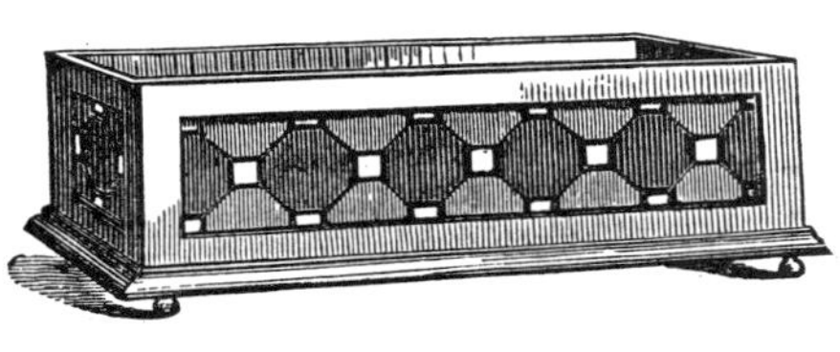

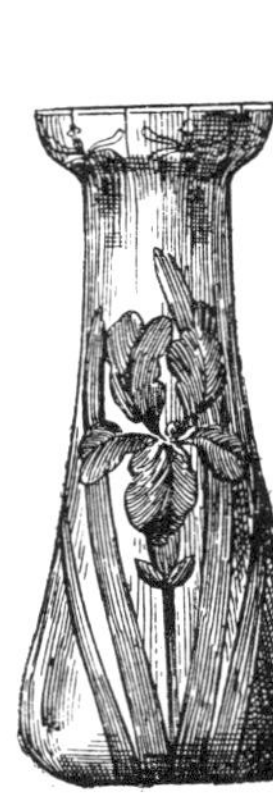

E. SEARS, SC.

E. SEARS

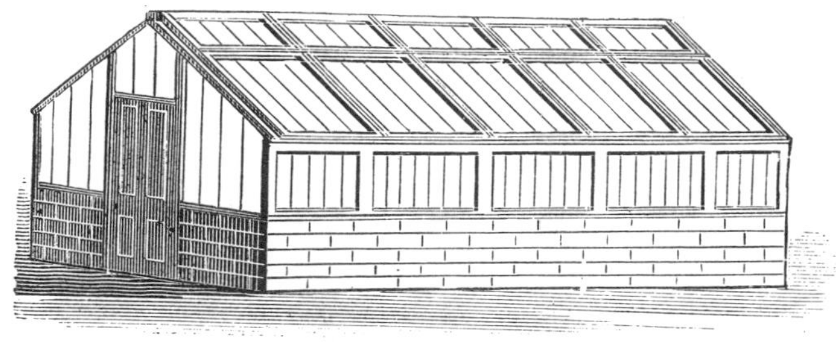

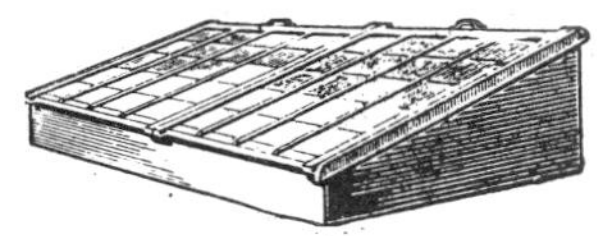

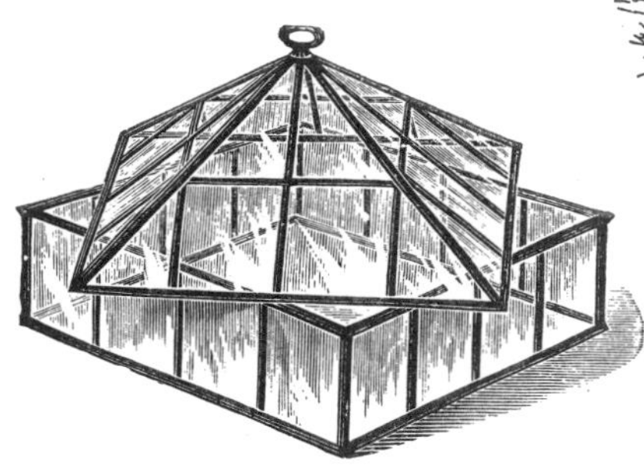

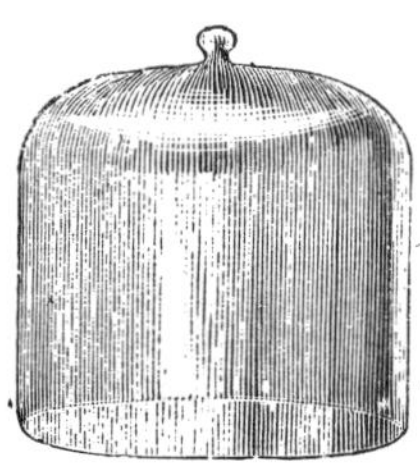

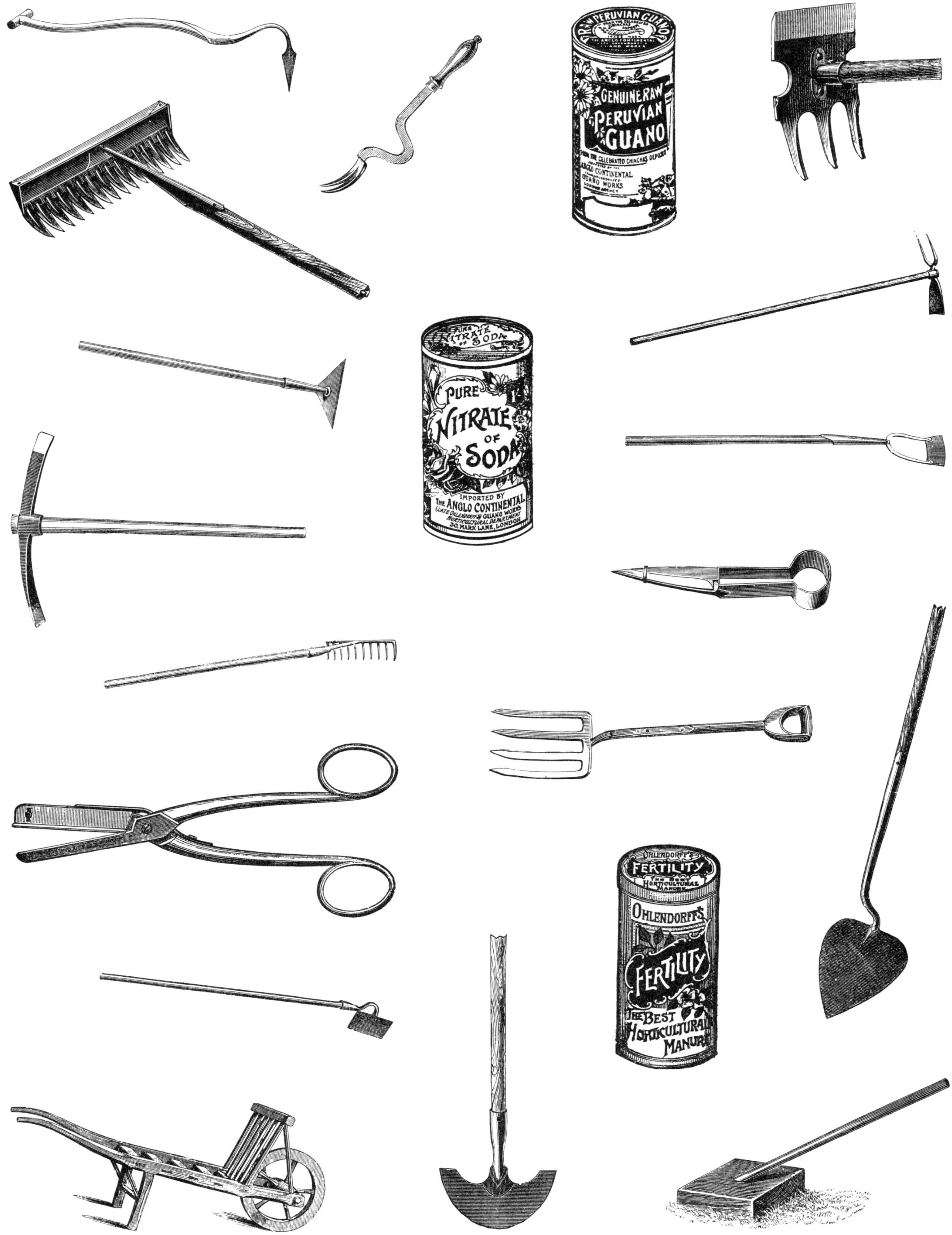

RAW PERUVIAN GUANO
GENUINE RAW
PERUVIAN
GUANO
FROM THE CELEBRATED CHINCHAS DEPOSIT
ANGLO CONTINENTAL
GUANO WORKS
PURE
NITRATE
OF
SODA
IMPORTED BY
THE ANGLO CONTINENTAL
(LATE OHLENDORFF'S) GUANO WORKS
HORTICULTURAL DEPARTMENT
30, MARK LANE, LONDON
OHLENDORFF'S
FERTILITY
OHLENDORFF'S
FERTILITY
THE BEST
HORTICULTURAL
MANURE

APPENDIX E

Decorative Borders and Motifs

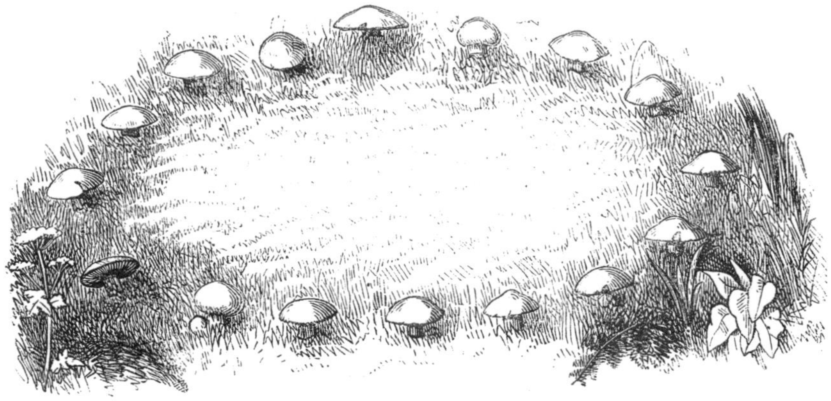

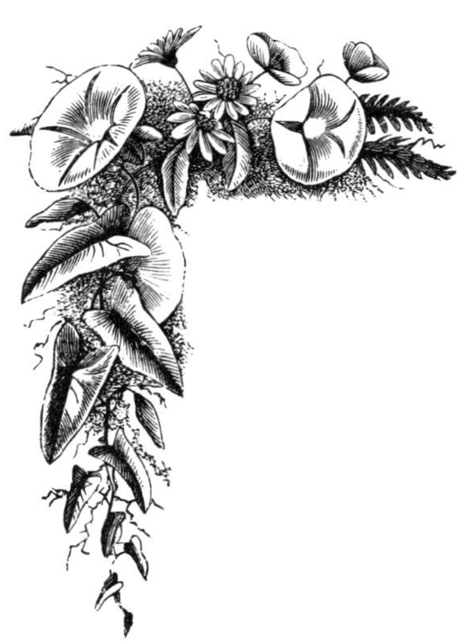

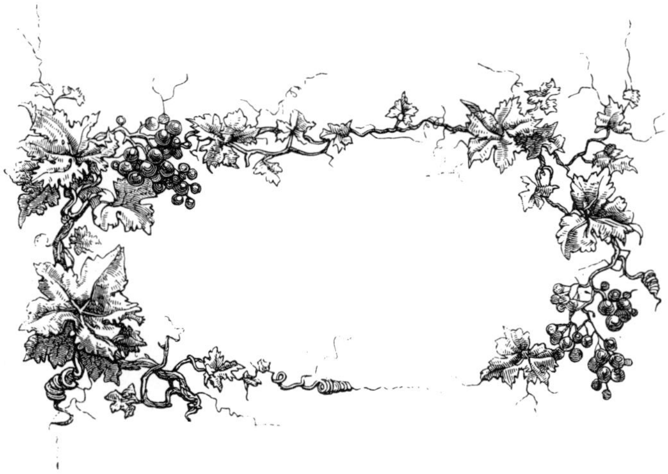

HOCHSTEIN DEL.
S.F.ARS Sc

GLOSSARY OF PLATE REFERENCES

This Glossary provides the species name or common identification for the botanical images and appendices in this book. To use the Glossary, locate the plate number next to the botanical image on a particular page, and then turn to the listing for that page in the Glossary. The description following the plate number will identify the plant or image.

SECTION 1

Botanical Images
Rafflesia arnoldi *(Rafflesiaceae)*

PAGE 2. ***Acanthaceae***

1. *Crossandra undulefolia*
2. *Thunbergia laurifolia*
3. *Sanchezia nobilis glaucophylla*
4. Soft-leaved acanthus
5. *Acanthus latifolius*
6. Spiny acanthus

PAGE 3. ***Aceraceae (maples)***

1. *Acer campestre,* the common or field maple
2. *Acer rubrum,* leaf of red maple
3. *Acer platanoides,* Norway maple
4. *Acer pseudoplatanus,* sycamore maple
5. *Acer negundo,* ash-leaved maple
6. *Acer campestre,* common european maple
7. *Acer pseudoplatanus,* sycamore maple
8. *Acer saccharum,* sugar maple
9. *Acer saccharum,* sugar maple
10. *Acer negundo,* ash-leaved maple

PAGE 4. ***Agaricaceae (mushrooms, toadstools)***

1. *Cantharellus cibarius,* the chantarelle mushroom
2. *Agaricus campestris,* the common mushroom
3. Unidentified mushroom
4. Miscellaneous mushrooms
5. *Lycoperdon gemmatum*
6. *Marasmius oreades,* the champignon
7. *Agaricus procerus,* parasol mushroom
8. *Agaricus gambosus,* St. George's mushroom
9. *Hydnum repandum*
10. *Agaricus muscarius,* fly agaric mushroom

PAGE 5. ***Agaricaceae (mushrooms, toadstools)***

1. *Clavaria aurea*
2. *Daedalea quercina*
3. *Morchella esculenta,* morel mushroom
4. *Marasmius oreades,* fairy ring champignon
5. *Craterellus clavatus*
6. *Hydnum imbricatum*
7. *Marasmius perforans*
8. *Agaricus arvensis,* horse mushroom
9. Common boletus mushroom
10. *Polyporus perennis*
11. *Agaricus campestris,* the common mushroom
12. *Agaricus procerus,* parasol mushroom
13. *Amanita phalloides*

PAGE 6. ***Agaricaceae (mushrooms, toadstools) and other primitive plants***

1. *Saccharomyces,* a yeast
2. *Saccharomyces pastorianus,* a yeast (alcoholic ferment of wine)
3. *Saccharomyces reesaii,* ferment of red wine
4. *Saccharomyces ellipsoideus*
5. *Saccharomyces cerevisiae,* yeast of surface beer
6. *Saccharomyces exiguus*
7. *Saccharomyces conglomeratus*
8. *Mucor racemosus,* penicillin
9. Mistletoe
10. Fireblast or smut, on the maize plant
11. *Tillandsia usneoides,* long or Spanish moss
12. *Geaster hygrometricus*
13. *Peziza coccinea fungus*
14. *Tremella mesenterica,* the warty nostoc fungus
15. *Equisetum sylvaticum,* horsetail
16. *Lecanora esculenta,* edible air-borne lichen
17. *Cetraria islandica,* a lichen
18. *Lecanora tartarea,* a lichen
19. *Sticta pulmonaria,* a lichen
20. *Sphagnum acutifolium,* peat moss
21. *Lycoperdon giganteum,* giant puff-ball

PAGE 7. ***Agavaceae (agaves)***

1. *Agave americana,* American aloe or century plant
2. *Agave victoria regina*
3. *Agave celsiana*
4. *Agave yuccaefolia*

5. *Agave densiflora*
6. *Agave americana,* American aloe or century plant
7. *Agave americana,* American aloe or century plant

PAGE 8. *Agavaceae (agaves)*

1. *Cordyline stricta congesta*
2. *Dracaena indivisa*
3. *Cordyline magnifica*
4. *Dracaena cannaefolia*
5. *Dracaena terminalis*
6. *Dracaena indivisa*

PAGE 9. *Agavaceae (agaves)*

1. *Cordyline cannaefolia*
2. *Yucca filamentosa*
3. *Cordyline indivisa*
4. Thread-leaved pine, agaves, and yucca

PAGE 10. *Agavaceae (agaves)*

1. *Furcraea gigantea*
2. *Furcraea cubensis*
3. *Furcraea gigantea*
4. *Phormium tenax,* New Zealand flax
5. *Phormium tenax,* New Zealand flax
6. *Doryanthes excelsa*

PAGE 11. *Agavaceae (agaves)*

1. *Dracaena indivisa*
2. *Polianthes tuberosa,* tuberose flower
3. *Polianthes tuberosa,* tuberose (single variety)
4. *Phormium tenax,* New Zealand flax
5. *Dracaena bausel*
6. *Polianthes tuberosa,* tuberose plant
7. *Polianthes tuberosa,* double tuberose

PAGE 12. *Agavaceae (dracaenas)*

1. *Dracaena mooreana,* greenhouse dracaena
2. *Agave americana,* American aloe or century plant
3. *Cordyline terminalis*
4. *Dracaena shepherdii*
5. *Dracaena congesta*
6. *Dracaena goldieana*

PAGE 13. *Agavaceae (yuccas)*

1. *Yucca gloriosa*
2. *Yucca filamentosa*
3. *Yucca flexilis ensifolia*
4. Three-valved pod of yucca
5. *Yucca filifera*
6. *Yucca gloriosa recurvifolia*
7. *Yucca filamentosa*

PAGE 14. *Agavaceae (yuccas)*

1. *Yucca filamentosa*
2. *Yucca filamentosa*
3. *Yucca gloriosa*
4. *Yucca angustifolia stricta*
5. *Yucca treculeana*

PAGE 15. *Aizoaceae*

1. *Mesembryanthemum minutum*
2. *Mesembryanthemum criniflorum*
3. *Mesembryanthemum crystallinum*
4. *Mesembryanthemum mutabile*
5. *Mesembryanthemum testiculatum*
6. *Mesembryanthemum tigrinum*
7. *Mesembryanthemum densum*

PAGE 16. *Amaranthaceae (amaranths cockscombs, celosias)*

1. *Amaranthus caudatus*
2. Hunch-backed amaranth
3. *Celosia huttonii*
4. *Iresine herbstii aureoreticulata*
5. *Iresine herbstii aureoreticulata*
6. *Celosia cristata variegata,* feathered cockscomb
7. Unidentified member of Amaranthaceae
8. *Celosia argentea*
9. *Amarante gigantesque,* giant amaranth
10. *Amaranthus caudatus*
11. *Celosia cristata variegata,* feathered cockscomb
12. *Amaranthus salicifolius*
13. *Celosia cristata,* Cockscomb

PAGE 17. *Amaryllidaceae (amaryllis, daffodils)*

1. *Clivia miniata*
2. *Amaryllis vittata hybrida*
3. Hybrid hippeastrums
4. Scarlet amaryllis
5. Purple amaryllis
6. *Amaryllis formosissima*
7. *Clivia miniata*

PAGE 18. *Amaryllidaceae (amaryllis, daffodils)*

1. *Amaryllis* sp.
2. *Sternbergia lutea*
3. *Bomarea edulis*
4. *Amaryllis belladonna*
5. *Urceolina pendula*
6. *Eucharis* sp.
7. *Crinum capense*
8. *Crinum kirkii*
9. *Bomarea carderi*

PAGE 19. *Amaryllidaceae (amaryllis, daffodils)*

1. Elves' snowdrop
2. *Galanthus elwesii*
3. *Galanthus nivalis reflexus*
4. *Ixiolirion tataricum brachyantherum*
5. *Imantophyllum cyrtanthiflorum*
6. *Hymenocallis andreana*
7. *Galanthus nivalis*
8. *Ixiolirion tataricum brachyantherum*
9. *Imantophyllum cyrtanthiflorum*

PAGE 20. ***Amaryllidaceae (narcissus, gathanthus)***

1. *Narcissus* sp. (unidentified variety)
2. *Narcissus jonquilla*, jonquil
3. *Narcissus poeticus*, double poet's narcissus
4. Various varieties of narcissus
5. *Galanthus nivalis*
6. *Narcissus poeticus*, poet's narcissus (single variety)
7. Large-flowered all-white narcissus

PAGE 21. ***Amaryllidaceae (narcissus)***

1. Unidentified variety of narcissus
2. *Narcissus monophyllus clusii*
3. *Narcissus bulbocodium*
4. Unidentified variety of narcissus
5. *Narcissus poeticus*
6. Trumpet major narcissus
7. *Narcissus cyclamineus*
8. *Narcissus horsfieldi*
9. *Narcissus bulbocodium*
10. Unidentified variety of narcissus

PAGE 22. ***Amaryllidaceae***

1. *Pancratium illyricum*
2. Unidentified variety of pancratium
3. *Vallota purpurea*
4. *Sternbergia lutea*
5. *Pancratium guianensis*

PAGE 23. ***Anacardiaceae (cashews, mangoes, poison ivies), and Apocynaceae (periwinkles, oleanders)***

1. *Vinca Rosea* (Apocynaceae)
2. *Rhus venenata*, poison sumach (Anacardiaceae)
3. *Rhus glabra*, smooth sumach (Anacardiaceae)
4. *Plumeria tricolor* (Apocynaceae)
5. *Vinca rosea* (Apocynaceae)
6. *Vinca rosea* (Apocynaceae)
7. *Rhus toxicodendron*, poison ivy (Anacardiaceae)
8. *Nerium oleander*, oleander (Apocynaceae)
9. *Nerium oleander*, double oleander (Apocynaceae)
10. *Dipladenia insignis* (Apocynaceae)

PAGE 24. ***Aquifoliaceae (Holly)***

1. *Ilex opaca*, American holly
2. *Ilex aquifolium*, European holly
3. *Ilex aquifolium*, European holly
4. *Ilex aquifolium crassifolia*
5. *Ilex aquifolium pyramidalis*
6. *Ilex aquifolium doningtonensis*
7. *Ilex cornuta*, Chinese holly
8. *Ilex cornuta*, Chinese holly
9. *Ilex aquifolium ferox*
10. *Ilex aquifolium argentea medio-picta*
11. *Ilex aquifolium bressoni*
12. *Ilex dipyrena*
13. *Ilex aquifolium ovata*
14. *Ilex crenata variegata*
15. *Ilex aquifolium tortuosa*
16. *Ilex verticillata*, winterberry

PAGE 25. ***Araceae***

1. *Arisaema fimbriatum*
2. *Arum maculatum*
3. *Ariopsis peltata*
4. *Colocasia esculenta*
5. Unidentified variety of caladiums
6. White calla or lily of the Nile

PAGE 26. ***Araceae***

1. *Dracunculus* sp.
2. Spotted leaf calla
3. Spotted leaf calla
4. *Zantedeschia aethiopica*
5. Arum lily
6. Jack-in-the-Pulpit
7. *Zantedeschia aethiopica*, arum lily
8. Unidentified variety of caladiums
9. Black calla

PAGE 27. ***Araceae***

1. *Rhektophythum mirabile*
2. *Colocasia esculenta*
3. *Rhektophythum mirabile*
4. *Philodendron andreanum*

PAGE 28. ***Araceae***

1. *Philodendron* sp.
2. *Philodendron mamei*
3. *Philodendron speciosum*
4. *Anthurium spendidum*
5. *Alocasia sanderiana*

PAGE 29. ***Araceae***

1. *Philodendron verrucosum*
2. *Philodendron verrucosum*
3. *Dieffenbachia regina*
4. *Dieffenbachia carderi*
5. *Xanthosoma sagittifolium*
6. *Anthurium scherzerianum maximum*

PAGE 30. ***Araceae***

1. *Schismatoglottis longispatha*
2. *Colocasia antiquorum*
3. *Aristolochia clematitis*
4. *Amorprophallus rivieri*
5. *Ariopsis peltata*
6. *Nephthytis picturata*
7. *Schismatoglottis*, unidentified variety
8. *Anthurium crystallinum*

PAGE 31. *Araceae (aroids) and Araliaceae (ivies, ginsengs)*

1. *Hedera helix regneriana,* variety of ivy (Arialiaceae)
2. *Hedera helix digitata* (Araliaceae)
3. *Fatsia japonica* (Araliaceae)
4. *Hedera helix dentata* (Araliaceae)
5. *Epipremnum mirabile* (Araceae)
6. *Fatsia papyrifera* (Araliaceae)
7. *Arisaema triphyllum* (Araceae)

PAGE 32. *Araceae (mainly caladiums)*

1. *Caladium comestible*
2. *Caladium bicolor varietäten*
3. *Caladium chantinii*
4. *Caladium esculentum*
5. *Caladium maculatum*
6. *Caladium esculentum*
7. Unidentified variety of caladium
8. *Colocasia odorata*

PAGE 33. *Araliaceae (ivies, ginsengs)*

1. *Oreopanax epremesnilianum*
2. *Aralia veitchii*
3. *Oreopanax peltatum*
4. *Trevesia eminens*

PAGE 34. *Araliaceae (ivies) and Aristolochiaceae*

1. *Hedera colchica,* asiatic ivy (Araliaceae)
2. Unidentified variety of ivy (Araliaceae)
3. Fruiting form of *Hedera helix* (Araliaceae)
4. *Hedera canariensis,* African ivy (Araliaceae)
5. *Hedera helix,* European Ivy (Araliaceae)
6. *Hedera helix lobata major* (Araliaceae)
7. *Hedera helix deltoidea* (Araliaceae)
8. *Aristolochia sipho,* Dutchman's pipe (Aristolochiaceae)

PAGE 35. *Asclepiadaceae (milkweeds, hoyas)*

1. *Ceropegia gardneril*
2. *Hoya carnosa variegata*
3. *Stephanotis floribunda*
4. *Physianthus albens*
5. *Asclepias variegata,* variegated milkweed
6. *Asclepias variegata,* variegated milkweed
7. *Hoya carnosa,* wax plant
8. *Stapelia* sp.
9. *Stapelia grandiflora*

PAGE 36. *Asclepiadaceae (impatiens), Balsaminaceae (balsams), and Begoniaceae (begonias)*

1. Balsam (Balsaminaceae)
2. Balsam (Balsaminaceae)
3. Balsam from the camellia gardens (Balsaminaceae)
4. Balsam
5. *Hoya bella* (Asclepiadaceae)
6. Tuberous-rooted begonias (Begoniaceae)
7. *Impatiens hawkeri* (Balsaminaceae)

PAGE 37. *Begoniaceae (begonias)*

1. *Begonia corallina*
2. *Begonia corallina*
3. *Begonia roezli rosea*
4. Double hybrid tuberous begonias
5. *Begonia veitchii*
6. Worth begonia
7. *Begonia vernon,* dark purple begonia
8. Froebel begonia
9. Perpetual flowering begonia
10. Perpetual flowering begonia
11. Tuberous begonias

PAGE 38. *Begoniaceae (begonias)*

1. *Begonia davisii*
2. *Begonia maculata*
3. *Begonia diadema*
4. *Begonia heracleifolia*
5. *Begonia semperflorens*
6. *Begonia maculata*
7. *Begonia veitchii*
8. *Begonia pearcei*

PAGE 39. *Begoniaceae (begonias)*

1. Begonia Queen of Whites
2. *Begonia rex*
3. *Begonia maculata*

PAGE 40. *Begoniaceae (begonias) and Berberidaceae (barberries, mayapples)*

1. *Berberidopsis corallina* (Berberidaceae)
2. *Begonia semperflorens* Frau Maria Brandt (Begoniaceae)
3. *Podophyllum peltatum* (Berberidaceae)
4. Single tuberous begonia (Begoniaceae)
5. *Berberis stenophylla* (Berberidaceae)
6. *Berberis wallichiana* (Berberidaceae)

PAGE 41. *Betulaceae (birch, alder trees)*

1. *Alnus glutinosa,* European alder
2. Cut-leaved weeping birch
3. *Betula papyrifera,* paper or white birch
4. *Alnus glutinosa,* European alder
5. Unidentified variety of birch
6. Weeping birch
7. *Betula pendula,* European white birch

PAGE 42. *Bignoniaceae (catalpas)*

1. Large-flowered incarvillea
2. *Bignonia magnifica*
3. *Incarvillea delavayi*
4. *Tecoma radicans*
5. *Incarvillea olgae*
6. *Catalpa syringifolia*

PAGE 43. *Boraginaceae (forget-me-nots, borages)*

1. *Echioides longiflorum,* prophet flower

2. *Borage* sp.
3. *Symphytum asperrimum*
4. *Symphytum officinale luteo-marginatum*
5. *Myosotis alpestris* (with leaf and flower)
6. *Anchusa sempervirens,* evergreen alkanet (with flower)
7. *Anchusa capensis*
8. *Pulmonaria saccharata*
9. *Pulmonaria officinalis*
10. *Anchusa capensis*
11. *Myosotis dissitiflora elegantissima,* forget-me-not

PAGE 44. *Bromeliaceae (pineapples, bromeliads)*

1. *Karatas humilis*
2. *Aechmea fulgens*
3. *Karatas scheremktiewi*
4. *Tillandsia splendens*
5. *Bonapartea* sp.
6. *Tillandsia Regina*
7. *Massangea hieroglyphica*
8. *Canistrum aurantiacum*

PAGE 45. Cactaceae (*cactuses*)

1. *Cereus ctenoides*
2. *Cereus enneacanthus*
3. *Cereus leptacanthus*
4. *Mammillaria elephantidens*
5. *Mammillaria subpolyhedra*

PAGE 46. *Cactaceae* (*cactuses*)

1. *Mammillaria micromeris*
2. *Mammillaria fissurata*
3. *Pilocereus brunnowii*
4. *Mammillaria sulcolanata*
5. *Echinocactus texensis*
6. *Mammillaria macromeris*
7. *Echinocactus horizonthalonius*

PAGE 47. *Cactaceae* (*cactuses*)

1. *Echinopsis*
2. *Melocactus communis*
3. Unidentified variety of cactus
4. *Echinocactus visnaga*
5. *Mammillaria haageana*
6. *Mammillaria ottonis*
7. *Echinocactus* sp.
8. Unidentified variety of cereus cactus
9. *Echinocactus cornigerus*

PAGE 48. *Cactaceae* (*cactuses*)

1. *Echinocactus coptonogonus*
2. *Cereus multiplex*
3. *Mammillaria sanguinea*
4. *Cereus caespitosus*
5. *Malacocarpus erinaceus*
6. *Mammillaria dolichocentra*
7. *Melocactus miquelii*

PAGE 49. *Cactaceae* (*cactuses*)

1. *Mammillaria echinus*
2. *Pilocereus dautwitzii*
3. *Echinocactus pottsii*
4. *Pelecyphora aselliformis*
5. *Astrophyton myriostigma*
6. *Mammillaria vivipara radiosa*
7. *Mammillaria longimamma*

PAGE 50. *Cactaceae* (*cactuses*)

1. *Phyllocactus roseus grandiflorus*
2. *Echinocactus wislizeni*
3. *Opuntia vulgaire*
4. *Mammillaria schelhasii*
5. *Pelecyphora pectinata*
6. *Pereskia zinniaeflora*
7. *Mammillaria sempervivi*

PAGE 51. *Cactaceae* (*cactuses*)

1. *Opuntia macrorhiza*
2. *Opuntia* sp., prickly pear cactus
3. *Opuntia tuna*
4. *Opuntia basilaris,* beaver-tail prickly pear
5. *Opuntia ficus-indica,* Indian fig
6. *Opuntia rafinesquii*
7. Unidentified variety of opuntia
8. *Opuntia tuna*

PAGE 52. *Cactaceae* (*cactuses*)

1. *Cereus procumbens*
2. *Opuntia boliviana*
3. *Cereus berlandieri*
4. *Nopal opuntia*
5. *Opuntia rosea*
6. Various cacti and century plant

PAGE 53. *Cactaceae* (*cactuses*)

1. *Pilocereus senilis,* old man cactus
2. *Cactus grandiflorus*
3. *Rhipsalis sarmentacea*
4. *Opuntia brachyarthra*
5. *Cactus flagelliformis*
6. *Phyllocactus latifrons*
7. *Cactus melocactus*
8. Group of cacti
9. *Echinocactus scopa cristatus*

PAGE 54. *Cactaceae* (*cactuses*)

1. Saguaro cactus and other plants in Northern Mexico
2. *Echinocactus crispatus*
3. Variety of opuntia
4. *Carnegiea gigantea,* saguaro cactus
5. *Opuntia platyacantha*
6. Unidentified cacti in pots
7. *Echinopsis pentlandi scheerii*
8. *Carnegiea gigantea,* saguaro cactus

PAGE 55. ***Campanulaceae* (campanulas, bellflowers)**

1. Double Canterbury bells
2. *Campanula garganica*
3. *Campanula celtidifolia*
4. Large-flowered campanula
5. *Campanula macrostyla*
6. *Campanula pyramidalis*
7. Lorey campanula
8. *Campanula laciniata*
9. *Campanula carpathica pelviformis*
10. *Campanula canarina*
11. *Campanula grosseckii heuffel*

PAGE 56. ***Campanulaceae* (campanulas, bellflowers)**

1. *Lobelia fulgens*
2. *Cyanthus lobatus*
3. *Centropogon fastuosus*
4. *Campanula carpathica turbinata*
5. *Phyteuma charmelii*
6. Tall campanula
7. Tall campanula
8. *Lobelia cardinalis*
9. *Campanula*, tall
10. *Lobelia ermus*, dwarf lobelia
11. *Wahlenbergia tenuifolia*

PAGE 57. ***Cannaceae* (cannas)**

1. *Canna speciosa*
2. *Canna indica*, Indian shot
3. *Canna annei*
4. *Canna indica*, Indian shot
5. *Canna annei*
6. *Canna gigantea*
7. *Canna coccinea*

PAGE 58. ***Caprifoliaceae* (viburnums, honeysuckles)**

1. *Viburnum acerifolium*, maple-leaved viburnum
2. *Viburnum pubescens*
3. *Weigela florida*
4. *Weigela florida*
5. *Lonicera flexuosa*, a variety of honeysuckle
6. *Viburnum macrocephalum keteleeri*
7. *Viburnum plicatum*, snowball
8. *Lonicera japonica 'Halliana,'* Hall's Japan honeysuckle
9. *Viburnum tinus*, Laurustinus viburnum
10. *Lonicera sempervirens*, a variety of honeysuckle

PAGE 59. ***Caryophyllaceae* (carnations, pinks)**

1. Dwarf hybrid Haage lychnis, with flower
2. *Lychnis fulgens sieboldi*
3. *Lychnis chalcedonica*
4. Haage lychnis
5. *Lychnis fulgens*
6. Pink fantasy, a variety of carnation
7. *Agrostemma coeli-rosa*
8. *Gypsophila elegans*
9. *Agrostemma flos-jovis*
10. *Silene asterias*, large-flowered
11. *Agrostemma coronaria*
12. *Selenicereus*, 'Good Luck'

PAGE 60. ***Caryophyllaceae* (carnations, pinks)**

1. *Dianthus caryophyllus*
2. *Dianthus caryophyllus*
3. *Dianthus caryophyllus*
4. Picotee pink
5. *Dianthus caryophyllus*
6. Florist's pink
7. *Dianthus chinensis heddewigii*
8. Group of border pinks
9. *Dianthus chinensis*, double Chinese pink

PAGE 61. ***Caryophyllaceae* (carnations, pinks)**

1. Carnation
2. Picotee pink
3. Single sweet William
4. Pink
5. Carnations
6. Double sweet William
7. *Dianthus superbus cardneri*, cut-flowered Chinese pink
8. *Dianthus superbus grandiflorus*, double-fringed pink
9. Double sweet William
10. Carnations

PAGE 62. ***Celastraceae* (spindle trees), *Cistaceae* (rock roses), *Combretaceae* (combretums), *Commelinaceae* (spiderworts), and *Compositae* (asters, sunflowers, dandelions, chrysanthemums)**

1. *Quisqualis indica* (Combretaceae)
2. *Achillea clavennae*, with flower (Compositae)
3. *Antennaria margaritacea*, with flower (Compositae)
4. *Celastrus scandens*, waxwork (Celastraceae)
5. *Arnica montana* (Compositae)
6. *Barnadesia rosea* (Compositae)
7. *Agathaea coelestis* (Compositae)
8. *Cistus creticus linne*, helianthemum (Cistaceae)
9. *Tradescantia warscewicziana* (Commelinaceae)
10. *Commelina coelestis*, plant and flower (Commelinaceae)

PAGE 63. ***Compositae* (asters)**

1. Dwarf tapering aster 'Queen Marguerite'
2. *Callistephus chinensis*, Washington nadel-aster
3. Unidentified variety of aster
4. Victoria aster
5. Various asters

PAGE 64. *Compositae (asters)*

1. *Callistephus chinensis,* comet aster
2. *Aster ericoides*
3. *Aster amellus bessarabicus*
4. *Aster alpinus*
5. Dwarf tapering aster 'Queen Marguerite'
6. Dwarf tapering aster 'Queen Marguerite'
7. Victoria aster
8. Truffault's paeony-flowered aster
9. *Aster corymbosus,* with flower
10. Chrysanthemum flowered aster
11. Unidentified variety of aster

PAGE 65. *Compositae (chrysanthemums)*

1. Unidentified variety of single flowered chrysanthemum
2. *Chrysanthemum carinatum*
3. *Chrysanthemum carinatum* Burridgeanum
4. Unidentified variety of chrysanthemum
5. Various chrysanthemums
6. Double-flowered recurvate chrysanthemum
7. Unidentified variety of chrysanthemum

PAGE 66. *Compositae (chrysanthemums)*

1. Incurved-flowered chrysanthemum
2. *Chrysanthemum indicum*
3. Recurved chrysanthemum Dr. Sharpe
4. Pompone chrysanthemum
5. Laciniathm chrysanthemum
6. Large double-flowered chrysanthemum
7. *Chrysanthemum carinatum* Lord Beaconsfield
8. White chrysanthemum
9. *Chrysanthemum frutescens,* Marguerite or Paris daisies

PAGE 67. *Compositae (chrysanthemums, cinerarias)*

1. *Cineraria cruenta webberiana*
2. Quilled pompone chrysanthemum
3. *Chrysanthemum segetum grandiflorum*
4. *Cineraria maritima*
5. Japanese chrysanthemum chinaman
6. Large-flowered hybrid cineraria
7. Double cineraria Mr. Thomas Lloyd

PAGE 68. *Compositae (chrysanthemums and others)*

1. *Chrysanthemum frutescens,* gold star chrysanthemum
2. *Chrysanthemum frutescens*
3. *Brachycome iberidifolia*
4. *Brachycome iberidifolia*
5. *Centaurea dealbata*
6. *Ptilostemon diacantha*
7. *Centaurea macrocephala*
8. *Ptilostemon casabònae*
9. *Chrysanthemum frutescens*
10. *Centaurea cyanus*
11. Double-flowered hybrid cineraria
12. Early-flowering chrysanthemum
13. *Coreopsis tinctoria nana*
14. Small hybrid cineraria with large dusty-rose flowers

PAGE 69. *Compositae (dahlias)*

1. *Dahlia imperialis*
2. Single flowered dahlias
3. Cactus-flowered decorative dahlias
4. *Dahlia coccinea*
5. Juarez dahlia
6. *Dahlia imperialis*
7. Dahlias: magpie and freedom
8. Dwarf-feathered single dahlia
9. Large-flowered double dahlias

PAGE 70. *Compositae (dahlias)*

1. Dahlias: Dr. Moffat and danger
2. Single flowered dahlia
3. *Dahlia juarezii*
4. Show dahlia
5. Cactus-flowered dahlia
6. Dahlias: beacon and utility

PAGE 71. *Compositae (mainly daisies)*

1. *Erigeron glauque,* with flower
2. *Bellis perennis prolifera,* hen and chickens daisy
3. Large-flowered painted daisy
4. *Bellis perennis,* double daisy, with flower
5. Oxeye daisy
6. Unidentified daisy
7. *Bellis perennis*
8. Double painted daisy
9. *Bellis perennis,* double daisy
10. *Erigeron* sp., orange
11. Painted daisy
12. Painted daisy 'Aurora Borealis'

PAGE 72. *Compositae (helianthus, sunflowers)*

1. *Helianthus argophyllus*
2. *Helianthus globosus fistulosus*
3. Double sunflower
4. Double California sunflower
5. *Helianthus annuus californicus plenissimus*
6. Sunflower with cucumber leaves
7. Dwarf single sunflower
8. *Helianthus annuus,* common sunflower
9. *Helianthus salicifolius*
10. *Helianthus annuus californicus plenissimus*
11. *Helianthus decapetalus multiflorus*
12. *Helianthus globosus Fistulosus*
13. Dwarf single sunflower
14. *Helianthus multiflorus*

PAGE 73. *Compositae (marigolds, tagetes, and others)*

1. Dwarf Indian single marigold 'Legion of Honor'
2. *Tagetes erecta*, African marigold (with flower)

3. *Calendula officinalis*
4. Dwarf Indian single marigold 'Legion of Honor'
5. Indian double marigold
6. *Tagetes patula,* French marigold
7. *Tagetes erecta,* African marigold
8. *Tagetes signata pumila*
9. Pyrethre Parth, remarkable double pyramidal
10. *Rhodanthe manglesi,* everlasting
11. *Tagetes signata pumila*
12. *Xanthocephalum gymnospermoides*

PAGE 74. *Compositae (marigolds, zinnias, and others)*

1. Tagetes African El Dorado, marigold
2. *Senecio pulcher*
3. *Tagetes fistulosa lutka,* with flower
4. Dwarf gold striped marigold, with flower
5. Scotch prize marigold
6. *Rhodanthe manglesi*
7. *Senecio macroglossus,* German ivy
8. Scarlet gem, double zinnia
9. Farquhar's Exhibition prize zinnia
10. *Waitzia aurea*

PAGE 75. *Compositae (thistles and others)*

1. *Liatris spicata,* with flower
2. *Leontopodium alpinum*
3. *Leontopodium alpinum*
4. *Carlina acaulis*
5. *Humea elegans*
6. *Circium vulgare,* common thistle
7. *Polycalymaa stuartii*
8. *Circium arvense,* Canada thistle, with flower buds
9. *Gundelia tournefortii*

PAGE 76. *Compositae (zinnias)*

1. *Zinnia elegans,* double zinnia
2. *Zinnia elegans,* double zinnia
3. *Zinnia elegans,* double zinnia
4. *Zinnia elegans*
5. *Zinnia darwini,* double-flowered
6. *Zinnia elegans,* single zinnia
7. *Zinnia haageana*
8. *Zinnia elegans,* double zinnia
9. *Zinnia elegans robusta grandiflora*

PAGE 77. *Compositae*

1. *Immortelle annuelle*
2. *Helichrysum bracteatum compositum*
3. *Immortelle annuelle multiflore*
4. *Coreopsis drummondi*
5. *Gnaphalium decurrens*
6. *Gnaphalium decurrens*
7. *Coreopsis verticillata,* with flower
8. *Echinops commutatus*
9. *Leptosyne maritima*
10. *Helichrysum bracteatum aureum*
11. *Helichrysum foetidum*
12. Jameson's gerbera daisy

PAGE 78. *Compositae*

1. *Inula helenium*
2. *Petasites fragrans,* winter heliotrope
3. *Inula glandulosa*
4. *Eupatorium* sp., bone set
5. *Tussilago farfara variegata*
6. *Verbesina pinnatifida*
7. *Montanoa bipinnatifida*

PAGE 79. *Compositae*

1. *Pyrethrum roseum*
2. *Podolepis gracilis,* with flower
3. Large-flowered purple coneflower
4. *Rudbeckia laciniata*
5. Mangles rodanthe
6. Dwarf double pyrethrum 'Ball of Gold'
7. Large-flowered double pyrethrum
8. *Sanvitalia procumbens*
9. Dwarf double pyrethrum 'Ball of Gold'
10. *Rhodanthe maculata*
11. *Rhodanthe manglesi,* Austrian rhodanthe
12. *Senecio balbisianus,* piedmont groundsel

PAGE 80. *Convolvulaceae (morning glories, convolvuluses)*

1. *Ipomoea purpurea*
2. *Ipomoea rubrocaerulea*
3. *Convolvulus arvensis*
4. *Exogonium purga,* jalap
5. Ivy-leaved morning glory, with flower
6. *Mina lobata*
7. Scarlet morning glory
8. *Nolana paradoxa*

PAGE 81. *Convolvulaceae (morning glories), Cornaceae (dogwoods), and Crassulaceae (stonecrops, houseleeks)*

1. *Garrya elliptica* (Cornaceae)
2. *Ipomoea* sp., morning glory (Convolvulaceae)
3. *Cornus florida,* flowering dogwood (Cornaceae)
4. *Echeveria secunda* (Crassulaceae)
5. *Grammanthes gentianoides* (Crassulaceae)
6. *Sempervivum tectorum,* common houseleek (Crassulaceae)
7. *Sempervivum arboreum,* tree houseleek (Crassulaceae)
8. *Convolvulus minor,* crimson-violet (Convolvulaceae)
9. *Sedum carneum variegatum* (Crassulaceae)
10. *Ipomoea* sp., morning glory (Convolvulaceae)
11. *Convolvulus tricolor* (Convolvulaceae)

PAGE 82. *Crassulaceae (stonecrops, houseleeks)*

1. *Sedum sieboldi*
2. *Sedum sieboldi*
3. *Cotyledon chrysantha*
4. *Sedum pulchellum,* purple American stonecrop
5. *Sedum maximowiczi*
6. *Sedum maximowiczi*
7. *Sedum coeruleum*
8. *Sempervivum tectorum,* houseleek
9. *Sempervivum tectorum,* houseleek
10. *Sedum spectabile*
11. *Echeverie glauque*
12. *Echeverie glauque*
13. *Sempervivum arachnoideum laggeri*
14. Unidentified variety of crassula
15. *Cotyledon agavoides*

PAGE 83. *Cruciferae (cabbages, mustards)*

1. *Cheiranthus cheiri*
2. *Cheiranthus,* sp., wall flower
3. *Cheiranthus* sp., wall flower
4. Wall flower 'Forty Cockades'
5. Wall flower 'Forty Cockades'
6. Wall flower 'Emperor' or 'Perpetual'
7. Dwarf hybrid thlaspia
8. Gibraltar thlaspia
9. *Iberis umbellata*
10. *Iberis umbellata*
11. Large-flowered aethioneme or stone cress
12. *Alyssum saxatile variegatum*
13. Large-flowered aethioneme or stone cress
14. *Alyssum saxatile variegatum*
15. *Alyssum saxatile*

PAGE 84. *Cruciferae (cabbages, mustards)*

1. Candytuft
2. *Brassica oleracea palmifolia*
3. *Brassica* sp., striped and variegated kales
4. Rose of Jericho, moist
5. *Brassica oleracea crispa*
6. *Aethionema coridifolium*
7. *Cheiranthus,* sp., summer wall flower 'Excelsior'
8. Rose of Jericho, dry
9. *Aubretia* sp.
10. *Arabis alpina*
11. *Aethionema coridifolium*
12. *Arabis alpina*
13. *Arabis arenosa,* sand arabis
14. *Malcolmia* sp., Virginian stock
15. *Arabis albida,* white rock cress
16. *Arabis albida,* white rock cress

PAGE 85. *Cucurbitaceae (cucumbers, squashes, gourds)*

1. Green citron melon
2. Pear-shaped colocynth
3. *Bryonia laciniosa*
4. Pear gourd
5. Miniature colocynth
6. *Cucurbita lagenaria*
7. Vegetable marrow
8. *Cucurbita lagenaria,* dipper gourd
9. Turk's cap gourd
10. Cucumber
11. Various fancy gourds
12. Club gourd
13. Pilgrim's gourd

PAGE 86. *Cucurbitaceae (cucumbers, squashes, gourds)*

1. *Melothrie scabre*
2. Waterspout gourd
3. Wild cucumber with lobed leaves
4. Snake cucumber
5. Waterspout gourd
6. *Trichosanthes anguina*
7. Antilles cucumber
8. *Cucurbita pepo,* pumpkin
9. *Cucumis sativus,* common cucumber
10. *Cucurbita depressa striata*
11. *Cucurbita pepo,* leaf
12. *Cucurbita pepo,* male and female flowers

PAGE 87. *Cycadaceae*

1. *Cycas circinalis*
2. *Cycas rumphii,* sago palm
3. *Cycas rumphii,* sago palm
4. *Cycas rumphii,* sago palm
5. *Cycas revoluta*
6. *Cycas revoluta*
7. *Cycas revoluta*
8. *Zamia integrifolia*

PAGE 88. *Diapensiaceae (shortias), Dioscoreaceae (yams), Dipsaceae (teasels, scabiouses), and Droseraceae (sundews, Venus's-flytraps)*

1. *Scabiosa caucasica* (Dipsaceae)
2. Purple scabious (Dipsaceae)
3. Purple scabious (Dipsaceae)
4. *Dionaea muscipula,* Venus's-flytrap (Droseraceae)
5. *Scabiosa atropurpurea* (Dipsaceae)
6. *Galax aphylla,* with flower (Diapensiaceae)
7. *Dionaea muscipula,* Venus's-flytrap (Droseraceae)
8. *Dipsacus sylvestris,* wild teasel (Dipsaceae)
9. *Scabiosa palaestina* (Dipsaceae)
10. Small blue Japanese scabious (Dipsaceae)
11. Small blue Japanese scabious (Dipsaceae)
12. *Testudinaria elephantipes* (Dioscoreaceae)

PAGE 89. *Droseraceae (sundews, Venus's-flytraps) and carnivorous plants of other families*

1. Nepenthe or monkey-cup (Nepenthaceae)
2. (1) *Sarracenia melanorhoda,* (2) *Sarracenia formosa* (Sarraceniaceae)
3. *Cephalotus follicularis,* Australian pitcher plant (Saxifragaceae)

4. *Sarracenia drummondii* (Sarraceniaceae)
5. *Heliamphora* sp., Venezuela pitcher plant (Sarraceniaceae)
6. *Cephalotus follicularis,* Australian pitcher plant (Saxifragaceae)
7. *Sarracenia flava,* yellow flowered huntsman's horn (Sarraceniaceae)

PAGE 90. ***Droseraceaè (sundews, Venus's-flytraps) and carnivorous plants of other families***

1. *Nepenthes rafflesiana insignis* (Nepenthaceae)
2. *Drosera filiformis,* thread-leaved sundew (Droseraceae)
3. *Sarrancenia purpurea* (Sarraceniaceae)
4. *Darlingtonia californica,* California pitcher plant (Sarraceniaceae)
5. *Nepenthes northiana* (Nepenthaceae)

PAGE 91. ***Droseraceae (sundews, Venus's-flytraps) and carnivorous plants of other families***

1. *Drosophyllum lusitanicum* (Droseraceae)
2. *Nepenthes distillatoria* (Nepenthaceae)
3. Unidentified pitcher plant (Nepenthaceae)
4. *Sarracenia courti* (Sarraceniaceae)

PAGE 92. ***Droseraceae (sundews, Venus's-flytraps) and carnivorous plants of other families***

1. *Cephalotus follicularis,* Australian pitcher plant (Saxifragaceae)
2. *Dionaea muscipula,* Venus's-flytrap (Droseraceae)
3. *Aldrovandia vesiculosa* (Droseraceae)
4. *Nepenthes villosa, Sarracenia variolaris, Sarracenia lacinata,* and *Darlingtonia californica*
5. Round-leaved sundew (Droseraceae)
6. *Darlingtonia californica* (Sarraceniaceae)

PAGE 93. ***Ericaceae (azaleas, rhododendrons)***

1. *Rhododendron mucronatum*
2. *Rhododendron ponticum*
3. *Rhododendron taylori*
4. *Rhododendron indicum balsaminiflorum*

PAGE 94. ***Ericaceae (heaths, heathers, rhododendrons, azaleas)***

1. *Erica cerinthoides*
2. *Erica cerinthoides*
3. *Erica rubrocalyx*
4. *Erica fairieana*
5. *Cassiope tetragona*
6. *Erica cinerea,* pine-leaved heath
7. *Erica massonii*
8. *Erica vestita coccinea*
9. *Erica vestita coccinea*
10. *Erica hybrida*
11. *Erica grandiflora*
12. *Erica grandiflora*

PAGE 95. ***Ericaceae (heathers, rhododendrons)***

1. *Pernettya mucronata*
2. *Vaccinium vitis-idaea*
3. *Gaultheria procumbens,* wintergreen
4. *Gaylussacia resinosa,* black whortleberry
5. *Vaccinium corymbosum,* swamp huckleberry
6. *Gaultheria shallon*
7. *Oxydendrum arboreum,* sorrel tree
8. *Pernettya mucronata*

PAGE 96. ***Ericaceae (rhododendrons) and Euphorbiaceae***

1. *Euphorbia heterophylla* (Euphorbiaceae)
2. *Euphorbia variegata* (Euphorbiaceae)
3. *Ricinus cambogiensis* (Euphorbiaceae)
4. Poinsettia, double (Euphorbiaceae)
5. *Euphorbia variegata* (Euphorbiaceae)
6. *Rhododendron catawbiense* (Ericaceae)
7. *Ricinus sanguineus* (Euphorbiaceae)
8. *Rhododendron viscosum* (Ericaceae)
9. *Ricinus gibsoni* (Euphorbiaceae)

PAGE 97. ***Euphorbiaceae***

1. *Codiaeum pictum taeniosum*
2. Castor-oil plant from Zanzibar
3. *Codiaeum nestor*

PAGE 98. ***Euphorbiaceae***

1. *Codiaeum recurvifolium*
2. *Sapium sebiferum,* tallow tree
3. *Siphonia elastica*
4. *Codiaeum illustris*

PAGE 99. ***Fagaceae (oaks)***

1. *Quercus alba,* white oak
2. *Quercus rubra,* red oak
3. *Quercus alba,* white oak
4. *Quercus ilex,* evergreen or holm oak
5. *Quercus agrifolia,* California evergreen oak
6. *Quercus robur pedunculata,* penduncled or common oak
7. *Quercus cerris,* turkey or mossy-cupped oak
8. *Quercus robur sessilifora,* sessile-fruited oak
9. *Quercus robur pedunculata,* peduncled or common oak
10. *Quercus cerris,* turkey or mossy-cupped oak
11. *Quercus prinus palustris,* chestnut oak
12. *Quercus robur sessiliflora,* sessile-fruited oak

PAGE 100. ***Fagaceae (oaks)***

1. *Quercus pedunculata*
2. *Quercus robur sessiliflora,* sessile-fruited oak
3. *Quercus robur sessiliflora,* sessile-fruited oak
4. *Quercus sessiliflora*
5. Giant oak near Cranbourne Tower
6. *Quercus aegilops,* valonia oak
7. *Quercus pedunculata*
8. *Quercus robur pedunculata,* peduncled or common oak

PAGE 101. *Fagaceae (oaks, chestnuts, beeches)*

1. *Quercus tomentosa,* swamp white oak
2. *Quercus macrocarpa,* burr oak or over-cup white oak
3. *Quercus palustris,* marsh or pin oak
4. *Quercus obtusiloba,* post or rough white oak
5. *Quercus phellos,* willow oak
6. *Quercus virginiana,* live oak
7. *Quercus prinus monticol.,* rock chestnut oak
8. *Quercus ilicifolia,* bear or black scrub oak
9. William the Conqueror's oak in Windsor Great Park

PAGE 102. *Fagaceae (oaks, chestnuts, beeches)*

1. *Castanea sativa,* sweet or Spanish chestnut
2. Weeping beech
3. *Fagus sylvatica,* European beech
4. *Fagus sylvatica,* European beech
5. *Fagus sylvatica,* European beech
6. *Fagus sylvatica,* European beech
7. *Fagus sylvatica,* European beech
8. *Fagus sylvatica,* European beech
9. *Castanea dentata,* American chestnut
10. *Castanea sativa,* sweet or Spanish chestnut

PAGE 103. *Filices (ferns)*

1. Unidentified fern tree
2. *Struthiopteris germanica,* ostrich fern
3. *Cyathea dealbata*
4. *Athyrium filix foemina*
5. *Adiantum pedatum*
6. Arborescent ferns of Brazil

PAGE 104. *Filices (ferns)*

1. *Hemitelia speciosa*
2. *Davallia parallela*
3. Dead tree fern
4. *Todea barbara*
5. *Dicksonia berteroana*
6. *Nephrodium leuzeanum*
7. *Dicksonia antarctica,* tree fern
8. *Alsophila crinita,* Ceylon tree fern

PAGE 105. *Filices (ferns)*

1. *Polypodium heracleum*
2. *Dicksonia davallioides youngii*
3. *Nephrodium leuzeanum*
4. *Aspidium aculeatum*
5. *Asplenium fontanum*
6. Section of a tree fern
7. Stem of a tree fern
8. *Alsophila rebeccae*

PAGE 106. *Filices (Ferns)*

1. *Asplenium radicans*
2. *Gymnogramme decomposita*
3. *Nephrodium filix-mas*
4. *Osmunda regalis,* royal fern
5. *Davallia parvula*
6. Sporangia of the male fern
7. *Struthiopteris germanica,* ostrich fern
8. *Davallia tenuifolia veitchiana*

PAGE 107. *Filices (ferns)*

1. *Davallia fijensis*
2. *Polypodium dryopteris*
3. *Aspidium filix-mas*
4. *Cheilanthes clevelandi*
5. *Todea superba*
6. *Pteris quadriaurita argyraea*
7. *Polypodium angustatum*

PAGE 108. *Filices (ferns)*

1. *Asplenium trichomanes cristatum*
2. *Gymnogramme tartarea*
3. *Davallia repens*
4. *Gymnogramme elegantissima*

PAGE 109. *Filices (ferns)*

1. *Gymnogramme calomelanos peruviana*
2. *Nephrodium molle grandiceps*
3. *Polypodium lingua heteractis*
4. *Davallia heterophylla*
5. *Nephrodium fragrans*
6. *Gymnogramme andersoni*
7. *Nephrolepis refescens tripinnatifida*
8. *Adiantum capillus-veneris daphnites*

PAGE 110. *Filices (ferns)*

1. *Pellaea hastata*
2. *Scolopendrium vulgare erectum,* tall Hart's tongue
3. *Platycerium alcicorne*
4. *Camptosorus rhizophyllus,* walking leaf
5. *Scolopendrium vulgare crispum,* crisped Hart's tongue
6. *Asplenium ceterach*
7. *Osmunda regalis corymbifera*

PAGE 111. *Filices (ferns)*

1. *Scolopendrium vulgare kelwayi*
2. *Gleichenia circinata semi-vestita*
3. *Lindsaya reniformis*
4. *Gymnogramme cordata*
5. *Blechnum longifolium*
6. *Adiantum diaphanum*
7. *Adiantum novae-caledoniae*

PAGE 112. *Fucaceae (kelps, seaweeds) and other algae*

1. Unidentified seaweeds
2. *Porphyra vulgaris*
3. Kelp
4. *Fucus siliquosus* (Fucaceae)
5. *Thalassophyllum*
6. *Ulva latissima*

7. *Agarum gmelini*
8. *Fucus saccharinus* (Fucaceae)
9. *Fucus vesiculosus* (Fucaceae)

PAGE 113. *Fucaceae (kelps, seaweeds) and other algae*

1. *Fucus serratus* (Fucaceae)
2. *Laminaria digitata*
3. *Fucus bacciferus,* sargassum or swimming fucus (Fucaceae)
4. *Enteromorpha electa*
5. *Gemeines seegras*
6. Sea wrack

PAGE 114. *Fumariaceae and Gentianaceae*

1. *Corydalis nobilis* (Fumariaceae)
2. *Erythraea muhlenbergi* (Gentianaceae)
3. *Corydalis solida* (Fumariaceae)
4. Dicentra, with flower (Fumariaceae)
5. *Gentiana cruciata* (Gentianaceae)
6. *Gentiana pheumonanthe* (Gentianaceae)
7. Gentian flower 'Country Sabbath' (Gentianaceae)
8. Gentian 'Country Sabbath' (Gentianaceae)
9. *Corydalis bracteata* (Fumariaceae)
10. Dicentra 'Remarkable' (Fumariaceae)
11. Dicentra 'Remarkable' (Fumariaceae)
12. *Gentiana acaulis* (Gentianaeceae)

PAGE 115. *Geraniaceae (geraniums, pelargoniums)*

1. Zonal pelargoniums
2. Golden bronze geranium
3. Large-flowered geranium
4. Zonal geranium
5. Blood-red geranium
6. Cut-leaved geranium
7. Ivy-leaved geranium
8. Geranium 'Incomparable'
9. Unidentified geraniums
10. Geranium Mrs. Pollock

PAGE 116. *Gesneriaceae (gloxinias, gesneriads)*

1. Erect-flowered gloxinia
2. Various achimenes
3. *Tydaea hybrida nana*
4. *Gloxinia hybride erecta*
5. *Gesnera* sp.
6. *Gesnera refulgens*
7. *Gloxinia diversiflora*
8. *Stenogastra concinna*
9. *Koellikeria argyrostigma,* with flower
10. *Sinningia gesnerioides*

PAGE 117. *Gramineae (bamboos, other grasses)*

1. *Bambusa arundinàcea,* a variety of bamboo
2. *Panicum virgatum*
3. Unidentified variety of bamboo
4. *Panicum capillare*
5. *Elymus arenarius,* lyme grass
6. *Bambusa nana*
7. *Arundinaria simoni*

PAGE 118. *Gramineae (cultivated grains)*

1. *Hordeum jubatum*
2. *Zea mays,* Indian corn
3. *Zea mays,* corn
4. *Oryza sativa,* bearded rice variety
5. *Panicum* sp., *Sorghum* sp., and *Eleusine* sp.
6. Harvesting unidentified grain crop
7. *Oryza sativa,* beardless rice variety
8. *Saccharum officinarum*
9. *Sorghum vulgare saccharatum,* Chinese sugar cane

PAGE 119. *Gramineae (grasses, bamboos, cereals)*

1. *Bambusa falcata*
2. *Briza minor*
3. *Bambusa aurea,* golden bamboo
4. *Tricholaena* sp.
5. *Festuca glauca,* fescue grass
6. Pampas grass
7. *Saccharum aegyptiacum*

PAGE 120. *Gramineae (grasses)*

1. *Arundo donax*
2. *Erianthus ravennae*
3. *Panicum plicatum variegatum*
4. *Lagurus ovatus*
5. *Saccharum aegyptiacum*
6. *Phleum pratense,* Timothy grass
7. Large-leaved gymnothrix or 'Lady's Hair' grass
8. *Gynerium argenteum,* pampas grass

PAGE 121. *Gramineae (grasses)*

1. *Teosinte,* euchlaena
2. *Zea japonica variegata,* ornamental corn
3. *Dactylis* sp., orchard grass
4. *Gynerium argenteum,* pampas grass
5. *Bromus brizaeformis*
6. *Zea mays variegata,* a variety of corn
7. *Eulalia zebrina*
8. *Pennisetum latifolium,* gymnothrix

PAGE 122. *Gramineae (grasses)*

1. Honduras variety grain sorghum
2. *Anthoxanthum odoratum*
3. *Sorghum halepense*
4. *Hordeum nodosum*

PAGE 123. *Gramineae (grasses)*

1. *Paspalum ovatum*
2. *Phleum pratense,* Timothy

PAGE 124. *Gramineae (grasses)*

1. Bearded darnel

2. Bermuda grass
3. Blue grass
4. Buffalo grass
5. *Stipa viridula,* bunch grass
6. *Ereocoma cuspidata,* bunch grass
7. Chess
8. Crab grass
9. Gama grass
10. Great bunch grass
11. Gramma grass
12. Guinea grass
13. Herd's grass
14. Johnson grass
15. Kentucky blue grass
16. Lyme grass
17. Meadow fescue
18. Meadow foxtail
19. Nimble will
20. Orchard grass
21. Porcupine grass
22. Quick grass
23. Red top
24. Red-topped buffalo grass
25. Rye grass
26. Seneca grass
27. Sheep's fescue
28. Small reed grass
29. Squirrel-tail grass
30. Velvet grass
31. Vernal grass
32. Wood grass

PAGE 125. ***Gymnospermae: Cupressaceae (junipers, cypress, cedars) and Pinaceae***

1. *Pseudolarix kaempferi,* golden pine (Pinaceae)
2. *Juniperus communis hibernica* (Cupressaceae)
3. *Juniperus communis,* common juniper (Cupressaceae)
4. Cypress, Cupressaceae
5. *Thuja occidentalis,* American arborvitae, white cedar (Cupressaceae)
6. *Abies balsamea,* Balsam fir

PAGE 126. ***Gymnospermae: Pinaceae (pines, spruces) and Cupressaceae (cedars)***

1. *Thuja occidentalis sibirica,* Siberian arborvitae (Cupressaceae)
2. *Pinus aristata,* cone, a species of pine (Pinaceae)
3. *Cupressus lawsoniana* (Cupressaceae)
4. *Pinus cembra* (Pinaceae)
5. *Picea engelmannii,* Engelman spruce (Pinaceae)
6. *Picea glanca,* white spruce (Pinaceae)

PAGE 127. ***Gymnospermae: Pinaceae (pines, spruces, firs), Taxaceae (yews), and Taxodiacene (cypress)***

1. *Taxus baccata dovastoni,* a variety of yew (Taxaceae)
2. Unidentified variety of yew (Taxaceae)
3. *Abies anadensis,* hemlock fir (Pinaceae)
4. *Taxus baccata* (Taxaceae)
5. *Taxodium distichum,* bald cypress cone (Taxodiaceae)
6. *Pinus pungens* (Pinaceae)
7. *Abies mertensiana* (Pinaceae)

PAGE 128. ***Gymnospermae: Pinaceae (spruces, pines), Cupressaceae (arborvitae, cedars), and Taxodiaceae (cryptomeria)***

1. *Thuja gigantea* (Cupressaceae)
2. *Picea excelsa,* Norway spruce (Pinaceae)
3. *Pinus nigra laricio* (Pinaceae)
4. *Picea excelsa,* Norway spruce (Pinaceae)
5. *Biota orientalis macrocarpa,* Oriental arborvitae (Cupressaceae)
6. *Cryptomeria elegans* (Taxodiaceae)
7. *Picea smithiana* (Pinaceae)

PAGE 129. ***Gymnospermae: Pinaceae (pines), Cupressaceae (cypress), Taxaceae (torreya), and Taxodiaceae***

1. *Pinus pinea,* stone pine (Pinaceae)
2. *Cunninghamia sikensis,* with cone (Taxodiaceae)
3. *Cupressus horizontalis,* spreading cypress (Cupressaceae)
4. *Torreya taxifolia,* Florida torreya (Taxaceae)
5. *Picea mariana,* black spruce (Pinaceae)
6. *Cryptomeria japonica,* Japanese cedar (Taxodiaceae)
7. *Pinus sylvestris fastigiata* (Pinaceae)

PAGE 130. ***Gymnospermae: Pinaceae (larches, spruces, pines), Cupressaceae (junipers), and Taxodiaceae (sequoias)***

1. *Picea excelsa,* Norway spruce (Pinaceae)
2. Irish juniper (Cupressaceae)
3. *Sequoia gigantea,* giant sequoia (Taxodiaceae)
4. *Abies smithiana,* Himalayan spruce (Pinaceae)
5. Swedish juniper (Cupressaceae)
6. Unidentified conifer
7. *Picea pectinata compacta,* oblate dwarf silver fir (Pinaceae)
8. *Larix europa* (Pinaceae)
9. *Pinus flexilis* (Pinaceae)
10. *Pinus australis* (Pinaceae)

PAGE 131. ***Gymnospermae: Pinaceae (pines, cedars) and Taxodiaceae (sequoias, sciadopitys)***

1. Italian or stone pine (Pinaceae)
2. *Cedrus libani,* cedar of Lebanon (Pinaceae)
3. *Pinus strobus,* white pine (Pinaceae)
4. *Sciadopitys verticillata* (Taxodiaceae)
5. *Sciadopitys verticillata* (Taxodiaceae)
6. *Sequoia gigantea,* giant redwood (Taxodiaceae)

PAGE 132. *Gymnospermae: Pinaceae (pines, firs), Araucariaceae (chili pines), Taxaceae (yews), Cupressaceae (arborvitae), and Ginkgoales (ginkos)*

1. *Araucaria araucana,* Chili pine (Araucariaceae)
2. *Biota orientalis,* Oriental arborvitae (Cupressaceae)
3. *Pinus sylvestris,* Scotch pine (Pinaceae)
4. Yew tree at Derbyshire, England (Taxaceae)
5. Unidentified variety of fir (Pinaceae)
6. *Podocarpus japonica*
7. *Ginkgo biloba* (order: Ginkgoales, the only species in the order; there is no family)

PAGE 133. *Gymnospermae: Pinaceae (pines) and Taxaceae (yews)*

1. *Pinus sylvestris,* Scotch pine (Pinaceae)
2. *Pinus cembra* (Pinaceae)
3. *Pinus strobus,* white pine (Pinaceae)
4. *Picea mariana,* black spruce (Pinaceae)
5. Dwarf pines (Pinaceae)
6. *Pinus strobus,* white pine (Pinaceae)
7. *Pinus pinaster,* pinaster or cluster pine (Pinaceae)
8. Unidentified variety of pine cone (Pinaceae)
9. *Taxus baccata,* common yew (Taxaceae)

PAGE 134. *Gymnospermae: Pinaceae (pines, larches, firs, spruces)*

1. *Cedrus libani,* cedar of Lebanon (Pinaceae)
2. Common larch (Pinaceae)
3. *Picea pectinata,* silver fir (Pinaceae)
4. Old Scotch fir (Pinaceae)
5. *Pseudotsuga menziesii,* Douglas fir (Pinaceae)
6. *Cedrus libani,* cedar of Lebanon (Pinaceae)
7. *Larix europaea,* larch (Pinaceae)
8. *Cedrus libani,* cedar of Lebanon (Pinaceae)
9. *Picea abies,* Norway spruce (Pinaceae)

PAGE 135. *Hydrophyllaceae*

1. *Whitlavia grandiflora*
2. *Whitlavia grandiflora*
3. *Wigandia caracasana*
4. *Phacelia viscida,* with flower
5. *Nemophila maculata*
6. *Hydrolea spinosa*
7. *Wigandia vigieri*
8. *Wigandia urens*

PAGE 136. *Iridaceae (irises)*

1. Unidentified variety of iris
2. *Iris susiana*
3. *Iris germanica*
4. Unidentified variety of iris
5. *Iris susiana*
6. *Iris hispanica*
7. *Iris kempferi*

PAGE 137. *Iridaceae (irises)*

1. *Iris histrio*
2. Unidentified variety of iris
3. *Iris iberica*
4. Unidentified variety of iris
5. *Iris kempferi*
6. *Iris anglica*
7. *Iris variegata*
8. *Iris caucasica*
9. *Iris germanica,* German iris
10. *Iris alata*

PAGE 138. *Iridaceae (irises)*

1. *Iris ruthenica*
2. *Iris chamaeiris,* miniature iris
3. *Iris florentina,* Florentine iris
4. *Iris chamaeiris,* miniature iris
5. Hybrid iris
6. *Iris pumila*
7. *Iris pumila*
8. *Iris versicolor*
9. *Iris kempferi,* double flowers
10. *Iris xiphioide*
11. *Iris persica*

PAGE 139. *Iridaceae (irises)*

1. *Tigridia pavonia,* tiger flower
2. *Tigridia pavonia*
3. Scarlet schizostylis
4. *Tigridia meleagris*
5. *Tigridia pavonia*
6. *Babiana stricta rubrocyanea*
7. *Morea pavonia*
8. *Ixia* sp.
9. *Tritonia pottsii*
10. *Tigridia pavonia*
11. *Tritonia pottsii*
12. *Ixia maculata*
13. *Sisyrinchium grandiflorum*

PAGE 140. *Iridaceae (irises, crocuses)*

1. *Crocus imperati*
2. *Crocus boryi*
3. *Crocus iridiflorus*
4. *Freesia refracta alba*
5. *Crocus vernus*
6. *Crocus nudiflorus*
7. *Crocus versicolor*

PAGE 141. *Iridaceae (irises, gladiolus)*

1. *Gladiolus saundersoni*
2. *Gladiolus cardinalis,* with flower
3. Gladiolus 'Triumph of Paris'
4. Lemoine gladiolus
5. Nancy gladiolus
6. Gladiolus surprise
7. Common gladiolus

8. Hybrid Gandavensis gladiolus
9. *Gladiolus brenchleyensis*
10. *Hybrid Glabiolus*

PAGE 142. *Iridaceae (irises) and Labiatae (mints, sages)*

1. *Freesia refracta alba* (Iridaceae)
2. *Sparaxis* sp. (Iridaceae)
3. *Glechoma hederacea variegata* (Labiatae)
4. *Montbretia pottsi* (Iridaceae)
5. *Tritonia aurea* (Iridaceae)
6. Unidentified gladiolus (Iridaceae)
7. *Salvia officinalis,* sage (Labiatae)
8. *Montbretia crocusmiaeflora* (Iridaceae)
9. *Coleus* sp. (Labiatae)
10. Silver sage (Labiatae)

PAGE 143. *Labiatae (mints, sages) and Leguminosae (peas, beans, clovers)*

1. Early dwarf silver sage (Labiatae)
2. Early dwarf silver sage (Labiatae)
3. *Coleus hybride* (Labiatae)
4. *Teucrium chamaedrys* (Labiatae)
5. *Gardoquia betonicoides, Cedronella mexicana* (Labiatae)
6. *Physostegia virginiana* (Labiatae)
7. Nankin perilla with jagged leaves
8. *Dracocephalum grandiflorum,* dragon's head, with flower (Labiatae)
9. *Salvia pratensis,* meadow sage (Labiatae)
10. *Salvia argentea,* silver sage (Labiatae)
11. *Leonurus cardiaca,* motherwort (Labiatae)
12. *Perilla nankinensis* (Labiatae)
13. *Trifolium pratense perenne,* mammoth clover (Leguminosae)
14. *Trifolium repens,* white clover (Leguminosae)
15. *Trifolium repens,* white clover (Leguminosae)

PAGE 144. *Leeaceae and Leguminosae (legumes, peas, beans)*

1. *Wistaria chinensis* (Leguminosae)
2. *Faba vulgaris,* broad bean plant (Leguminosae)
3. *Phaseolus multiflorus,* runner or climbing kidney bean (Leguminosae)
4. *Cytisus scoparius* (Leguminosae)
5. *Ulex europaeus, furze or gorse* (Leguminosae)
6. Unidentified variety of clover (Leguminosae)
7. *Clianthus formosus* (Leguminosae)
8. *Leea amabilis* (Leeaceae)

PAGE 145. *Leguminosae (peas, beans, clovers)*

1. *Lathyrus odoratus,* sweet peas
2. White everlasting pea
3. *Astragalus monspessulanus*
4. *Lathyrus latifolius*
5. *Astragalus monspessulanus*
6. *Lathyrus odoratus,* sweet peas
7. *Lathyrus odoratus,* dwarf sweet pea
8. *Dolichos lablab,* hyacinth bean

PAGE 146. *Leguminosae (peas, beans)*

1. *Erythrina indica parcelli*
2. *Erythrina,* sp. coral plant
3. *Lupinus mutabilis*
4. *Lupinus hartwegi,* annual lupine
5. *Geinsta canariensis*
6. *Medicago* sp., alfalfa or lucerne

PAGE 147. *Leguminosae (peas, beans)*

1. Hardenbergia with oval leaves
2. *Camoensia maxima*
3. *Vicia sativa,* vetch
4. *Genista tinctoria,* rock broom or woodwaxen
5. *Genista tinctoria,* rock broom or woodwaxen
6. *Genista tinctoria,* rock broom or woodwaxen
7. *Erythrina vespertilio*

PAGE 148. *Leguminosae (peas, beans)*

1. *Mesquite* sp.
2. *Mimosa pudica*
3. *Dipterix odorata,* tonqua bean
4. *Robinia hispida*
5. *Tamarindus indica,* tamarind
6. *Sophora japonica pendula,* winter state
7. *Scorpiurus Vermiculata*
8. *Cassia marylandica*

PAGE 149. *Liliaceae (lilies)*

1. *Lilium candidum*
2. Easter lilies
3. *Atrosanguineum,* bulb
4. *Lilium martagon,* Turk's cap lily
5. Unidentified lilies
6. Parvum lily
7. *Lilium longiflorum*
8. *Lilium elegans*

PAGE 150. *Liliaceae (lilies)*

1. Bermuda Easter lily
2. *Lilium speciosum*
3. *Lilium martagon*
4. Unidentified variety of lily
5. *Lilium brownii*
6. *Lilium washingtonianum*
7. *Lilium concolor*
8. *Lilium auratum vittatum*
9. *Lilium auratum*
10. *Lilium candidum*

PAGE 151. *Liliaceae (lilies)*

1. Unidentified variety of lily
2. *Lilium hansoni*

3. *Lilium auratum*
4. *Lilium washingtonianum*
5. *Aloe socotrina*
6. *Lilium longiflorum*
7. *Aloe socotrina*
8. *Lilium krameri* or *japonicum*
9. *Lilium martagon lancifolium*
10. Unidentified variety of lilies

PAGE 152. *Liliaceae (lilies)*

1. *Chionodoxa lucillae*
2. *Colchicum parkinsoni*
3. *Brodiaea californica*
4. *Bulbocodium trigynum*
5. *Asphodele subalpin*, with flower
6. California tiger lily
7. *Calochortus venustus*, mariposa lily
8. *Calochortus* sp.
9. *Paradisea liliastrum major*, giant St. Bruno lily

PAGE 153. *Liliaceae (lilies)*

1. *Erythronium dens-canis*, dog-tooth violet, European fawn-lily
2. *Colchicum* sp.
3. *Ememurus elwesii*
4. *Colchicum montanum*
5. *Convallaria majalis*, lily of the valley
6. *Cyclobothea flava*
7. *Colchicum autumnale*
8. *Eremurus olgae*, with flower
9. *Convallaria majalis*, lily of the valley

PAGE 154. *Liliaceae (lilies)*

1. *Fritillaria pallidiflora*
2. *Fritillaria imperialis*, crown imperial
3. *Fritillaria aurea*
4. *Funkia lancifolia*
5. *Fritillaria recurva*
6. *Funkia subcordata*, plantain lily
7. *Funkia grandiflora*
8. *Funkia ovata*
9. *Erythronium dens-canis*, large white variety
10. *Fritillaria meleagris*
11. *Funkia sieboldiana*

PAGE 155. *Liliaceae (lilies)*

1. *Ornithogalum arabicum*
2. White Roman hyacinthus
3. *Kniphofia macowani*
4. *Lilium tigrinum*
5. Feathered hyacinthus
6. *Polygonatum* sp.
7. *Galtonia candicans*
8. *Kniphofia aloides nobilis*
9. *Kniphofia aloides nobilis*
10. *Lapageria* sp.
11. *Sansevieria* sp.
12. *Ornithogalum aureum*
13. *Hemerocallis fulva*
14. *Galtonia candicans*
15. *Muscari moschatum majus*, musk hyacinthus
16. *Ornithogalum aureum*
17. *Hyacinthus candicans*

PAGE 156. *Liliaceae (lilies)*

1. *Tritoma grandiflora major*
2. *Veratrum album*
3. *Scilla clusii*
4. *Scilla ughii*
5. *Scilla peruviana*
6. *Scilla agreable*, with flower
7. *Tricyrtis hirta*
8. *Triteleia uniflora*
9. Unidentified variety of fritillarias
10. *Scilla patula*

PAGE 157. *Liliaceae (lilies, hyacinths)*

1. Double-flowered Holland hyacinths
2. Double-flowered garden hyacinth
3. Simple-flowered Holland hyacinths
4. Unidentified variety of hyacinth
5. *Hyacinthus* sp.
6. *Hyacinthus* sp.
7. *Hyacinthus* sp.
8. *Hyacinthus* sp.

PAGE 158. *Liliaceae (tulips)*

1. Parrot tulips
2. *Tulipa greigii*, Turkestan tulip
3. *Tulipa greigii*, Turkestan tulip
4. Parrot tulips
5. Different varieties of tulips
6. Unidentified variety of tulip
7. Unidentified variety of tulip
8. Celestial star tulip
9. *Tulipa greigii*, Turkestan tulip
10. *Tulipa acuminata*, with flower
11. Double scarlet tournesol tulip

PAGE 159. *Liliaceae (tulips)*

1. *Tulipa gesneriana*
2. Parrot tulip
3. Tulip 'Duke of Thol'
4. Double flowered tulip
5. Unidentified variety of tulip
6. Single tulip
7. Single tulip
8. *Tulipa greigii*, Turkestan tulip
9. *Tulipa billietiana*
10. *Tulipa gesneriana*
11. Double show tulips

PAGE 160. *Linaceae, Lythraceae, Loasaceae, Lobeliaceae, and Lycopodiaceae*

1. *Blumenbachia chuquitensis* (Loasaceae)
2. *Linum grandiflorum*, Algerian flax (Linaceae)
3. Hybrid lobelia (Lobeliaceae)
4. *Mentzelia ornata* (Loasaceae)

5. *Lagerstroemia indica,* crape myrtle (Lythraceae)
6. Lobelie vivace hybride (Lobeliaceae)
7. *Selaginella involvens variegata* (Lycopodiaceae)

PAGE 161. ***Magnoliaceae (magnolias) and Malvaceae (mallows)***

1. *Magnolia conspicua* (Magnoliaceae)
2. *Liriodendron tulipifera,* tulip tree (Magnoliaceae)
3. *Magnolia grandiflora* (Magnoliaceae)
4. *Magnolia glauca,* laurel magnolia (Magnoliaceae)
5. *Magnolia conspicua* (Magnoliaceae)
6. *Magnolia glauca,* laurel magnolia (Magnoliaceae)
7. Unidentified variety of magnolia (Magnoliaceae)
8. *Hibiscus moscheutos* (Malvaceae)
9. Ketmia Manihot hibiscus with jagged leaves (Malvaceae)
10. *Abutilon* sp. (Malvaceae)
11. *Gossypium herbaceum,* a cotton ball (Malvaceae)
12. *Hibiscus trionum* (Malvaceae)
13. *Gossypium herbaceum,* cotton (Malvaceae)

PAGE 162. ***Malvaceae (mallows)***

1. *Sphaeralcea rivularis*
2. *Hibiscus syriacus*
3. *Hibiscus roseus*
4. Snow-white hibiscus, with flower
5. *Hibiscus rosa-sinenis*
6. *Lavatera arborea variegata*

PAGE 163. ***Marantaceae (arrowroots)***

1. *Stromanthe sanguinea*
2. *Calathea zebrina*
3. *Calathea zebrina*
4. *Thalia dealbata*
5. *Calathea veitchii*
6. *Thalia dealbata*
7. *Calathea massangeana*

PAGE 164. ***Marantaceae (arrowroots), Melastomataceae (melastomas), Meliaceae (mahoganies), and Moraceae (figs, mulberries)***

1. *Sphaerogyne* sp. (Melastomataceae)
2. Mahogany flower (Meliaceae)
3. *Melastoma malabathricum* (Melastomataceae)
4. Mahogany (Meliaceae)
5. *Sonerila* sp. (Melastomataceae)
6. Fig 'Osborn's prolific' (Moraceae)
7. *Phrynium variegatum* (Marantaceae)
8. Fig of *Ficus carica* (Moraceae)

PAGE 165. ***Moraceae (figs, mulberries)***

1. *Ficus elastica,* Indian rubber plant
2. *Ficus elastica,* Indian rubber plant
3. *Ficus cooperi*
4. *Maclura pomifera,* osage orange
5. *Broussonetia papyrifera,* paper mulberry
6. *Ficus exsculpta*

PAGE 166. ***Musaceae (bananas)***

1. *Musa cavendishii*
2. *Musa superba*
3. *Musa rosaceae,* plantain
4. Banana
5. *Musa rosaceae,* plantain
6. *Musa rosaceae,* plantain
7. *Musa ensete*
8. *Musa rosacea,* plantain
9. *Musa textilis,* manila hemp tree

PAGE 167. ***Myrsinaceae (ardisias) and Myrtaceae (myrtles, eucalyptuses)***

1. *Ardisia picta* (Myrsinaceae)
2. *Callistemon speciosus* (Myrtaceae)
3. *Psidium cattleyanum* (Myrtaceae)
4. *Myrtus communis,* common myrtle (Myrtaceae)
5. *Myrtus ugni* (Myrtaceae)

PAGE 168. ***Nymphaeaceae (water lilies) and water plants and water grasses of other families***

1. *Nymphaea odorata,* sweet-scented water lily (Nymphaeaceae)
2. *Nymphaea odorata,* sweet-scented water lily (Nymphaeaceae)
3. *Nelumbium luteum,* nelumbo (Nymphaeaceae)
4. *Nuphar advena,* yellow pond lily (Nymphaeaceae)
5. Egyptian lotus
6. *Nymphaea odorata,* sweet-scented water lily (Nymphaeaceae)
7. *Nuphar luteum (Nymphaeaceae)*
8. *Victoria regia,* the giant water lily

PAGE 169. ***Nymphaeaceae (water lilies) and water plants and water grasses of other families***

1. *Nymphaea lotus* (Nymphaeaceae)
2. *Nelumbium luteum nelumbo* (Nymphaeaceae)
3. *Brasenia peltata,* water shield (Nymphaeaceae)
4. *Sagittaria sagittifolia,* double-flowered arrowhead (Alismataceae)
5. *Lotus* sp. (Nymphaeaceae)
6. *Nympheae lutea* (Nymphaeaceae)
7. *Nelumbium,* sacred lotus (Nymphaeaceae)
8. *Nuphar advena* (Nymphaeaceae)
9. *Vallisneria spiralis* (Hydrocharitaceae)

PAGE 170. ***Nymphaeaceae (water lilies) and water plants and water grasses of other families***

1. *Sagittaria sagittifolia,* double-flowered arrowhead (Alismataceae)
2. *Acorus calamus* (Araceae)

3. *Aponogeton distachyon,* cape pond weed (Aponogetonaceae)
4. *Sagittaria sagittifolia,* double-flowered arrowhead (Alismataceae)
5. *Aponogeton spathaceum* (Aponogetonaceae)
6. *Aponogeton distachyon,* with flower (Aponogetonaceae)
7. *Scirpus* sp., club rushes (Cyperaceae)
8. *Typha latifolia,* cattail or reed mace (Typhaceae)
9. *Typha latifolia,* cattail or reed mace (Typhaceae)

PAGE 171. *Nymphaeaceae (water lilies) and water plants and water grasses of other families*

1. Unidentified species
2. *Typha latifolia,* cattail or reed mace (Typhaceae)
3. *Cyperus longus* (Cyperaceae)
4. *Typha* sp. (Typhaceae)
5. Bulrush (Typhaceae)
6. *Cyperus alternifolius* (Cyperaceae)
7. *Cyperus papyrus,* Egyptian papyrus (Cyperaceae)

PAGE 172. *Oleaceae (olives, ashes)*

1. *Fraxinus excelsior,* European ash
2. *Fraxinus ornus,* manna ash
3. *Fraximus* sp., ash tree
4. Remilly ash
5. Lilac 'Charles X'
6. *Fraxinus excelsior,* European ash, in winter state
7. *Osmanthus fragrans*
8. *Fraxinus excelsior,* European ash

PAGE 173. *Oleaceae (olives, lilacs)*

1. *Syringa japonica*
2. *Jasminum officinale affine*
3. *Forsythia suspensa*
4. *Jasminum grandiflorum*
5. *Ligustrum lucidum coriaceum*
6. *Chionanthus retusa*

PAGE 174. *Oleaceae (olives) and Onagraceae (evening primroses)*

1. *Syringa chinensis* (Oleaceae)
2. *Godetia* sp., tall variety (Onagraceae)
3. *Oenothera taraxacifolia* (Onagraceae)
4. *Oenothera macrocarpa,* Missouri evening primrose (Onagraceae)
5. Narrow-stalked evening primrose (Onagraceae)
6. *Clarkia elegans* (Onagraceae)
7. *Clarkia elegans* (Onagraceae)
8. Oenothera 'Lady Albemarle' (Onagraceae)
9. *Godetia whitney* (Onagraceae)
10. *Clarkia elegans* (Onagraceae)
11. *Jasminum hirsutum* (Oleaceae)
12. Unidentified variety of oenothera (Onagraceae)
13. Clarkia 'Mrs. Langtry' (Onagraceae)

PAGE 175. *Onagraceae (evening primroses, fuchsias)*

1. Fuchsia 'Day Dream'
2. *Fuchsia fulgens*
3. Unidentified variety of fuchsia
4. *Fuchsia coccinea*
5. Fuchsia 'Gipsy Queen'
6. Fuchsia 'Earl of Beaconsfield'
7. *Godetia lindleyana*
8. Fuchsia 'Beauty of Exeter'
9. *Fuchsia apetala*
10. Fuchsia 'Miss Lucy Finnis'
11. Unidentified variety of godetia
12. *Fuchsia erecta superba*

PAGE 176. *Orchidaceae (orchids)*

1. *Brassia lanceana*
2. *Brassia maculata*
3. *Cattleya citrina*
4. *Cymbidium giganteum*
5. Unidentified variety of orchid
6. *Cattleya trianae*
7. Unidentified variety of orchid
8. *Coelogyne cristata*
9. *Coelogyne lagenaria*

PAGE 177. *Orchidaceae (orchids)*

1. *Cymbidium eburneum*
2. *Cypripedium spectabile*
3. Unidentified variety of orchid
4. Unidentified variety of orchid
5. *Cypripedium oenanthum superbum*
6. *Cypripedium macranthum,* Siberian lady's slipper
7. *Cypripedium fairieanum*
8. *Cypripedium concolor*

PAGE 178. *Orchidaceae (orchids)*

1. *Cypripedium barbatum*
2. Unidentified orchid
3. *Cypripedium spectabile*
4. *Cypripedium selligerum*
5. *Cypripedium macranthum,* Siberian lady's slipper
6. *Miltonia spectabilis*

PAGE 179. *Orchidaceae (orchids)*

1. *Dendrobium superbiens*
2. Unidentified variety of orchid
3. *Miltonia warscewiczii*
4. *Miltonia phalaenopsis*
5. *Oncidium serratum*
6. *Maxillaria picta*

PAGE 180. *Orchidaceae (orchids)*

1. *Angraecum eburneum*
2. *Oncidium sphacelatum*

PAGE 181. *Orchidaceae (orchids)*

1. *Odontoglossum cirrhosum*
2. Unidentified variety of orchid
3. *Masdevallia tovarensis*
4. *Odontoglossum rossii*
5. *Laelia albida*
6. *Odontoglossum rossii*
7. *Maxillaria venusta*

PAGE 182. *Orchidaceae (orchids)*

1. *Orchis maculata*
2. *Masdevallia lindeni*
3. *Laelia anceps*
4. *Phalaenopsis esmeralda*
5. *Phalaenopsis schilleriana*
6. *Odontoglossum crispum*

PAGE 183. *Orchidaceae (orchids)*

1. *Trichopilia suavis*
2. Unidentified variety of orchid
3. Unidentified variety of orchid
4. Unidentified variety of orchid
5. *Trichopilia suavis*
6. *Selenipedium sedeni*
7. Unidentified variety of orchid
8. *Selenipedium schlimii*

PAGE 184. *Orchidaceae (orchids)*

1. *Chysis chelsoni*
2. *Vanda caerulescens*
3. *Dendrobium farmeri*
4. *Orchis fusca*
5. *Oncidium excavatum*
6. *Cypripedium calceolus*, English lady's slipper

PAGE 185. *Orchidaceae (orchids)*

1. *Zygopetalum rollissoni*
2. *Stanhopea insignis*
3. *Zygopetalum sedeni*
4. *Peristeria cerina*
5. *Peristeria cerina*
6. *Vanda tricolor patersoni*

PAGE 186. *Oxalidaceae (oxalis) and Paeoniaceae (peonies)*

1. Paeony 'Lady Bramwell' (Paeoniaceae)
2. Unidentified variety of peony (Paeoniaceae)
3. *Paeonia tenuifolia* (Paeoniaceae)
4. Unidentified variety of peony (Paeoniaceae)
5. *Oxalis versicolor* (Oxalidaceae)
6. *Oxalis cernua plena* (Oxalidaceae)
7. Oxalis 'Grand Duchess' (Oxalidaceae)
8. *Paeonia officinalis*, common paeony (Paeoniaceae)
9. *Oxalis lutea major* (Oxalidaceae)

PAGE 187. *Palmaceae (palms)*

1. *Phoenix dactylifera*
2. Wax palm
3. *Geonoma gracilis*
4. *Livistona australis*
5. Coconut palm and other tropical fruit trees
6. *Archontophoenix cunninghamiana*

PAGE 188. *Palmaceae (palms)*

1. *Latania borbonica*, bourbon palm
2. *Livistona chinensis*
3. *Jubaea spectabilis*, coquita palm
4. *Areca lutescens*
5. Fruits of date palm and two other palms

PAGE 189. *Palmaceae (palms)*

1. *Pritchardia vuylsteriana*
2. *Hedyscepe canterburyana*
3. *Chamaerops excelsa*, hardy palm
4. Nut of the wine-bearing mauritia palm
5. *Verschaffeltia splendida*
6. *Phoenix reclinata*
7. *Chamaedorea sartorii*
8. Wine-bearing maurita palm

PAGE 190. *Palmaceae (palms)*

1. *Hyphaene ruineensis*, ntefa palm
2. Coquilla nut palm
3. *Seaforthia elegans*
4. *Caryota sobolifera*
5. *Hyphaene thebaica*, doom palm of Egypt
6. Coconut
7. Fruit of the oil palm
8. Branch of the coconut palm
9. Coconut palm
10. *Arenga saccharifera*, sugar palm

PAGE 191. *Palmaceae (palms)*

1. *Livistona chinensis*, *Latania borbonica*
2. Coquilla nut
3. *Hyphaene thebaica*
4. *Areca baueri*
5. *Borassus flabelliformis*, palmyra palm
6. *Sabal palmetto*, cabbage palmetto
7. *Kentia belmoreana*
8. *Attalea funifera*, piassata palm
9. *Elaeis guineensis*, oil palm
10. *Hyphaene thebaica*, doom palm

PAGE 192. *Palmaceae (palms)*

1. *Elaeis guineensis*
2. *Hyphaene thebaica*, doom palm

PAGE 193. *Palmaceae (palms)*

1. *Raphia vinifera*
2. Fruit of lodoxia of the Seychelles

3. Stalk of lodoxia of the Seychelles
4. Lodoxia of the Seychelles
5. Bifurcated palm leaf
6. *Mauritia flexuosa*

PAGE 194. *Palmaceae (palms)*

1. *Thrinax radiata*
2. *Rhapis flabelliformis*
3. *Trachycarpus excelsus*
4. *Livistona australis*
5. Palmetto
6. *Cocos weddeliana*

PAGE 195. *Palmaceae (palms)*

1. *Hyophorbe verschaffeltii*
2. *Chamaerops fortunei*
3. *Cocos australis*
4. Unidentified palm
5. *Thrinax argentea*
6. *Chamaerops humilis*

PAGE 196. *Palmaceae (palms) and Pandanaceae (screw pines)*

1. *Pandanus houlletii* (Pandanaceae)
2. Screw pine (Pandanaceae)
3. *Pandanus furcatus* (Pandanaceae)
4. *Pandanus odoratissimus* (Pandanaceae)
5. *Pandanus candelabrum* (Pandanaceae)
6. *Pandanus candelabrum variegata* (Pandanaceae)
7. *Pandanus utilis* (Pandanaceae)
8. *Calamus rotang*, rattan palm (Palmaceae)
9. *Pandanus javanicus* (Pandanaceae)

PAGE 197. *Papaveraceae (poppies)*

1. Tulip poppy, with flower
2. *Argemone mexicana*
3. *Glaucium* sp., horned poppy
4. Corn-poppy with large single flower
5. *Papaver murselli*
6. *Papaver danebrog*
7. Oriental poppy
8. *Papaver somniferum*, opium poppy
9. *Eschscholzia californica*, California poppy
10. *Eschscholzia californica*, with flower
11. *Bocconia cordata*, plume poppy

PAGE 198. *Papaveraceae (poppies)*

1. *Eschscholzia californica*
2. *Glaucium* sp.
3. Farquhar's superb Iceland poppies, with flower
4. *Meconopsis wallichi*, blue Himalayan poppy
5. *Papaver rhoeas*
6. *Papaver umbrosum*
7. *Papaver orientale*
8. Tulip poppy
9. Hooker's single mixed poppy
10. Poppy, double white tipped with rose

PAGE 199. *Passifloraceae (passion flowers)*

1. *Passiflora caerulea*
2. *Passiflora caerulea*
3. *Passiflora* 'John Spalding'
4. *Passiflora caerulea*
5. *Passiflora antioquiensis*
6. *Passiflora caerulea*

PAGE 200. *Piperaceae (peppers)*

1. *Piper nigrum*, black pepper (Piperaceae)
2. *Proboscidea louisianica*, flower
3. *Proboscidea louisianica*
4. *Proboscidea louisianica*
5. *Proboscidea fragrans*
6. *Ibicella lutea*
7. *Piper porphyrophyllum* (Piperaceae)
8. *Piper betle*, betel pepper (Piperaceae)
9. *Ibicella lutea*
10. *Peperomia marmorata* (Piperaceae)
11. *Peperomia saundersii* (Piperaceae)

PAGE 201. *Plumbaginaceae (plumago, sea lavender), Polygalaceae (milkworts), Polygonaceae (buckwheats), and Phytolaccaceae (pokeweeds)*

1. *Statice elata* (Plumbaginaceae)
2. Large-leaved tapering statice (Plumbaginaceae)
3. Hybrid white statice (Plumbaginaceae)
4. *Statice sinuata* (Plumbaginaceae)
5. *Polygonum bistorta*, snakeweed with flower (Polygonaceae)
6. *Polygala chamaebuxus*, box-leaved milkwort with stem (Polygalaceae)
7. *Rivinia humilis* (Phytolaceaceae)
8. *Statice tatarica* (Plumbaginaceae)
9. *Muehlenbeckia complexa* (Polygalaceae)
10. *Statice suworowi* (Plumbaginaceae)
11. *Polygonum sachalinense* (Polygalaceae)

PAGE 202. *Polemoniaceae (phlox)*

1. Creeping phlox
2. *Cantua buxifolia*
3. *Gilia dichotome*
4. *Phlox drummondii*, with cuspidate flowers
5. *Polemonium confertum*
6. *Phlox drummondii*, with semi-double flowers
7. *Gilia* sp.
8. *Leptosiphon roseus*
9. Dwarf three-colored gilia
10. *Phlox drummondii*
11. *Cobaea scandens*, flower
12. *Phlox drummondii*, with large flowers

PAGE 203. *Polygonaceae (buckwheats), Pontederiaceae (water hyacinths), and Portulacaceae (portulacas)*

1. Unidentified portulaca (Portulacaceae)
2. Unidentified portulaca (Portulacaceae)

3. *Portulaca grandiflora,* purslane (Portulacaceae)
4. *Pontederia cordata,* pickerel weed (Pontederiaceae)
5. *Polygonum orientale (Polygonaceae)*
6. *Polygonum orientale (Polygonaceae)*
7. *Portulaca grandiflora,* purslane (Portulacaceae)
8. *Calandrinia speciosa* (Portulacaceae)
9. *Pontederia* sp. (Pontederiaceae)
10. *Rheum undulatum* (Polygonaceae)
11. Dockweed (Polygonaceae)
12. *Calandrinia speciosa* (Portulacaceae)
13. *Rheum palmatum,* palmated rhubarb (Polygonaceae)

PAGE 204. *Primulaceae (primroses)*

1. *Primula spectabilis wulfeniana*
2. *Primula cortusoides amoena*
3. Grey-edged auriculas
4. *Primula minima,* fairy primrose
5. *Primula denticulata cashmeriana*
6. *Primula marginata*
7. *Primula officinalis,* with flower
8. *Primula stuarti*
9. *Primula marginata*

PAGE 205. *Primulaceae (primroses)*

1. Primrose, with flower
2. Unidentified variety of primrose
3. Unidentified variety of primrose
4. Unidentified variety of primrose
5. *Primula verticillee*
6. *Primula obconica,* with double flowers
7. Giant fringed Chinese primrose
8. *Primula auricula*
9. Fringed Chinese primrose
10. Fringed Chinese primrose
11. *Primula auricula*

PAGE 206. *Primulaceae (primroses)*

1. *Primula sinensis,* with flower
2. *Lysimaque nummulaire*
3. *Primula sikkimensis*
4. *Anagallis monelli,* Italian pimpernel
5. *Primula sikkimensis*
6. *Primula capitata*
7. *Primula longiflora*
8. *Primula intermedia*
9. *Primula villosa*
10. *Primula denticulata*
11. *Androsace sarmentosa*

PAGE 207. *Primulaceae (primroses, cyclamens)*

1. *Dodecatheon clevelandi,* giant American cowslip
2. *Primula sinensis fimbriata*
3. *Primula sinensis fimbriata*
4. *Cyclamen persicum*
5. *Primula sinensis*
6. *Primula elatior,* ox lip
7. *Cyclamen persicum*
8. *Cyclamen persicum*

PAGE 208. *Primulaceae (primroses, cyclamens)*

1. *Cyclamen persicum papilio*
2. Large-flowered Persian cyclamen
3. *Cyclamen neapolitanum*
4. *Cyclamen coum*
5. Large-flowered Persian cyclamen

PAGE 209. *Ranunculaceae (buttercups)*

1. Semi-double Persian ranunculus
2. *Ranunculus asiaticus*
3. *Helleborus niger,* Christmas rose
4. *Ranunculus bulbosus,* with flower
5. *Ranunculus amplexicaulis,* with flower
6. *Helleborus foetidus*
7. *Clematis alpina*
8. *Helleborus olympicus*
9. *Ranunculus lingua,* great spearwort
10. *Ranunculus ficaria*

PAGE 210. *Ranunculaceae (buttercups)*

1. Double hybrid columbine
2. *Aquilegia olympica*
3. *Aquilegia vulgaris,* columbine
4. Dwarf columbine ‘Mount Olympus’
5. *Delphinium consolida,* branched larkspur
6. *Aquilegia olympica*
7. Dwarf columbine ‘Mount Olympus’
8. *Delphinium nudicaule*
9. *Delphinium ajacis,* rocket larkspur
10. Blue columbine
11. *Delphinium cashmerianum,* cashmerian larkspur
12. *Aquilegia sibirica*

PAGE 211. *Ranunculaceae (buttercups, anemones)*

1. Double-flowered Caen anemone
2. Japanese anemone
3. *Anemone coronaria*
4. Single-flowered Caen anemone
5. *Anemone coronaria,* poppy anemone
6. *Anemone japonica*
7. *Anemone fulgens*
8. Double anemone ‘Cardinal’s Hat’
9. Japanese anemone
10. Chrysanthemum-flowered anemone

PAGE 212. *Ranunculaceae (buttercups, clematis)*

1. *Clematis* sp., ‘John Gould Veitch’
2. *Clematis graveolens*
3. *Clematis jackmanii*
4. *Clematis fortunei*
5. *Nigella* sp., dwarf double

6. *Clematis coccinea*
7. *Clematis crispa*
8. *Clematis jackmanii*

PAGE 213. *Resedaceae (mignaneltes), Rhamnaceae (buckthorns), and Rosaceae (roses)*

1. Crimson rambler rose (Rosaceae)
2. *Zizyphus jujura (Rhamnaceae)*
3. *Rosa centifolia,* Provence or cabbage rose (Rosaceae)
4. *Reseda pyramidal machet* (Resedaceae)
5. *Reseda odorant,* with flower (Resedaceae)
6. *Reseda pyramidal machet* (Resedaceae)
7. Tea rose 'Sunset' (Rosaceae)
8. Standard rose (Rosaceae)
9. Large-flowered tapering migonette (Resedaceae)

PAGE 214. *Rosaceae (roses)*

1. Hybrid tea rose
2. Hybrid perpetual rose 'Coquette of the Alps'
3. *Rosa canina*
4. *Rosa* 'Glory of Dijon'
5. *Rosa* 'Field-Marshall Niel'
6. *Rosa* 'Pearl of the Garden'
7. *Rosa niphetos*

PAGE 215. *Rosaceae (roses)*

1. Polyantha rose
2. Tea rose
3. *Rosa* 'Glory of Dijon'
4. Unidentified variety of rose
5. *Rosa polyantha,* bramble rose
6. Moss rose
7. Unidentified variety of rose

PAGE 216. *Rosaceae (roses)*

1. Unidentified variety of rose
2. *Rosa* 'Father Gontier'
3. *Rosa indica*
4. *Rosa noisettiana*
5. Double rose noisette
6. *Rosa dinsmore*
7. *Rosa* 'Madame de Watteville'

PAGE 217. *Rosaceae (roses)*

1. *Rosa* 'Wm. Francis Bennett'
2. *Rosa gallica*
3. Unidentified variety of rose
4. Roses: hybrid tea, polyantha, tea, and hybrid perpetual
5. Sweetbrier rose
6. *Rosa* 'Baltimore Beauty'
7. *Rosa* 'Bourbon Rose'

PAGE 218. *Rosaceae (roses)*

1. *Spirea astilboides*
2. *Spirea tomentosa,* hardhack
3. *Spirea salicifolia,* meadow sweet
4. *Potentilla fruticosa*
5. *Spirea japonica*
6. *Geum montanum*
7. *Spirea palmata*
8. *Spirea ulmaria,* double meadow sweet
9. *Spirea astilboides*

PAGE 219. *Rosaceae (roses, almonds, strawberries)*

1. *Sorbus aucuparia,* mountain ash
2. *Pyrus sorbus,* service tree
3. *Prunus persica,* peach
4. Oak-leaved mountain ash
5. *Fragaria indica,* Indian strawberry
6. *Prunus laurocerasus,* cherry laurel
7. *Margyricarpus setosus*
8. Almond
9. *Fragaria vesca,* alpine strawberry
10. *Fragaria chilensis,* chili strawberry
11. Almond
12. *Spirea van houtteii*

PAGE 220. *Rosaceae (roses, cherries, apples)*

1. *Prunus chapronii*
2. Pear
3. *Cerasus sylvestris,* wild cherry
4. Cherry
5. *Cerasus sylvestris,* wild cherry
6. *Amygdalus communis,* almond
7. *Cerasus ilicifolia,* variety of cherry
8. *Pyrus malus,* apple
9. *Prunus biferum*

PAGE 221. *Rosaceae (roses, hawthorns)*

1. *Sorbus aucuparia,* mountain ash
2. *Crataegus laevigata,* hawthorn
3. *Pyracantha coccinea,* fruiting branch
4. *Pyrus Arii,* white beam tree
5. *Crataegus crus-galli,* cockspur hawthorn
6. *Crataegus crus-galli,* cockspur hawthorn
7. *Prunus spinoa,* blackthorn
8. Pear
9. *Cartaegus laevigata,* hawthorn
10. *Persica davidiana*
11. Apricot
12. White thorn

PAGE 222. *Rosaceae (roses, pears)*

1. *Pyrus malus bertini,* apple
2. Peach
3. *Pyrus leucocarpa*
4. Peach
5. *Pyrus triloba*
6. *Pyrus japonica*

7. *Pyrus malus crataegina*, apple
8. Pear trees
9. *Photinia japonica*
10. *Mespilus germanica*, medlar tree

PAGE 223. *Rubiaceae (gardenias, coffee)*

1. *Bouvardia hendersonii*
2. *Gardenia thunbergia*
3. *Gardenia thunbergia*
4. *Bouvardia* sp.
5. *Gardenia radicans variegata*
6. *Luculia pinceana*
7. *Nertera granadensis*, fruiting duckweed coral moss
8. *Pentas carnea*, with flower
9. *Posoqueria multiflora*
10. *Urceola elastica*, with flower
11. *Luculia gratissima*

PAGE 224. *Rubiaceae (gardenias) and Rutaceae (oranges, lemons)*

1. *Bouvardia* sp. (Rubiaceae)
2. *Citrus margarita*, bergamot (Rutaceae)
3. *Citrus medica* (Rutaceae)
4. Cape jasmine (Rubiaceae)
5. Jasmine or gardenia (Rubiaceae)
6. *Citrus aurantium*, orange (Rutaceae)
7. *Luculia* sp. (Rubiaceae)
8. *Bouvardia Alfred Neuher* (Rubiaceae)
9. Orange with horned fruit (Rutaceae)
10. *Cinchona condaminea* (Rubiaceae)

PAGE 225. *Rutaceae (oranges, lemons)*

1. Common orange
2. *Skimmia fragrans*
3. *Triphasia trifoliata*
4. *Skimmia japonica*
5. *Boronia megastigma*
6. *Calodendron capensis*

PAGE 226. *Salicaceae (poplars, willows)*

1. *Populus balsamifera*, balsam poplar
2. *Populus alba*, European white poplar
3. *Populus balsamifera*, young balsam poplar
4. *Populus graeca*, Athenian poplar
5. *Populus graeca*
6. *Populus nigra italica*, black Italian poplar
7. *Populus nigra italica*, Lombardy poplar
8. *Populus nigra*, black poplar

PAGE 227. *Salicaceae (poplars, willows)*

1. *Populus tremuloides*, trembling aspen
2. *Salix pentandra*, bay-leaved willow
3. *Salix fragilis*, crack willow
4. *Salix babylonica*, weeping willow
5. *Populus alba canescens*
6. *Salix* sp., willow
7. *Salix* sp., willow
8. *Populus nigra italica*, Lombardy poplar
9. *Salix lucida*, glossy willow
10. *Populus alba*, European white poplar
11. *Salix viminalis*
12. Pollard willows

PAGE 228. *Salicaceae (poplars, willows)*

1. *Salix russelliana*, Russell or Duke of Bedford's willow
2. White willow
3. *Salix caprea*, goat willow
4. Goat willow or large-leaved sallow
5. Unidentified variety of willow
6. Goat willow
7. *Salix alba*, white willow
8. *Salix russellinana*, Russell willow
9. *Salix fragilis*, crack or redwood willow

PAGE 229. *Saxifragaceae (saxifrages, hydrangeas)*

1. *Saxifraga cotyledon*
2. *Deutzia crenata*, with flower
3. *Saxifraga virginiensis*
4. *Saxifraga trifurcata*, with flower
5. *Saxifraga crassifolia*
6. *Hoteia japonica*
7. *Hydrangea hortensis*
8. *Saxifraga purpurascens*
9. *Saxifraga caesia*, with flower
10. *Saxifraga cymbalaria*, with flower
11. Astilbe 'Abbe David'

PAGE 230. *Saxifragaceae (saxifrages, hydrangeas)*

1. *Philadelphus coronarius*
2. *Saxifraga hosti*
3. *Philadelphus gordonianus*
4. *Heuchera glabra*
5. *Saxifraga sarmentosa tricolor*
6. *Saxifraga granulata*, meadow saxifrage
7. *Saxifraga pygmaea*
8. *Saxifraga rotundifolia*
9. *Hydrangea paniculata grandiflora*, with flower
10. *Saxifraga cordifolia*, with flower
11. *Saxifraga longifolia*
12. *Tiarella cordifolia*

PAGE 231. *Scrophulariaceae (foxgloves)*

1. *Calceolaria hybride*, slipper wort
2. *Alonsoa myrtifolia*, mask flower
3. *Salpiglossis*
4. Small-leaved foxglove, with flowers
5. Foxglove
6. *Antirrhinum asarina*, with flower
7. *Chelone lyoni*, with flower
8. *Calceolaria hybride*, slipper wort

PAGE 232. *Scrophulariaceae (foxgloves)*

1. *Penstemon hartwegi*
2. Hybrid copper monkey-flower
3. *Ourisia coccinea*
4. *Verbascum olympicum*
5. *Linaria multipunctata,* with flower
6. *Penstemon* sp.
7. *Asarina scandens,* with flower
8. *Asarina barclaiana,* flower
9. Dalmatian toadflax, with flower
10. *Antirrhinum* sp., snapdragons
11. *Veronica spicata,* spiked speedwell with flower
12. Dalmatian toadflax

PAGE 233. *Smilacaceae (smilax) and Solanaceae (nightshades, tomatoes, potatoes)*

1. *Capsicum* var. (Solanaceae)
2. Pimento (Solanaceae)
3. *Datura meteloides* (Solanaceae)
4. Chinese pimento (Solanaceae)
5. *Myrsiophyllum,* smilax (Smilacaceae)
6. *Datura arborea* (Solanaceae)
7. *Smilax rotundifolia,* greenbriar (Smilacaceae)
8. *Datura wrighti* (Solanaceae)
9. *Capsicum annuum* (Solanaceae)
10. *Smilax ornata* (Smilacaceae)

PAGE 234. *Solanaceae (nightshades)*

1. Large-fruited 'winking' nightshade, with fruit
2. Horned nightshade, with flower
3. *Solanum robustum*
4. *Solanum dulcamara,* bittersweet
5. Nightshade 'False Pimento'
6. *Solanum warscewiczii*
7. *Solanum maroniense*
8. *Solanum laciniatum,* with flower
9. Texas nightshade, with flower
10. 'Egg' nightshade, with fruit

PAGE 235. *Solanaceae (nightshades, petunias)*

1. Large-flowered spotted fringed petunia
2. Large-flowered, large-throated petunia
3. Petunia, large flowering single
4. Petunia, garden hybrid single
5. *Brugmansia suaveolens*
6. Unidentified variety of petunia
7. Dwarf hybrid petunia with flowers
8. Double garden petunia
9. Double fringed petunia
10. Single garden petunia
11. Double-flowered petunia

PAGE 236. *Solanaceae (nightshades, tobacco)*

1. *Nicotiana macrophylla,* variety of tobacco
2. *Nicotiana forgetiana*
3. *Nicotiana acutiflora*
4. *Nicotiana tabacum*
5. *Nicotiana suaveolens*
6. *Nicotiana forgetiana*
7. *Nicotiana forgetiana*
8. Tobacco leaves
9. *Nicotiana affinis*
10. Giant tobacco plant with fringed leaves

PAGE 237. *Strelitziaceae and Theaceae*

1. *Camellia japonica* (Theaceae)
2. *Camellia japonica* (Theaceae)
3. *Visnea mocanera* (Theaceae)
4. *Camellia oleifera* (Theaceae)
5. *Camellia japonica anemonaeflora* (Theaceae)
6. *Strelitzia regine,* bird of Paradise flower (Strelitziaceae)
7. *Heliconia bicolor* (Strelitziaceae)
8. *Ravenala madagascariensis* (Strelitziaceae)

PAGE 238. *Trilliaceae (trilliums) and Tropaeolaceae (nasturtiums)*

1. Hybrid Capucine nasturtium 'Madame Gunter' (Tropaeolaceae)
2. *Trillium erectum* (Trilliaceae)
3. *Trillium grandiflorum* (Trilliaceae)
4. *Tropaeolum majus,* dwarf (Tropaeolaceae)
5. Asparagus-shaped trillium (Trilliaceae)
6. Dwarf Capucine camellia, with flowers (Tropaeolaceae)
7. *Tropaeolum lobbianum* (Tropaeolaceae)
8. Asparagus-shaped trillium (Trilliaceae)
9. Canaris Capucine nasturtium (Tropaeolaceae)

PAGE 239. *Ulmaceae (elms)*

1. *Ulmus glabra,* Scotch elm or Wych elm
2. *Celtis occidentalis,* hackberry, with leaf
3. *Ulmus glabra,* Scotch elm
4. Unidentified variety of elm
5. Washington elm, Cambridge, Massachusetts
6. *Ulmus procera,* English elm
7. *Ulmus montana,* mountain elm
8. *Ulmus campestris,* English or small leaved elm

PAGE 240. *Umbelliferae (carrots, parsley) and Urticaceae (nettles)*

1. *Cecropia* sp., embauba plant (Urticaceae)
2. *Eryngium bromeliaefolium* (Umbelliferae)
3. *Eryngium giganteum* (Umbelliferae)
4. *Cudrania triloba* (Urticaceae)
5. Cow tree (Urticaceae)
6. *Heracleum sibiricum* (Umbelliferae)
7. *Eryngium eburneum* (Umbelliferae)
8. *Boehmeria nivea* (Urticaceae)
9. *Humulus japonicus* (Urticaceae)
10. *Heracleum sibiricum* (Umbelliferae)

PAGE 241. ***Verbenaceae (verbenas)***

1. *Clerodendrum balfouri*
2. *Amasonia punicea* Vahl.
3. *Clerodendrum squamatum*, with flower
4. Striped verbena
5. *Amasonia punicea* Vahl.
6. Lantana hybride
7. Large-flowered hybrid verbena 'Commander Marchaud'

PAGE 242. ***Verbenaceae (verbenas)* and *Zingiberaceae (gingers)***

1. Farquhar's mammoth hybrid verbena (Verbenaceae)
2. Italian hybrid verbena (Verbenaceae)
3. Garden variety verbena (Verbenaceae)
4. Garden hybrid verbena (Verbenaceae)
5. Striped verbena (Verbenaceae)
6. Garden hybrid verbena (Verbenaceae)
7. Verbenas (Verbenaceae)
8. *Kaempferia gilbertii* (Zingiberaceae)

PAGE 243. ***Violaceae (violets, pansies)***

1. *Viola cucullata*
2. King of violets
3. *Viola canadensis*, with flower
4. *Viola tricolor*, pansy
5. Pansy flowers
6. Large-flowered show pansies
7. Pansy
8. Pansy

PAGE 244. ***Violaceae (violets, pansies)***

1. Large-spotted Parisian pansy
2. Scented cyclops violet, with flower
3. Pansies
4. *Viola munbyana*, Algerian violet with flower
5. Scented Luxonne violet
6. *Viola pedata*, bird's-foot violet
7. Pansies
8. French scented violet, with flower
9. Pansies
10. Scented violet 'Princess of Wales'

PAGE 245. ***Violaceae (violets), Vitaceae (virginia creepers), and Zingiberaceae (gingers)***

1. *Ampelopsis veitchii* (Vitaceae)
2. *Hedychium gardnerianum* (Zingiberaceae)
3. *Ammobium alatum* (Zingiberaceae)
4. *Parthenocissus quinquefolia*, virginia creeper (Vitaceae)
5. *Hedychium gardnerianum* (Zingiberaceae)
6. *Amomum grana paradisi* (Zingiberaceae)
7. Violet 'Princess Beatrice' (Violaceae)
8. *Alpinia vittata* (Zingiberaceae)

SECTION 2

Appendices of Botanical Images
Giant puffball

PAGE 248. ***Appendix A: Additional trees***

Ficus indica, banyan tree

PAGE 249. ***Additional trees***

1. *Rhizophora mangrove*, mangrove (Rhizophoraceae)
2. Breadfruit (Moraceae)
3. Breadfruit tree (Moraceae)
4. *Pandanus odoratissimus* (Pandanaceae)
5. *Ficus elastica* (Moraceae)
6. Australian bottle tree (Sterculiaceae)
7. *Rhizophora mangrove* (Rhizophoraceae)

PAGE 250. ***Additional trees***

1. *Carica papaya* (Caricaceae)
2. *Carica spinosa* (Caricaceae)
3. Fruit of *Pandanus odoratissimus* (Pandanaceae)
4. *Papayero comun*
5. Shea tree (Sapotaceae)
6. Unidentified variety of *Ficus* (Moraceae)
7. Croton tree (Euphorbiaceae)

PAGE 251. ***Additional trees***

1. Banyan tree (Moraceae)
2. *Olea europaea*, olive (Oleaceae)
3. *Siphonia elastica*, caoutchouc tree
4. *Isonandra gutta*, gutta-percha tree (Sapotaceae)
5. Olive branch (Oleaceae)
6. Brazilian silk-cotton tree

PAGE 252. ***Additional trees***

1. Yucca tree and saguaro cactus
2. Cream of tartar tree (Australia)
3. Brazilian silk-cotton tree

PAGE 253. ***Additional trees***

1. *Carya alba*, shell-bark hickory (Juglandaceae)
2. *Juglans regia*, common walnut (Juglandaceae)
3. *Magnolia conspicua*, Chinese white magnolia
4. *Tilia americana*, American linden (Tiliaceae)
5. Dwarf orange tree (Rutaceae)
6. *Aesculus hippocastanum*, horse-chestnut (Hippocastanaceae)

PAGE 254. ***Additional trees***

1. *Catalpa bungei* (Bignoniaceae)
2. *Robinia pseudacacia*, black locust or false acacia (Leguminosae)
3. *Pyrus malus acerba*, crab apple (Rosaceae)
4. *Carpinus betulus*, common hornbeam (Betulaceae)
5. *Styphnolobium japonicum* (Leguminosae)
6. *Styphnolobium japonicum pendula*, weeping sophora (Leguminosae)

PAGE 255. ***Additional trees***

1. Cork tree of Fernana (North West Africa)
2. *Aesculus hippocastanum,* horse-chestnut (Hippocastanaceae)
3. *Sassafras albidum,* sassafras
4. *Fraxinus exelsior,* common ash
5. Unidentified variety of oak (Fagaceae)

PAGE 256. ***Additional trees***

1. *Acer pseudoplatanus,* sycamore maple (Aceraceae)
2. *Liriodendron tulipifera,* whitewood or tulip tree
3. *Pavia flava* or *Aesculus flava,* Ohio buckeye or yellow horse-chestnut
4. *Ulmus montana* (Ulmaceae)
5. *Morus rubra,* American red mulberry (Moraceae)
6. *Betula verrucosa* (Betulaceae)
7. *Nyssa biflora,* tupelo or peperidge tree (Nyssaceae)
8. *Tilia parvifolia* (Tiliaceae)
9. European horse-chestnut (Hippocastanaceae)
10. *Populus tremuloides,* trembling aspen (Salicaceae)

PAGE 257. ***Additional trees***

1. *Platanus occidentalis,* western plane tree (Platanaceae)
2. *Platanus racemosus,* California plane tree (Platanaceae)
3. *Populus canescens,* gray poplar (Salicaceae)
4. *Platanus occidentalis,* western plane tree (Platanaceae)
5. *Populus graeca,* Athenian poplar (Salicaceae)
6. *Populus tremuloides,* aspen or trembling poplar (Salicaceae)
7. *Populus tremuloides,* trembling aspen (Salicaceae)
8. *Populus alba,* white poplar (Salicaceae)
9. *Platanus orientalis,* oriental plane (Platanaceae)

PAGE 258. ***Additional trees***

1. *Ulmus suberosa,* cork-barked elm (Ulmaceae)
2. Lime tree (Tiliaceae)
3. *Ulmus campestris,* English or small-leaved elm (Ulmaceae)
4. *Ulmus glabra,* mountain, Wych, or Scotch elm (Ulmaceae)
5. *Ulmus montana vegeta,* Chichester elm (Ulmaceae)
6. *Ulmus glabra,* Scotch or Wych elm (Ulmaceae)
7. *Tilia americana,* American basswood or linden (Tiliaceae)
8. *Ulmus glabra,* Wych or Scotch elm (Ulmaceae)
9. *Tilia europaea,* European linden (Tiliaceae)

PAGE 259. ***Additional trees***

1. *Carpinus betulus,* common hornbean (Betulaceae)
2. *Magnolia tripetela,* umbrella magnolia (Magnoliaceae)
3. *Carpinus betulus,* common hornbean (Betulaceae)
4. *Tilia rubra,* red-barked linden (Tiliaceae)
5. *Chionanthus virginica,* Virginia fringe tree
6. *Juglans regia,* black walnut (Juglandaceae)
7. *Betula alba,* white birch (Betulaceae)

PAGE 260. ***Additional trees***

1. *Ficus religiosa,* pagoda fig (Moraceae)
2. Cedar of Lebanon (Pinaceae)

PAGE 261. ***Additional trees***

1. *Castanea vulgaris,* chestnut tree of Mount Aetna (Fagaceae)
2. *Dracaena draco,* dragon's blood tree

PAGE 262. ***Additional trees***

1. *Pinus sylvestris,* Scotch pine (Pinaceae)
2. *Quercus sessiliflora* (Fagaceae)

PAGE 263. ***Additional trees***

1. Tree from Santa Maria del Tule
2. *Quercus palestinae,* oak of Abraham (Fagaceae)

PAGE 264. ***Additional trees***

1. *Tilia europaea,* European linden (Tiliaceae)
2. *Betula pendula,* European white birch (Betulaceae)

PAGE 265. ***Additional trees***

1. *Platanus orientalis,* Oriental plane tree (Platanaceae)
2. *Adansonia gigantea,* baobab tree (Bombacaceae)

PAGE 266. ***Additional trees***

1. *Salix alba,* white willow (Salicaceae)
2. *Juglans* sp., walnut tree (Juglandaceae)

PAGE 267. ***Additional trees***

1. Chapel oak of Allouville, Normandy (Fagaceae)
2. Lime tree of the Battle of Morat (Tiliaceae)

PAGE 268. ***Additional trees***

1. *Laurus camphora,* camphor tree (Lauraceae)
2. *Isonandra gutta,* gutta-percha tree (Sapotaceae)

PAGE 269. ***Additional trees***

1. *Antiaris toxicaria,* poison or upas tree (Moraceae)
2. *Castanea vulgaris,* chestnut tree (Fagaceae)

PAGE 270. ***Additional trees***

1. Baobab forest (Bombacaceae)
2. Ficus with trellised climbing roots (Moraceae)

PAGE 271. ***Additional trees***

1. *Ficus benjamina* (Moraceae)
2. *Eucalyptus* sp. (Myrtaceae)

PAGE 272. ***Additional trees***

1. Virgin forest in Equatorial regions
2. Mangroves (Rhizophoraceae)

PAGE 273. ***Additional trees***

1. An Indian forest
2. A Brazilian forest

PAGE 274. ***Appendix B: Edible foods, Nuts, Fruits, Vegetables, Legumes, Grains, Beverages, Herbs and Spices***

Ribes oxyacanthoides

PAGE 275. ***Edible foods: Nuts***

1. Sweet chestnut
2. Small-fruited walnut
3. Walnut
4. Thick-shelled hickory
5. Brazil nut
6. Pecan
7. Gibbou's walnut
8. Almond
9. Walnut meat
10. Butternut or white walnut
11. Hazel nut
12. Filbert
13. Hales' paper-shell hickory
14. Barthere walnut

PAGE 276. ***Edible foods: Nuts, Fruits***

1. Cashew nut
2. Pistachio
3. Pecan
4. Colmar pear
5. Easter pear
6. Pear 'Winter Gray'
7. Fulton pear (oblate shape)
8. Amanlis pear
9. Pear 'Duchess of Angouleme'
10. Pear 'No More'
11. Bartlett pear (pyriform shape)
12. Winter banana apple
13. Brown pear
14. Wismers's dessert apple

PAGE 277. ***Edible foods: Fruits***

1. Portugal quince
2. Sterckmans pear
3. Unidentified variety of pear
4. Bosc pear
5. Autumn bergamot pear
6. Pear Uvedale's St. Germaine
7. Pear 'End of Sadness'
8. Pear Williams 'Good Christian'
9. Easter pear
10. Unidentified variety of apple
11. Gray rennet apple
12. Apple 'Short-hanging Fruit'
13. White Norman apple
14. Canadian rennet apple

PAGE 278. ***Edible foods: Fruits***

1. Cherries
2. Apricot
3. Chinese date plum
4. Nectarine
5. Unidentified variety of plum
6. Greengage plum
7. Green's Tartarian cherry
8. Clingstone nectarine
9. Peach
10. Persimmon

PAGE 279. ***Edible foods: Fruits***

1. Windsor cherry
2. Chili strawberry
3. York State prune
4. Quetsche plum or German prune
5. Peach
6. Apricot
7. Strawberries
8. Napoleon cherry
9. Manchester strawberry
10. Strawberries
11. Crimson cluster strawberry

PAGE 280. ***Edible foods: Fruits***

1. Chautauqua gooseberry
2. Red currant
3. Fay's currant
4. Black currant
5. Gooseberry
6. Cranberry
7. Parry strawberry
8. Chili strawberry
9. Strawberries

PAGE 281. ***Edible foods: fruits***

1. Cuthbert red raspberry
2. Raspberry
3. Dewberry
4. Herstine raspberry
5. New Rochelle blackberry
6. Agawam blackberry
7. Minnewaska blackberry
8. New Iceberg blackberry
9. Kansas black raspberry

PAGE 282. ***Edible foods: Grapes***

1. Wild grape
2. Black Hamburg grapes
3. Unidentified variety of grape
4. Black monukka grapes
5. Royal muscadine grapes
6. Strawberry grapes
7. Black corinth grapes

PAGE 283. ***Edible foods: Fruits***

1. Moore's early grape
2. Olive
3. Unidentified variety of grape
4. Guava
5. Pomegranate
6. Fig
7. Olive
8. Papaw
9. Passion flower fruit
10. Mango, Custard apple

PAGE 284. ***Edible foods: Fruits***

1. Banana tree
2. Pineapple
3. Bread-fruit
4. Pomegranate
5. Black Bourjassotte figs
6. Banana
7. Fig tree
8. Figs
9. Date
10. Pineapple
11. Mango

PAGE 285. ***Edible foods: Citrus fruits***

1. Common orange
2. Kumquat
3. Mandarin orange
4. Shaddock
5. Orange
6. Lemon
7. Orange
8. Citron

PAGE 286. ***Edible foods: Vegetables***

1. Cabbage
2. Cos lettuce
3. Savoy cabbage
4. Early York cabbage
5. Curled-leaved endive
6. Cabbage lettuce
7. Flat Dutch cabbage
8. Green fringed salamander lettuce
9. Oxheart cabbage
10. Albino cabbage
11. Cabbage
12. Belleville sorrel

PAGE 287. ***Edible foods: Vegetables***

1. Henderson's early summer cabbage
2. Collard green
3. Midsummer cabbage
4. Early Wakefield cabbage
5. Savoy-leaved spinach
6. Ohio cabbage lettuce
7. Borecole, dwarf green curled Scotch kale
8. Mustard green
9. Borecole, brown curled kale
10. Express cabbage
11. Broad-leaved endive
12. Spinach

PAGE 288. ***Edible foods: Vegetables***

1. Boston market celery
2. Henderson's early snowball cauliflower
3. Half dwarf celery
4. White plume celery
5. Common celery
6. Brussel sprouts
7. Broccoli
8. Broccoli
9. Cauliflower
10. Brussel sprouts

PAGE 289. ***Edible foods: Vegetables***

1. Sea kale
2. Asparagus
3. Artichoke
4. Martynia
5. Water cress
6. Water chestnut
7. Okra
8. Cardoon
9. Globe artichoke
10. Rhubarb
11. Chicory 'Capucin's Beard'
12. Chicory
13. Upland cress

PAGE 290. ***Edible foods: Vegetables***

1. Green pepper
2. Potato leaf tomato
3. Red and green peppers
4. Grape tomatoes
5. Tomato
6. Round capsicum
7. Grape tomato
8. Pear tomatoes
9. Dwarf tomato
10. Long capsicum
11. Tomatoes
12. Long purple eggplant
13. Varieties of cucumber
14. Pear tomato
15. Round eggplant

PAGE 291. ***Edible foods: Melons***

1. Prize jumbo melon
2. Gray monarch watermelon
3. Kolb's gem watermelon
4. Blenheim orange melon
5. Green citron melon
6. Pride of Georgia, rattlesnake, and black Spanish melons
7. Superior musk melon
8. Vicks early watermelon
9. Watermelons
10. Perfection musk melon

PAGE 292. ***Edible foods: Melons, gourds, squash***

1. Cantaloupe melon
2. Citron watermelon
3. Coulommier's melon
4. Persian melon
5. Embroidered market melon
6. Carolina watermelon
7. Winter melon
8. Figari melon
9. Queen Anne's pocket or Dudaim melon
10. Large musk melon
11. Nutmet gourd of Marseilles
12. Naples gourd
13. Hubbard squash
14. Pumpkin
15. Custard gourd
16. Crook-neck squash
17. Patagonian gourd

PAGE 293. ***Edible foods: Legumes***

1. Bush lima beans
2. Maule's butter wax beans
3. Unidentified variety of pea
4. Stratagem pea
5. Broad bean
6. King of the garden pole lima bean
7. Unidentified variety of pea
8. Peanut
9. Peas
10. Round pod valentine bean

PAGE 294. ***Edible foods: Legumes***

1. Lentil
2. Dwarf or French bean
3. Unidentified variety of pea
4. Lentil
5. Pods and seed of broad bean
6. Unidentified variety of pea
7. String beans
8. Peanuts

PAGE 295. ***Edible foods: Grains***

1. Japanese buckwheat
2. *Triticum spelta,* a variety of wheat
3. Wheat
4. Sugar corn
5. Corn
6. Rice
7. Oats
8. Queen's golden pop corn
9. Indian corn
10. Indian corn
11. Barley
12. Millet

PAGE 296. ***Edible foods: Radishes, Carrots***

1. Long black Spanish radishes
2. China rose radish
3. Rose China winter radish
4. Turnip, early white, scarlet, and white tipped scarlet radishes
5. Yellow malta turnip radish
6. Long scarlet radishes
7. Olive scarlet, olive white, and French breakfast radishes
8. Long white Naples radish
9. Chartier, white Strasburg, and red rocket radishes
10. Half-long Luc carrot
11. Red turnip radish
12. Long red coreless carrot
13. Half-long scarlet carentan carrot
14. Early rose globe radish

PAGE 297. ***Edible foods***

1. American purple top rutabaga
2. Blood turnip beet
3. Sugar beet
4. Rampion
5. White leaf beet
6. Red beet
7. Parsnip
8. Early strap-leaved white stone turnip
9. Kohlrabi
10. Orange jelly turnip

PAGE 298. ***Edible foods***

1. Horse-radish
2. Horse-radish
3. Celeriac
4. Chervil
5. Chinese yam
6. Jerusalem artichoke
7. Turnip-rooted celery
8. Yam
9. Jerusalem artichoke
10. Potatoes
11. Potatoes
12. Potato
13. Potato
14. Potato plant

PAGE 299. ***Edible foods***

1. Yellow Danvers onion
2. Extra early red onion
3. Chives

4. Leek
5. Garlic
6. White Spanish onions
7. Yellow Dutch onions
8. Top onions
9. Trebons onions
10. Garlic
11. Naples giant Rocca onion
12. Silver skin onion
13. Unidentified onion
14. Prizetaker onion
15. Potato or multiplier onions
16. Globe Danvers onions

PAGE 300. ***Edible foods***

1. Mate
2. Coffee
3. Tea culture in China
4. Coffee
5. *Thea chinensis,* tea
6. *Theobroma cacao,* cocoa
7. *Coffea arabica,* coffee
8. Tea
9. Fruit-bearing cocoa plant with flowers and fruit

PAGE 301. ***Edible foods: Spices***

1. Asafoetida
2. Allspice
3. *Ceratonia siliqua,* carob
4. Clove
5. Coriander
6. Basil
7. Red cardamom
8. Caraway
9. Black cardamom
10. Cinnamon
11. Cumin
12. Fennel

PAGE 302. ***Edible foods: Herbs, Spices***

1. Liquorice
2. Mustard
3. *Ferula tingitana,* a variety of fennel
4. Nutmeg
5. Marjoram
6. Ginger
7. Black pepper
8. Single parsley
9. Double curled parsley

PAGE 303. ***Edible foods***

1. Rosemary
2. Sugar cane
3. Savory
4. Sarsaparilla
5. Sunflower
6. Sage
7. Sesame
8. Tapioca plant
9. Thyme
10. Thyme
11. Safflower
12. Turmeric, long and round varieties
13. Vanilla

PAGE 304. ***Appendix C: Medicinal Herbs, Narcotic and Psychotropic Plants, Plants with Miscellaneous Uses***
Rheum palmatum, rhubarb

PAGE 305. ***Medicinal herbs***

1. *Aloe vera*
2. American wormseed
3. American wormseed
4. *Pimpinella anisum,* anise
5. *Arnica montana*
6. *Frasera carolinensis,* American colombo
7. *Cimicifuga racemosa,* black cohosh
8. *Berberis vulgaris,* barberry
9. *Copaifera officinalis, balsam copaiba*
10. *Veratrum viride,* American hellebore

PAGE 306. ***Medicinal herbs***

1. *Eupatorium perfoliatum,* boneset
2. *Spartium scoparium,* broom
3. *Myrica cerifera,* bayberry
4. *Lycopus virginicus,* bugle-weed
5. *Bryonia dioica,* bryony
6. *Barosma crenata,* buchu
7. *Rhamnus catharticus,* buckthorn
8. *Lycopus virginicus,* bugle-weed
9. *Sanguinaria canadensis,* blood-root
10. *Melaleuca cajuputi,* cajeput
11. *Physostigma venenosum,* calabar bean
12. *Erigeron canadense,* Canada fleabane

PAGE 307. ***Medicinal herbs***

1. *Asarum canadense,* Canada snakeroot
2. Castor oil plant
3. *Anthemis nobilis,* chamomile
4. *Cephaelis ipecacuanha*
5. *Tussilago farfara,* coltsfoot
6. *Cinchona cordifolia*
7. Centaury
8. Colocynth
9. Chicory
10. *Actaea spicata,* cohosh

PAGE 308. ***Medicinal herbs***

1. *Geranium maculatum,* cranesbill
2. *Digitalis purpurea,* foxglove
3. *Rhus copallina,* copal
4. *Symphytum officinale,* comfrey
5. *Leptandra virginica,* Culver's root
6. *Cornus florida,* dogwood
7. *Hedera helix,* English ivy
8. *Croton tiglium*
9. *Linum usitatissimum,* flax
10. *Taraxacum officinale,* dandelion
11. *Chionanthus virginica,* fringe tree

PAGE 309. *Medicinal herbs*

1. *Hydrastis canadensis,* golden seal
2. *Gentiana lutea,* yellow gentian
3. *Coptis trifolia,* golden thread
4. *Gingko biloba,* gingko tree
5. *Aralia quinquefolia,* ginseng
6. *Zingiber officinale,* ginger
7. *Solidago canadensis,* goldenrod
8. *Guaiacum officinale*
9. *Spiraea tomentosa*
10. *Humulus lupulus,* hops
11. *Althaea rosea,* hollyhock

PAGE 310. *Medicinal herbs*

1. *Equisetum arvense,* horsetail
2. *Hyssopus officinalis,* hyssop
3. *Aesculus hippocastanum,* common horse-chestnut
4. *Apocynum cannabinum,* Indian help
5. Jeffersonia
6. Male fern
7. *Lavandula* sp., lavender
8. *Pulmonaria saccharata,* lungwort
9. *Lobelia inflata,* lobelia
10. Jaborandi

PAGE 311. *Medicinal herbs*

1. *Althaea officinalis,* marsh-mallow
2. *Leonurus cardiaca,* motherwort
3. *Pistacia lentiscus,* mastic plant
4. *Aconitum napellus,* monkshood
5. *Ceanothus americanus,* New Jersey tea
6. *Podophyllum peltatum,* mandrake or May apple
7. *Verbascum thapeus,* common mullein
8. *Strychnos nux vomica*
9. *Viscum album,* mistletoe
10. *Urtica urena,* nettle
11. *Rubia tinctorum,* madder

PAGE 312. *Medicinal herbs*

1. *Spigelia marilandica,* pink-root
2. *Xanthoxylum fraxineum,* prickly ash
3. *Asclepias tuberosa,* pleurisy root
4. *Rheum officinale,* rhubarb
5. *Hedeoma pulegioides,* pennyroyal
6. *Phytolacca decandra,* poke
7. *Ruta graveolens,* garden rue
8. *Cucurbita pepo,* pumpkin

PAGE 313. *Medicinal herbs*

1. *Nerium oleander,* rose bay
2. *Sassafras officinale*
3. *Scutellaria lateriolia,* skull cap
4. *Carex umbellata,* sedge
5. *Polygala senega,* seneca snakeroot
6. *Symplocarpus foetidus,* skunk cabbage
7. *Cassia acutifolia,* senna
8. *Collinsonia canadensis,* stone-root
9. *Cochlearia officinalis,* scurvy grass
10. *Rhus glabra,* smooth sumach

PAGE 314. *Medicinal herbs*

1. *Urginea maritima,* squill, sea-onion, closely related to *Scilla*
2. *Mentha viridis,* spearmint
3. *Tanacetum vulgare,* tansy
4. *Aristolochia serpentaria,* Virginia snakeroot
5. *Valeriana officinalis,* valerian
6. *Celastrus scandens,* waxwork
7. *Hamamelis virginiana,* witch hazel
8. *Gelsemium sempervirens,* yellow jessamine
9. *Gaultheria procumbens,* wintergreen
10. *Artemisia absinthium,* wormwood
11. Nasturtium, water cress
12. *Achillea millefolium,* yarrow

PAGE 315. *Narcotic and psychotropic plants*

1. *Cannabis indica*
2. *Atropa belladonna*
3. *Conium maculatum,* poison hemlock
4. *Amanita muscaria*
5. *Cannabis sativa*
6. *Cannabis sativa*
7. *Datura stramonium*

PAGE 316. *Narcotic and psychotropic plants*

1. *Mandragora officinarum,* mandrake
2. *Datura stramonium*
3. Opium poppy
4. *Cannabis sativa*
5. *Datura stramonium*
6. *Solanum nigrum,* common nightshade*
7. *Hyoscyamus niger,* henbane
8. *Mandragora officinarum,* mandrake

PAGE 317. *Plants with miscellaneous uses*

1. *Corchorus olitorius,* jute
2. Mahogany
3. *Quercus suber,* cork oak
4. Cotton
5. Papyrus
6. *Styrax benzoin*
7. *Tectona grandis,* teak
8. Picking cotton
9. *Gossypium herbaceum,* cotton

PAGE 318. *Plants with miscellaneous uses*

1. *Santalum album,* sandalwood
2. *Crocus sativus,* saffron crocus
3. Myrrh and frankincense
4. *Pogostemon patchouly,* patchouli
5. Balm of Gilead
6. *Nepeta cataria,* catnip
7. *Indigofera tinctoria,* indigo

* Historically, nightshade has been used as a psychotropic drug in small doses. It is now considered poisonous.

8. *Stillingia sebifera,* tallow tree
9. *Fatsia papyrifera,* rice paper tree
10. *Camphora officinarum*
11. *Isonandra gutta,* gutta percha

PAGE 319. ***Appendix D: Vases and Urns, Decorative Flowers and Plants, Window Gardens, Greenhouses, Gardening, and Gardening Tools***

PAGE 320. ***Vases and urns***

PAGE 321. ***Decorative flowers and plants***

PAGE 322. ***Decorative flowers and plants***

PAGE 323. ***Decorative flowers and plants***

PAGE 324. ***Decorative flowers and plants***

PAGE 325. ***Decorative flowers and plants***

PAGE 326. ***Decorative flowers and plants***

PAGE 327. ***Decorative flowers and plants***

PAGE 328. ***Decorative flowers and plants***

PAGE 329. ***Window gardens, greenhouses, and gardening tools***

PAGE 330. ***Greenhouses***

PAGE 331. ***Greenhouses***

PAGE 332. ***Gardening tools***

PAGE 333. ***Appendix E: Decorative Borders and Motifs***

PAGE 334. ***Decorative borders and motifs***

PAGE 335. ***Decorative borders and motifs***

PAGE 336. ***Decorative borders and motifs***

PAGE 337. ***Decorative borders and motifs***

PAGE 338. ***Decorative borders and motifs***

PAGE 339. ***Decorative borders and motifs***

BIBLIOGRAPHY

Farquhar's Garden Annual, Boston, 1908.

Figuier, Louis, *The Vegetable World,* Cassell, Petter, and Galpin, New York and London.

Les Fleurs de Pleine Terre, Vilmorin-Andrieux and Co., Paris, 1893.

Fruit Guide and Catalog for the year 1904, Green's Nursery Co., Rochester, New York, 1904.

Fuller, Andrew S., *Practical Forestry,* Orange Judd Co., New York, 1895.

Gardening Illustrated, for Town and Country, Vol. 1, London, 1880.

Gartenflora, Zeitschrift fur Garten und Blumenkunde, Verlag von Paul Parey, Berlin, selected volumes 1880s.

Greiner, T., *How to Make the Garden Pay,* Wm. Henry Maule, Philadelphia, 1894.

Henderson, Peter, *Garden and Farm Topics,* Peter Henderson and Co., New York, 1884.

Henderson, Peter, *Henderson's Handbook of Plants and General Horticulture,* Peter Henderson and Co., New York, 1904.

Hoopes, Josiah, *The Book of Evergreens: A Practical Treatise on the Coniferae or Cone Bearing Plants,* Orange Judd Co., New York.

Jones, C. S., and Williams, Henry T., *Household Elegancies; Suggestions in Household Art and Tasteful Decorations,* Henry T. Williams, New York, 1877.

Long, Elias A., *The Home Florist,* Chas. A. Reeser, Springfield, Ohio, 1886.

Minshull, J., *Land, Sea, and Sky, or Wonders of Life and Nature,* Ward, Lock and Co., London.

Nicholson, George, ed., *The Illustrated Dictionary of Gardening,* L. Upcott Gill, London, 1887.

Pierce, R. V., *The Peoples Common Sense Medical Adviser in Plain English; or Medicine Simplified,* World's Dispensary Printing Office and Bindery, Buffalo, New York, 1895.

Pouchet, *The Universe; or the Infinitely Great and the Infinitely Small,* Blackie and Son, London, 1874.

Rakel, Friedrich, *Volkerkunde,* Verlag des Bibliographischen Instituts, Leipzig, 1885.

Ripley, George and Dana, Charles A., *The American Cyclopaedia, A Popular Dictionary of General Knowledge,* D. Appleton and Co., New York and London, 1881.

Robinson, W., *The English Flower Garden,* John Murray, London, 1883.

Scott, Frank J., *Suburban Home Grounds,* American Book Exchange, New York, 1881.

Selby, Prideaux John, et al., *A History of British Forest-Trees, Indigenous and Introduced,* John Van Voorst, London, 1842.

Vaughan's Seed Store, Autumn Bulbs and Plants, New York and Chicago, 1892.

Vick's Illustrated Monthly, James Vick, Rochester, New York, selected volumes beginning 1878.

von Marilaun, Anton Kerner, *Pflanzenleben,* Verlag des Bibliographischen Instituts, Leipzig and Vienna, 1890.

Williams, Henry T., ed., *Window Gardening,* Henry T. Williams, New York, 1875.